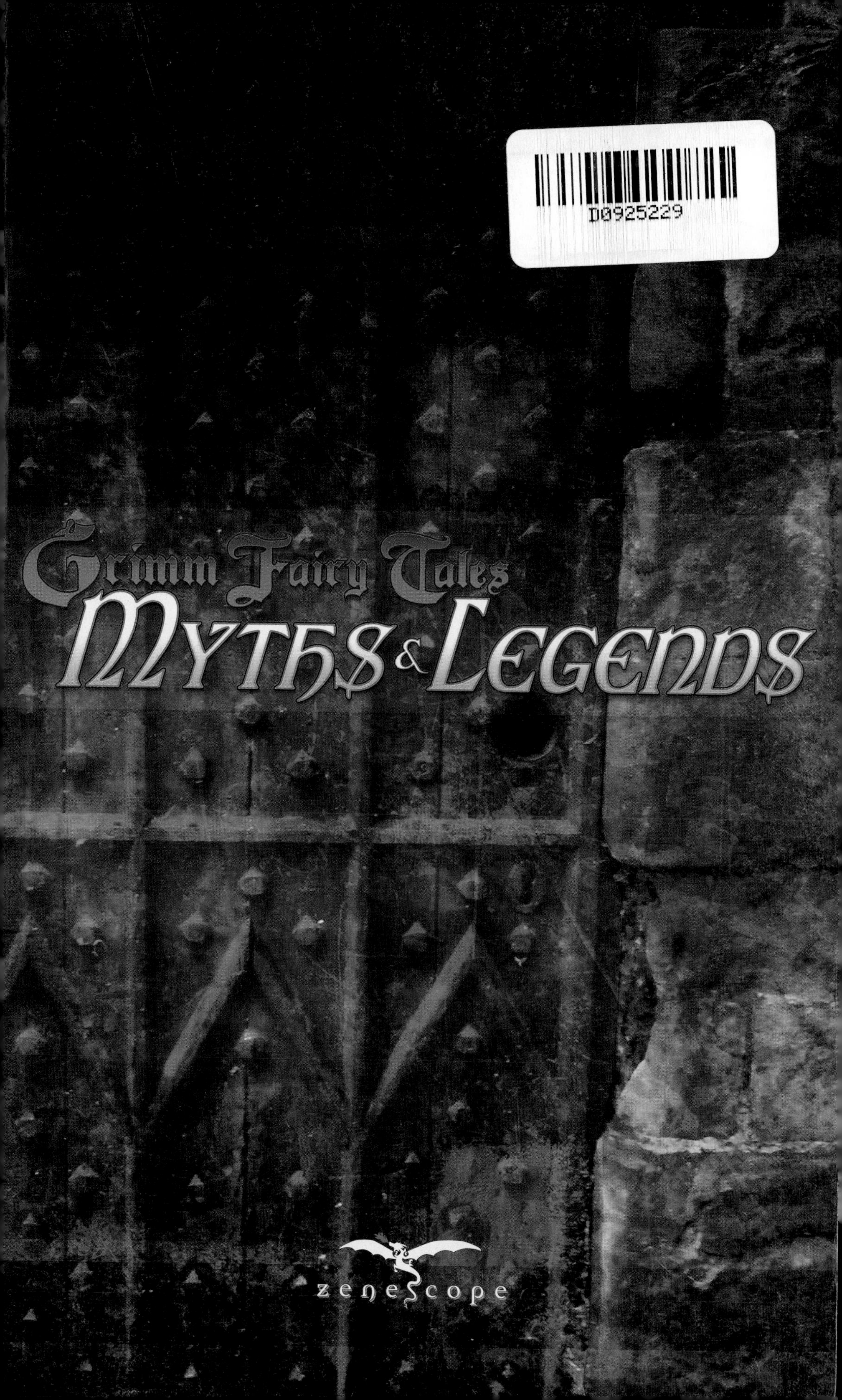
D0925229
Grimm Fairy Tales
Myths & Legends
zenescope

## Grimm Fairy Tales
# MYTHS & LEGENDS

CREATED AND STORY BY
### RAVEN GREGORY
### JOE BRUSHA
### RALPH TEDESCO

TRADE DESIGN BY
### CHRISTOPHER COTE

TRADE EDITED BY
### RALPH TEDESCO
### MATT ROGERS

THIS VOLUME REPRINTS THE COMIC
SERIES GRIMM FAIRY TALES MYTHS
& LEGENDS ISSUES #12-15 AND
GRIMM FAIRY TALES ISSUES #13
& 14 PUBLISHED BY ZENESCOPE
ENTERTAINMENT.

WWW.ZENESCOPE.COM

FIRST EDITION, MAY 2012
ISBN: 978-1-937068-41-7

### zenescope
WWW.ZENESCOPE.COM
FACEBOOK.COM/ZENESCOPE

**ZENESCOPE ENTERTAINMENT, INC.**

**Joe Brusha** • President & Chief Creative Officer
**Ralph Tedesco** • Editor-in-Chief
**Jennifer Bermel** • Director of Licensing & Business Development
**Raven Gregory** • Executive Editor
**Anthony Spay** • Art Director
**Christopher Cote** • Production Manager
**Dave Franchini** • Direct Market Sales & Customer Service
**Stephen Haberman** • Marketing Manager

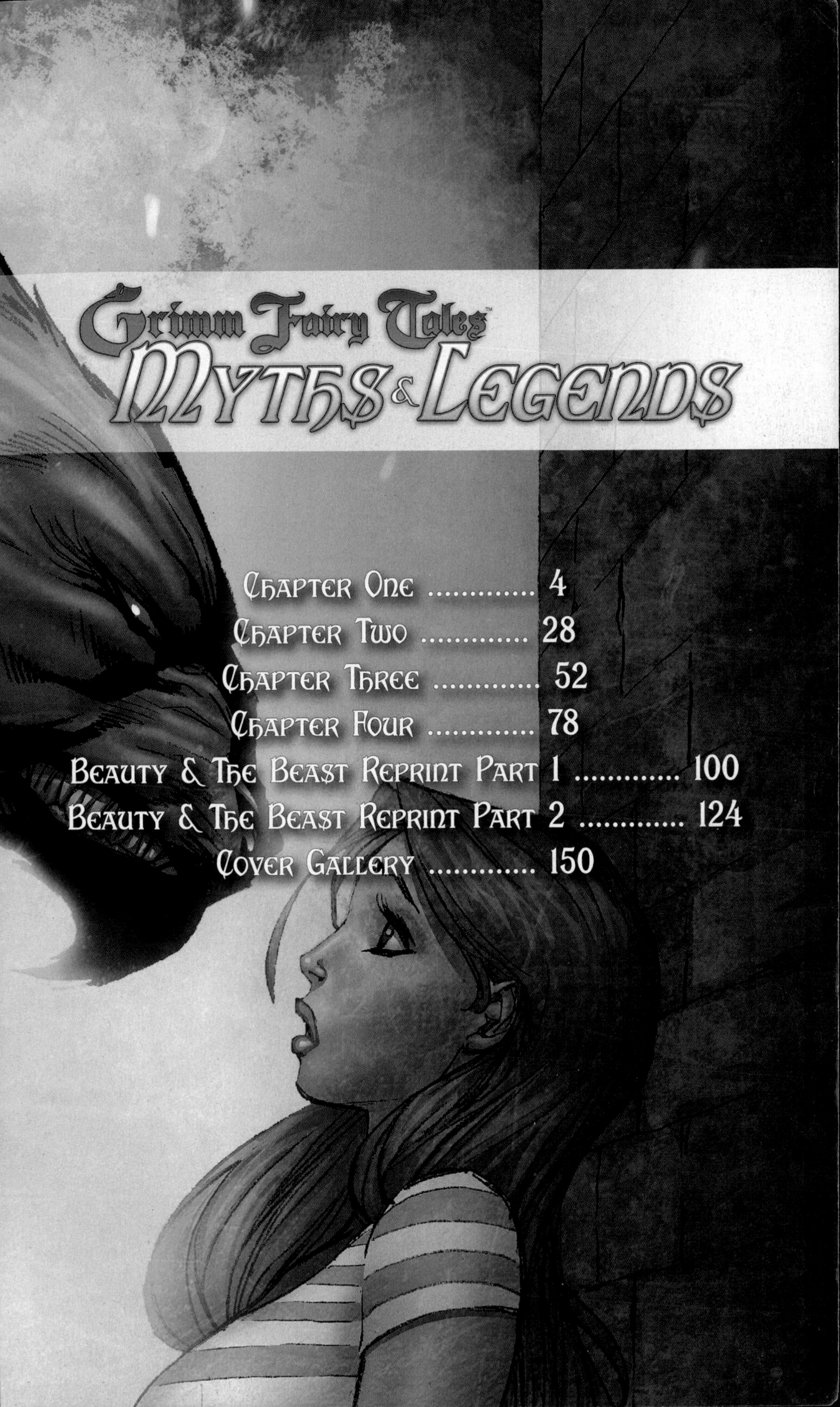

# Grimm Fairy Tales™ Myths & Legends

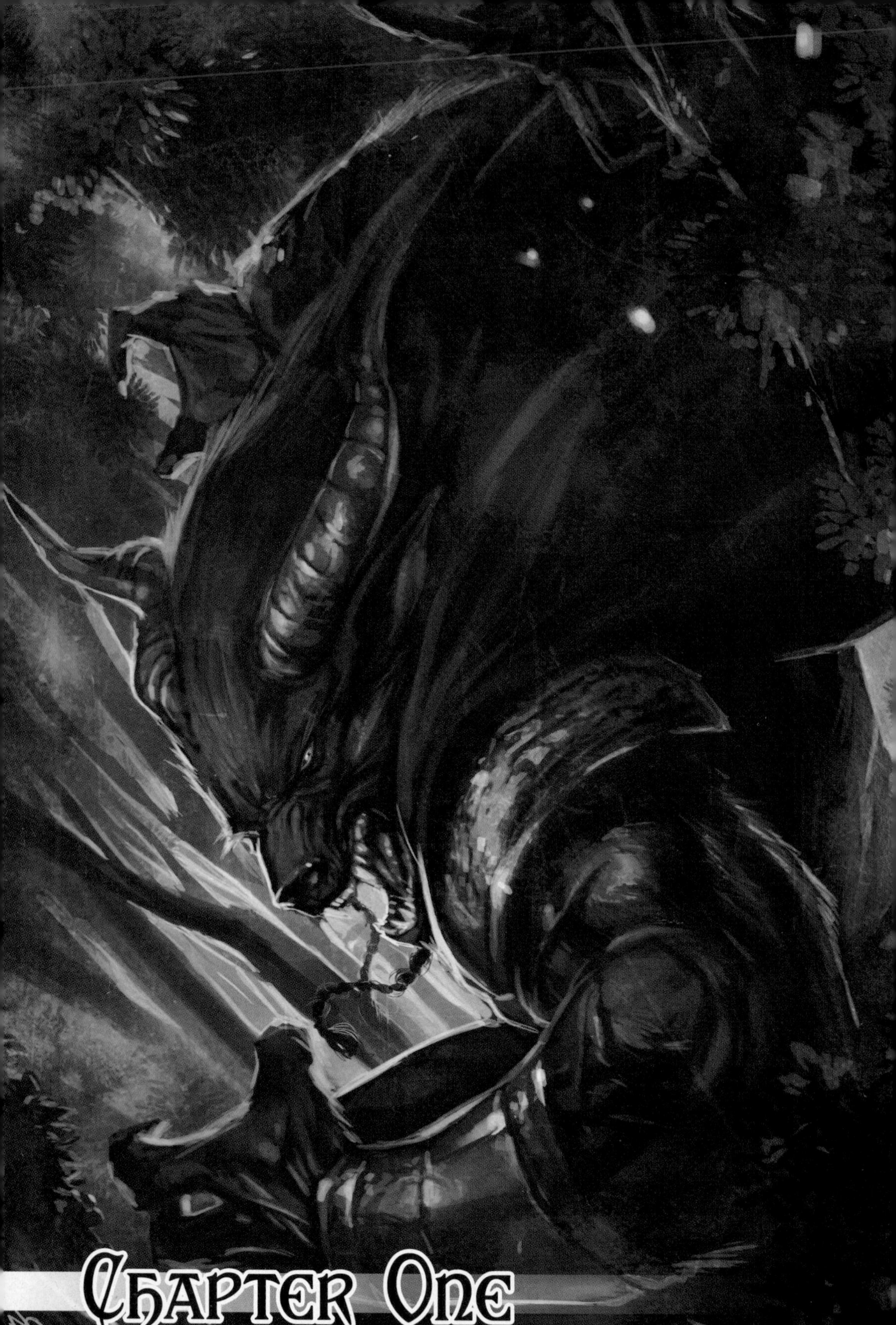

# Chapter One

Story by Raven Gregory, Joe Brusha and Ralph Tedesco

Written by Raven Gregory • Art by Juanan Ramirez

Colors by Jason Embury, Andrew Elder and Tim Yates • Letters by Jim Campbell

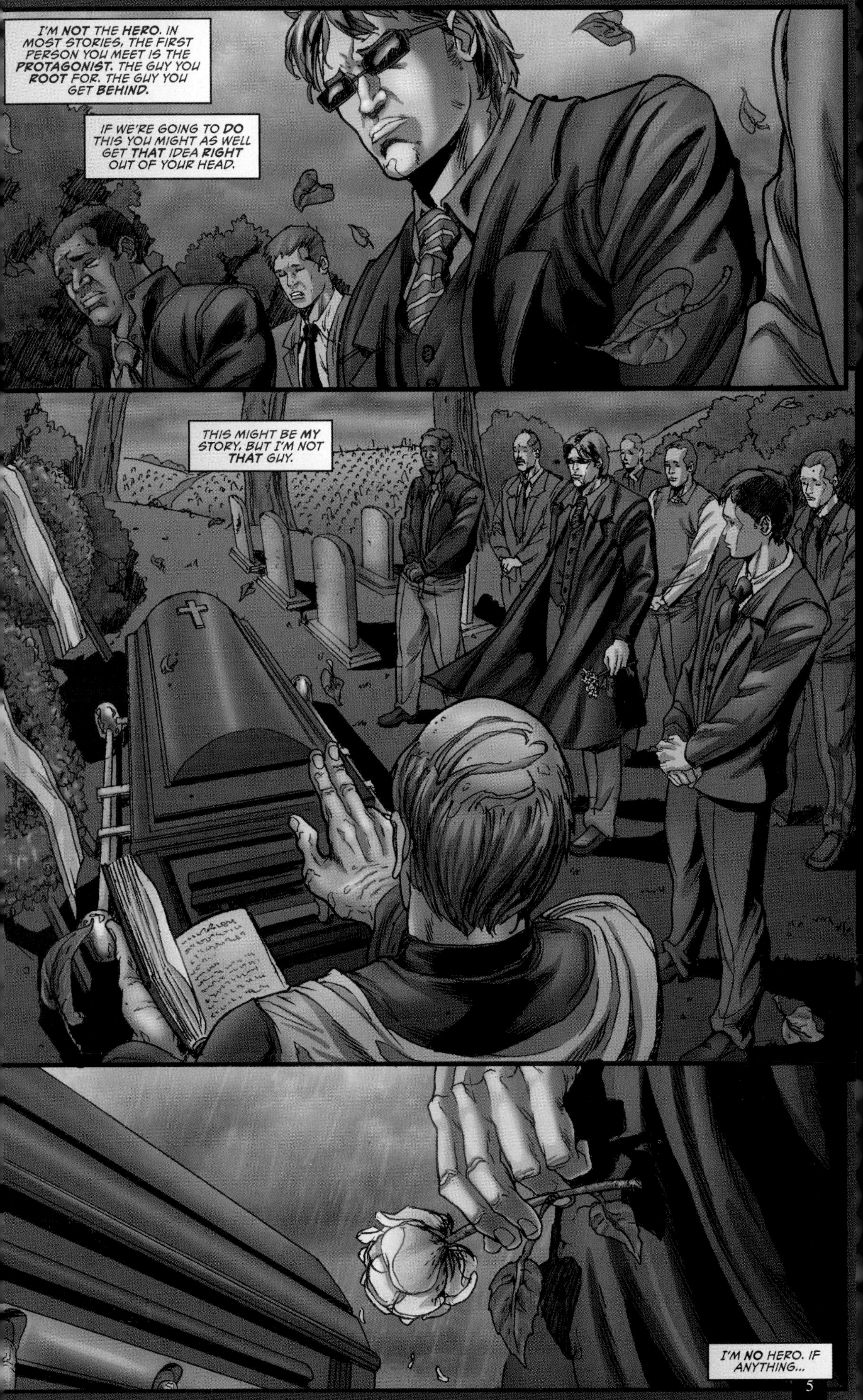
I'M NOT THE HERO. IN MOST STORIES, THE FIRST PERSON YOU MEET IS THE PROTAGONIST. THE GUY YOU ROOT FOR. THE GUY YOU GET BEHIND.
IF WE'RE GOING TO DO THIS YOU MIGHT AS WELL GET THAT IDEA RIGHT OUT OF YOUR HEAD.
THIS MIGHT BE MY STORY, BUT I'M NOT THAT GUY.
I'M NO HERO. IF ANYTHING...

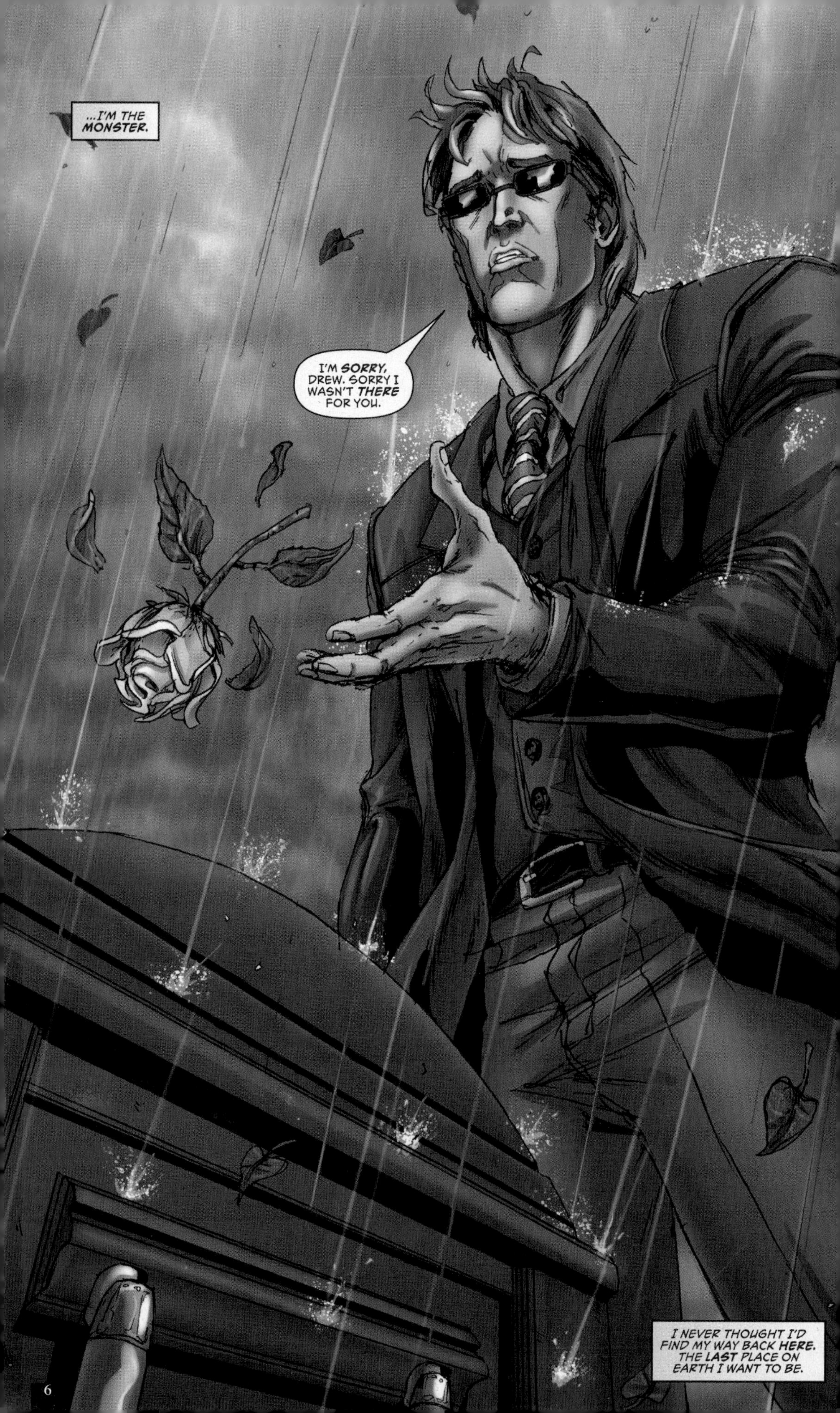
...I'M THE MONSTER.
I'M SORRY, DREW. SORRY I WASN'T THERE FOR YOU.
I NEVER THOUGHT I'D FIND MY WAY BACK HERE. THE LAST PLACE ON EARTH I WANT TO BE.

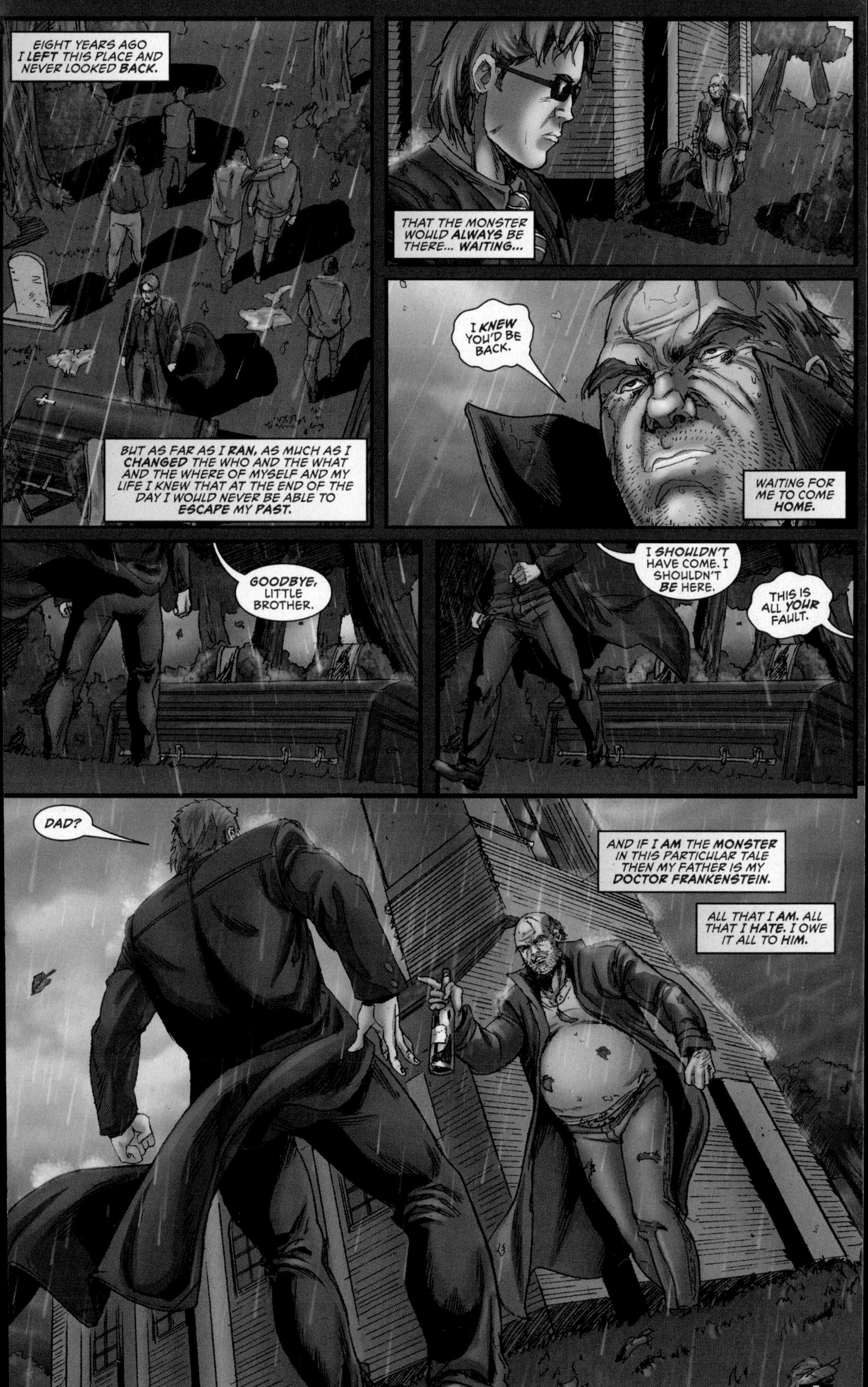
EIGHT YEARS AGO I LEFT THIS PLACE AND NEVER LOOKED BACK.
BUT AS FAR AS I RAN, AS MUCH AS I CHANGED THE WHO AND THE WHAT AND THE WHERE OF MYSELF AND MY LIFE I KNEW THAT AT THE END OF THE DAY I WOULD NEVER BE ABLE TO ESCAPE MY PAST.
THAT THE MONSTER WOULD ALWAYS BE THERE... WAITING...
I KNEW YOU'D BE BACK.
WAITING FOR ME TO COME HOME.
GOODBYE, LITTLE BROTHER.
I SHOULDN'T HAVE COME. I SHOULDN'T BE HERE.
THIS IS ALL YOUR FAULT.
DAD?
AND IF I AM THE MONSTER IN THIS PARTICULAR TALE THEN MY FATHER IS MY DOCTOR FRANKENSTEIN.
ALL THAT I AM. ALL THAT I HATE. I OWE IT ALL TO HIM.

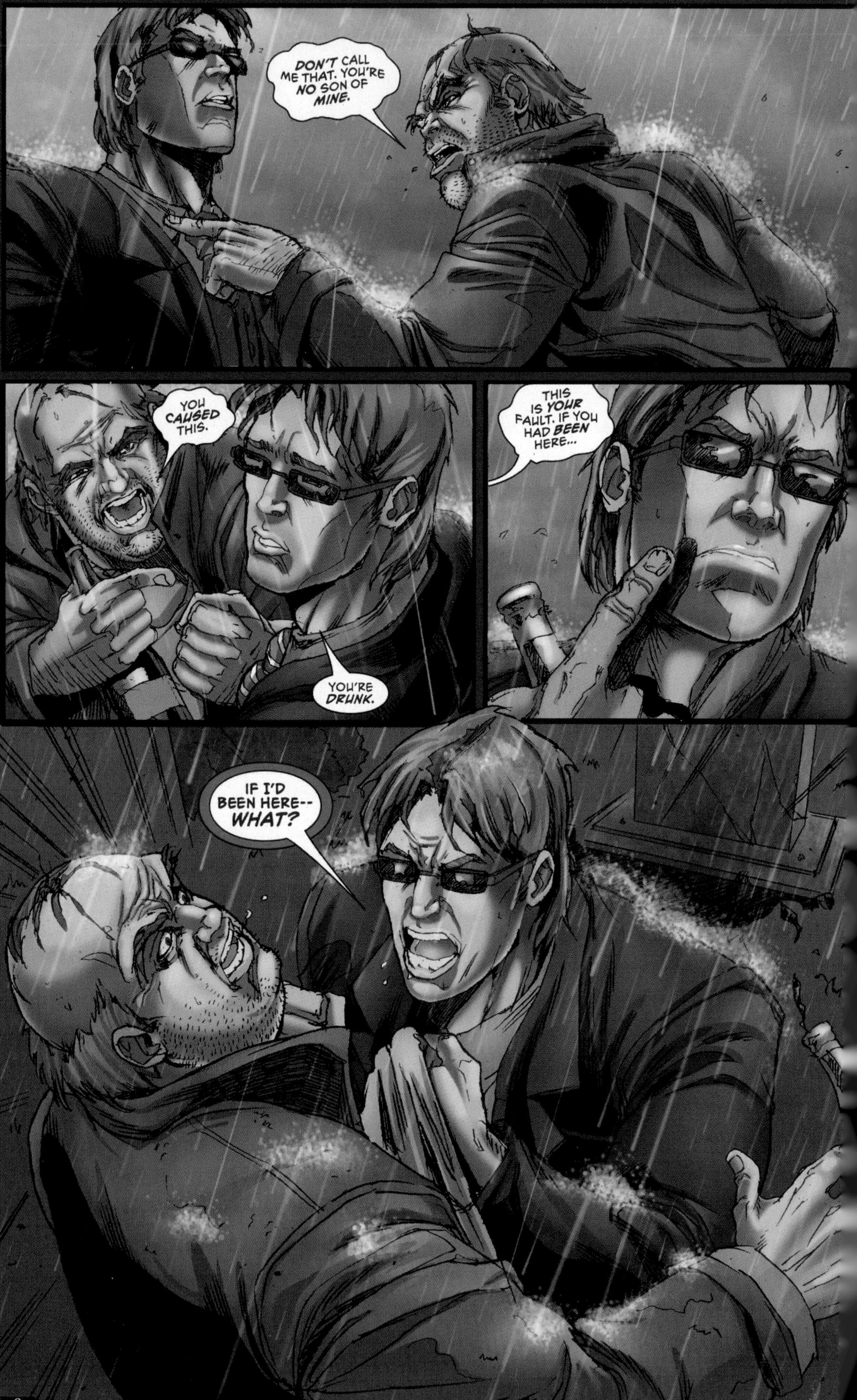
DON'T CALL ME THAT. YOU'RE NO SON OF MINE.
YOU CAUSED THIS.
YOU'RE DRUNK.
THIS IS YOUR FAULT. IF YOU HAD BEEN HERE...
IF I'D BEEN HERE-- WHAT?

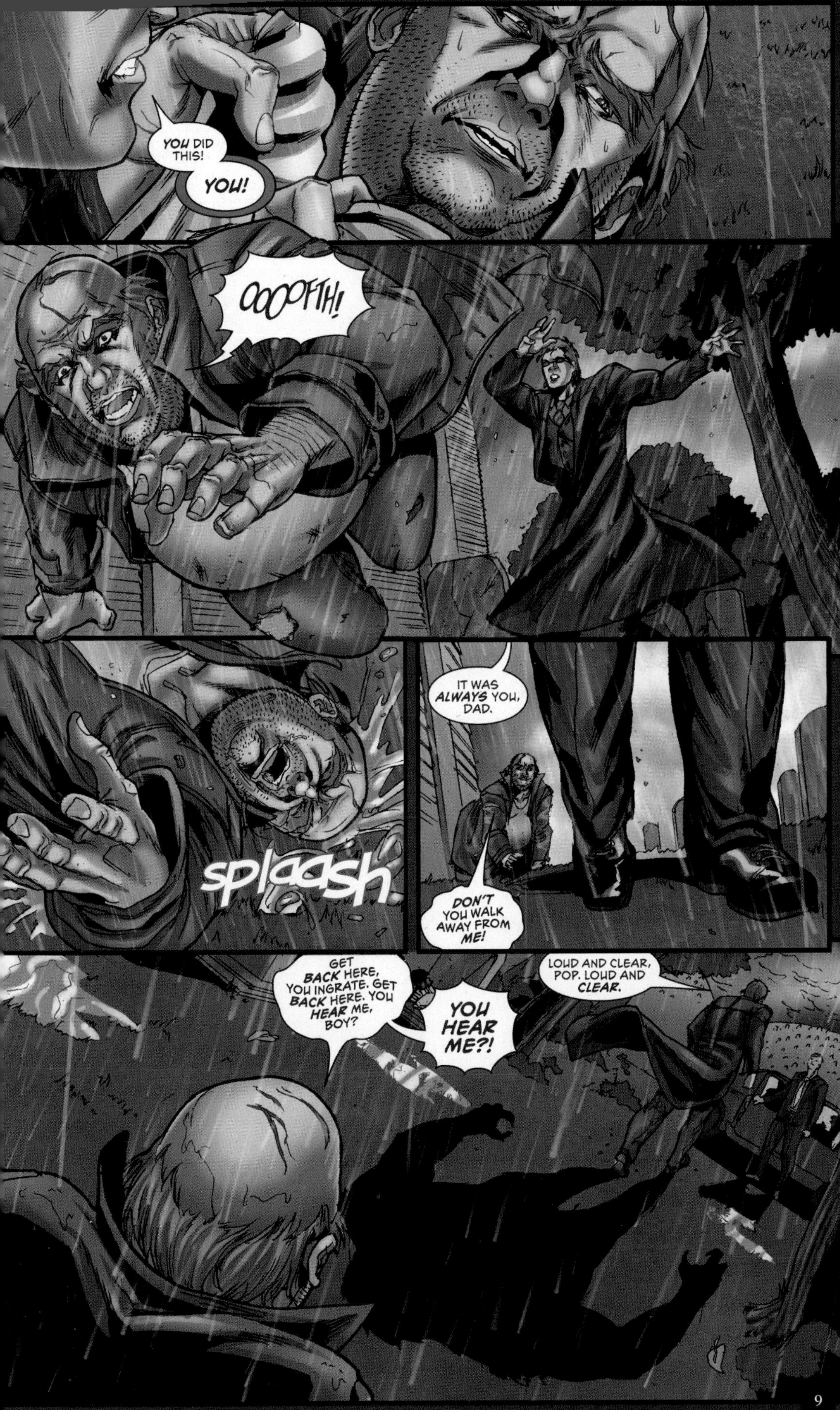
YOU DID THIS!
YOU!
OOOOFTH!
splaash
IT WAS ALWAYS YOU, DAD.
DON'T YOU WALK AWAY FROM ME!
GET BACK HERE, YOU INGRATE. GET BACK HERE. YOU HEAR ME, BOY?
YOU HEAR ME?!
LOUD AND CLEAR, POP. LOUD AND CLEAR.

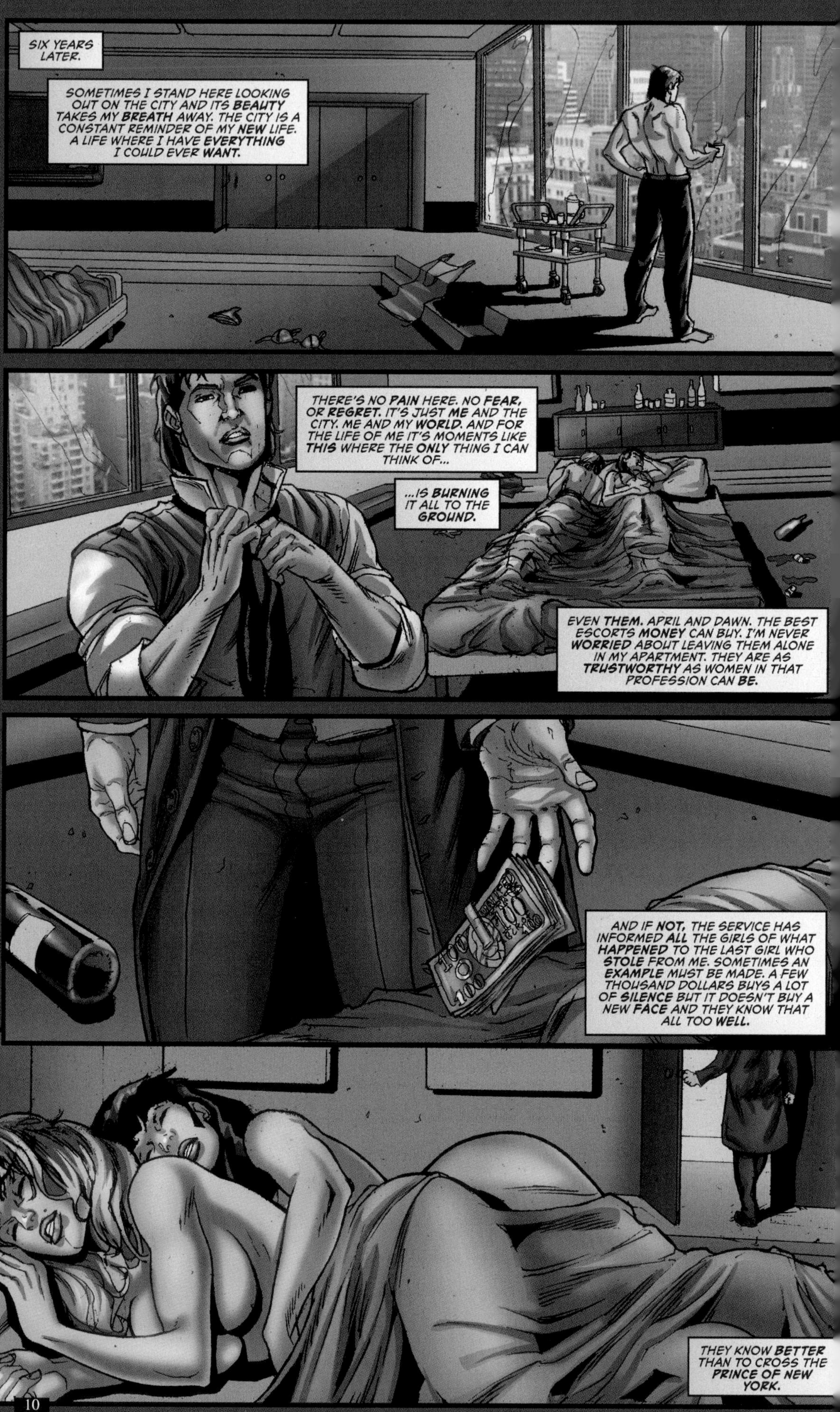
SIX YEARS LATER.
SOMETIMES I STAND HERE LOOKING OUT ON THE CITY AND ITS BEAUTY TAKES MY BREATH AWAY. THE CITY IS A CONSTANT REMINDER OF MY NEW LIFE. A LIFE WHERE I HAVE EVERYTHING I COULD EVER WANT.
THERE'S NO PAIN HERE. NO FEAR, OR REGRET. IT'S JUST ME AND THE CITY. ME AND MY WORLD. AND FOR THE LIFE OF ME IT'S MOMENTS LIKE THIS WHERE THE ONLY THING I CAN THINK OF...
...IS BURNING IT ALL TO THE GROUND.
EVEN THEM. APRIL AND DAWN. THE BEST ESCORTS MONEY CAN BUY. I'M NEVER WORRIED ABOUT LEAVING THEM ALONE IN MY APARTMENT. THEY ARE AS TRUSTWORTHY AS WOMEN IN THAT PROFESSION CAN BE.
AND IF NOT, THE SERVICE HAS INFORMED ALL THE GIRLS OF WHAT HAPPENED TO THE LAST GIRL WHO STOLE FROM ME. SOMETIMES AN EXAMPLE MUST BE MADE. A FEW THOUSAND DOLLARS BUYS A LOT OF SILENCE BUT IT DOESN'T BUY A NEW FACE AND THEY KNOW THAT ALL TOO WELL.
THEY KNOW BETTER THAN TO CROSS THE PRINCE OF NEW YORK.

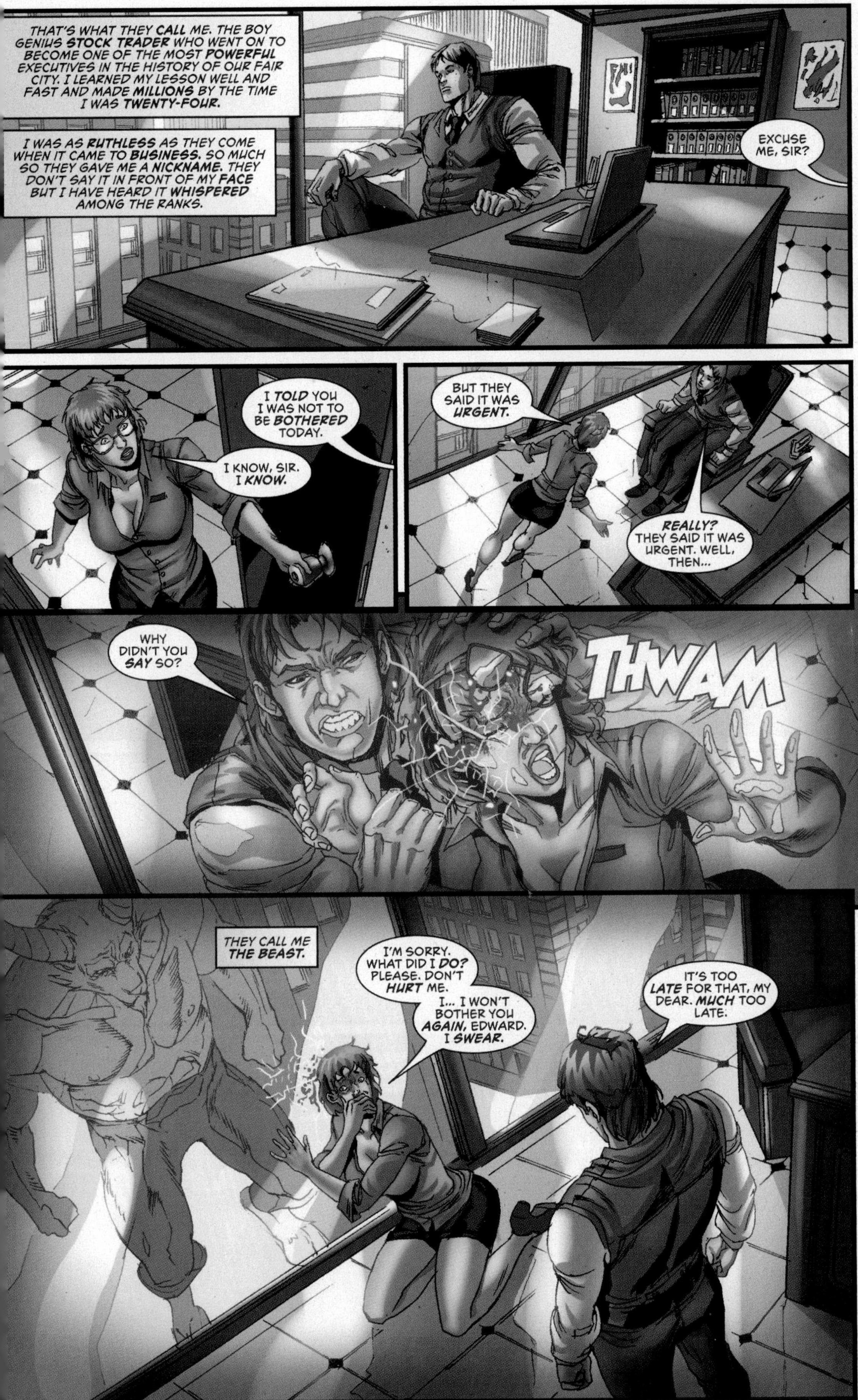
THAT'S WHAT THEY CALL ME. THE BOY GENIUS STOCK TRADER WHO WENT ON TO BECOME ONE OF THE MOST POWERFUL EXECUTIVES IN THE HISTORY OF OUR FAIR CITY. I LEARNED MY LESSON WELL AND FAST AND MADE MILLIONS BY THE TIME I WAS TWENTY-FOUR.
I WAS AS RUTHLESS AS THEY COME WHEN IT CAME TO BUSINESS. SO MUCH SO THEY GAVE ME A NICKNAME. THEY DON'T SAY IT IN FRONT OF MY FACE BUT I HAVE HEARD IT WHISPERED AMONG THE RANKS.
EXCUSE ME, SIR?
I TOLD YOU I WAS NOT TO BE BOTHERED TODAY.
I KNOW, SIR. I KNOW.
BUT THEY SAID IT WAS URGENT.
REALLY? THEY SAID IT WAS URGENT. WELL, THEN...
WHY DIDN'T YOU SAY SO?
THWAM
THEY CALL ME THE BEAST.
I'M SORRY. WHAT DID I DO? PLEASE. DON'T HURT ME.
I... I WON'T BOTHER YOU AGAIN, EDWARD. I SWEAR.
IT'S TOO LATE FOR THAT, MY DEAR. MUCH TOO LATE.

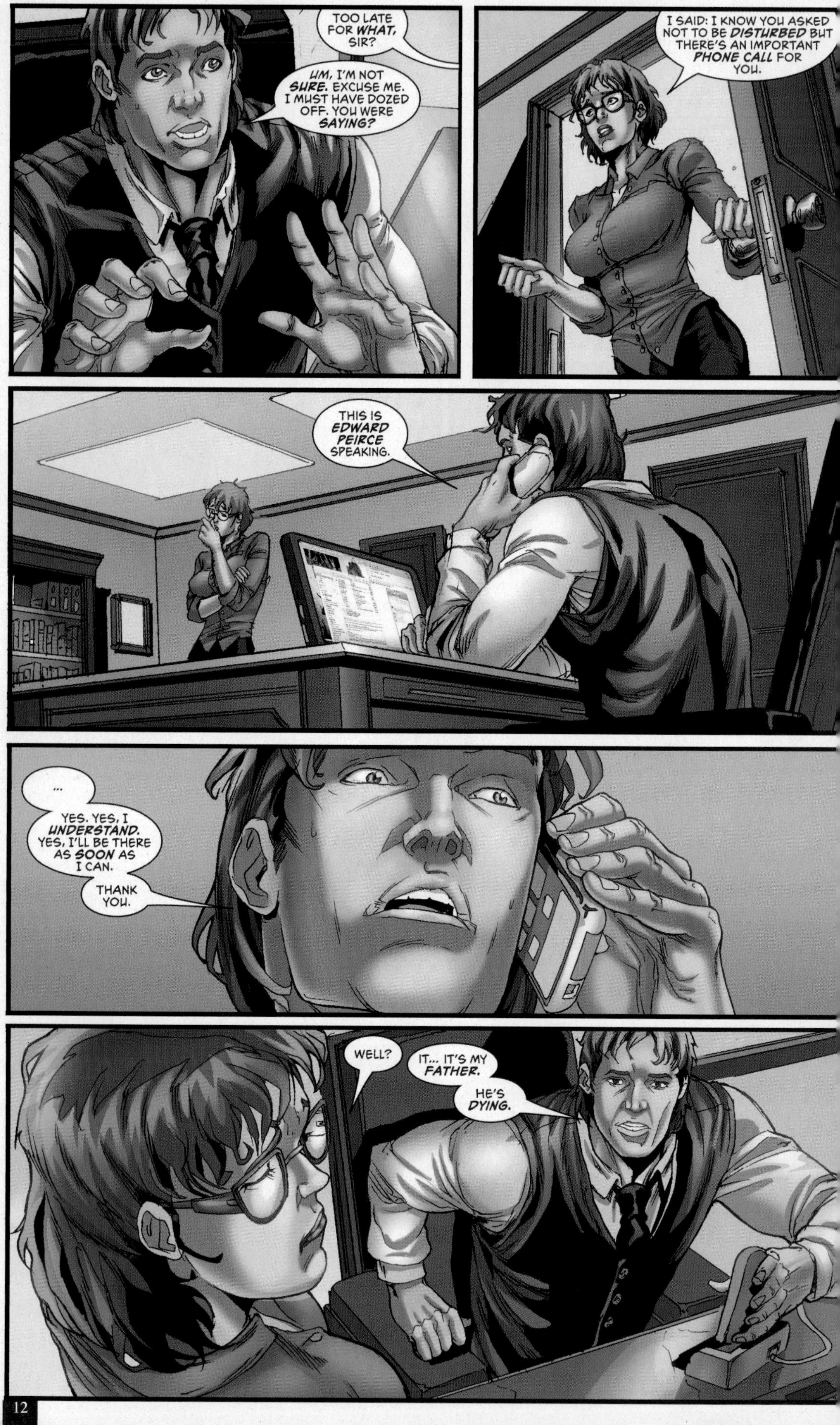
TOO LATE FOR WHAT, SIR?
UM, I'M NOT SURE. EXCUSE ME. I MUST HAVE DOZED OFF. YOU WERE SAYING?
I SAID: I KNOW YOU ASKED NOT TO BE DISTURBED BUT THERE'S AN IMPORTANT PHONE CALL FOR YOU.
THIS IS EDWARD PEIRCE SPEAKING.
...
YES. YES, I UNDERSTAND. YES, I'LL BE THERE AS SOON AS I CAN.
THANK YOU.
WELL?
IT... IT'S MY FATHER.
HE'S DYING.

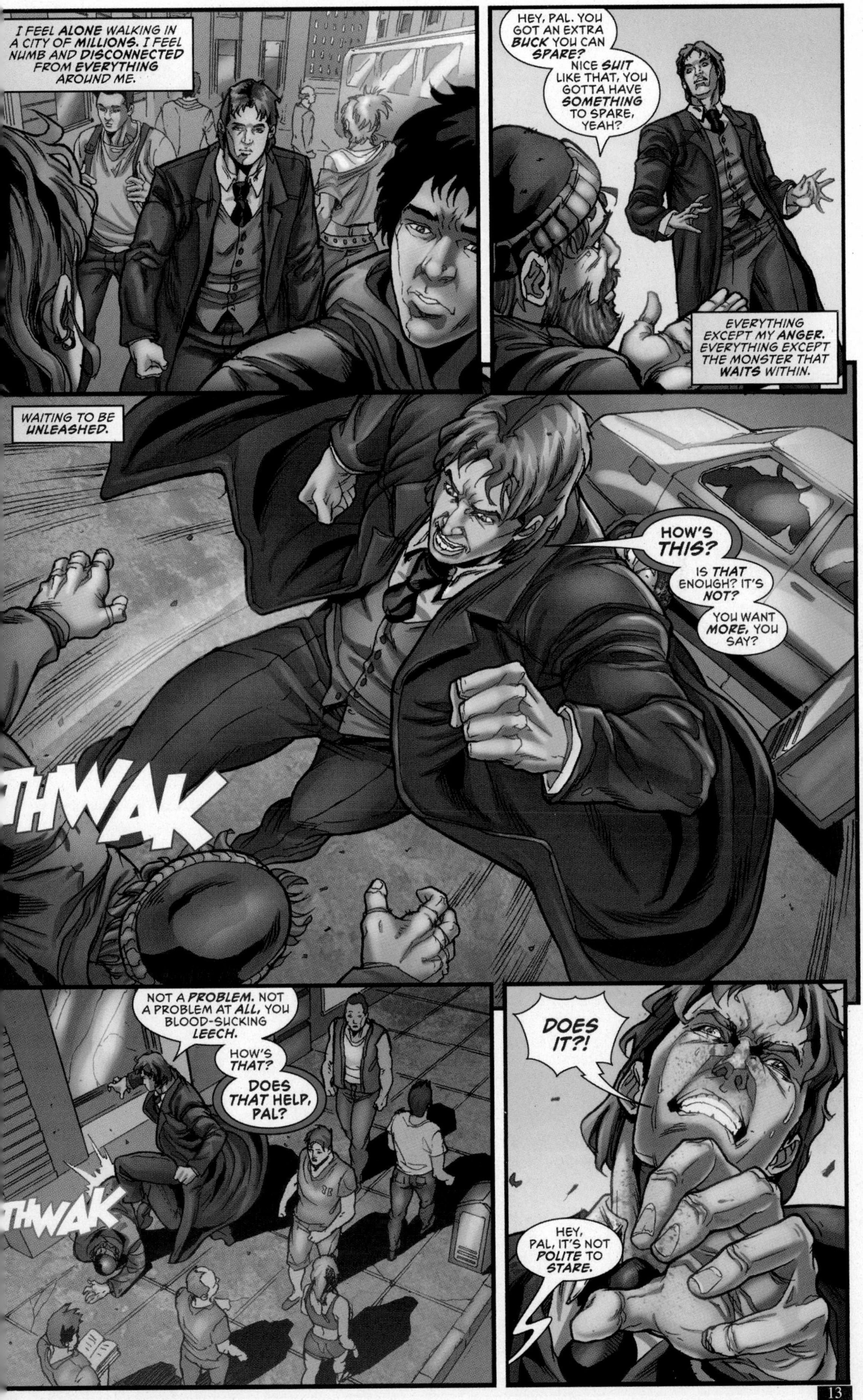
I FEEL ALONE WALKING IN A CITY OF MILLIONS. I FEEL NUMB AND DISCONNECTED FROM EVERYTHING AROUND ME.
HEY, PAL. YOU GOT AN EXTRA BUCK YOU CAN SPARE?
NICE SUIT LIKE THAT, YOU GOTTA HAVE SOMETHING TO SPARE, YEAH?
EVERYTHING EXCEPT MY ANGER. EVERYTHING EXCEPT THE MONSTER THAT WAITS WITHIN.
WAITING TO BE UNLEASHED.
HOW'S THIS?
IS THAT ENOUGH? IT'S NOT?
YOU WANT MORE, YOU SAY?
THWAK
NOT A PROBLEM. NOT A PROBLEM AT ALL, YOU BLOOD-SUCKING LEECH.
HOW'S THAT?
DOES THAT HELP, PAL?
THWAK
DOES IT?!
HEY, PAL, IT'S NOT POLITE TO STARE.

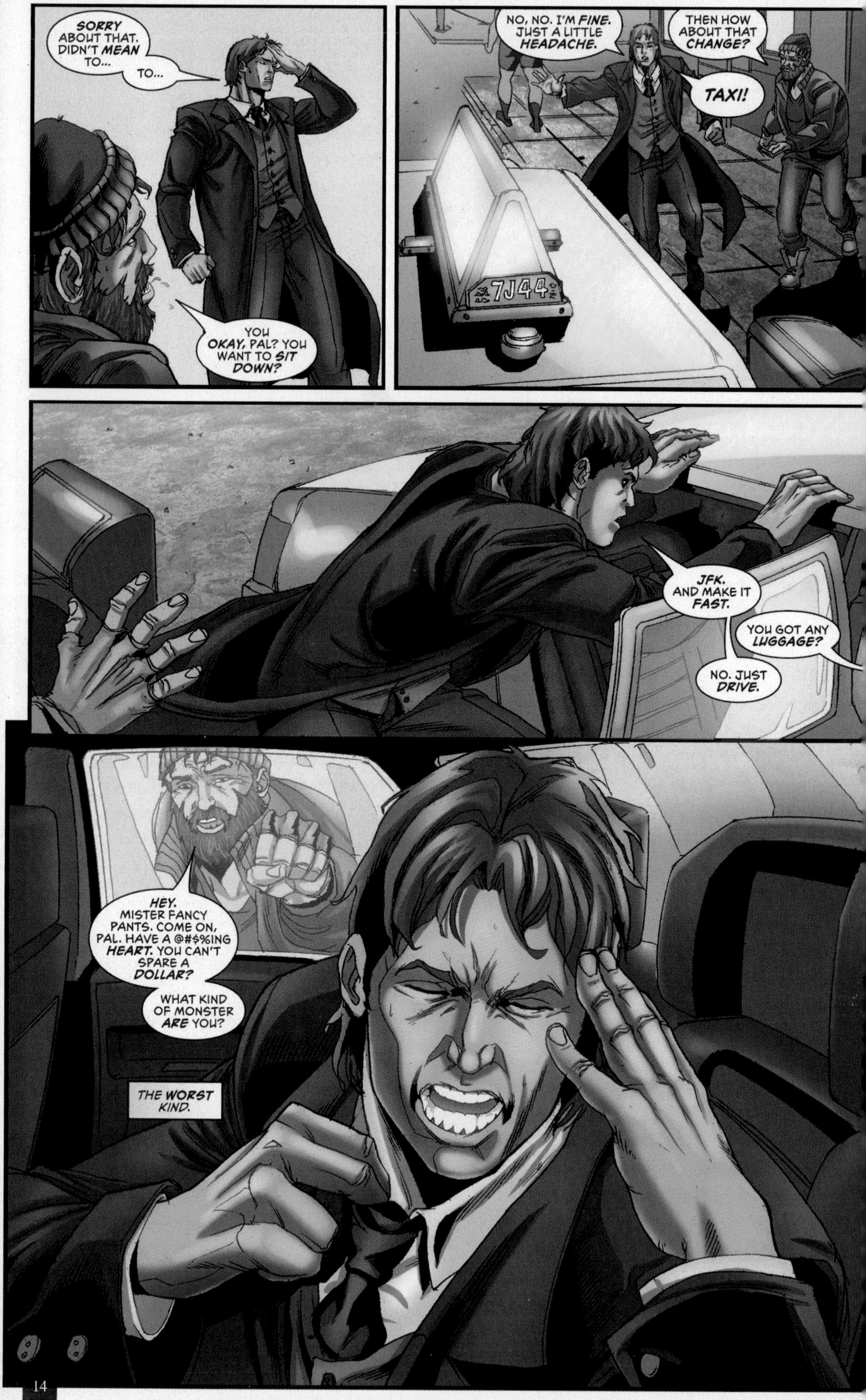
SORRY ABOUT THAT. DIDN'T MEAN TO...
TO...
YOU OKAY, PAL? YOU WANT TO SIT DOWN?
NO, NO. I'M FINE. JUST A LITTLE HEADACHE.
THEN HOW ABOUT THAT CHANGE?
TAXI!
7J44
JFK. AND MAKE IT FAST.
YOU GOT ANY LUGGAGE?
NO. JUST DRIVE.
HEY. MISTER FANCY PANTS. COME ON, PAL. HAVE A @#$%ING HEART. YOU CAN'T SPARE A DOLLAR?
WHAT KIND OF MONSTER ARE YOU?
THE WORST KIND.

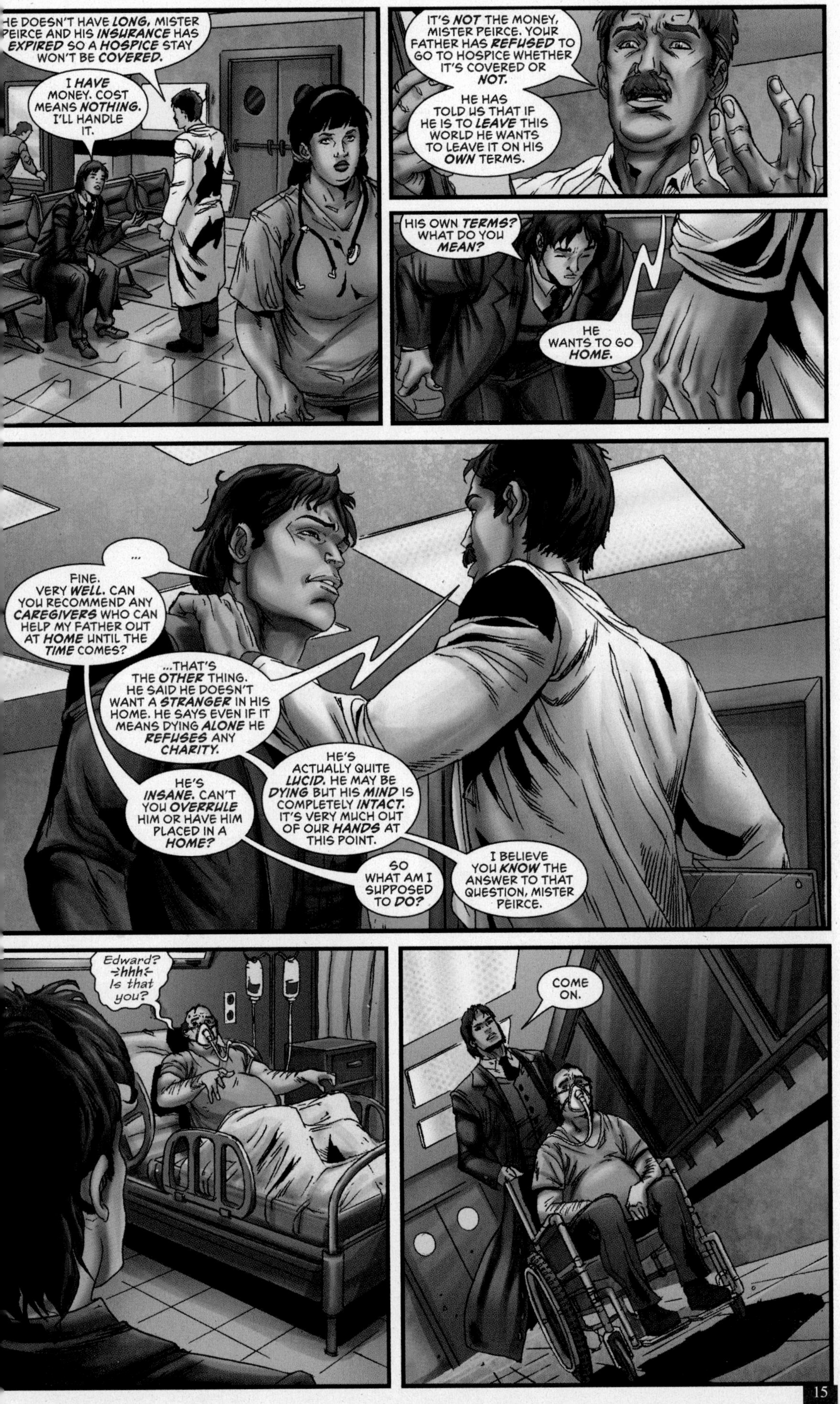

HE DOESN'T HAVE LONG, MISTER PEIRCE AND HIS INSURANCE HAS EXPIRED SO A HOSPICE STAY WON'T BE COVERED.
I HAVE MONEY. COST MEANS NOTHING. I'LL HANDLE IT.
IT'S NOT THE MONEY, MISTER PEIRCE. YOUR FATHER HAS REFUSED TO GO TO HOSPICE WHETHER IT'S COVERED OR NOT.
HE HAS TOLD US THAT IF HE IS TO LEAVE THIS WORLD HE WANTS TO LEAVE IT ON HIS OWN TERMS.
HIS OWN TERMS? WHAT DO YOU MEAN?
HE WANTS TO GO HOME.
...
FINE. VERY WELL. CAN YOU RECOMMEND ANY CAREGIVERS WHO CAN HELP MY FATHER OUT AT HOME UNTIL THE TIME COMES?
...THAT'S THE OTHER THING. HE SAID HE DOESN'T WANT A STRANGER IN HIS HOME. HE SAYS EVEN IF IT MEANS DYING ALONE HE REFUSES ANY CHARITY.
HE'S INSANE. CAN'T YOU OVERRULE HIM OR HAVE HIM PLACED IN A HOME?
HE'S ACTUALLY QUITE LUCID. HE MAY BE DYING BUT HIS MIND IS COMPLETELY INTACT. IT'S VERY MUCH OUT OF OUR HANDS AT THIS POINT.
SO WHAT AM I SUPPOSED TO DO?
I BELIEVE YOU KNOW THE ANSWER TO THAT QUESTION, MISTER PEIRCE.
Edward? ≈hhh≈ Is that you?
COME ON.

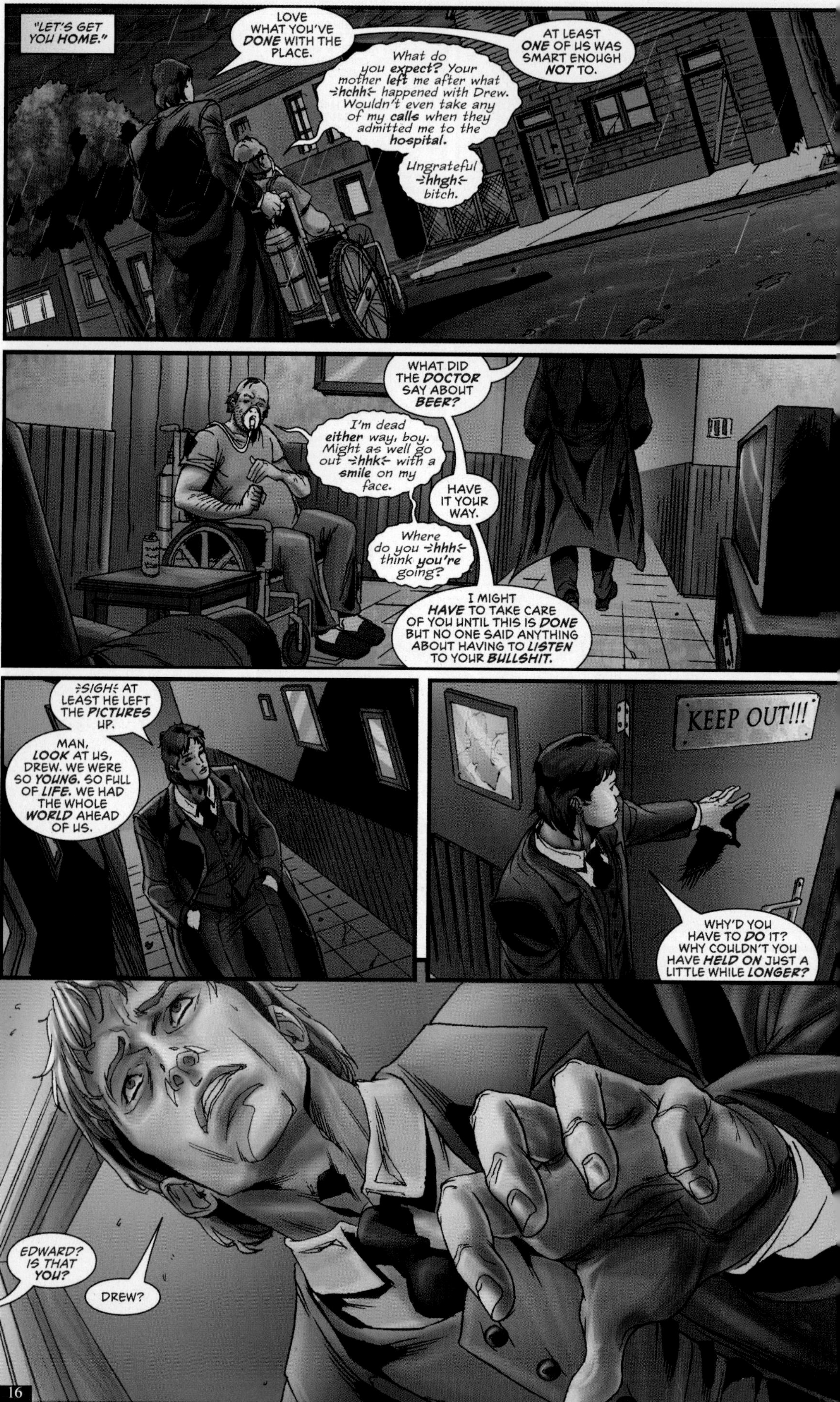
"LET'S GET YOU HOME."
LOVE WHAT YOU'VE DONE WITH THE PLACE.
What do you expect? Your mother left me after what -hchh- happened with Drew. Wouldn't even take any of my calls when they admitted me to the hospital.
Ungrateful -hhgh- bitch.
AT LEAST ONE OF US WAS SMART ENOUGH NOT TO.
WHAT DID THE DOCTOR SAY ABOUT BEER?
I'm dead either way, boy. Might as well go out -hhk- with a smile on my face.
HAVE IT YOUR WAY.
Where do you -hhh- think you're going?
I MIGHT HAVE TO TAKE CARE OF YOU UNTIL THIS IS DONE BUT NO ONE SAID ANYTHING ABOUT HAVING TO LISTEN TO YOUR BULLSHIT.
-SIGH- AT LEAST HE LEFT THE PICTURES UP.
MAN, LOOK AT US, DREW. WE WERE SO YOUNG. SO FULL OF LIFE. WE HAD THE WHOLE WORLD AHEAD OF US.
KEEP OUT!!!
WHY'D YOU HAVE TO DO IT? WHY COULDN'T YOU HAVE HELD ON JUST A LITTLE WHILE LONGER?
EDWARD? IS THAT YOU?
DREW?

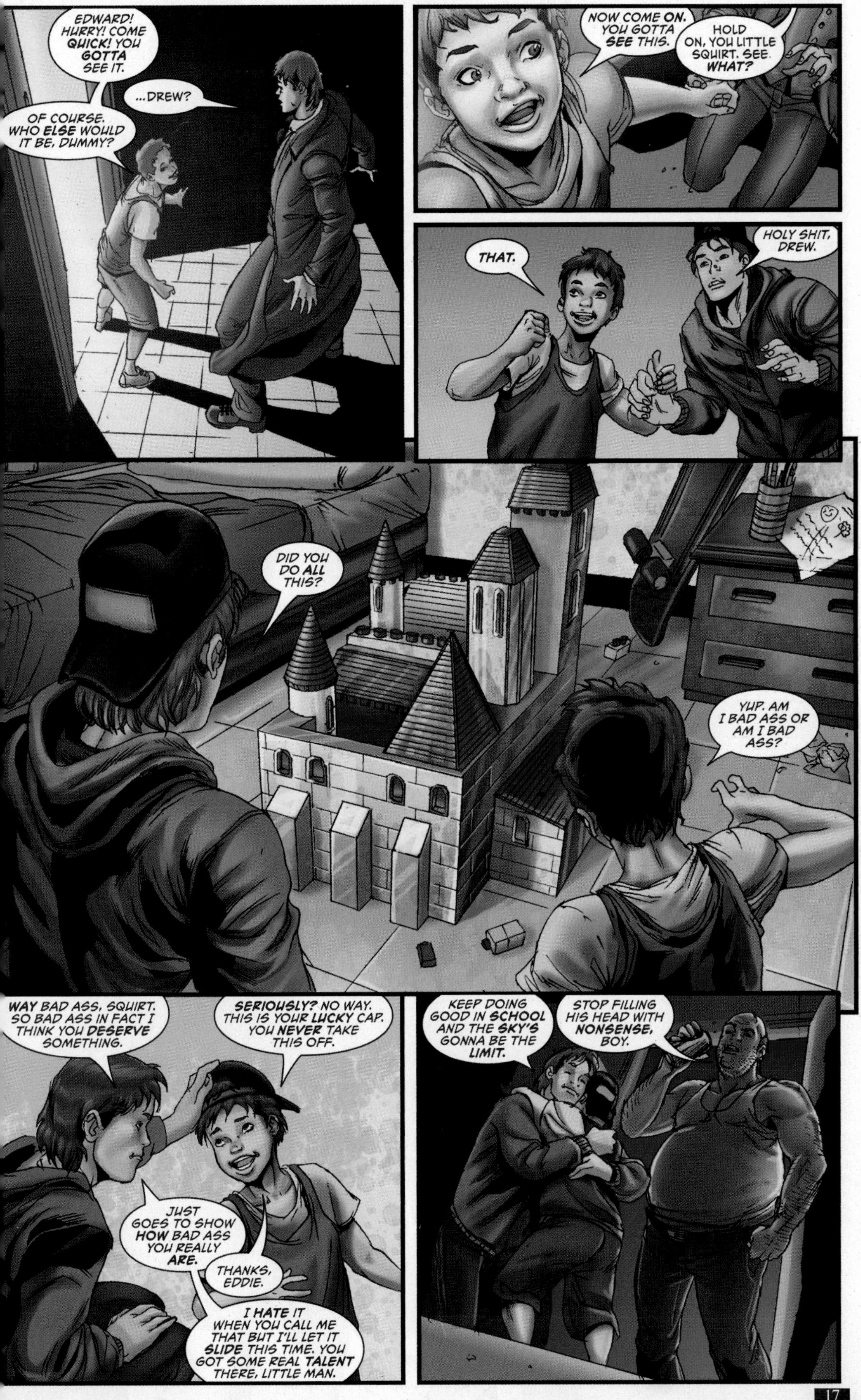
EDWARD! HURRY! COME QUICK! YOU GOTTA SEE IT.
...DREW?
OF COURSE. WHO ELSE WOULD IT BE, DUMMY?
NOW COME ON. YOU GOTTA SEE THIS.
HOLD ON, YOU LITTLE SQUIRT. SEE WHAT?
THAT.
HOLY SHIT, DREW.
DID YOU DO ALL THIS?
YUP. AM I BAD ASS OR AM I BAD ASS?
WAY BAD ASS, SQUIRT. SO BAD ASS IN FACT I THINK YOU DESERVE SOMETHING.
SERIOUSLY? NO WAY. THIS IS YOUR LUCKY CAP. YOU NEVER TAKE THIS OFF.
JUST GOES TO SHOW HOW BAD ASS YOU REALLY ARE.
THANKS, EDDIE.
I HATE IT WHEN YOU CALL ME THAT BUT I'LL LET IT SLIDE THIS TIME. YOU GOT SOME REAL TALENT THERE, LITTLE MAN.
KEEP DOING GOOD IN SCHOOL AND THE SKY'S GONNA BE THE LIMIT.
STOP FILLING HIS HEAD WITH NONSENSE, BOY.

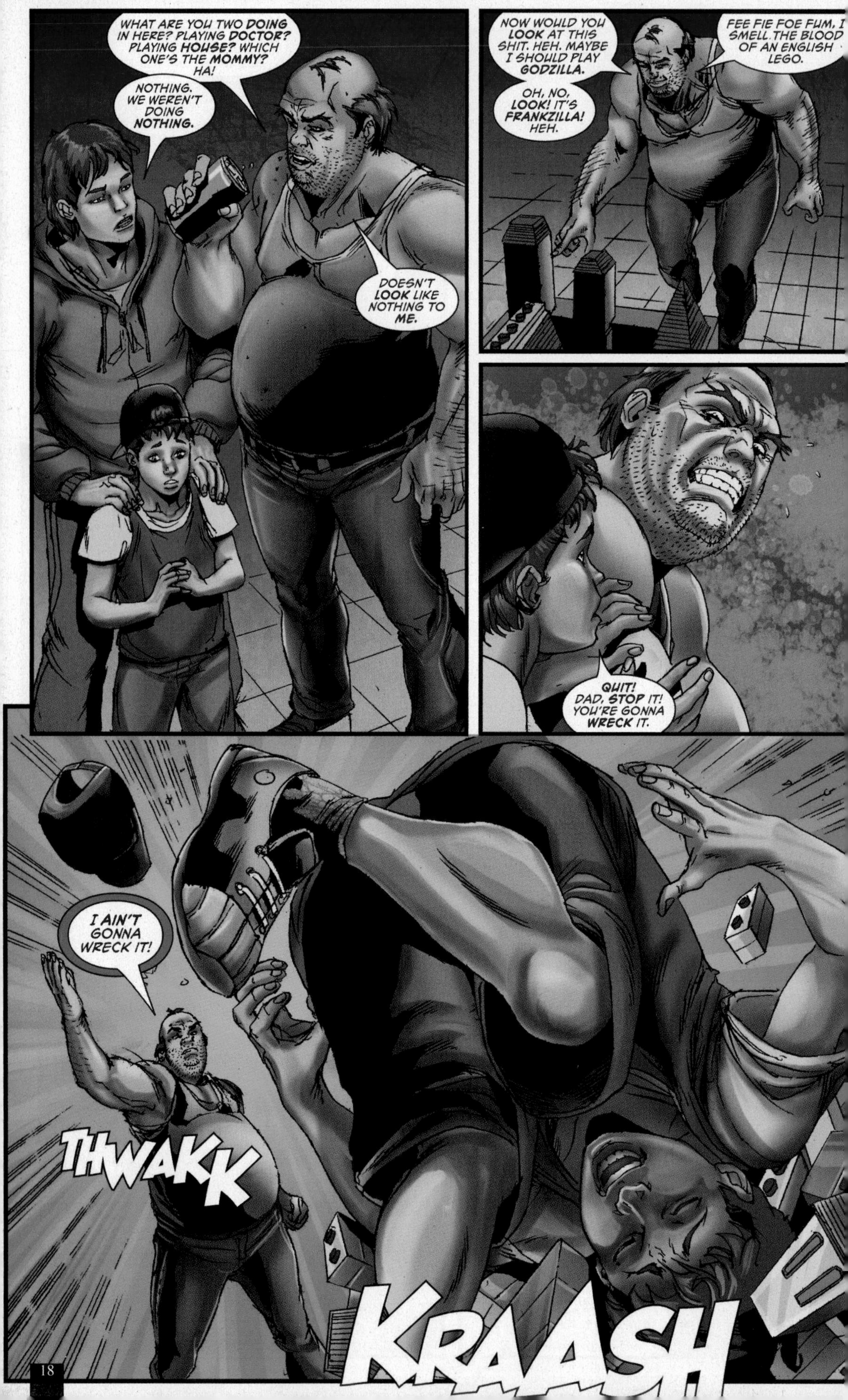
WHAT ARE YOU TWO DOING IN HERE? PLAYING DOCTOR? PLAYING HOUSE? WHICH ONE'S THE MOMMY? HA!
NOTHING. WE WEREN'T DOING NOTHING.
DOESN'T LOOK LIKE NOTHING TO ME.
NOW WOULD YOU LOOK AT THIS SHIT. HEH. MAYBE I SHOULD PLAY GODZILLA.
OH, NO, LOOK! IT'S FRANKZILLA! HEH.
FEE FIE FOE FUM. I SMELL THE BLOOD OF AN ENGLISH LEGO.
QUIT! DAD, STOP IT! YOU'RE GONNA WRECK IT.
I AIN'T GONNA WRECK IT!
THWAKK
KRAASH

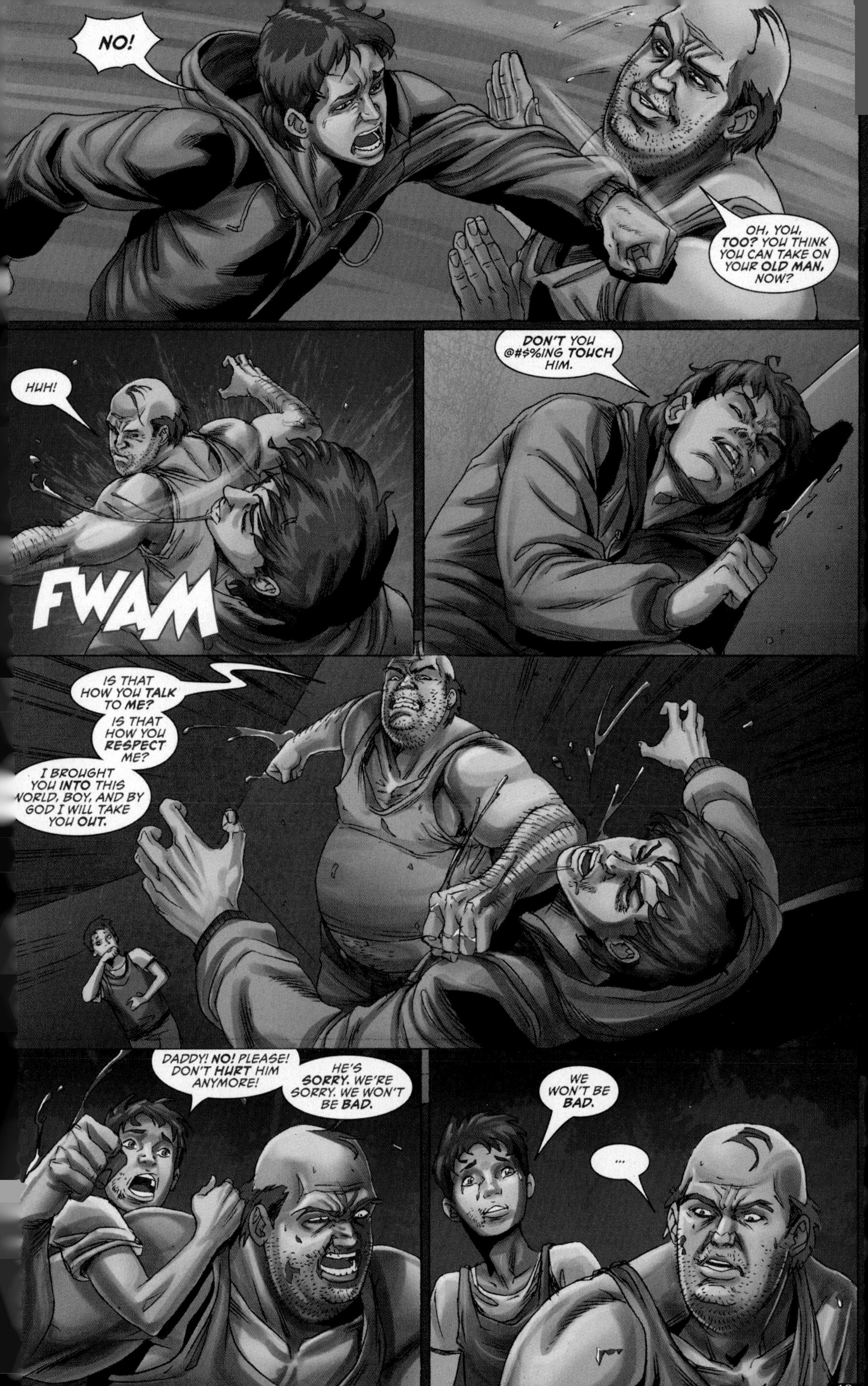
NO!
OH, YOU, TOO? YOU THINK YOU CAN TAKE ON YOUR OLD MAN, NOW?
HUH!
FWAM
DON'T YOU @#$%ING TOUCH HIM.
IS THAT HOW YOU TALK TO ME?
IS THAT HOW YOU RESPECT ME?
I BROUGHT YOU INTO THIS WORLD, BOY, AND BY GOD I WILL TAKE YOU OUT.
DADDY! NO! PLEASE! DON'T HURT HIM ANYMORE!
HE'S SORRY. WE'RE SORRY. WE WON'T BE BAD.
WE WON'T BE BAD.
...

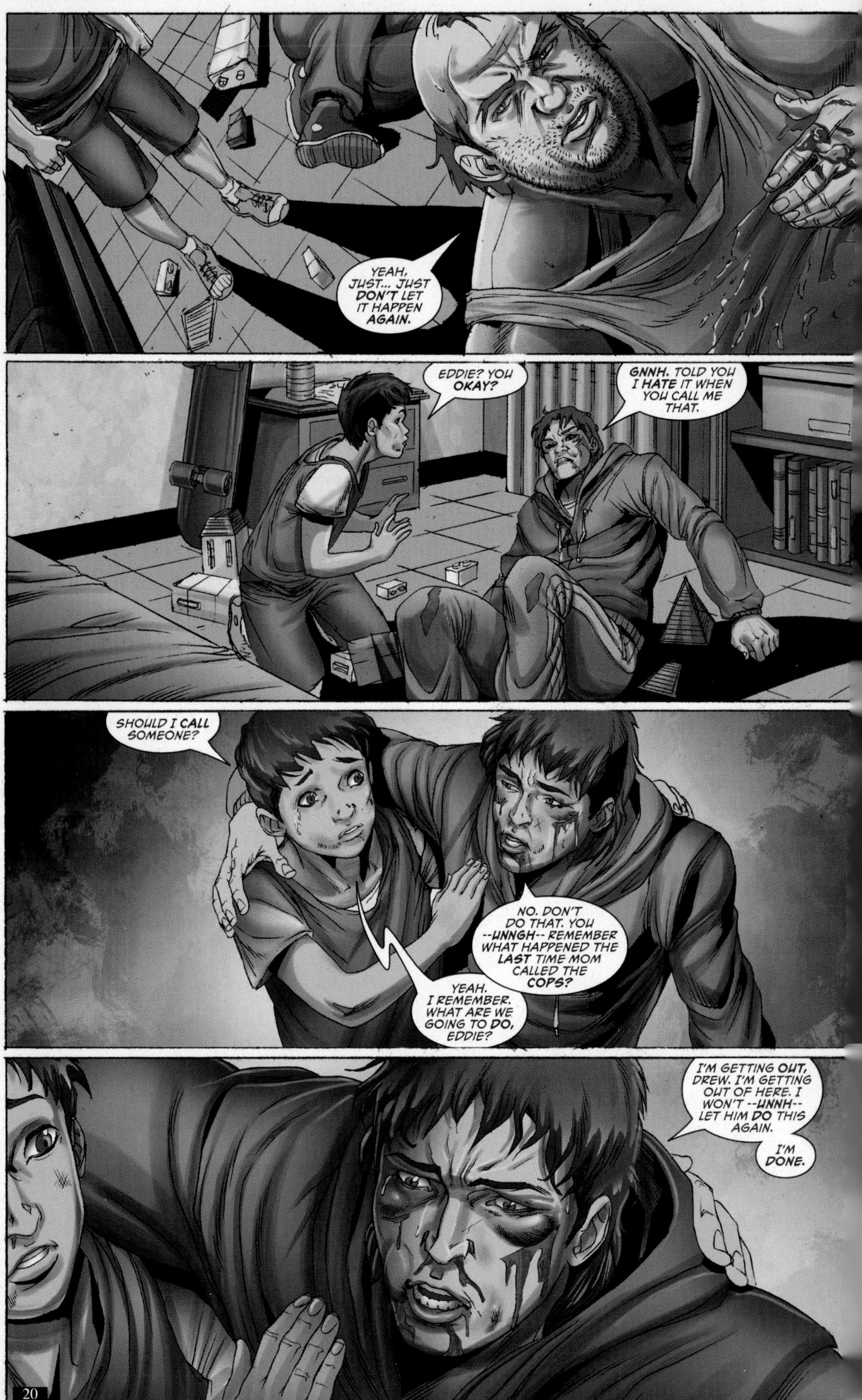
YEAH, JUST... JUST DON'T LET IT HAPPEN AGAIN.
EDDIE? YOU OKAY?
GNNH. TOLD YOU I HATE IT WHEN YOU CALL ME THAT.
SHOULD I CALL SOMEONE?
NO. DON'T DO THAT. YOU --UNNGH-- REMEMBER WHAT HAPPENED THE LAST TIME MOM CALLED THE COPS?
YEAH. I REMEMBER. WHAT ARE WE GOING TO DO, EDDIE?
I'M GETTING OUT, DREW. I'M GETTING OUT OF HERE. I WON'T --UNNH-- LET HIM DO THIS AGAIN.
I'M DONE.

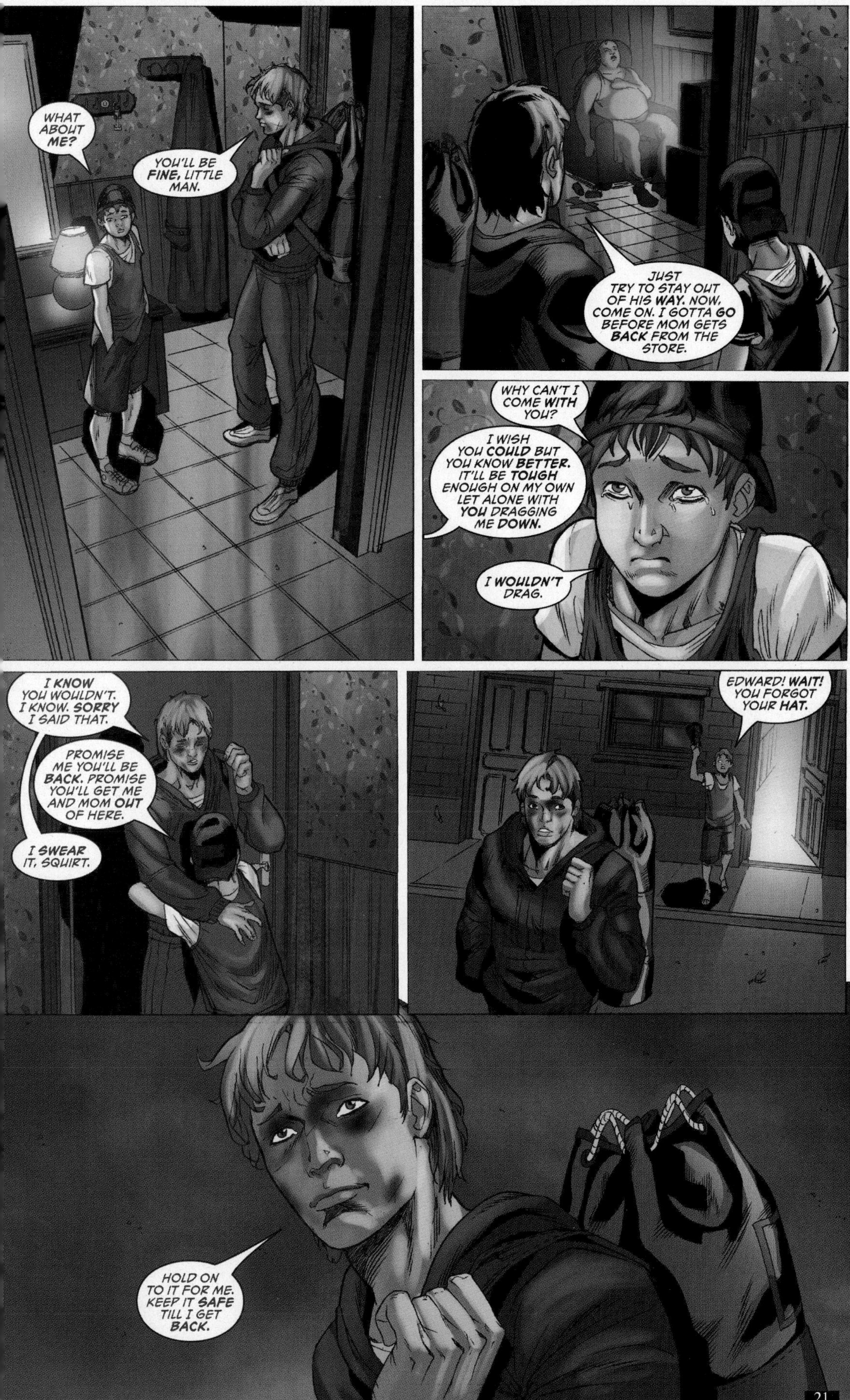
WHAT ABOUT ME?
YOU'LL BE FINE, LITTLE MAN.
JUST TRY TO STAY OUT OF HIS WAY. NOW, COME ON. I GOTTA GO BEFORE MOM GETS BACK FROM THE STORE.
WHY CAN'T I COME WITH YOU?
I WISH YOU COULD BUT YOU KNOW BETTER. IT'LL BE TOUGH ENOUGH ON MY OWN LET ALONE WITH YOU DRAGGING ME DOWN.
I WOULDN'T DRAG.
I KNOW YOU WOULDN'T. I KNOW. SORRY I SAID THAT.
PROMISE ME YOU'LL BE BACK. PROMISE YOU'LL GET ME AND MOM OUT OF HERE.
I SWEAR IT, SQUIRT.
EDWARD! WAIT! YOU FORGOT YOUR HAT.
HOLD ON TO IT FOR ME. KEEP IT SAFE TILL I GET BACK.

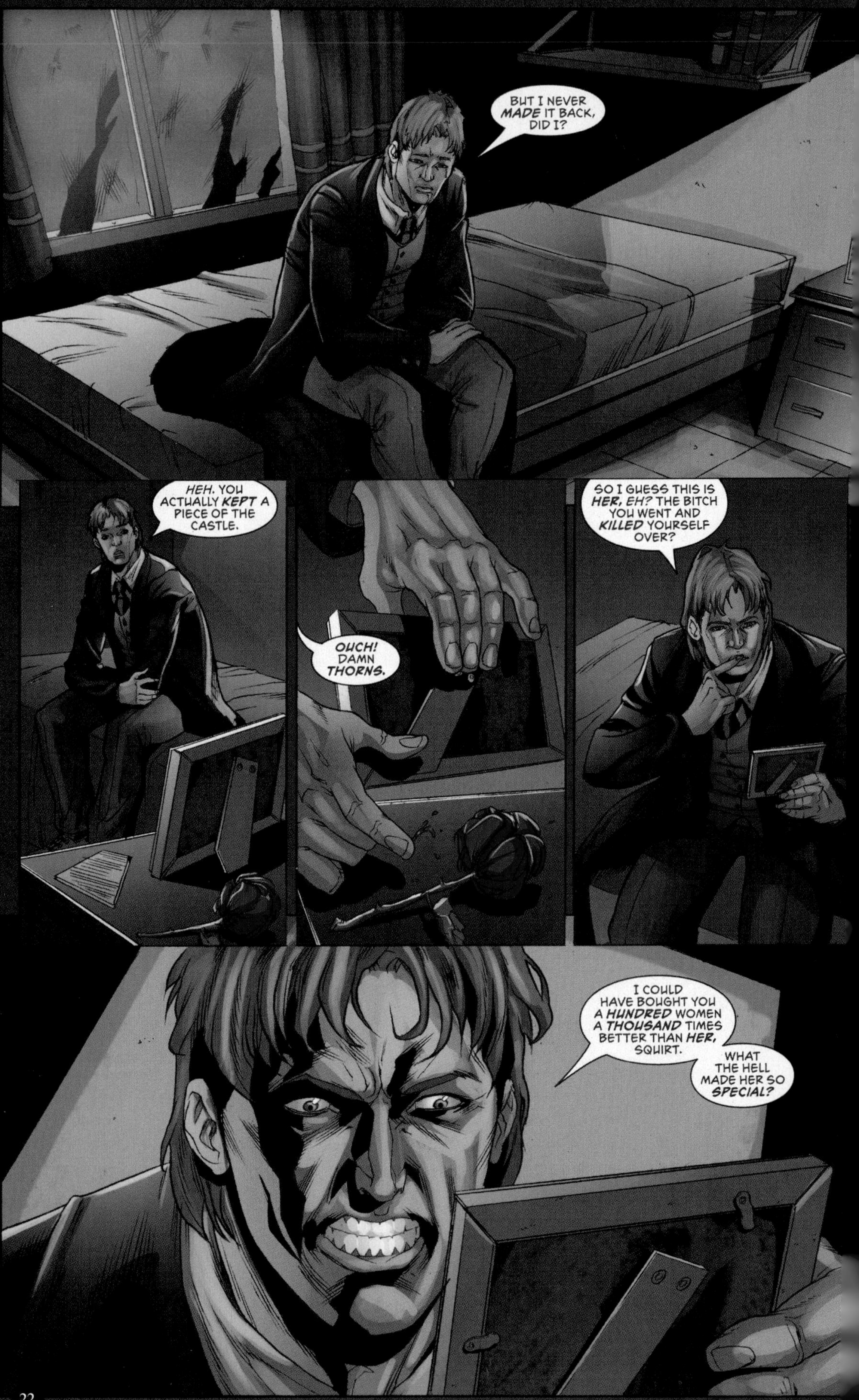
BUT I NEVER MADE IT BACK, DID I?
HEH. YOU ACTUALLY KEPT A PIECE OF THE CASTLE.
OUCH! DAMN THORNS.
SO I GUESS THIS IS HER, EH? THE BITCH YOU WENT AND KILLED YOURSELF OVER?
I COULD HAVE BOUGHT YOU A HUNDRED WOMEN A THOUSAND TIMES BETTER THAN HER, SQUIRT.
WHAT THE HELL MADE HER SO SPECIAL?

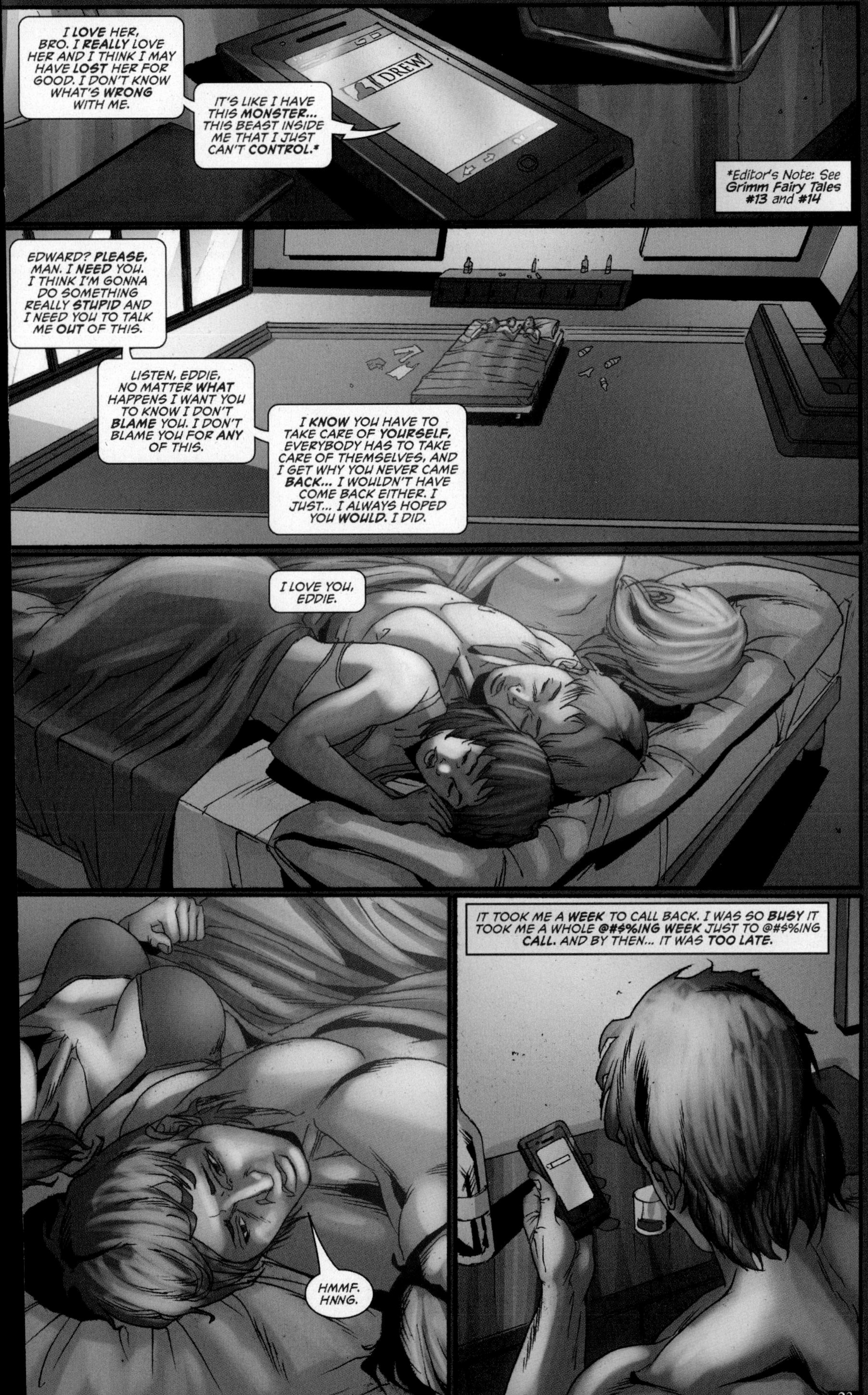
I LOVE HER, BRO. I REALLY LOVE HER AND I THINK I MAY HAVE LOST HER FOR GOOD. I DON'T KNOW WHAT'S WRONG WITH ME.
DREW
IT'S LIKE I HAVE THIS MONSTER... THIS BEAST INSIDE ME THAT I JUST CAN'T CONTROL.*
*Editor's Note: See Grimm Fairy Tales #13 and #14
EDWARD? PLEASE, MAN. I NEED YOU. I THINK I'M GONNA DO SOMETHING REALLY STUPID AND I NEED YOU TO TALK ME OUT OF THIS.
LISTEN, EDDIE, NO MATTER WHAT HAPPENS I WANT YOU TO KNOW I DON'T BLAME YOU. I DON'T BLAME YOU FOR ANY OF THIS.
I KNOW YOU HAVE TO TAKE CARE OF YOURSELF, EVERYBODY HAS TO TAKE CARE OF THEMSELVES, AND I GET WHY YOU NEVER CAME BACK... I WOULDN'T HAVE COME BACK EITHER. I JUST... I ALWAYS HOPED YOU WOULD. I DID.
I LOVE YOU, EDDIE.
HMMF. HNNG.
IT TOOK ME A WEEK TO CALL BACK. I WAS SO BUSY IT TOOK ME A WHOLE @#$%ING WEEK JUST TO @#$%ING CALL. AND BY THEN... IT WAS TOO LATE.

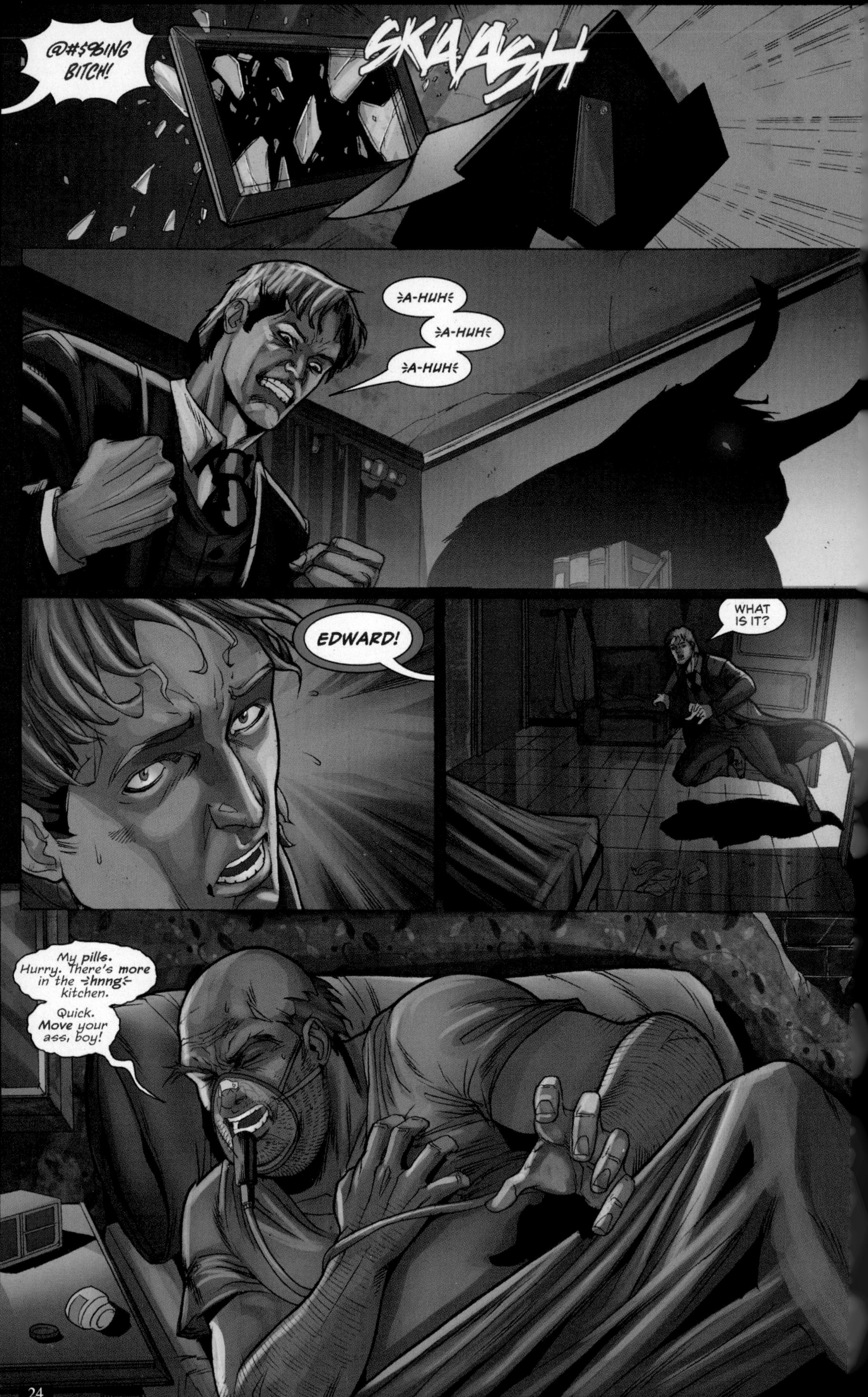
@#$%ING BITCH!
SKAASH
=A-HUH=
=A-HUH=
=A-HUH=
EDWARD!
WHAT IS IT?
My pills. Hurry. There's more in the =hnng= kitchen.
Quick. Move your ass, boy!

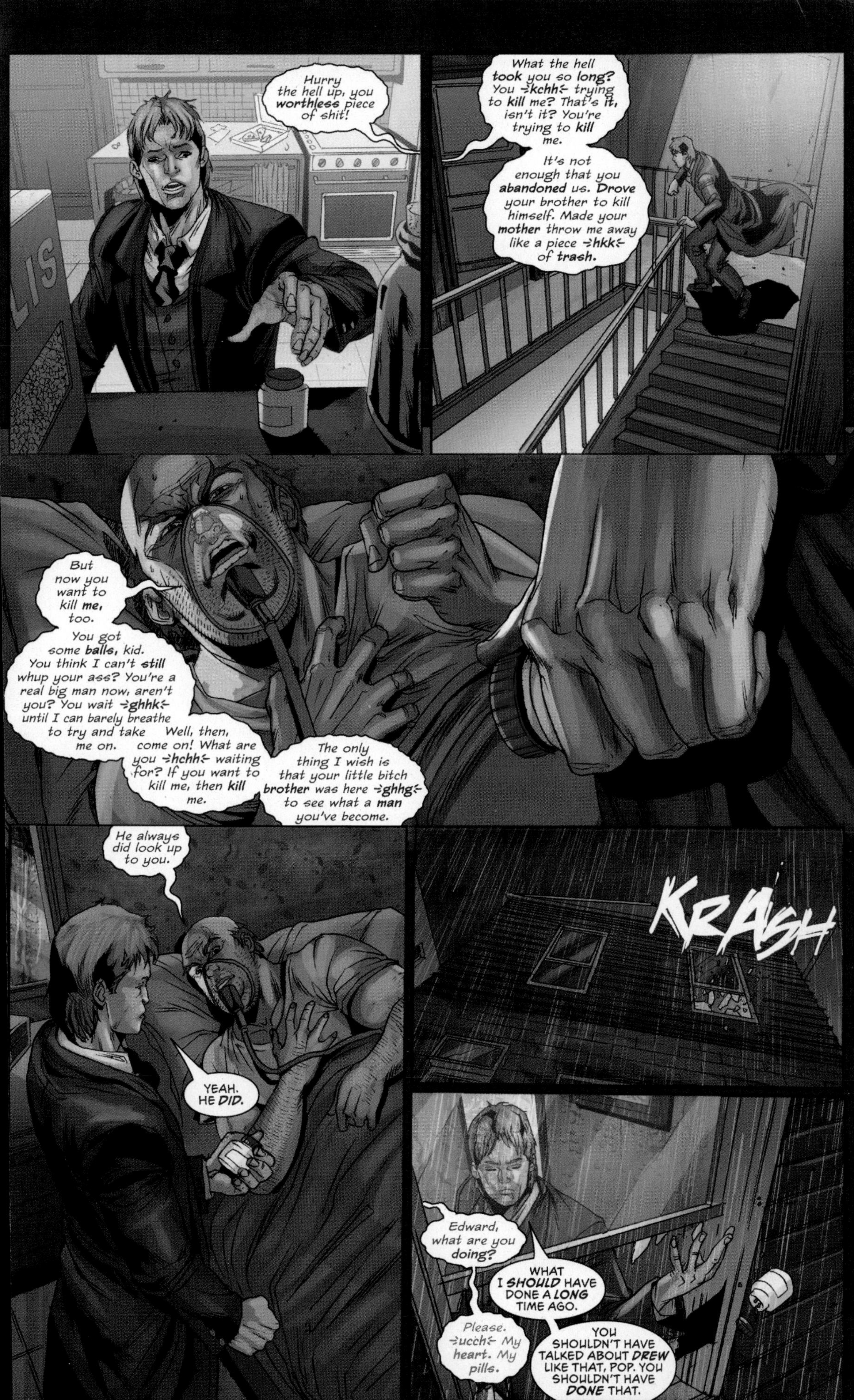
Hurry the hell up, you worthless piece of shit!
What the hell took you so long? You ⇛kchh⇚ trying to kill me? That's it, isn't it? You're trying to kill me.
It's not enough that you abandoned us. Drove your brother to kill himself. Made your mother throw me away like a piece ⇛hkk⇚ of trash.
But now you want to kill me, too.
You got some balls, kid. You think I can't still whup your ass? You're a real big man now, aren't you? You wait ⇛ghhk⇚ until I can barely breathe to try and take me on.
Well, then, come on! What are you ⇛hchh⇚ waiting for? If you want to kill me, then kill me.
The only thing I wish is that your little bitch brother was here ⇛ghhg⇚ to see what a man you've become.
He always did look up to you.
YEAH. HE DID.
KRASH
Edward, what are you doing?
WHAT I SHOULD HAVE DONE A LONG TIME AGO.
Please. ⇛ucch⇚ My heart. My pills.
YOU SHOULDN'T HAVE TALKED ABOUT DREW LIKE THAT, POP. YOU SHOULDN'T HAVE DONE THAT.

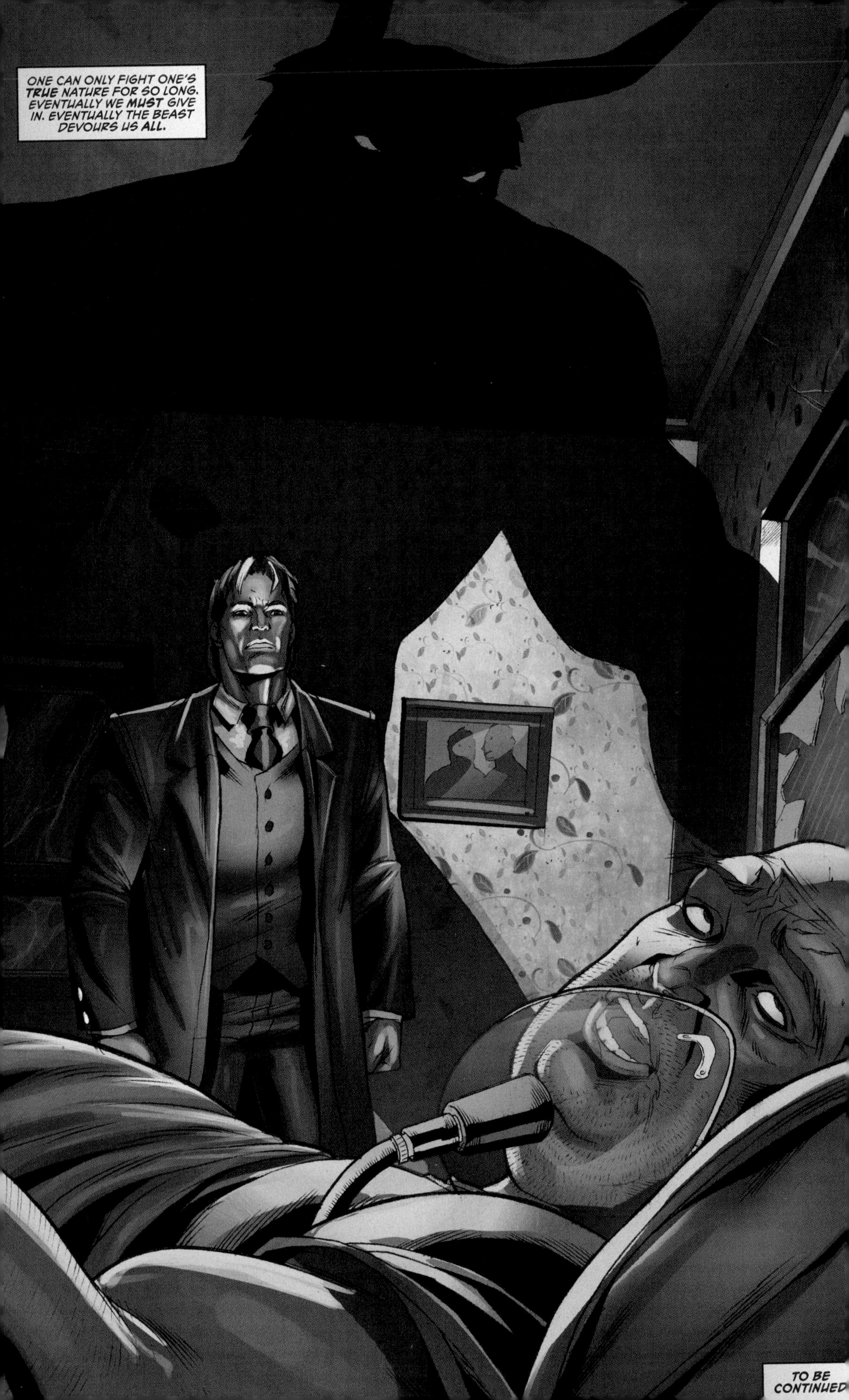
ONE CAN ONLY FIGHT ONE'S TRUE NATURE FOR SO LONG. EVENTUALLY WE MUST GIVE IN. EVENTUALLY THE BEAST DEVOURS US ALL.
TO BE CONTINUED

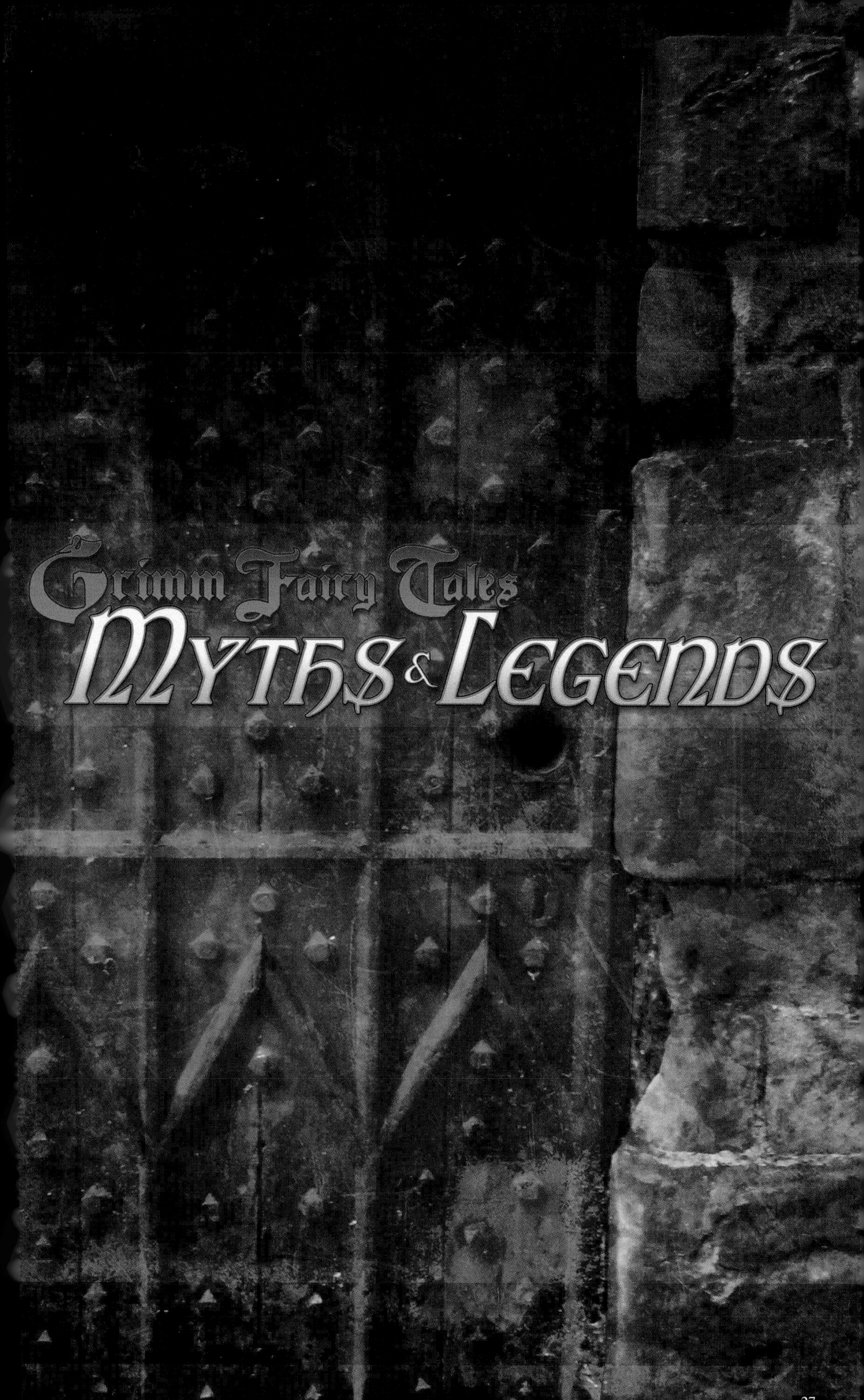
Grimm Fairy Tales
Myths & Legends

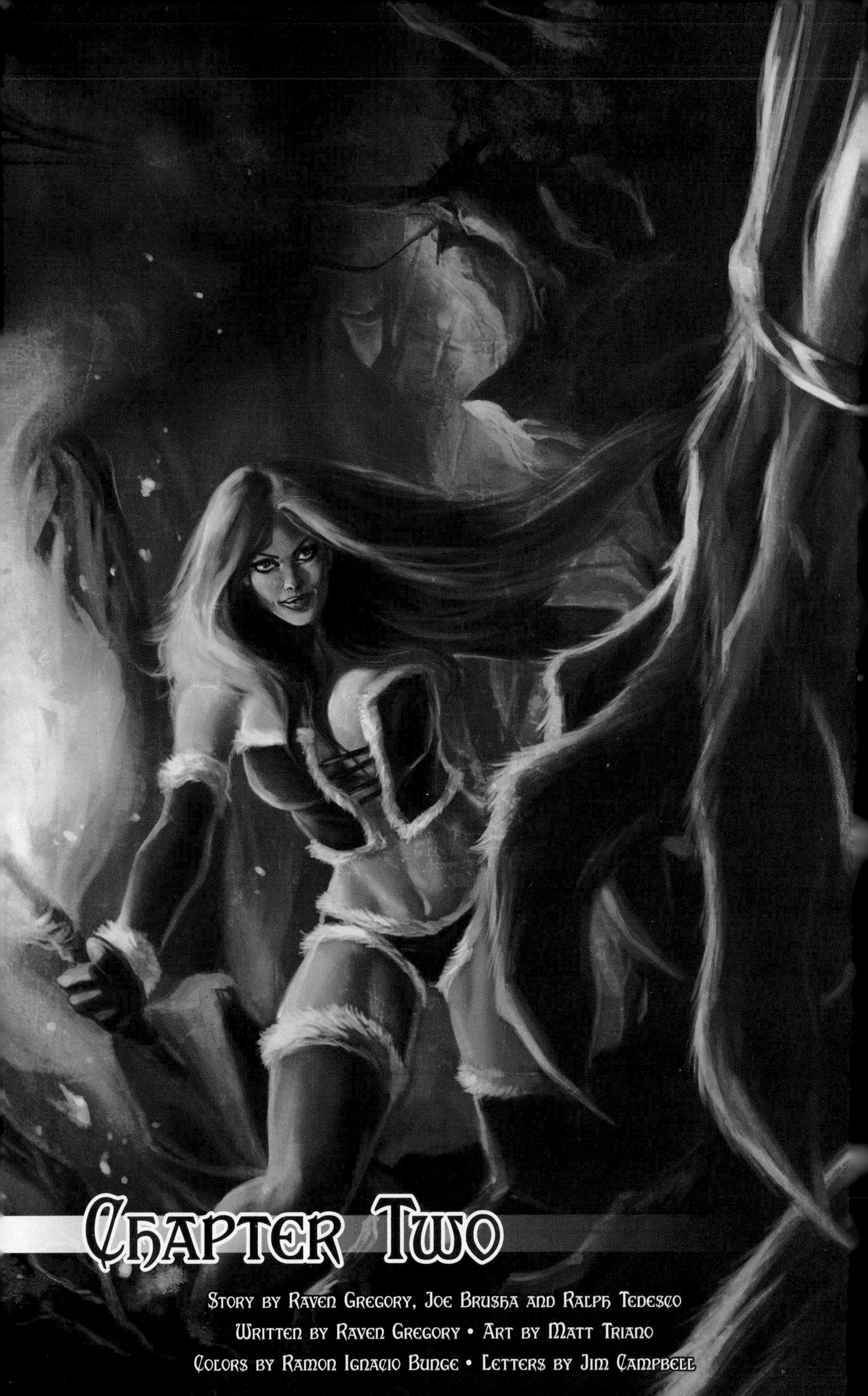

# Chapter Two

Story by Raven Gregory, Joe Brusha and Ralph Tedesco

Written by Raven Gregory • Art by Matt Triano

Colors by Ramon Ignacio Bunge • Letters by Jim Campbell

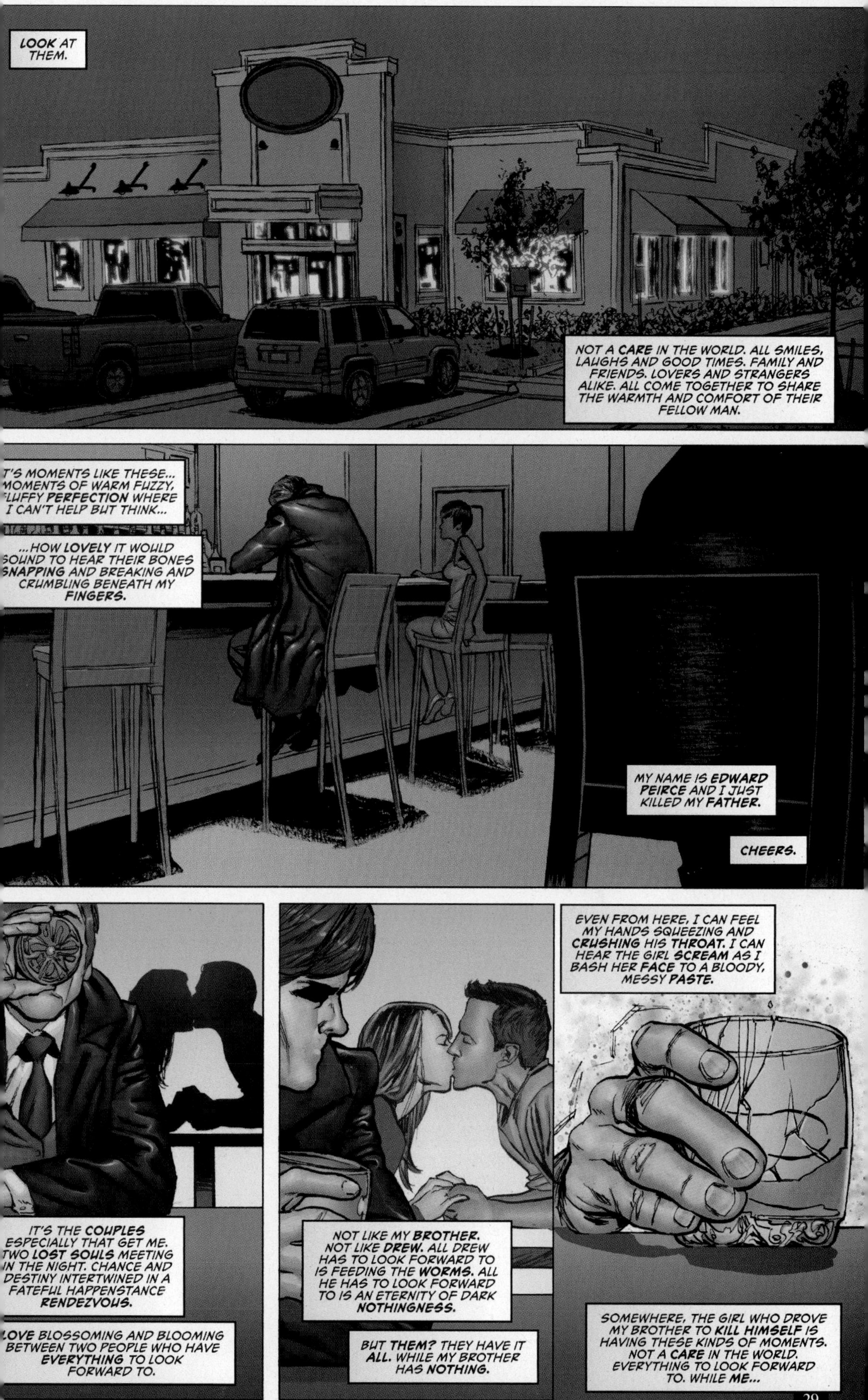
LOOK AT THEM.
NOT A CARE IN THE WORLD. ALL SMILES, LAUGHS AND GOOD TIMES. FAMILY AND FRIENDS. LOVERS AND STRANGERS ALIKE. ALL COME TOGETHER TO SHARE THE WARMTH AND COMFORT OF THEIR FELLOW MAN.
T'S MOMENTS LIKE THESE... MOMENTS OF WARM FUZZY, FLUFFY PERFECTION WHERE I CAN'T HELP BUT THINK...
...HOW LOVELY IT WOULD SOUND TO HEAR THEIR BONES SNAPPING AND BREAKING AND CRUMBLING BENEATH MY FINGERS.
MY NAME IS EDWARD PEIRCE AND I JUST KILLED MY FATHER.
CHEERS.
IT'S THE COUPLES ESPECIALLY THAT GET ME. TWO LOST SOULS MEETING IN THE NIGHT. CHANCE AND DESTINY INTERTWINED IN A FATEFUL HAPPENSTANCE RENDEZVOUS.
LOVE BLOSSOMING AND BLOOMING BETWEEN TWO PEOPLE WHO HAVE EVERYTHING TO LOOK FORWARD TO.
NOT LIKE MY BROTHER. NOT LIKE DREW. ALL DREW HAS TO LOOK FORWARD TO IS FEEDING THE WORMS. ALL HE HAS TO LOOK FORWARD TO IS AN ETERNITY OF DARK NOTHINGNESS.
BUT THEM? THEY HAVE IT ALL. WHILE MY BROTHER HAS NOTHING.
EVEN FROM HERE, I CAN FEEL MY HANDS SQUEEZING AND CRUSHING HIS THROAT. I CAN HEAR THE GIRL SCREAM AS I BASH HER FACE TO A BLOODY, MESSY PASTE.
SOMEWHERE, THE GIRL WHO DROVE MY BROTHER TO KILL HIMSELF IS HAVING THESE KINDS OF MOMENTS. NOT A CARE IN THE WORLD. EVERYTHING TO LOOK FORWARD TO. WHILE ME...

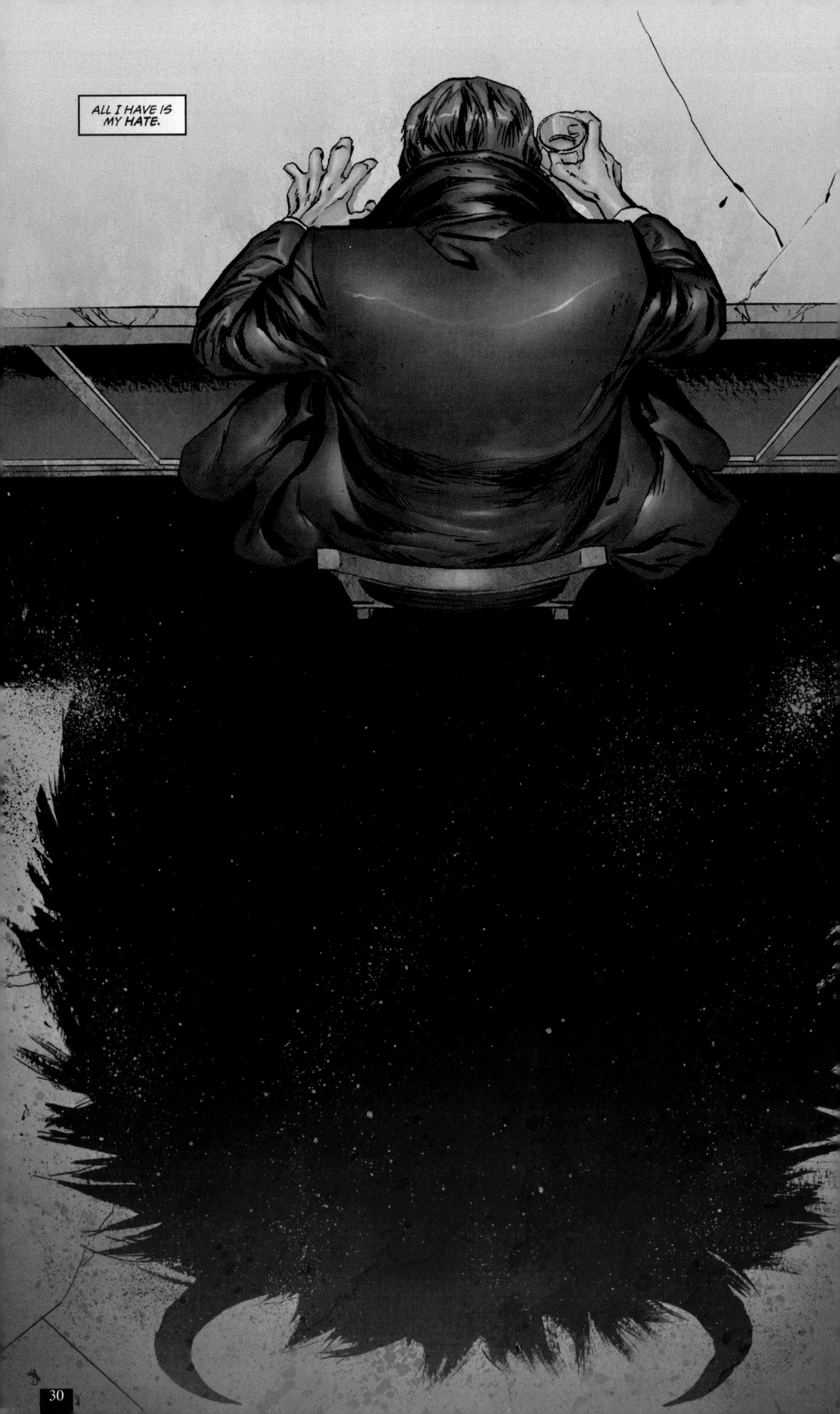
ALL I HAVE IS MY HATE.

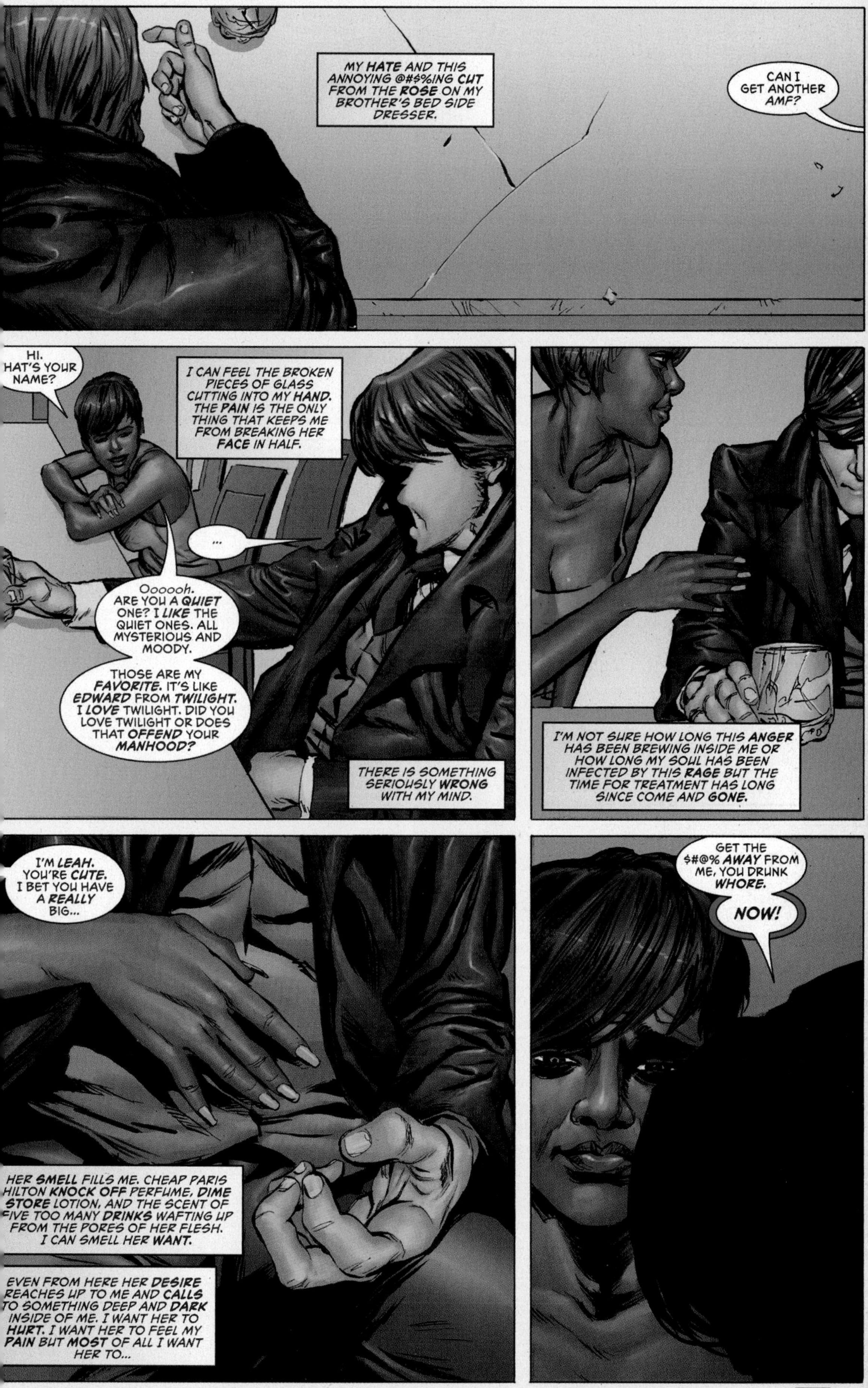

MY HATE AND THIS ANNOYING @#$%ING CUT FROM THE ROSE ON MY BROTHER'S BED SIDE DRESSER.
CAN I GET ANOTHER AMF?
HI. HAT'S YOUR NAME?
I CAN FEEL THE BROKEN PIECES OF GLASS CUTTING INTO MY HAND. THE PAIN IS THE ONLY THING THAT KEEPS ME FROM BREAKING HER FACE IN HALF.
...
Oooooh. ARE YOU A QUIET ONE? I LIKE THE QUIET ONES. ALL MYSTERIOUS AND MOODY.
THOSE ARE MY FAVORITE. IT'S LIKE EDWARD FROM TWILIGHT. I LOVE TWILIGHT. DID YOU LOVE TWILIGHT OR DOES THAT OFFEND YOUR MANHOOD?
THERE IS SOMETHING SERIOUSLY WRONG WITH MY MIND.
I'M NOT SURE HOW LONG THIS ANGER HAS BEEN BREWING INSIDE ME OR HOW LONG MY SOUL HAS BEEN INFECTED BY THIS RAGE BUT THE TIME FOR TREATMENT HAS LONG SINCE COME AND GONE.
I'M LEAH. YOU'RE CUTE. I BET YOU HAVE A REALLY BIG...
HER SMELL FILLS ME. CHEAP PARIS HILTON KNOCK OFF PERFUME, DIME STORE LOTION, AND THE SCENT OF FIVE TOO MANY DRINKS WAFTING UP FROM THE PORES OF HER FLESH. I CAN SMELL HER WANT.
EVEN FROM HERE HER DESIRE REACHES UP TO ME AND CALLS TO SOMETHING DEEP AND DARK INSIDE OF ME. I WANT HER TO HURT. I WANT HER TO FEEL MY PAIN BUT MOST OF ALL I WANT HER TO...
GET THE $#@% AWAY FROM ME, YOU DRUNK WHORE.
NOW!

≠SOB≠

≠SOB≠

≠SOB≠

LEAH? HEY.

YOU *OKAY?* WHAT HAPPENED?

HEY, BUDDY. WHAT'S YOUR *PROBLEM?* SHE WAS JUST HAVING A LITTLE *FUN.* YOU DIDN'T HAVE TO *INSULT* THE LADY.

IN MY HEAD I HEAR THE WORDS I *SHOULD* BE SPEAKING TO HER CONVENIENTLY FOUND *KNIGHT* IN SHINING ARMOR.

THAT HE SHOULD TAKE HIS FRIENDS AND *GET LOST* BEFORE THEY DO SOMETHING THEY'LL *REGRET.* THAT THEY HAVE *NO* IDEA WHO OR WHAT THEY ARE *PROVOKING.*

I THINK YOU OWE HER AN *APOLOGY.*

NO. I'M *NOT* GONNA JUST LET IT GO. GUY'S RUDE TO MY *FRIEND* AND THINKS HE CAN GET *AWAY* WITH IT.

BOHN, JUST LET IT *GO* AND LET'S GET OUT OF HERE.

NO. *Uh uh. NOT* GONNA HAPPEN. THIS @#$% IS GONNA SAY HE'S *SORRY* ONE WAY OR *ANOTHER.*

BUT I DON'T SAY A *WORD.* I LET THEM KEEP *TALKING.* I LET THEM KEEP *POKING.*

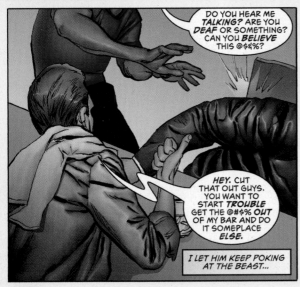

DO YOU HEAR ME *TALKING?* ARE YOU *DEAF* OR SOMETHING? CAN YOU *BELIEVE* THIS @$¢%?

HEY. *CUT* THAT OUT GUYS. YOU WANT TO START *TROUBLE* GET THE @#$% *OUT* OF MY BAR AND DO IT SOMEPLACE *ELSE.*

I LET HIM KEEP POKING AT THE BEAST...

*WHATEVER.* COME ON, GUYS. LET'S GET OUT OF HERE. THIS GUY IS *NOTHING* BUT A LITTLE OLD *BITCH.*

...UNTIL IT FINAL[L]Y WAKES UP.

WHO'S THE LITTLE BITCH *NOW,* BOHN?

*AAAAAAH!*

KRUNNCH

MY HAND'S BLEEDING NOW. I CAN FEEL THE SHATTERED PIECES OF BROKEN GLASS STABBING INTO MY FLESH.

MY *HAND.* THAT MOTHER@#$%ER @#$%ED UP MY HAND.

YOU GONNA *REGRET* THAT &@%$, BRAH.

IT FEELS *GOOD.* IT FEELS *RIGHT.* THE HURT FEEDS MY *ANGER.* MY ANGER FEEDS THE *RAGE* AND THE RAGE...

*UNLEASHES* THE BEAST.

THEY DON'T STAND A CHANCE.

HEY. TAKE IT *EASY,* MAN. WE WERE JUST MESSING AROUND. WE DIDN'T *MEAN* ANYTHING BY IT.

IT WAS A *JOKE.* IT WAS ALL JUST A BIG *JOKE.*

I CAN SEE OTHER PATRONS OUT OF THE SIDE OF MY EYE RUSHING TO *HELP.* I HEAR THEIR FOOTSTEPS MOVING URGENTLY IN MY DIRECTION. I SMELL THEIR *FEAR* AND TASTE THEIR *HORROR* IN THE AIR AROUND US. I CAN FEEL THEM MOVING CLOSER AND CLOSER.

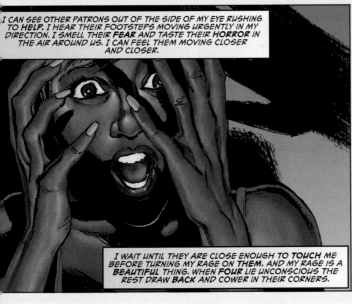

I WAIT UNTIL THEY ARE CLOSE ENOUGH TO *TOUCH* ME BEFORE TURNING MY RAGE ON *THEM.* AND MY RAGE IS A *BEAUTIFUL* THING. WHEN *FOUR* LIE UNCONSCIOUS THE REST DRAW *BACK* AND COWER IN THEIR CORNERS.

IT'S STILL NOT ENOUGH.

AN *EXAMPLE* MUST BE MADE.

AND THEN AS QUICKLY AS IT BEGAN... IT'S OVER. THE **BEAST** SHUFFLES AWAY TO WHATEVER PLACE IT CALLS HOME AND I'M LEFT ALONE IN THE **AFTERMATH** OF ITS WRATH.

WITHOUT THE **HATE** I FEEL **EMPTY** INSIDE. I FEEL HOLLOW. WITHOUT THE HATE TO GIVE ME PURPOSE I FEEL **NOTHING.** NOTHING BUT THE LOSS OF MY **BROTHER.**

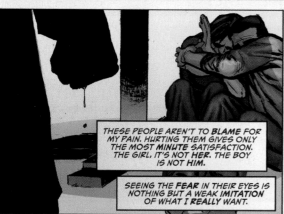

THESE PEOPLE AREN'T TO **BLAME** FOR MY PAIN. HURTING THEM GIVES ONLY THE MOST **MINUTE** SATISFACTION. THE GIRL, IT'S NOT **HER.** THE BOY IS NOT **HIM.**

SEEING THE **FEAR** IN THEIR EYES IS NOTHING BUT A WEAK IMITATION OF WHAT I REALLY WANT.

...HERE ...FOR YOUR TROUBLES.

THERE'S **MORE** THAN ENOUGH TO COVER THE **DAMAGES** AND TO **COMPENSATE** YOUR CUSTOMERS.

BUT IF I WAS YOU I'D LEAVE **ANY** MENTION OF ME OUT OF ANY **POLICE REPORT** THAT MIGHT COME YOUR WAY. YOU'LL FIND IT MUCH BETTER FOR YOUR **HEALTH.**

Hmmm? WHAT'S THIS?

AND THAT'S WHEN IT BECOMES **CLEAR.** AS CLEAR AS THE PHOTO OF MY **BROTHER'S EX-GIRLFRIEND.**

THERE'S ONLY ONE PERSON IN THE **WORLD** WHO CAN GIVE ME WHAT I WANT.

AND THAT'S **HER.**

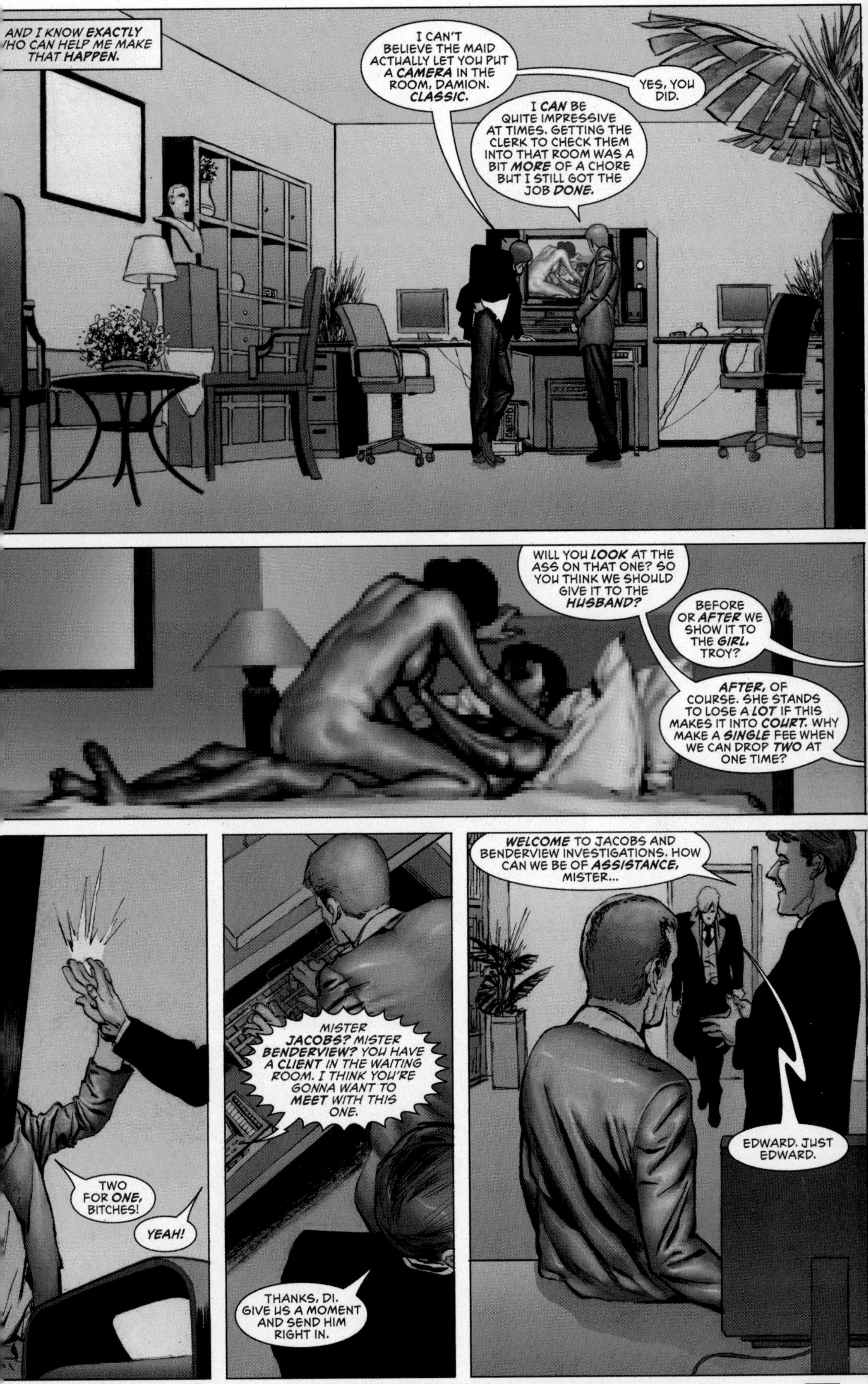
AND I KNOW EXACTLY WHO CAN HELP ME MAKE THAT HAPPEN.
I CAN'T BELIEVE THE MAID ACTUALLY LET YOU PUT A CAMERA IN THE ROOM, DAMION. CLASSIC.
YES, YOU DID.
I CAN BE QUITE IMPRESSIVE AT TIMES. GETTING THE CLERK TO CHECK THEM INTO THAT ROOM WAS A BIT MORE OF A CHORE BUT I STILL GOT THE JOB DONE.
WILL YOU LOOK AT THE ASS ON THAT ONE? SO YOU THINK WE SHOULD GIVE IT TO THE HUSBAND?
BEFORE OR AFTER WE SHOW IT TO THE GIRL, TROY?
AFTER, OF COURSE. SHE STANDS TO LOSE A LOT IF THIS MAKES IT INTO COURT. WHY MAKE A SINGLE FEE WHEN WE CAN DROP TWO AT ONE TIME?
TWO FOR ONE, BITCHES!
YEAH!
MISTER JACOBS? MISTER BENDERVIEW? YOU HAVE A CLIENT IN THE WAITING ROOM. I THINK YOU'RE GONNA WANT TO MEET WITH THIS ONE.
THANKS, DI. GIVE US A MOMENT AND SEND HIM RIGHT IN.
WELCOME TO JACOBS AND BENDERVIEW INVESTIGATIONS. HOW CAN WE BE OF ASSISTANCE, MISTER...
EDWARD. JUST EDWARD.

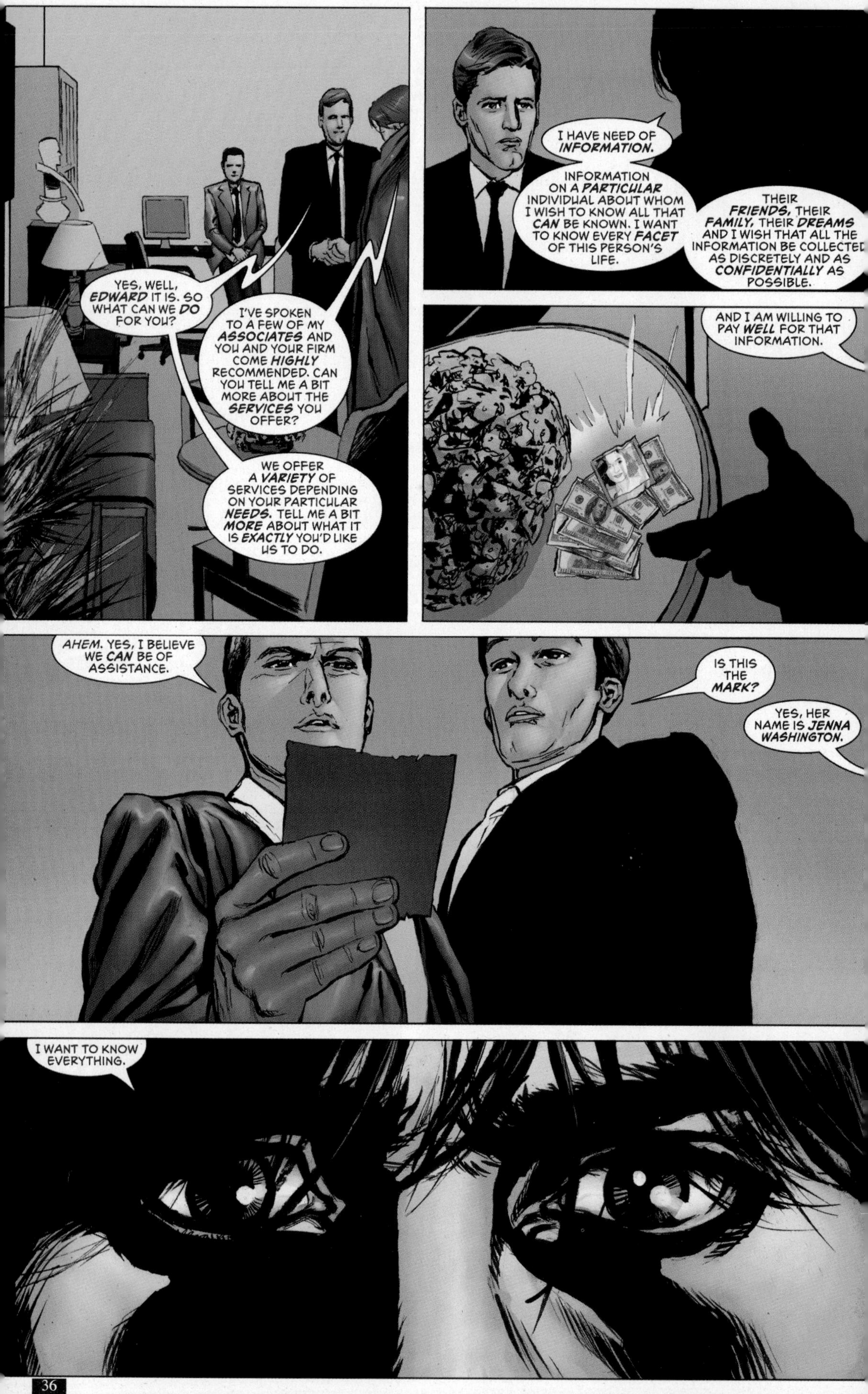
YES, WELL, EDWARD IT IS. SO WHAT CAN WE DO FOR YOU?
I'VE SPOKEN TO A FEW OF MY ASSOCIATES AND YOU AND YOUR FIRM COME HIGHLY RECOMMENDED. CAN YOU TELL ME A BIT MORE ABOUT THE SERVICES YOU OFFER?
WE OFFER A VARIETY OF SERVICES DEPENDING ON YOUR PARTICULAR NEEDS. TELL ME A BIT MORE ABOUT WHAT IT IS EXACTLY YOU'D LIKE US TO DO.
I HAVE NEED OF INFORMATION.
INFORMATION ON A PARTICULAR INDIVIDUAL ABOUT WHOM I WISH TO KNOW ALL THAT CAN BE KNOWN. I WANT TO KNOW EVERY FACET OF THIS PERSON'S LIFE.
THEIR FRIENDS, THEIR FAMILY, THEIR DREAMS AND I WISH THAT ALL THE INFORMATION BE COLLECTED AS DISCRETELY AND AS CONFIDENTIALLY AS POSSIBLE.
AND I AM WILLING TO PAY WELL FOR THAT INFORMATION.
AHEM. YES, I BELIEVE WE CAN BE OF ASSISTANCE.
IS THIS THE MARK?
YES, HER NAME IS JENNA WASHINGTON.
I WANT TO KNOW EVERYTHING.

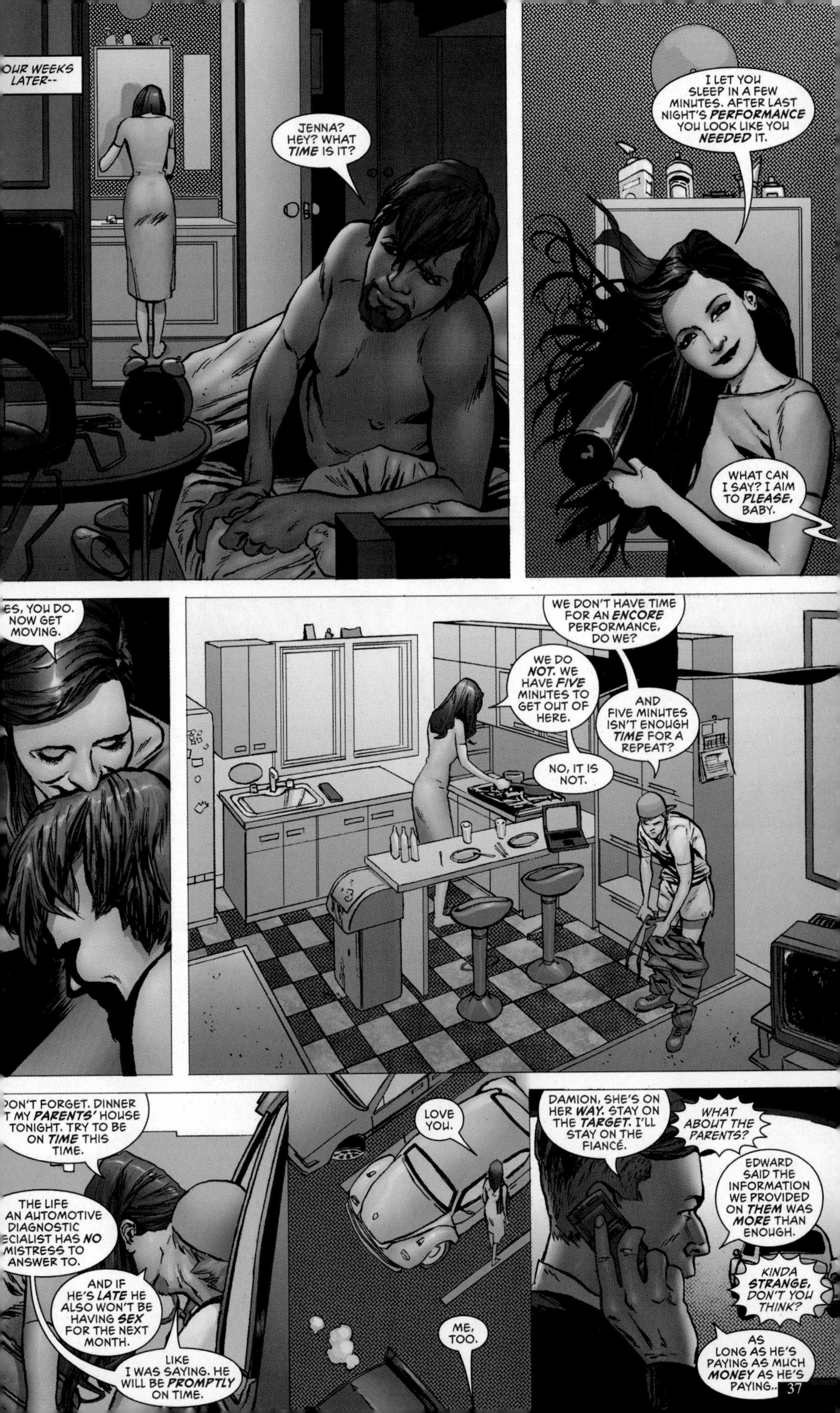
OUR WEEKS LATER--
JENNA? HEY? WHAT TIME IS IT?
I LET YOU SLEEP IN A FEW MINUTES. AFTER LAST NIGHT'S PERFORMANCE YOU LOOK LIKE YOU NEEDED IT.
WHAT CAN I SAY? I AIM TO PLEASE, BABY.
ES, YOU DO. NOW GET MOVING.
WE DON'T HAVE TIME FOR AN ENCORE PERFORMANCE, DO WE?
WE DO NOT. WE HAVE FIVE MINUTES TO GET OUT OF HERE.
AND FIVE MINUTES ISN'T ENOUGH TIME FOR A REPEAT?
NO, IT IS NOT.
DON'T FORGET. DINNER T MY PARENTS' HOUSE TONIGHT. TRY TO BE ON TIME THIS TIME.
THE LIFE AN AUTOMOTIVE DIAGNOSTIC ECIALIST HAS NO MISTRESS TO ANSWER TO.
AND IF HE'S LATE HE ALSO WON'T BE HAVING SEX FOR THE NEXT MONTH.
LIKE I WAS SAYING. HE WILL BE PROMPTLY ON TIME.
LOVE YOU.
ME, TOO.
DAMION, SHE'S ON HER WAY. STAY ON THE TARGET. I'LL STAY ON THE FIANCÉ.
WHAT ABOUT THE PARENTS?
EDWARD SAID THE INFORMATION WE PROVIDED ON THEM WAS MORE THAN ENOUGH.
KINDA STRANGE, DON'T YOU THINK?
AS LONG AS HE'S PAYING AS MUCH MONEY AS HE'S PAYING..

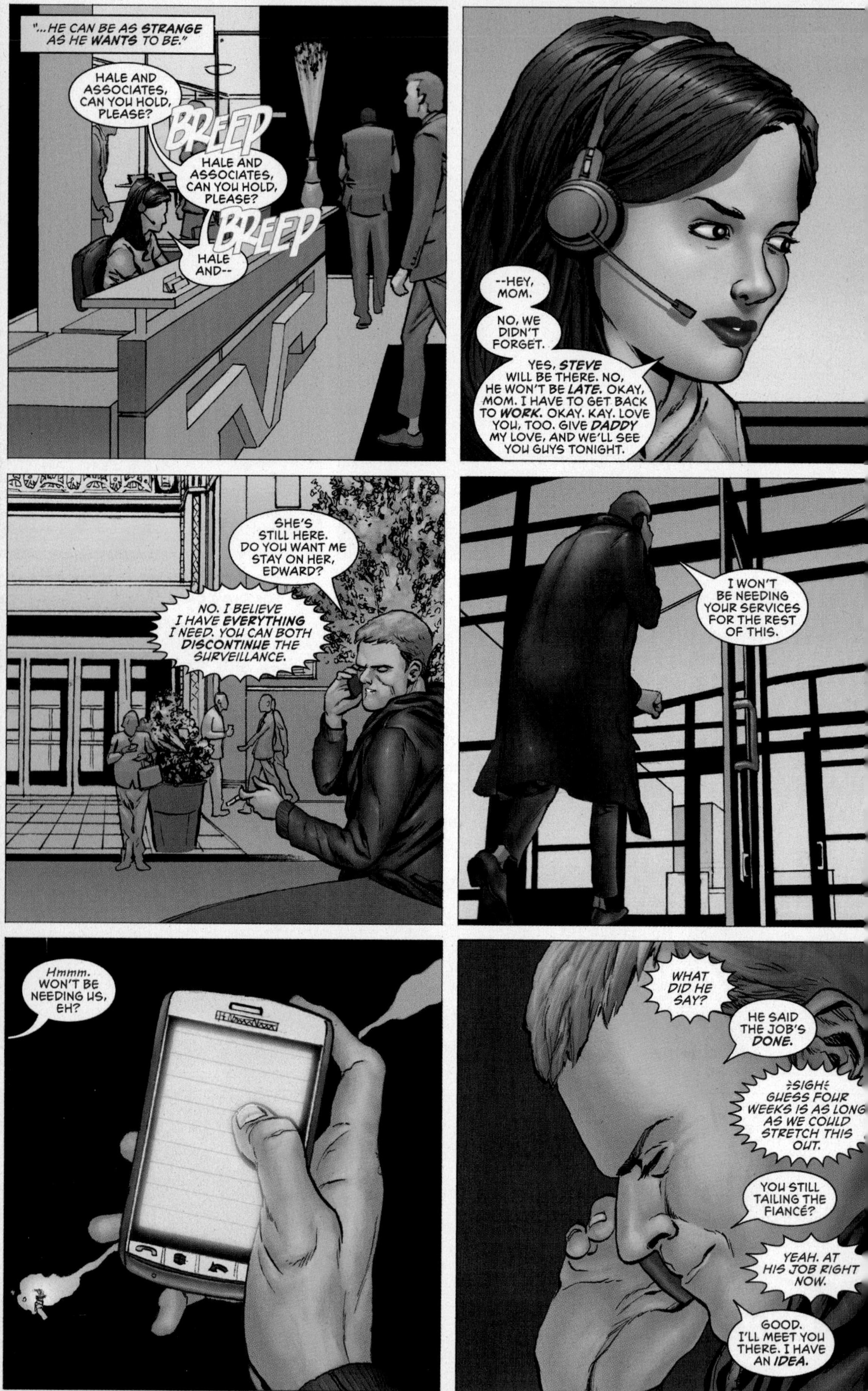

"...HE CAN BE AS STRANGE AS HE WANTS TO BE."
HALE AND ASSOCIATES, CAN YOU HOLD, PLEASE?
BREEP
HALE AND ASSOCIATES, CAN YOU HOLD, PLEASE?
BREEP
HALE AND--
--HEY, MOM.
NO, WE DIDN'T FORGET.
YES, STEVE WILL BE THERE. NO, HE WON'T BE LATE. OKAY, MOM. I HAVE TO GET BACK TO WORK. OKAY. KAY. LOVE YOU, TOO. GIVE DADDY MY LOVE, AND WE'LL SEE YOU GUYS TONIGHT.
SHE'S STILL HERE. DO YOU WANT ME STAY ON HER, EDWARD?
NO. I BELIEVE I HAVE EVERYTHING I NEED. YOU CAN BOTH DISCONTINUE THE SURVEILLANCE.
I WON'T BE NEEDING YOUR SERVICES FOR THE REST OF THIS.
Hmmm. WON'T BE NEEDING US, EH?
WHAT DID HE SAY?
HE SAID THE JOB'S DONE.
SIGH GUESS FOUR WEEKS IS AS LONG AS WE COULD STRETCH THIS OUT.
YOU STILL TAILING THE FIANCÉ?
YEAH. AT HIS JOB RIGHT NOW.
GOOD. I'LL MEET YOU THERE. I HAVE AN IDEA.

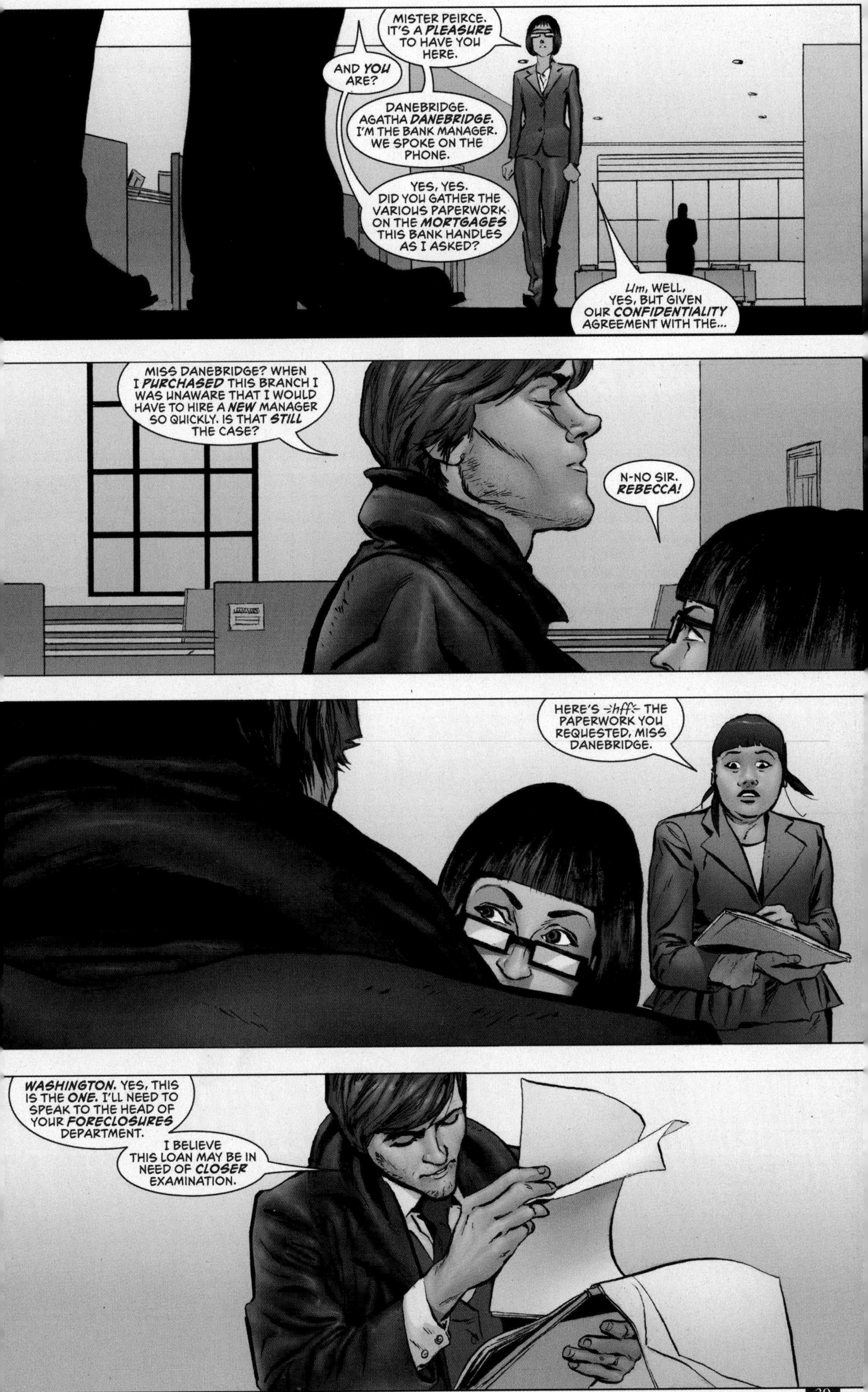
MISTER PEIRCE. IT'S A PLEASURE TO HAVE YOU HERE.
AND YOU ARE?
DANEBRIDGE. AGATHA DANEBRIDGE. I'M THE BANK MANAGER. WE SPOKE ON THE PHONE.
YES, YES. DID YOU GATHER THE VARIOUS PAPERWORK ON THE MORTGAGES THIS BANK HANDLES AS I ASKED?
UM, WELL, YES, BUT GIVEN OUR CONFIDENTIALITY AGREEMENT WITH THE...
MISS DANEBRIDGE? WHEN I PURCHASED THIS BRANCH I WAS UNAWARE THAT I WOULD HAVE TO HIRE A NEW MANAGER SO QUICKLY. IS THAT STILL THE CASE?
N-NO SIR. REBECCA!
HERE'S =hff= THE PAPERWORK YOU REQUESTED, MISS DANEBRIDGE.
WASHINGTON. YES, THIS IS THE ONE. I'LL NEED TO SPEAK TO THE HEAD OF YOUR FORECLOSURES DEPARTMENT.
I BELIEVE THIS LOAN MAY BE IN NEED OF CLOSER EXAMINATION.

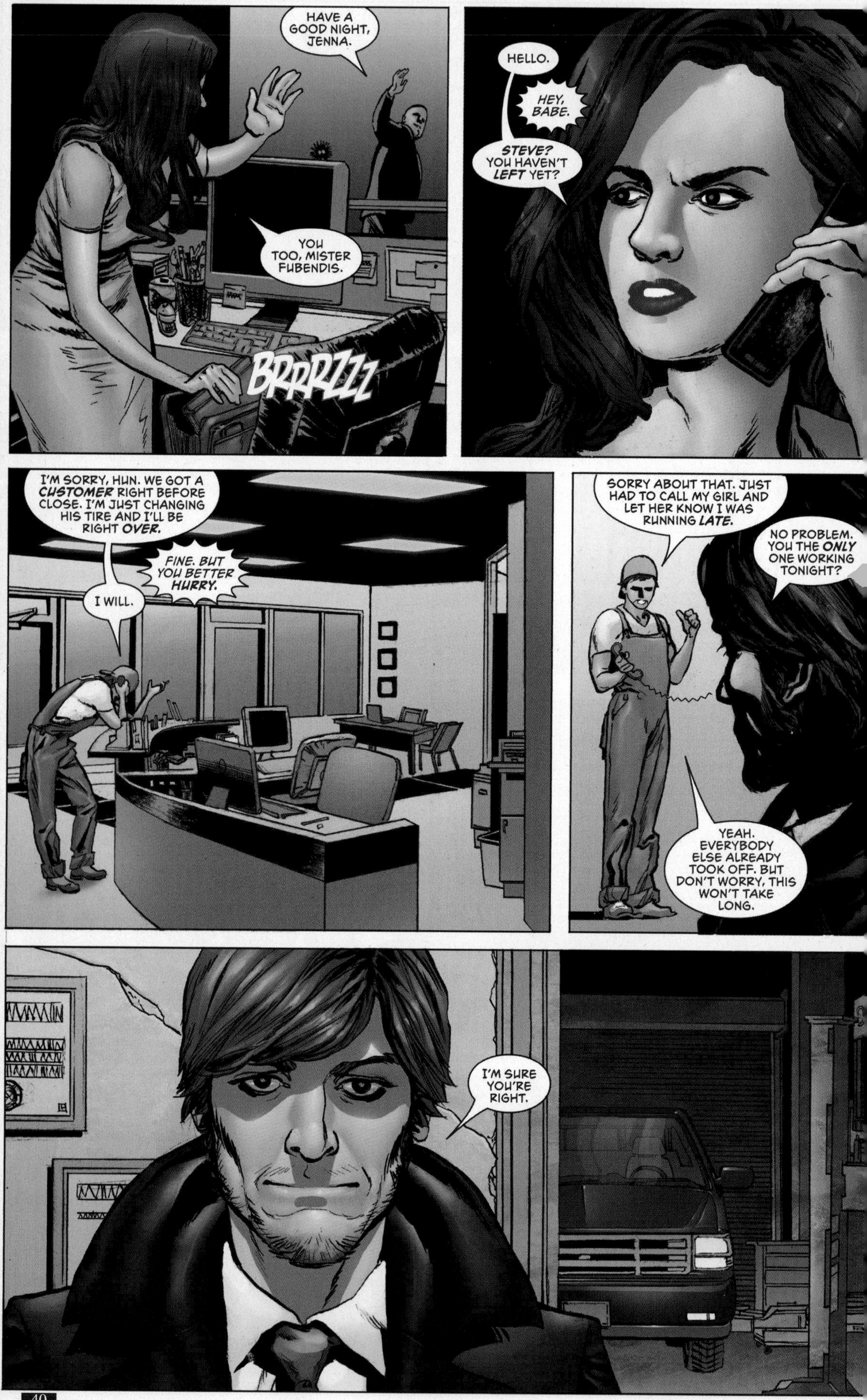
HAVE A GOOD NIGHT, JENNA.
YOU TOO, MISTER FUBENDIS.
BRRRZZZ
HELLO.
HEY, BABE.
STEVE? YOU HAVEN'T LEFT YET?
I'M SORRY, HUN. WE GOT A CUSTOMER RIGHT BEFORE CLOSE. I'M JUST CHANGING HIS TIRE AND I'LL BE RIGHT OVER.
FINE. BUT YOU BETTER HURRY.
I WILL.
SORRY ABOUT THAT. JUST HAD TO CALL MY GIRL AND LET HER KNOW I WAS RUNNING LATE.
NO PROBLEM. YOU THE ONLY ONE WORKING TONIGHT?
YEAH. EVERYBODY ELSE ALREADY TOOK OFF. BUT DON'T WORRY, THIS WON'T TAKE LONG.
I'M SURE YOU'RE RIGHT.

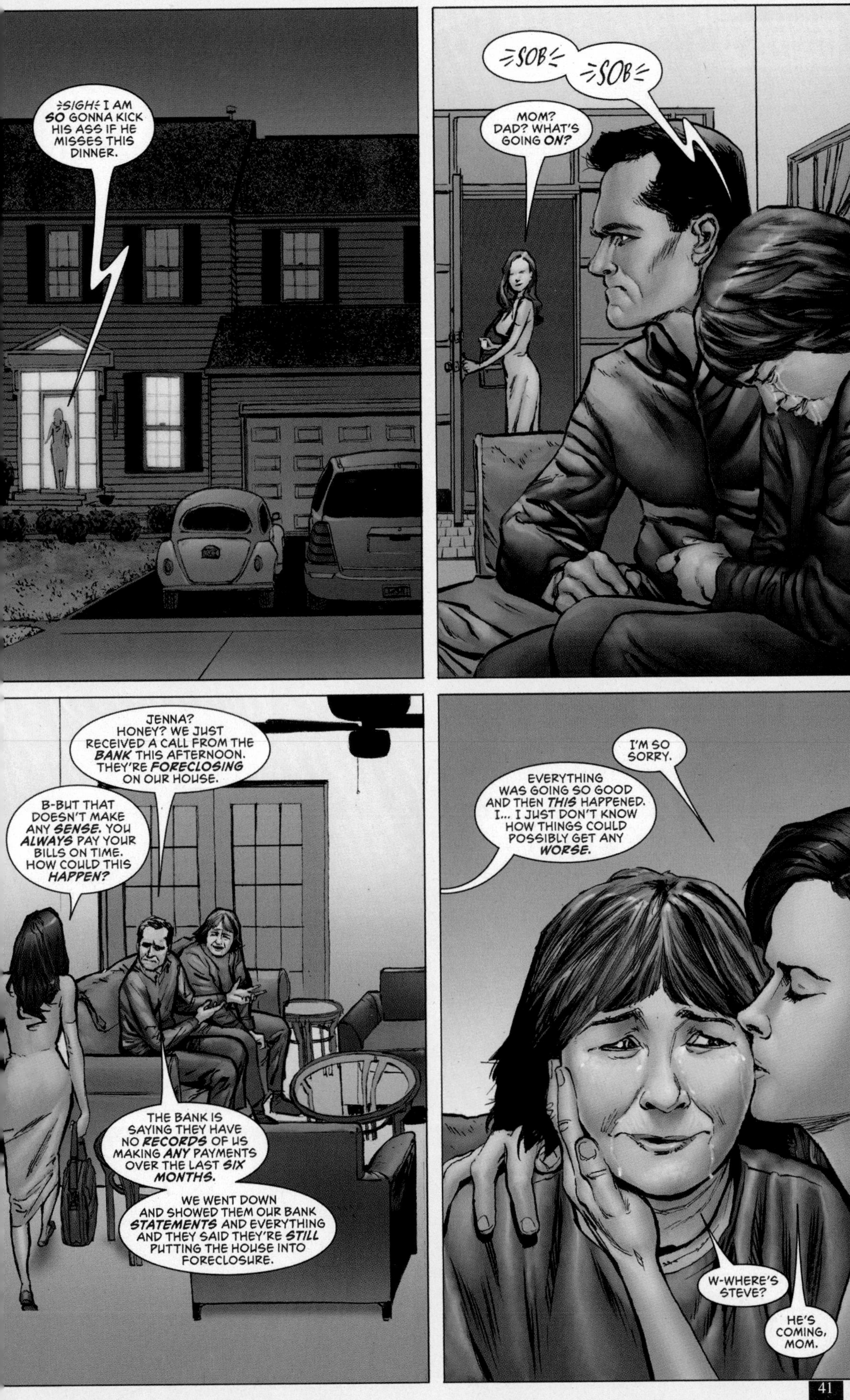

SIGH I AM SO GONNA KICK HIS ASS IF HE MISSES THIS DINNER.
SOB
SOB
MOM? DAD? WHAT'S GOING ON?
JENNA? HONEY? WE JUST RECEIVED A CALL FROM THE BANK THIS AFTERNOON. THEY'RE FORECLOSING ON OUR HOUSE.
B-BUT THAT DOESN'T MAKE ANY SENSE. YOU ALWAYS PAY YOUR BILLS ON TIME. HOW COULD THIS HAPPEN?
THE BANK IS SAYING THEY HAVE NO RECORDS OF US MAKING ANY PAYMENTS OVER THE LAST SIX MONTHS.
WE WENT DOWN AND SHOWED THEM OUR BANK STATEMENTS AND EVERYTHING AND THEY SAID THEY'RE STILL PUTTING THE HOUSE INTO FORECLOSURE.
I'M SO SORRY.
EVERYTHING WAS GOING SO GOOD AND THEN THIS HAPPENED. I... I JUST DON'T KNOW HOW THINGS COULD POSSIBLY GET ANY WORSE.
W-WHERE'S STEVE?
HE'S COMING, MOM.

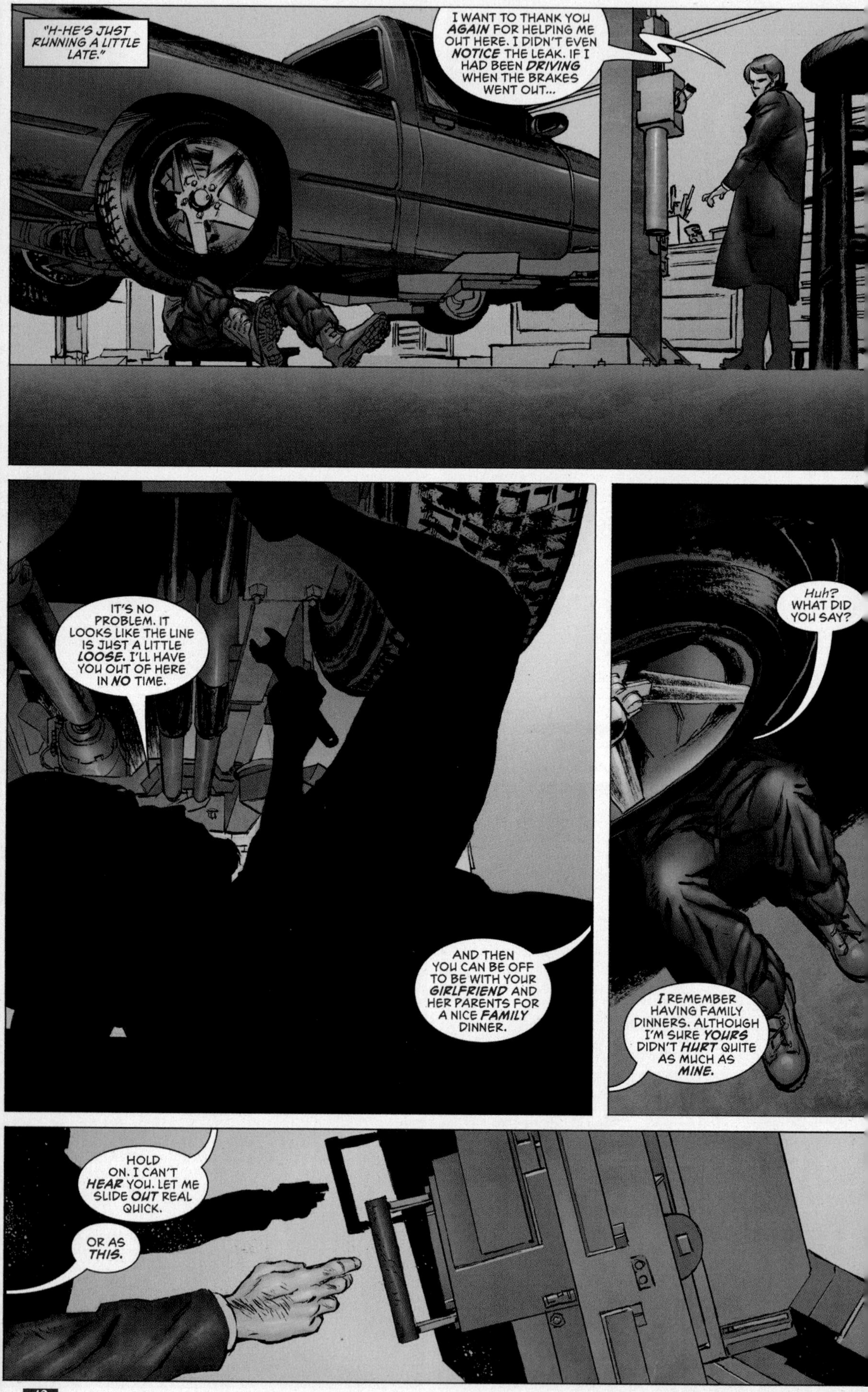
"H-HE'S JUST RUNNING A LITTLE LATE."
I WANT TO THANK YOU AGAIN FOR HELPING ME OUT HERE. I DIDN'T EVEN NOTICE THE LEAK. IF I HAD BEEN DRIVING WHEN THE BRAKES WENT OUT...
IT'S NO PROBLEM. IT LOOKS LIKE THE LINE IS JUST A LITTLE LOOSE. I'LL HAVE YOU OUT OF HERE IN NO TIME.
AND THEN YOU CAN BE OFF TO BE WITH YOUR GIRLFRIEND AND HER PARENTS FOR A NICE FAMILY DINNER.
Huh? WHAT DID YOU SAY?
I REMEMBER HAVING FAMILY DINNERS. ALTHOUGH I'M SURE YOURS DIDN'T HURT QUITE AS MUCH AS MINE.
HOLD ON. I CAN'T HEAR YOU. LET ME SLIDE OUT REAL QUICK.
OR AS THIS.

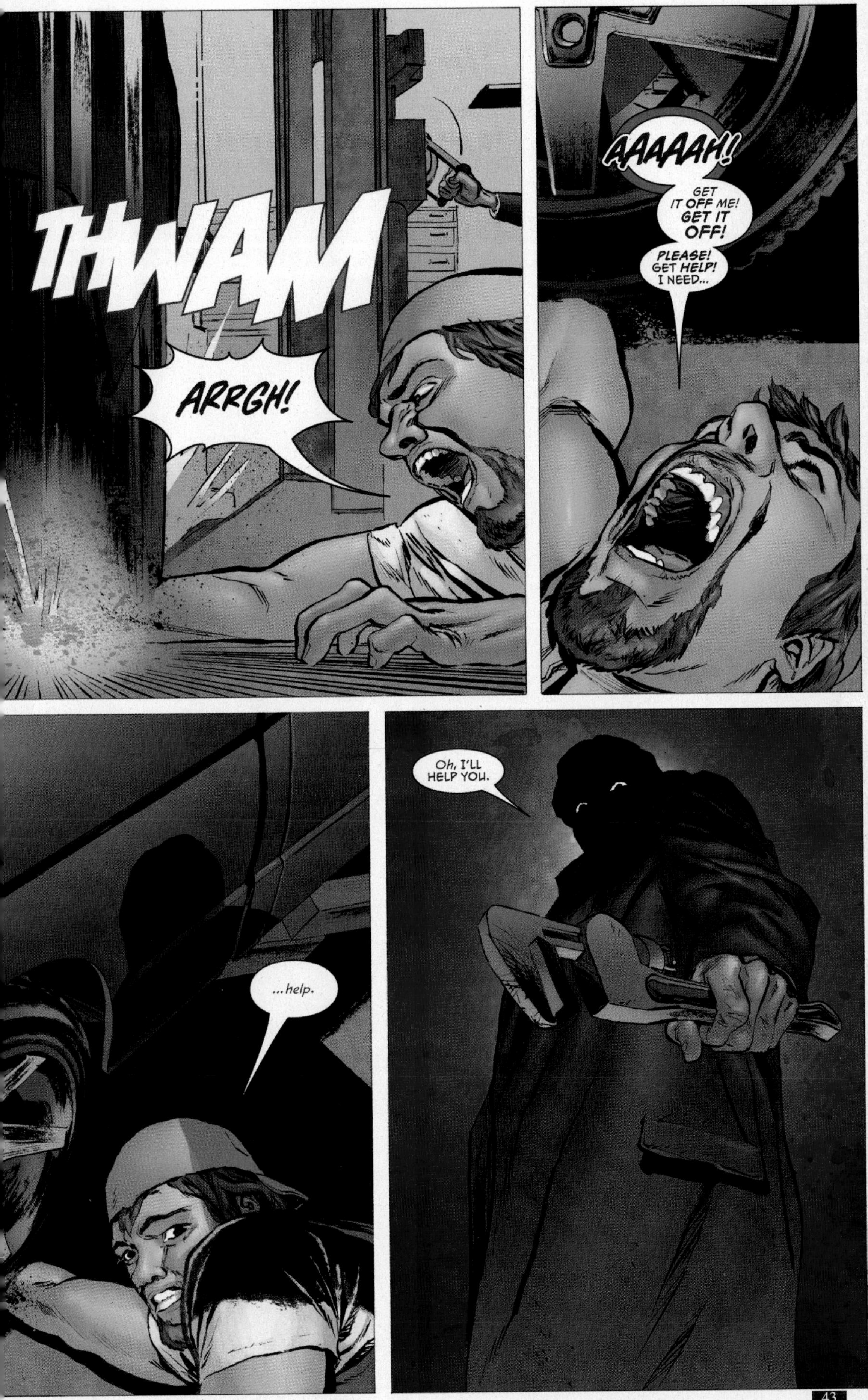
THWAM
ARRGH!
AAAAAH!
GET IT OFF ME! GET IT OFF!
PLEASE! GET HELP! I NEED...
...help.
Oh, I'LL HELP YOU.

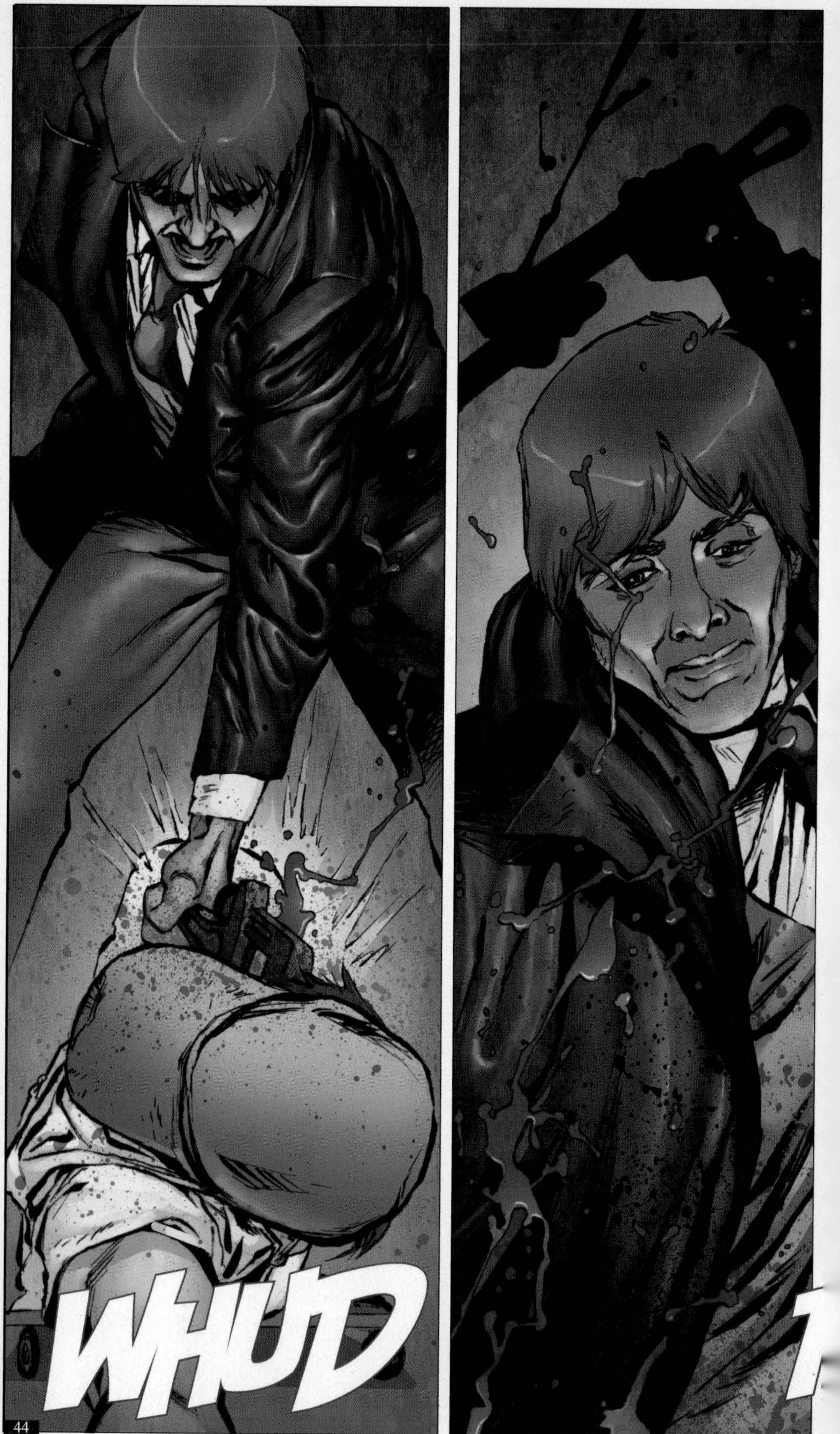
WHUD

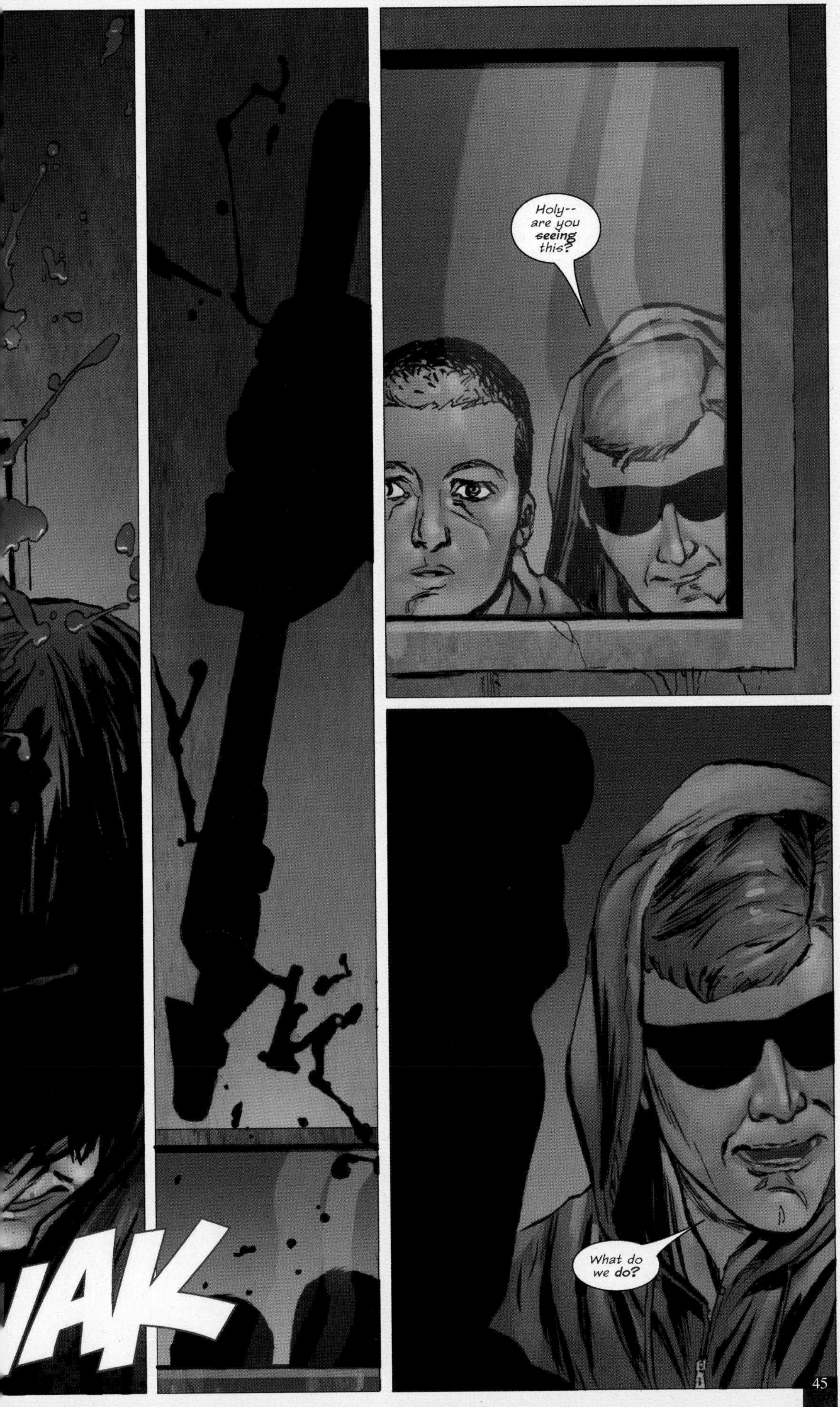
AK
Holy--
are you
seeing
this?
What do
we do?

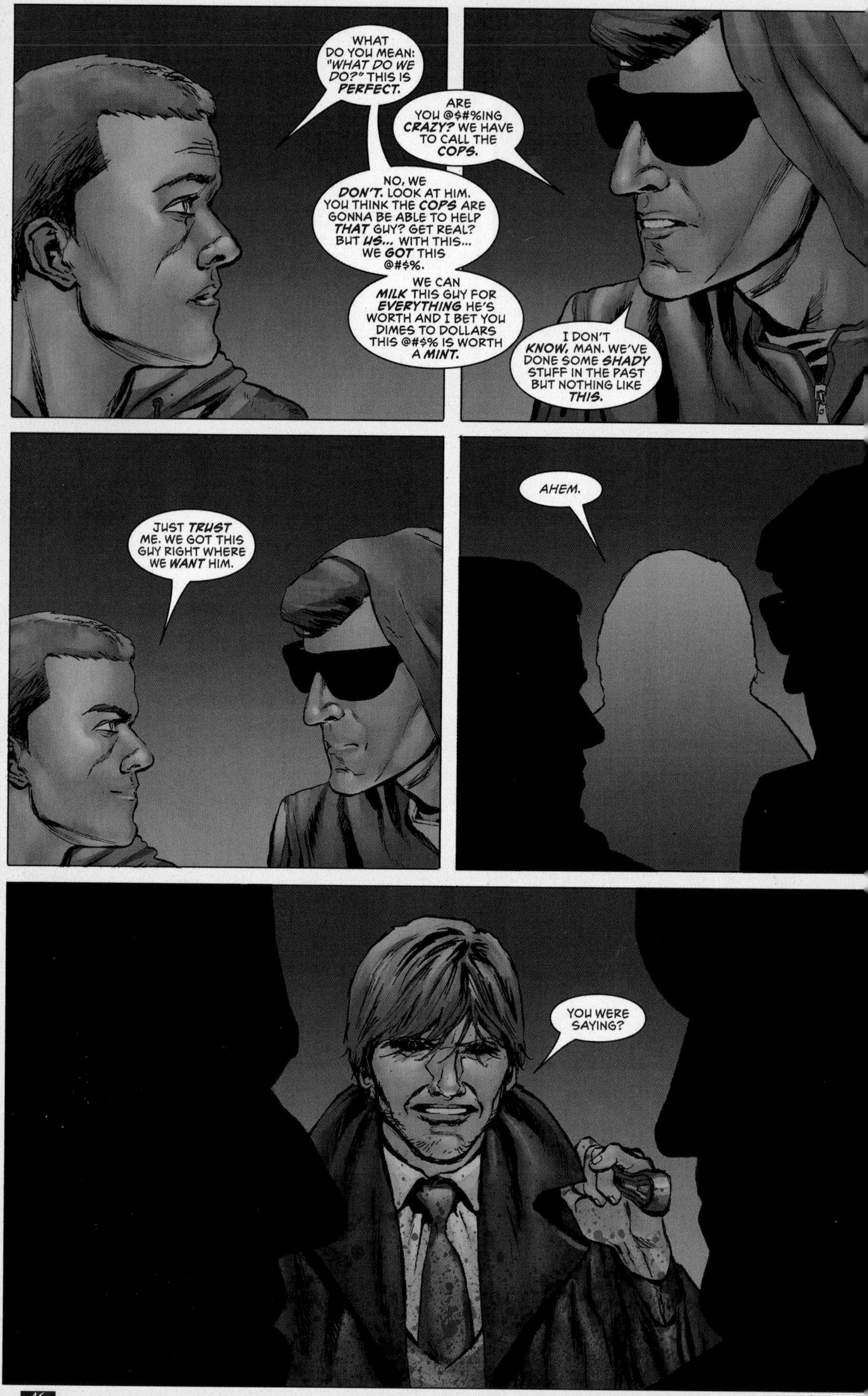
WHAT DO YOU MEAN: "WHAT DO WE DO?" THIS IS PERFECT.
ARE YOU @$#%ING CRAZY? WE HAVE TO CALL THE COPS.
NO, WE DON'T. LOOK AT HIM. YOU THINK THE COPS ARE GONNA BE ABLE TO HELP THAT GUY? GET REAL? BUT US... WITH THIS... WE GOT THIS @#$%.
WE CAN MILK THIS GUY FOR EVERYTHING HE'S WORTH AND I BET YOU DIMES TO DOLLARS THIS @#$% IS WORTH A MINT.
I DON'T KNOW, MAN. WE'VE DONE SOME SHADY STUFF IN THE PAST BUT NOTHING LIKE THIS.
JUST TRUST ME. WE GOT THIS GUY RIGHT WHERE WE WANT HIM.
AHEM.
YOU WERE SAYING?

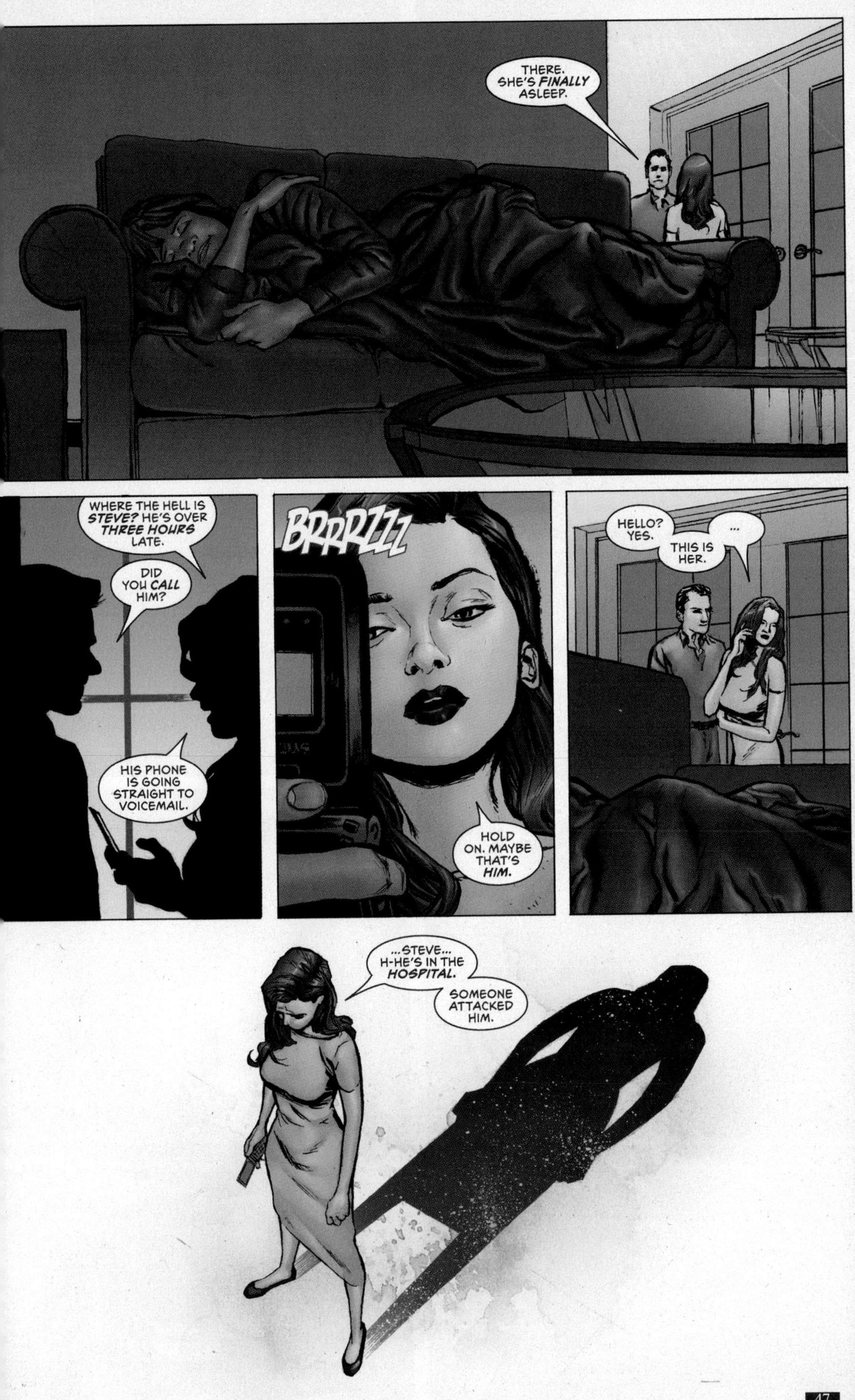
THERE. SHE'S FINALLY ASLEEP.
WHERE THE HELL IS STEVE? HE'S OVER THREE HOURS LATE.
DID YOU CALL HIM?
HIS PHONE IS GOING STRAIGHT TO VOICEMAIL.
BRRRZZZZ
HOLD ON. MAYBE THAT'S HIM.
HELLO? YES.
THIS IS HER.
...
...STEVE... H-HE'S IN THE HOSPITAL.
SOMEONE ATTACKED HIM.

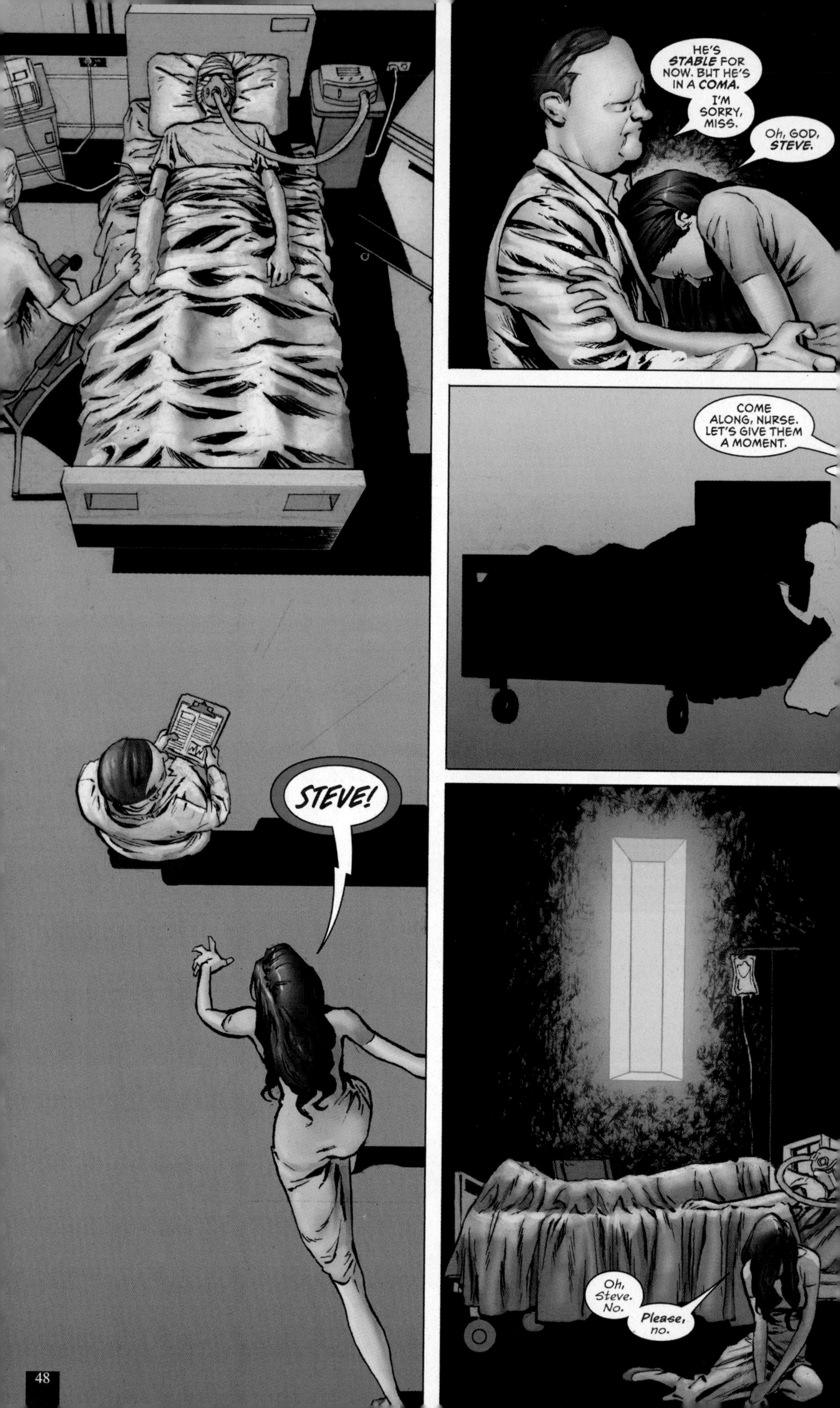
STEVE!
HE'S STABLE FOR NOW. BUT HE'S IN A COMA.
I'M SORRY, MISS.
Oh, GOD, STEVE.
COME ALONG, NURSE. LET'S GIVE THEM A MOMENT.
Oh, Steve. No.
Please, no.

THE BEAST IS FINALLY SILENT. ITS RAGE SPENT, IT NOW SLUMBERS IN SOME DARK RECESS OF MY MIND.

HURTING THE BOY BROUGHT ME NO JOY.

TAKING HER PARENTS' HOME FROM THEM LEAVES ME WITH NO PLEASURE.

BUT KNOWING THE PAIN IT WILL BRING HER...

...KNOWING THE ANGUISH AND SUFFERING SHE'S FEELING RIGHT NOW MAKES ME FEEL SOMETHING I HAVE NOT FELT IN YEARS.

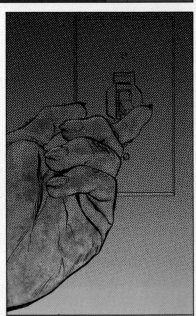

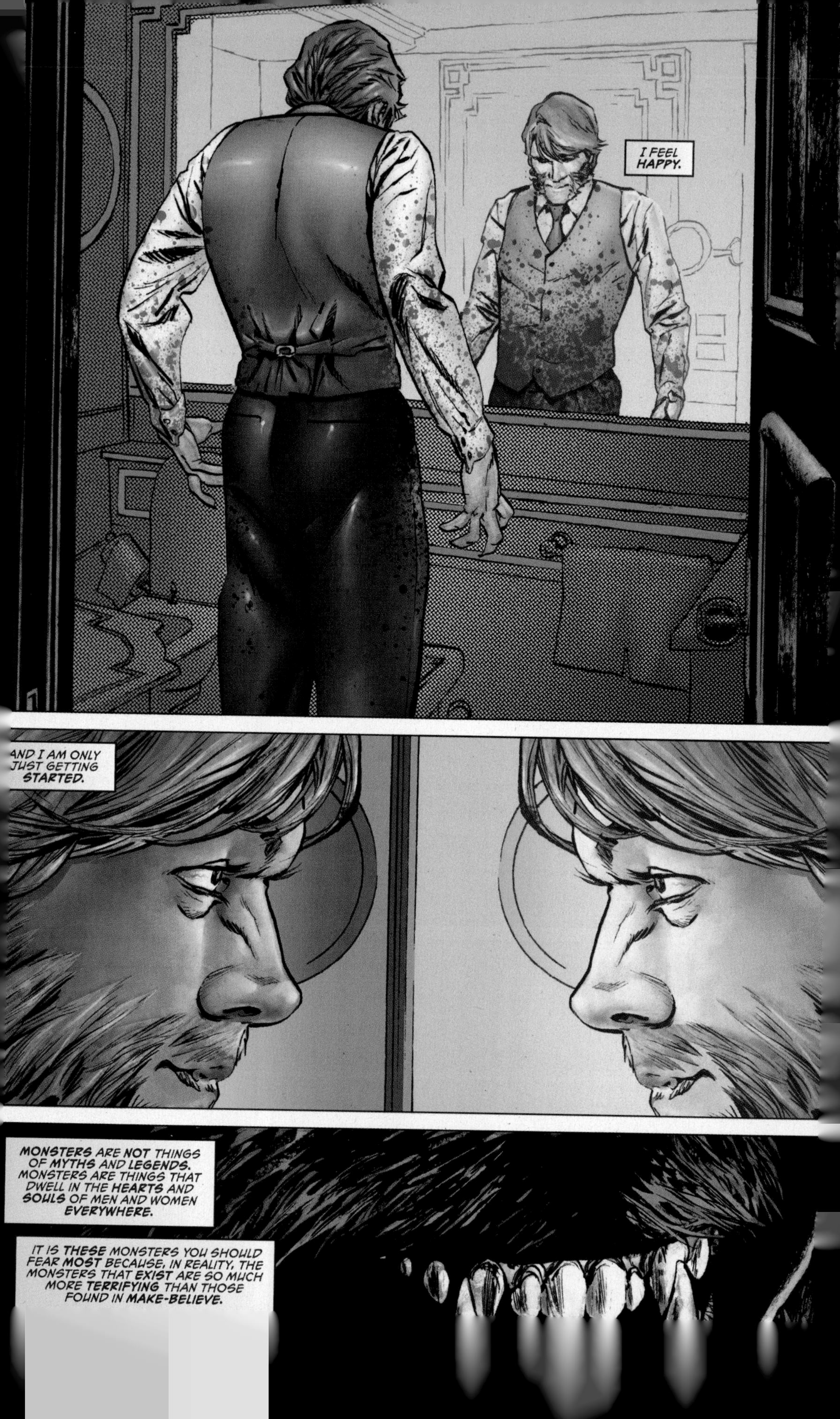
I FEEL HAPPY.
AND I AM ONLY JUST GETTING STARTED.
MONSTERS ARE NOT THINGS OF MYTHS AND LEGENDS. MONSTERS ARE THINGS THAT DWELL IN THE HEARTS AND SOULS OF MEN AND WOMEN EVERYWHERE.
IT IS THESE MONSTERS YOU SHOULD FEAR MOST BECAUSE, IN REALITY, THE MONSTERS THAT EXIST ARE SO MUCH MORE TERRIFYING THAN THOSE FOUND IN MAKE-BELIEVE.

# Grimm Fairy Tales
# Myths & Legends

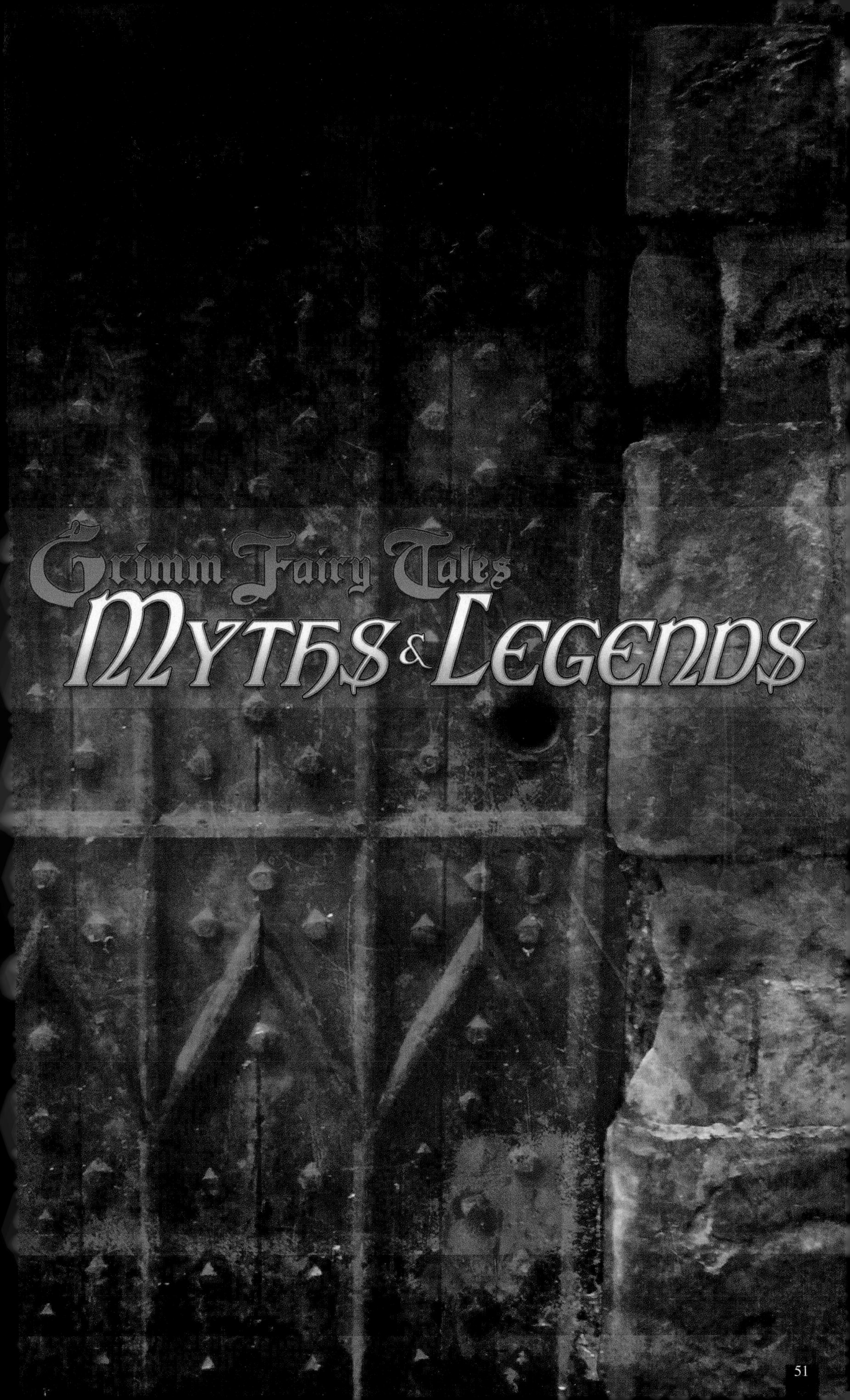

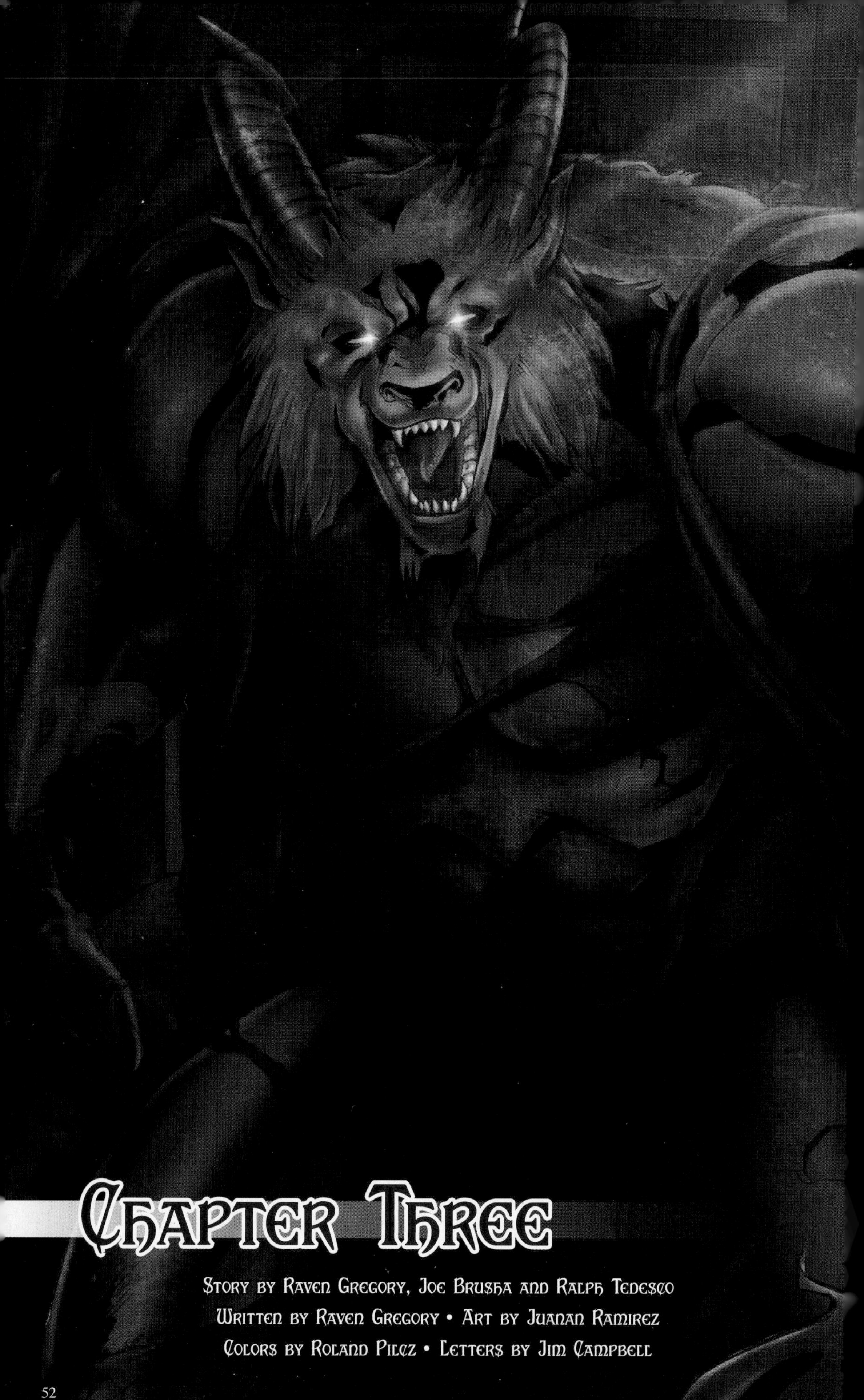

# Chapter Three

Story by Raven Gregory, Joe Brusha and Ralph Tedesco
Written by Raven Gregory • Art by Juanan Ramirez
Colors by Roland Pilcz • Letters by Jim Campbell

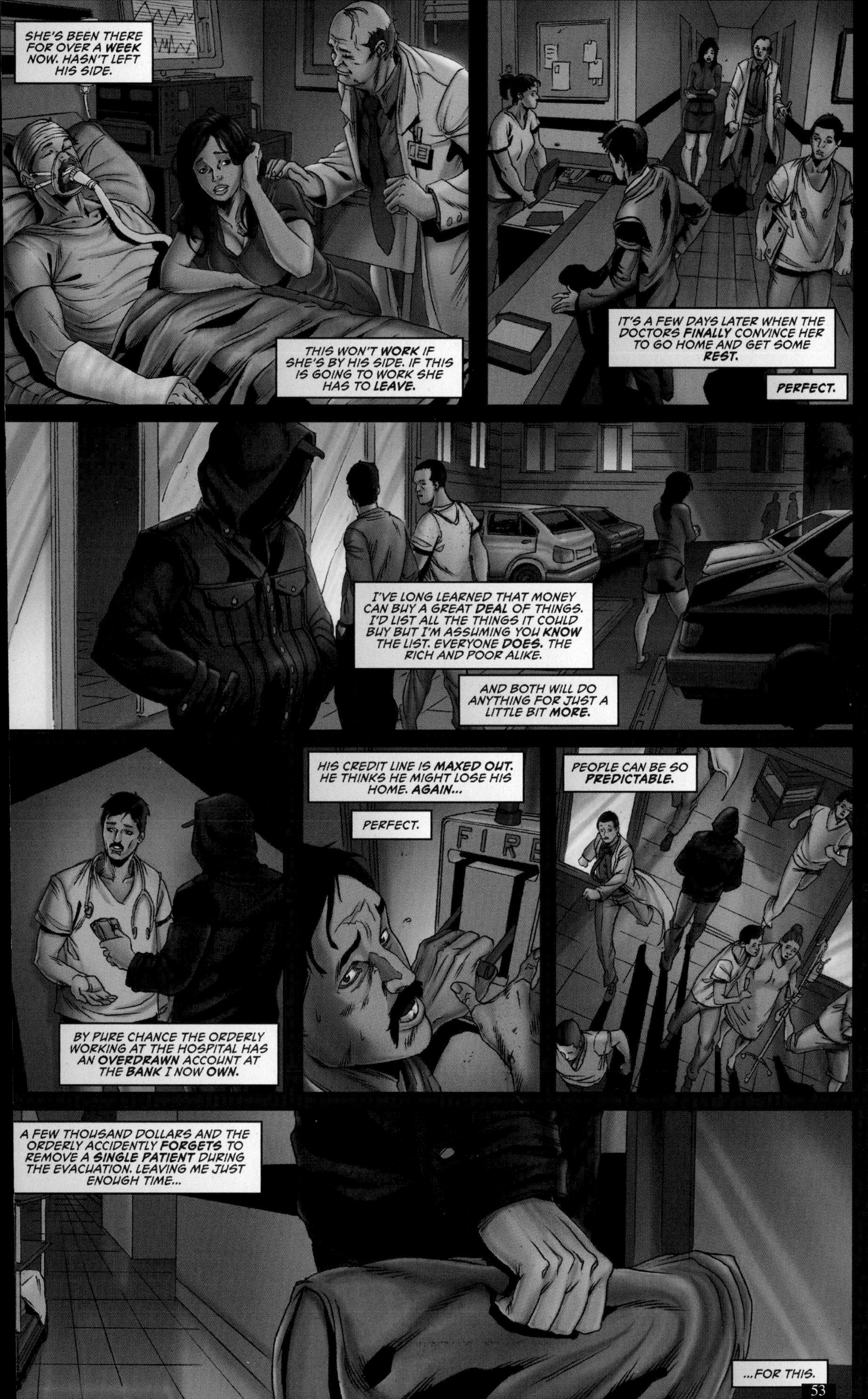
SHE'S BEEN THERE FOR OVER A WEEK NOW. HASN'T LEFT HIS SIDE.
THIS WON'T WORK IF SHE'S BY HIS SIDE. IF THIS IS GOING TO WORK SHE HAS TO LEAVE.
IT'S A FEW DAYS LATER WHEN THE DOCTORS FINALLY CONVINCE HER TO GO HOME AND GET SOME REST.
PERFECT.
I'VE LONG LEARNED THAT MONEY CAN BUY A GREAT DEAL OF THINGS. I'D LIST ALL THE THINGS IT COULD BUY BUT I'M ASSUMING YOU KNOW THE LIST. EVERYONE DOES. THE RICH AND POOR ALIKE.
AND BOTH WILL DO ANYTHING FOR JUST A LITTLE BIT MORE.
BY PURE CHANCE THE ORDERLY WORKING AT THE HOSPITAL HAS AN OVERDRAWN ACCOUNT AT THE BANK I NOW OWN.
HIS CREDIT LINE IS MAXED OUT. HE THINKS HE MIGHT LOSE HIS HOME. AGAIN...
PERFECT.
FIRE
PEOPLE CAN BE SO PREDICTABLE.
A FEW THOUSAND DOLLARS AND THE ORDERLY ACCIDENTLY FORGETS TO REMOVE A SINGLE PATIENT DURING THE EVACUATION. LEAVING ME JUST ENOUGH TIME...
...FOR THIS.

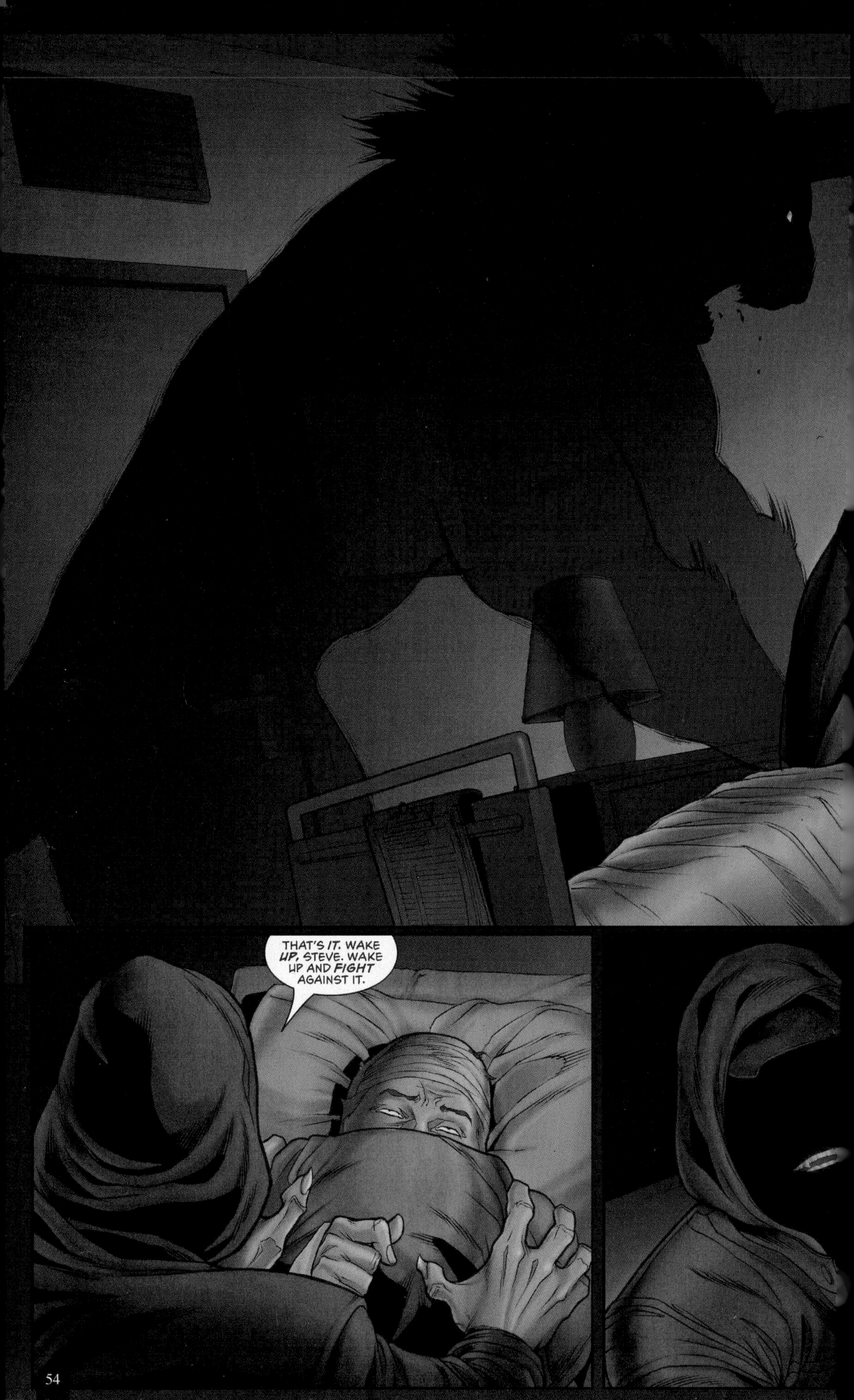
THAT'S *IT.* WAKE *UP,* STEVE. WAKE UP AND *FIGHT* AGAINST IT.

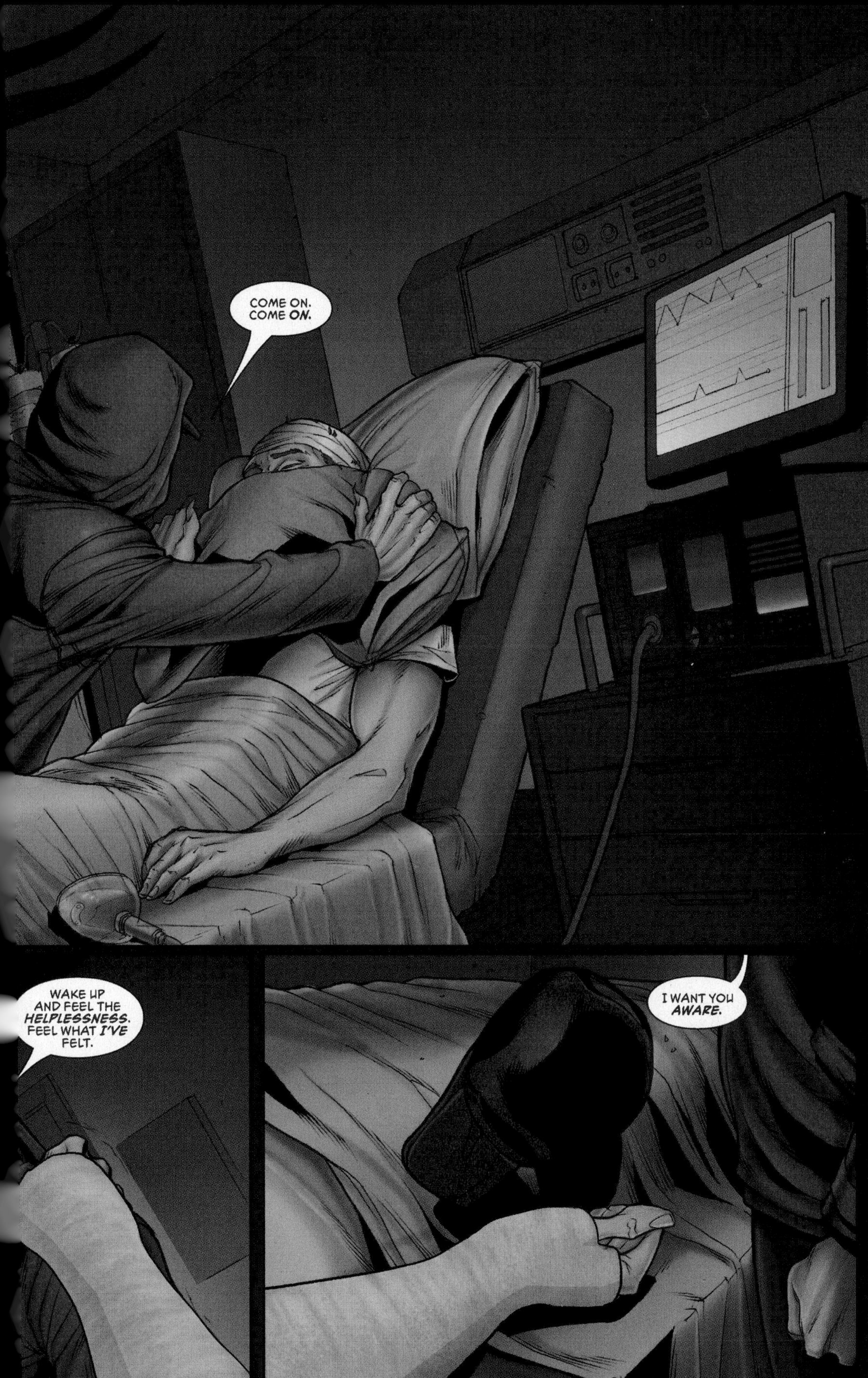
COME ON.
COME *ON*.
WAKE UP AND FEEL THE *HELPLESSNESS*. FEEL WHAT *I'VE* FELT.
I WANT YOU *AWARE*.

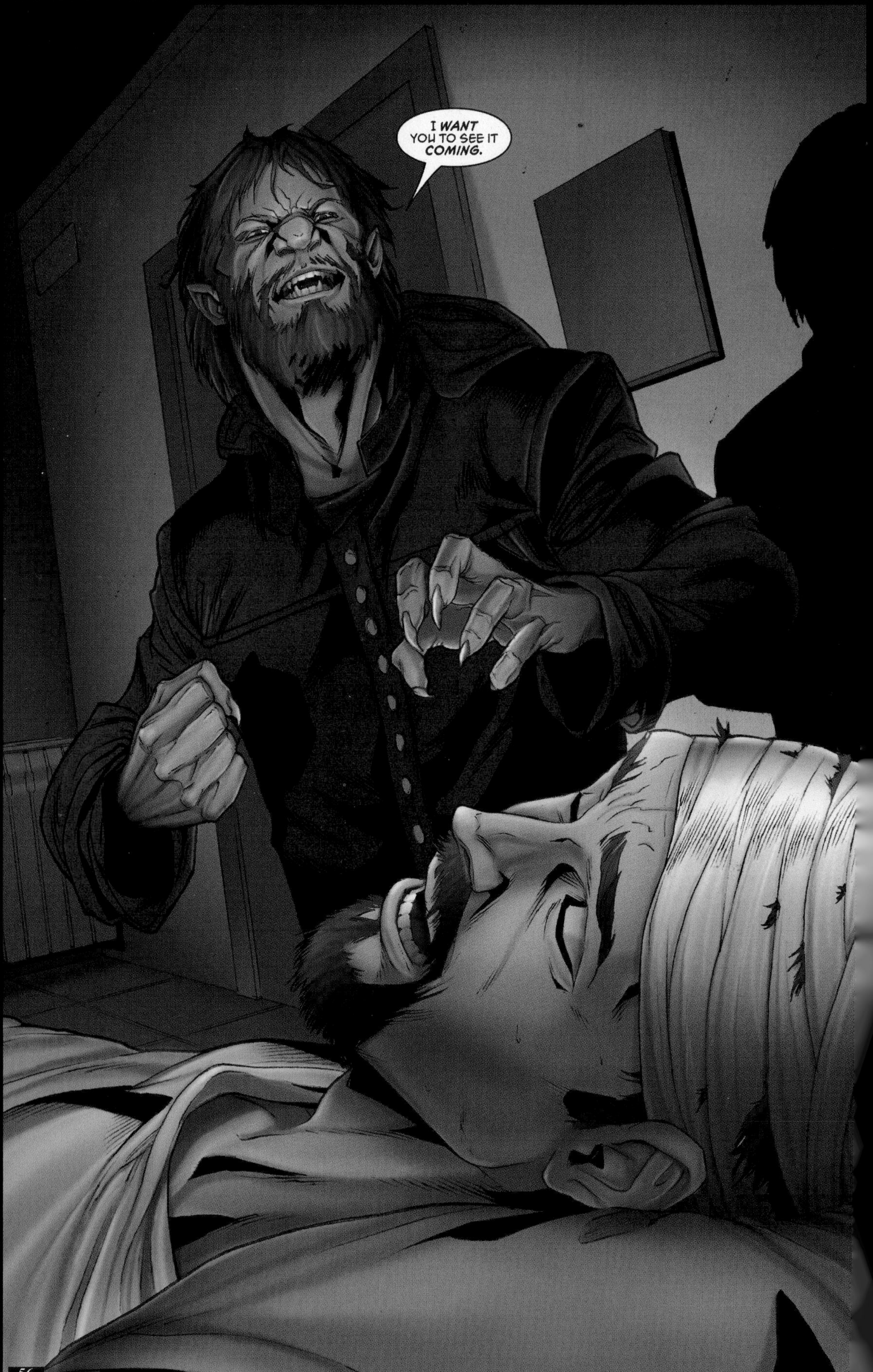
I WANT YOU TO SEE IT COMING.

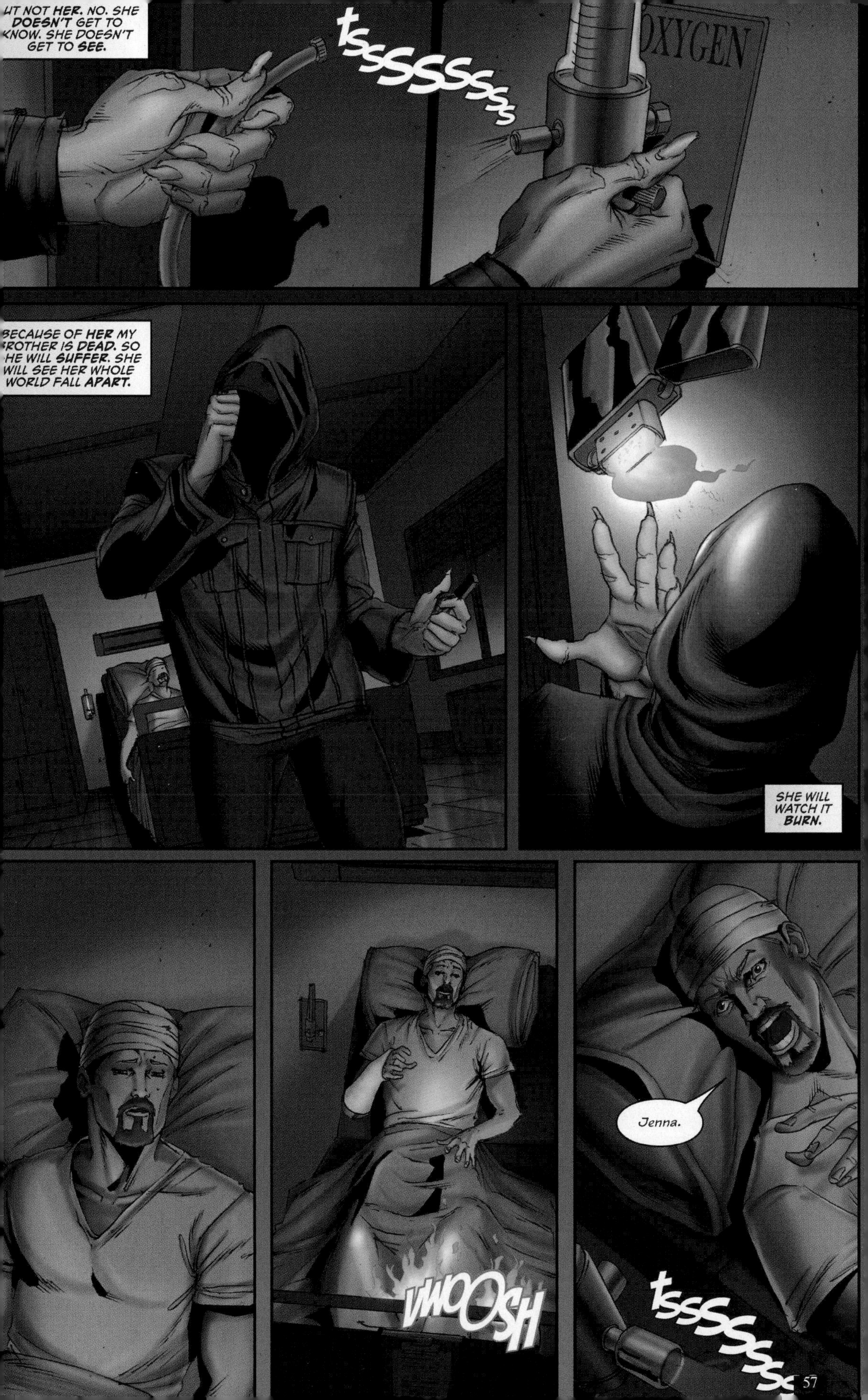
UT NOT HER. NO. SHE DOESN'T GET TO KNOW. SHE DOESN'T GET TO SEE.
tsssssssss
OXYGEN
BECAUSE OF HER MY ROTHER IS DEAD. SO HE WILL SUFFER. SHE WILL SEE HER WHOLE WORLD FALL APART.
SHE WILL WATCH IT BURN.
VWOOSH
Jenna.
tssssssss

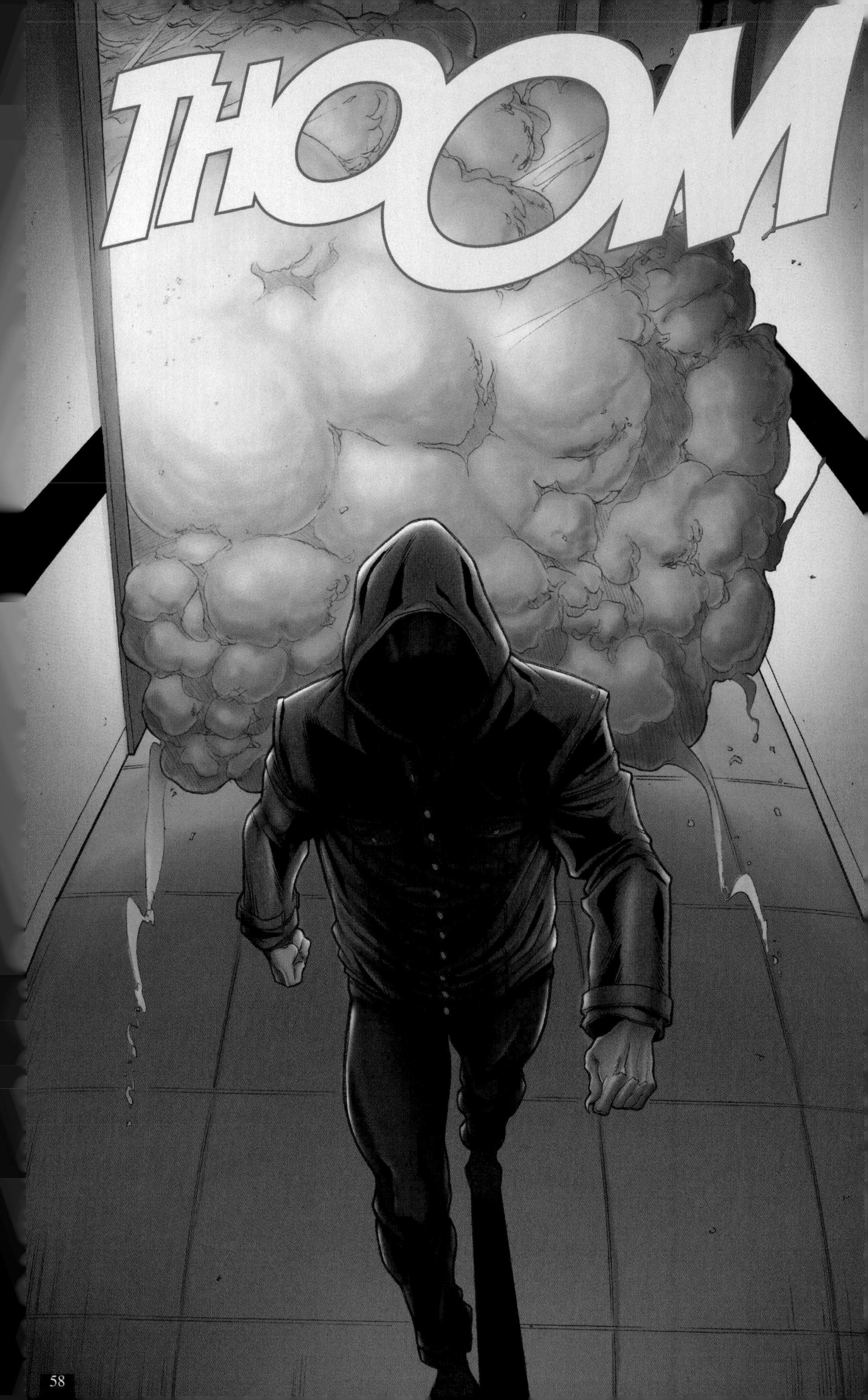
THOOM

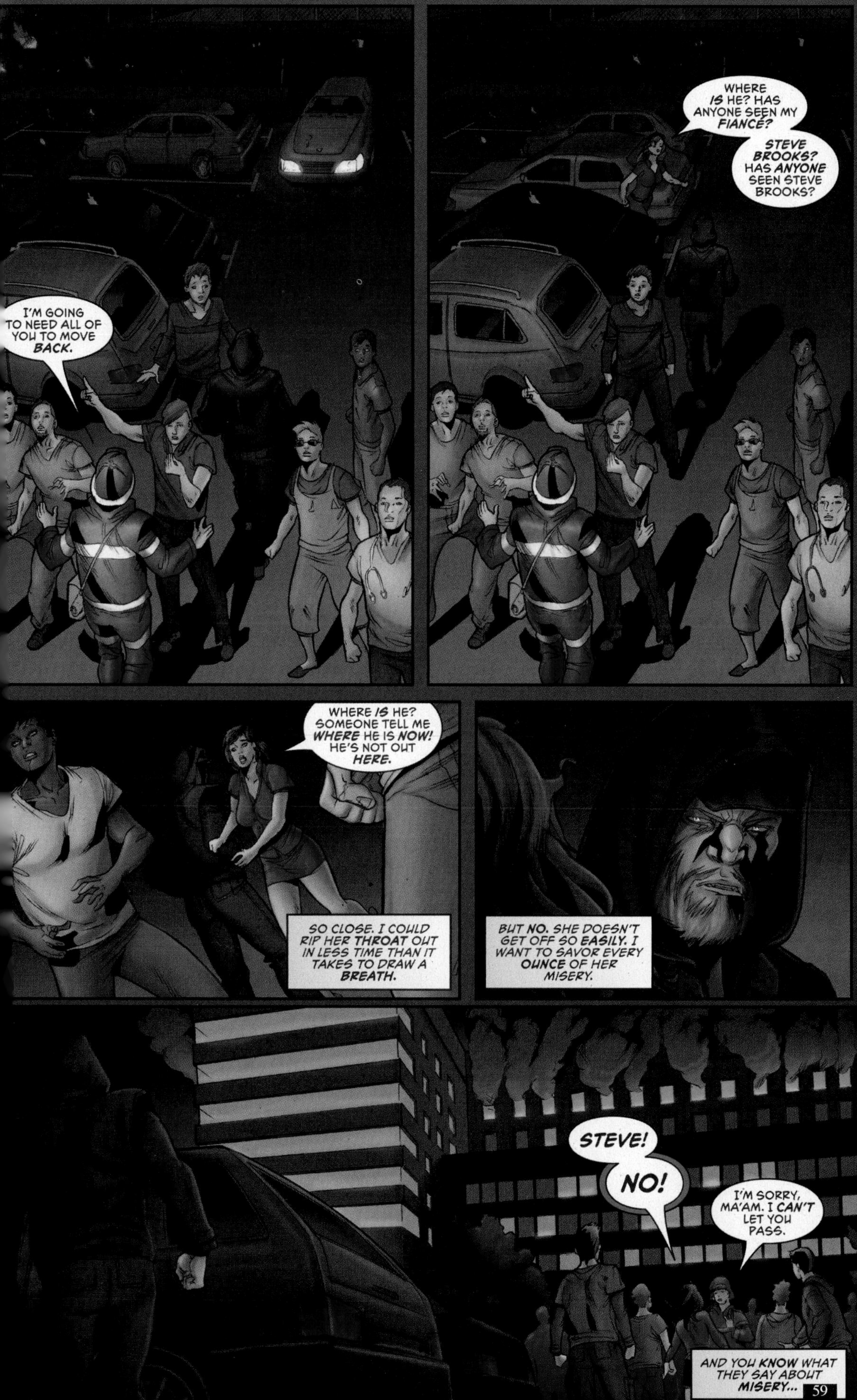
I'M GOING TO NEED ALL OF YOU TO MOVE BACK.
WHERE IS HE? HAS ANYONE SEEN MY FIANCÉ?
STEVE BROOKS? HAS ANYONE SEEN STEVE BROOKS?
WHERE IS HE? SOMEONE TELL ME WHERE HE IS NOW! HE'S NOT OUT HERE.
SO CLOSE. I COULD RIP HER THROAT OUT IN LESS TIME THAN IT TAKES TO DRAW A BREATH.
BUT NO. SHE DOESN'T GET OFF SO EASILY. I WANT TO SAVOR EVERY OUNCE OF HER MISERY.
STEVE!
NO!
I'M SORRY, MA'AM. I CAN'T LET YOU PASS.
AND YOU KNOW WHAT THEY SAY ABOUT MISERY...

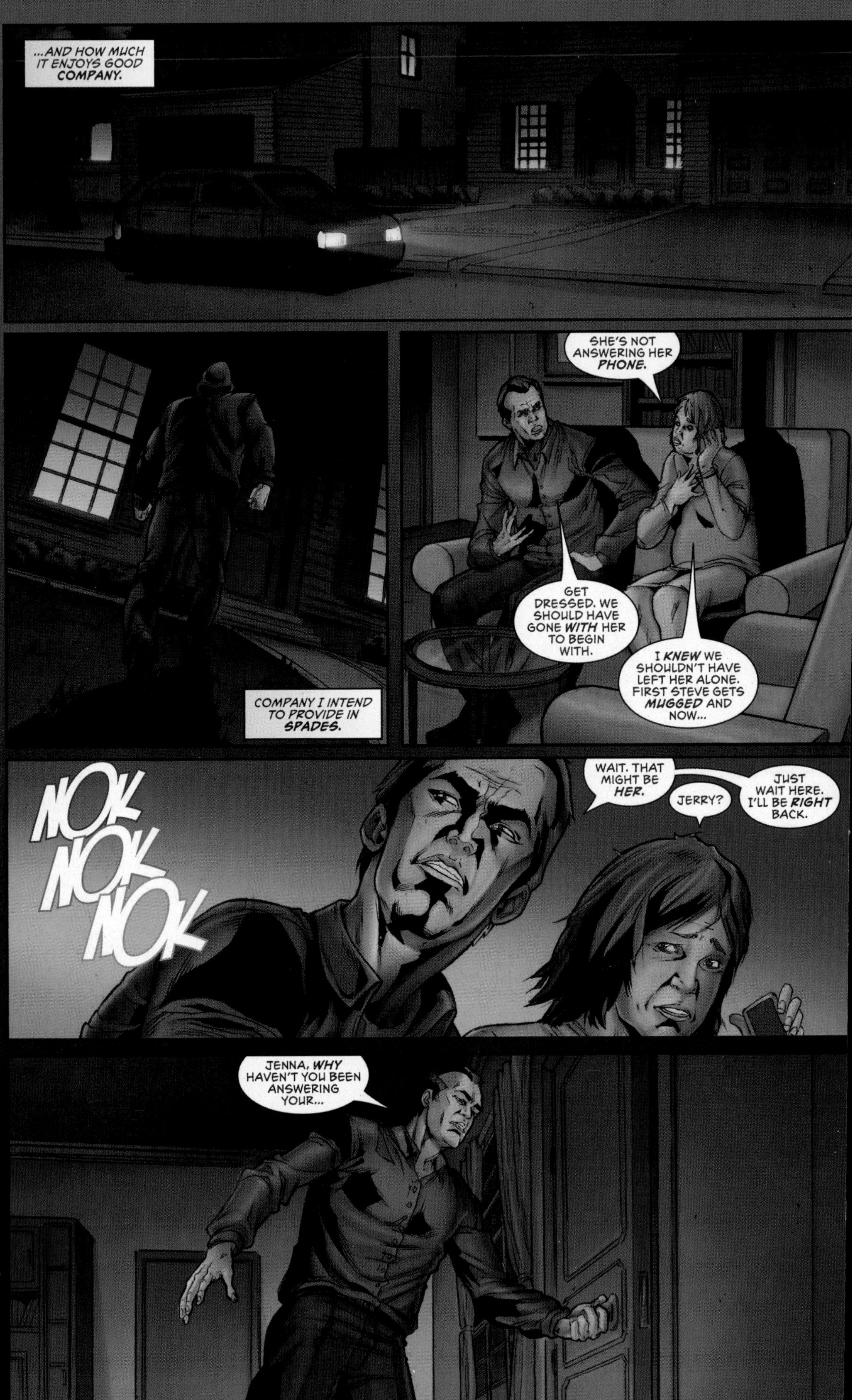
...AND HOW MUCH IT ENJOYS GOOD COMPANY.
COMPANY I INTEND TO PROVIDE IN SPADES.
SHE'S NOT ANSWERING HER PHONE.
GET DRESSED. WE SHOULD HAVE GONE WITH HER TO BEGIN WITH.
I KNEW WE SHOULDN'T HAVE LEFT HER ALONE. FIRST STEVE GETS MUGGED AND NOW...
NOK NOK NOK
WAIT. THAT MIGHT BE HER.
JERRY?
JUST WAIT HERE. I'LL BE RIGHT BACK.
JENNA, WHY HAVEN'T YOU BEEN ANSWERING YOUR...

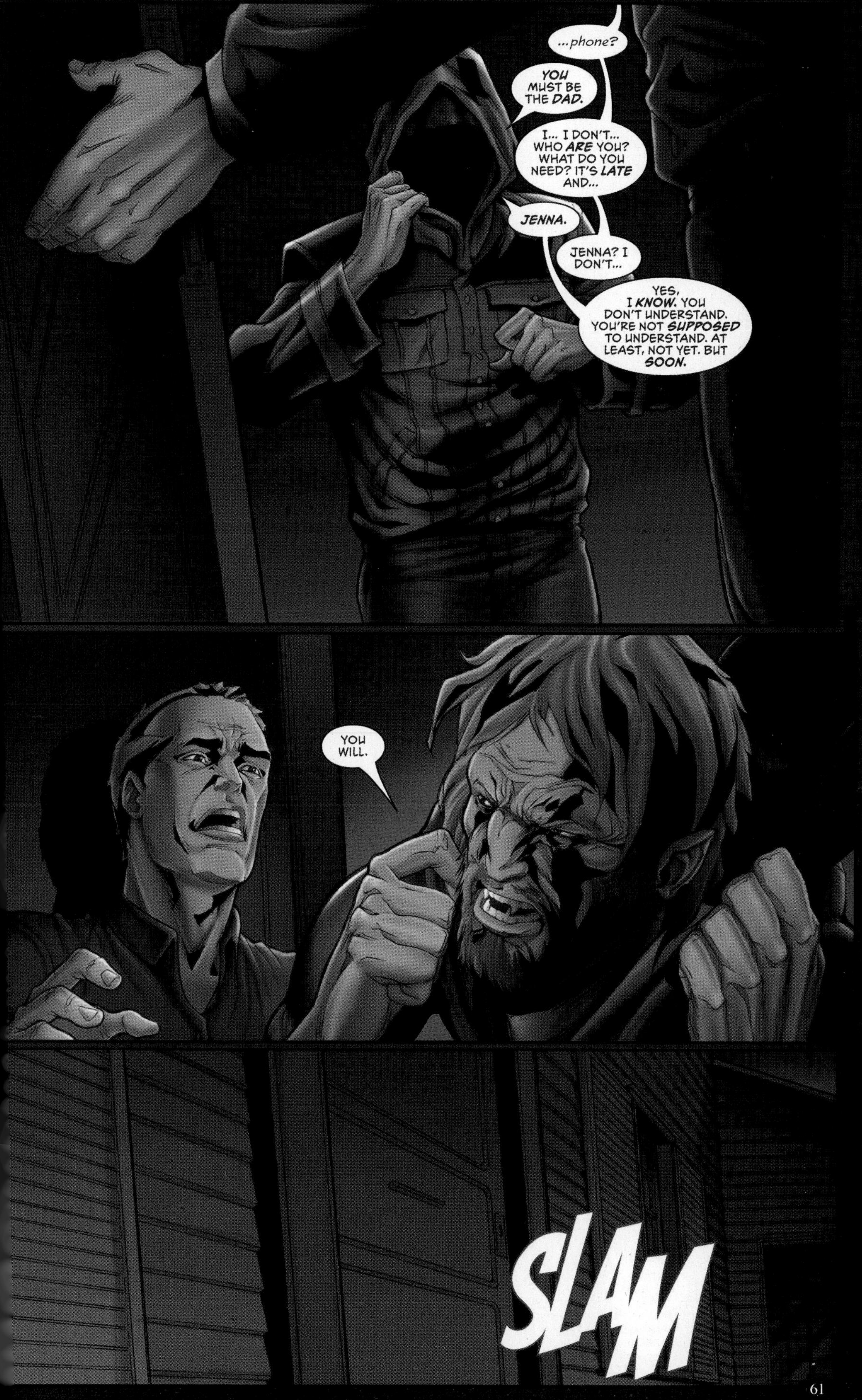

...phone?
YOU MUST BE THE DAD.
I... I DON'T... WHO ARE YOU? WHAT DO YOU NEED? IT'S LATE AND...
JENNA.
JENNA? I DON'T...
YES, I KNOW. YOU DON'T UNDERSTAND. YOU'RE NOT SUPPOSED TO UNDERSTAND. AT LEAST, NOT YET. BUT SOON.
YOU WILL.
SLAM

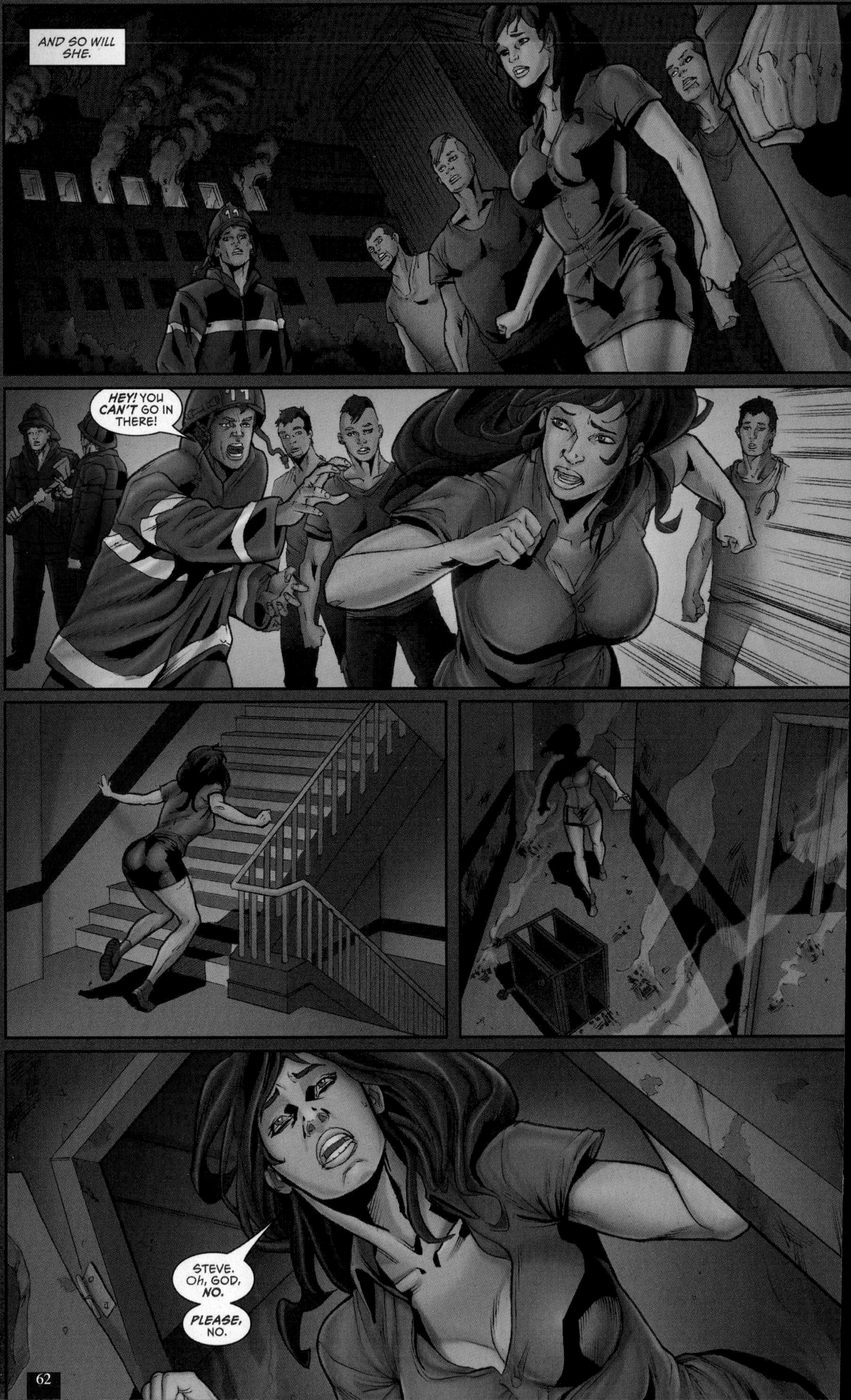
AND SO WILL SHE.
HEY! YOU CAN'T GO IN THERE!
STEVE. Oh, GOD, NO.
PLEASE, NO.

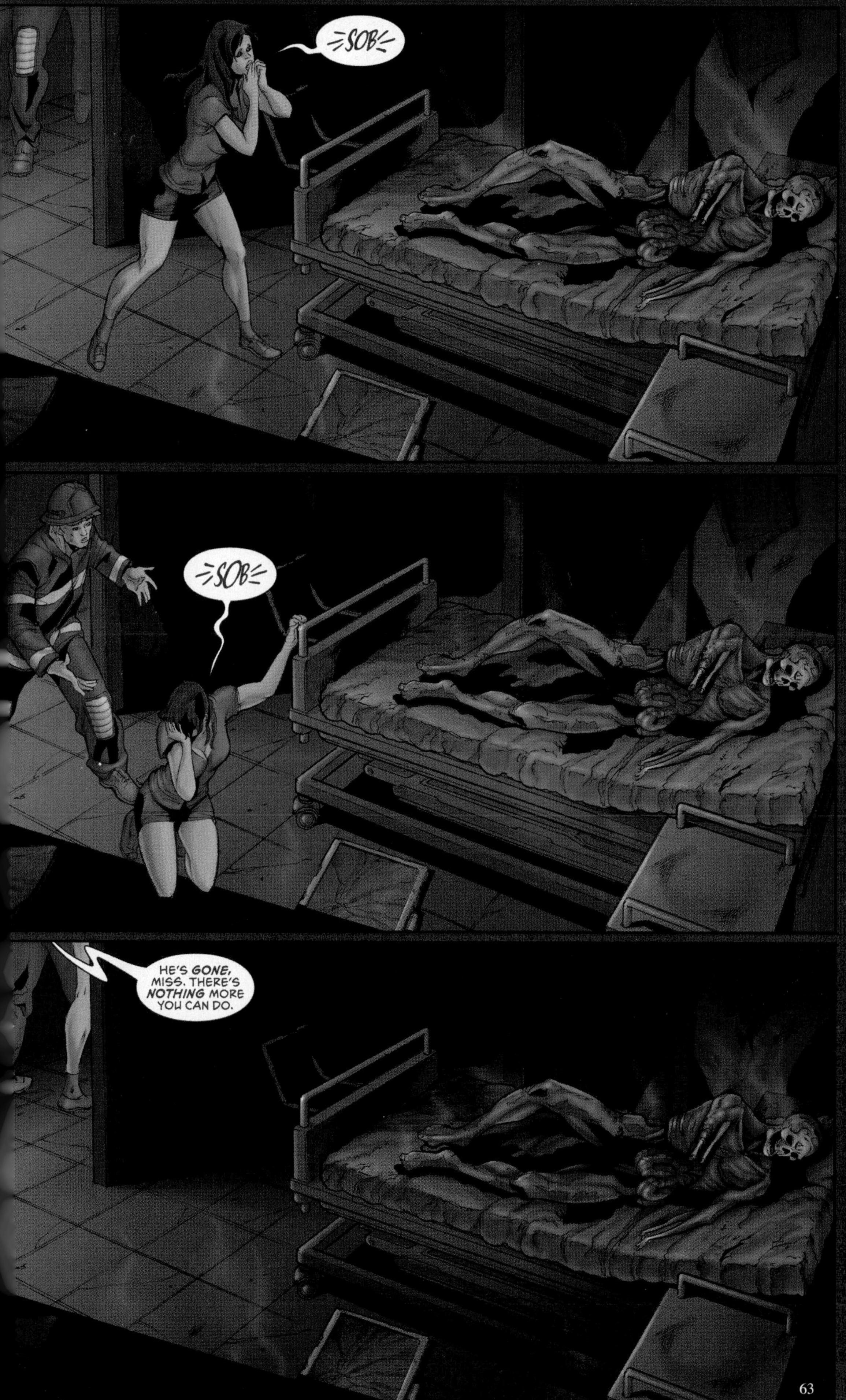
SOB
SOB
HE'S GONE, MISS. THERE'S NOTHING MORE YOU CAN DO.

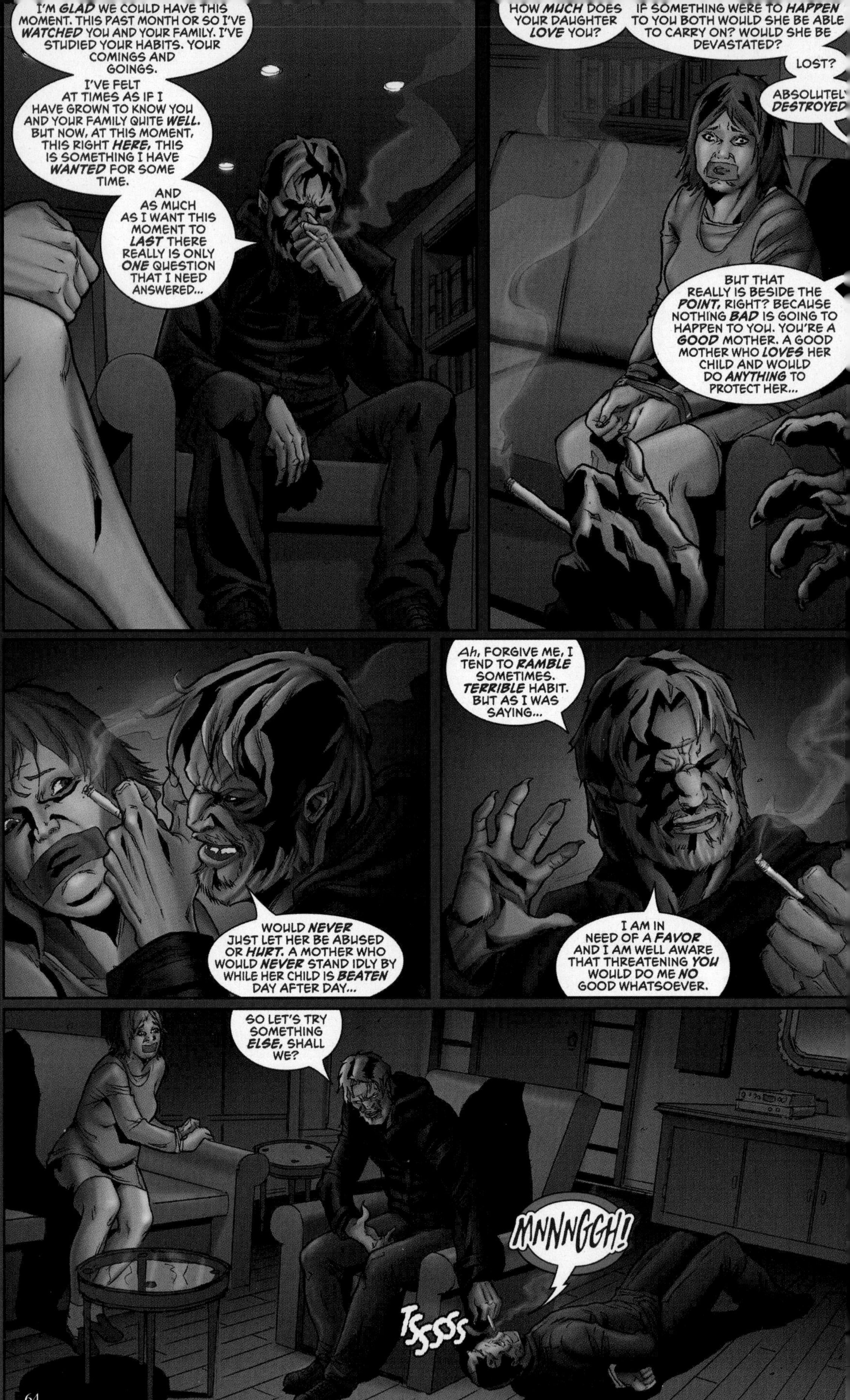
I'M GLAD WE COULD HAVE THIS MOMENT. THIS PAST MONTH OR SO I'VE WATCHED YOU AND YOUR FAMILY. I'VE STUDIED YOUR HABITS. YOUR COMINGS AND GOINGS.
I'VE FELT AT TIMES AS IF I HAVE GROWN TO KNOW YOU AND YOUR FAMILY QUITE WELL. BUT NOW, AT THIS MOMENT, THIS RIGHT HERE, THIS IS SOMETHING I HAVE WANTED FOR SOME TIME.
AND AS MUCH AS I WANT THIS MOMENT TO LAST THERE REALLY IS ONLY ONE QUESTION THAT I NEED ANSWERED...
HOW MUCH DOES YOUR DAUGHTER LOVE YOU?
IF SOMETHING WERE TO HAPPEN TO YOU BOTH WOULD SHE BE ABLE TO CARRY ON? WOULD SHE BE DEVASTATED?
LOST?
ABSOLUTEL DESTROYED
BUT THAT REALLY IS BESIDE THE POINT, RIGHT? BECAUSE NOTHING BAD IS GOING TO HAPPEN TO YOU. YOU'RE A GOOD MOTHER. A GOOD MOTHER WHO LOVES HER CHILD AND WOULD DO ANYTHING TO PROTECT HER...
WOULD NEVER JUST LET HER BE ABUSED OR HURT. A MOTHER WHO WOULD NEVER STAND IDLY BY WHILE HER CHILD IS BEATEN DAY AFTER DAY...
Ah, FORGIVE ME, I TEND TO RAMBLE SOMETIMES. TERRIBLE HABIT. BUT AS I WAS SAYING...
I AM IN NEED OF A FAVOR AND I AM WELL AWARE THAT THREATENING YOU WOULD DO ME NO GOOD WHATSOEVER.
SO LET'S TRY SOMETHING ELSE, SHALL WE?
MNNNGGH!
TSSSS

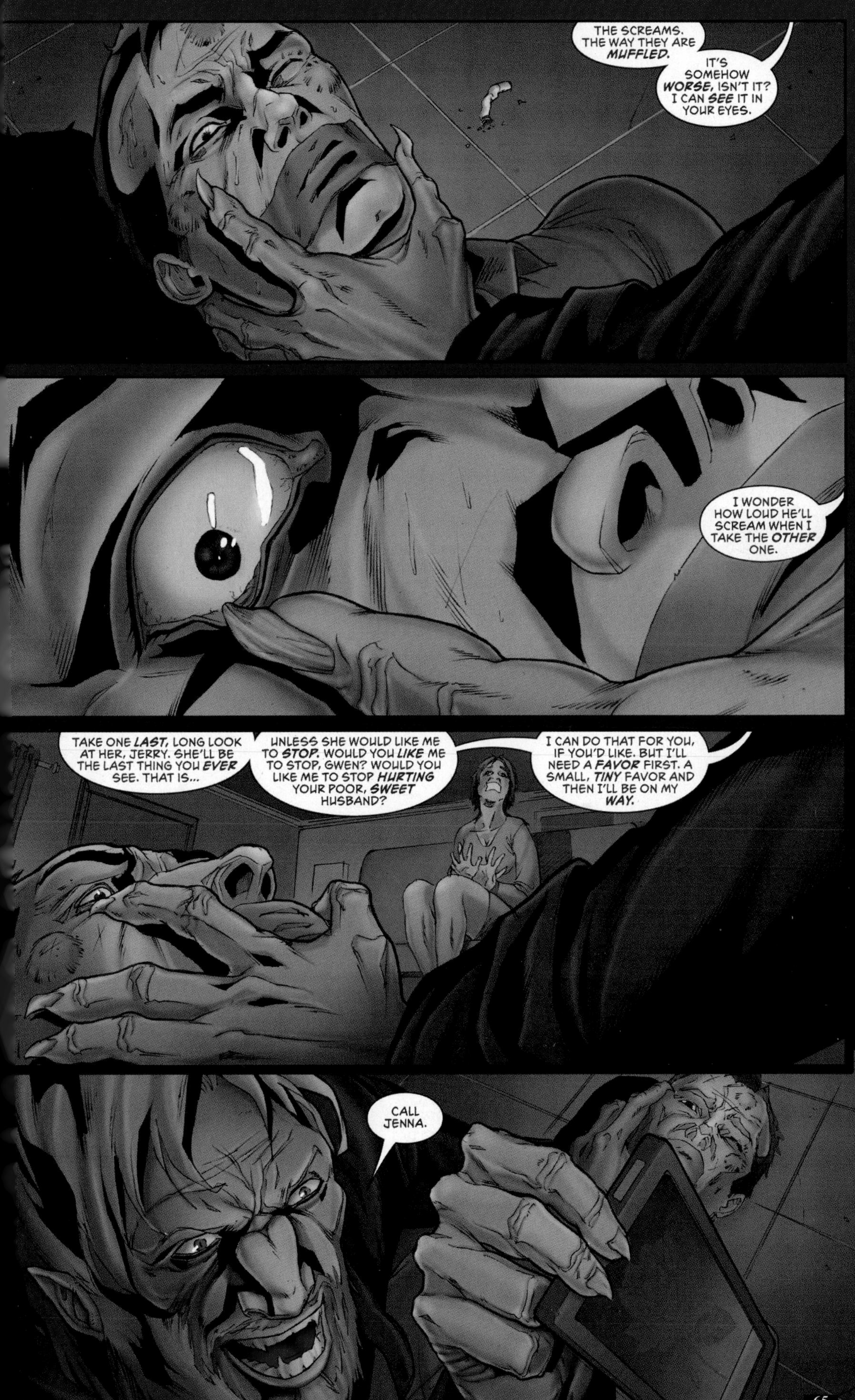
THE SCREAMS. THE WAY THEY ARE MUFFLED.
IT'S SOMEHOW WORSE, ISN'T IT? I CAN SEE IT IN YOUR EYES.
I WONDER HOW LOUD HE'LL SCREAM WHEN I TAKE THE OTHER ONE.
TAKE ONE LAST, LONG LOOK AT HER, JERRY. SHE'LL BE THE LAST THING YOU EVER SEE. THAT IS...
UNLESS SHE WOULD LIKE ME TO STOP. WOULD YOU LIKE ME TO STOP, GWEN? WOULD YOU LIKE ME TO STOP HURTING YOUR POOR, SWEET HUSBAND?
I CAN DO THAT FOR YOU, IF YOU'D LIKE. BUT I'LL NEED A FAVOR FIRST. A SMALL, TINY FAVOR AND THEN I'LL BE ON MY WAY.
CALL JENNA.

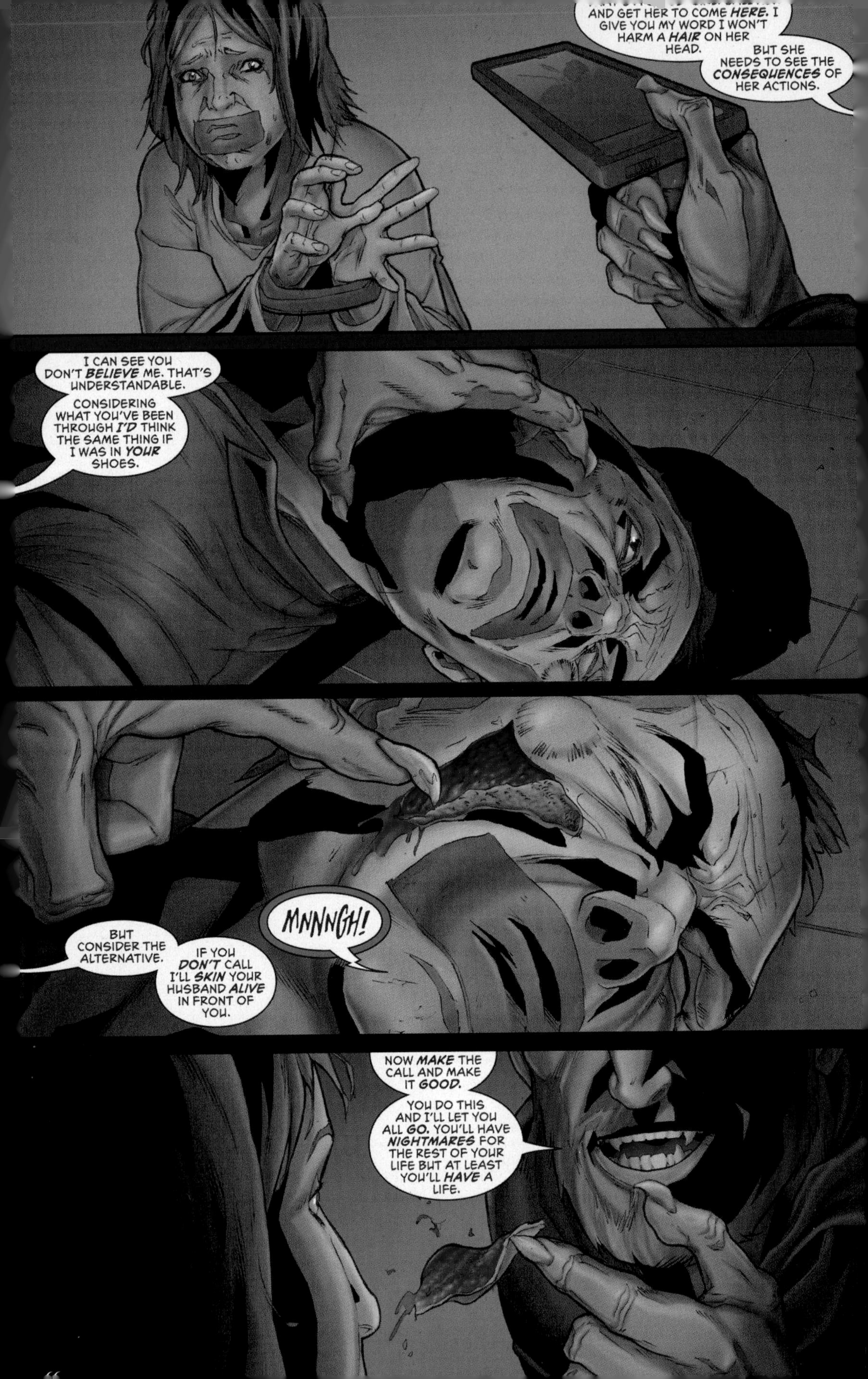
AND GET HER TO COME HERE. I GIVE YOU MY WORD I WON'T HARM A HAIR ON HER HEAD.
BUT SHE NEEDS TO SEE THE CONSEQUENCES OF HER ACTIONS.
I CAN SEE YOU DON'T BELIEVE ME. THAT'S UNDERSTANDABLE.
CONSIDERING WHAT YOU'VE BEEN THROUGH I'D THINK THE SAME THING IF I WAS IN YOUR SHOES.
MNNNGH!
BUT CONSIDER THE ALTERNATIVE.
IF YOU DON'T CALL I'LL SKIN YOUR HUSBAND ALIVE IN FRONT OF YOU.
NOW MAKE THE CALL AND MAKE IT GOOD.
YOU DO THIS AND I'LL LET YOU ALL GO. YOU'LL HAVE NIGHTMARES FOR THE REST OF YOUR LIFE BUT AT LEAST YOU'LL HAVE A LIFE.

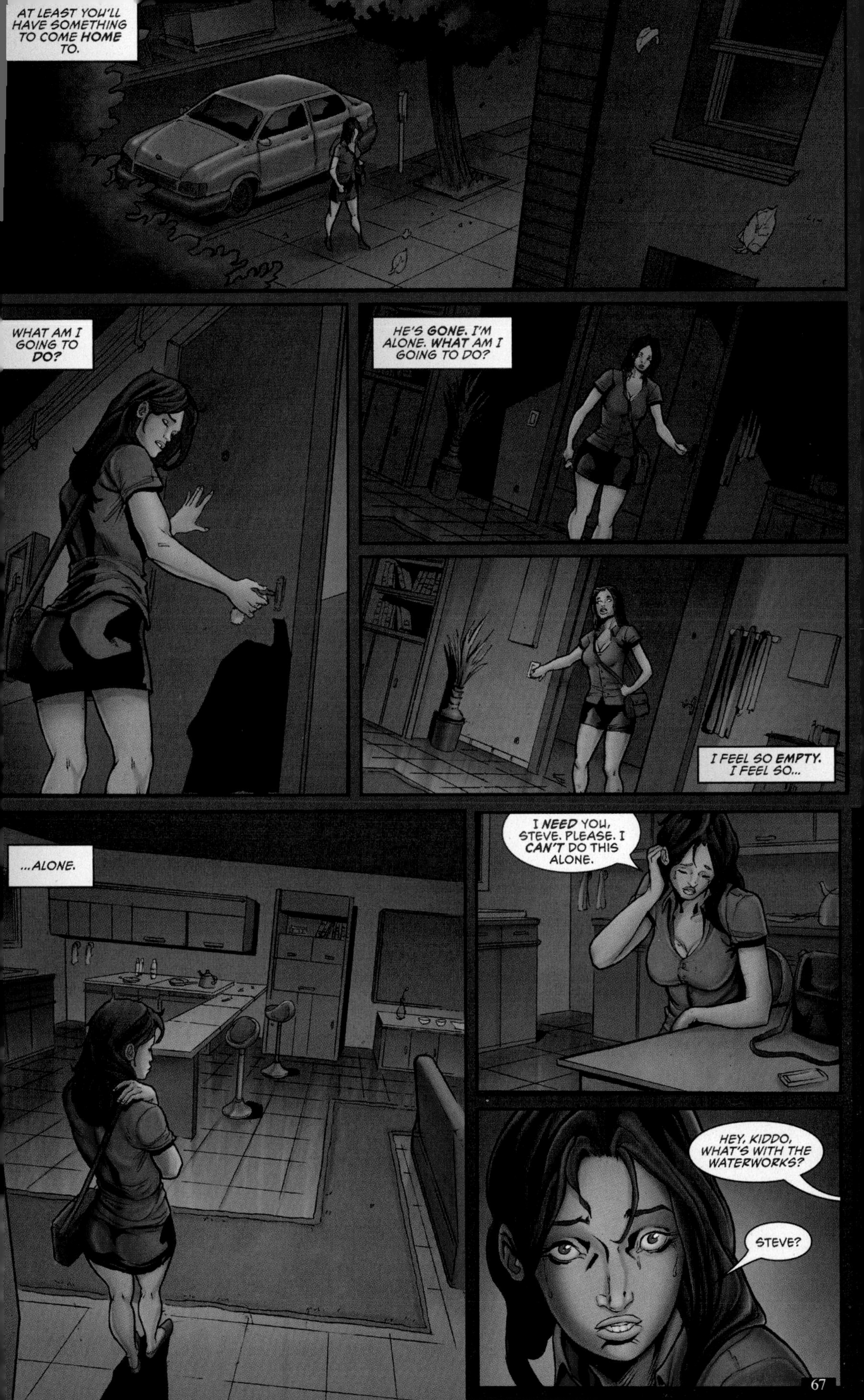
AT LEAST YOU'LL HAVE SOMETHING TO COME HOME TO.
WHAT AM I GOING TO DO?
HE'S GONE. I'M ALONE. WHAT AM I GOING TO DO?
I FEEL SO EMPTY. I FEEL SO...
...ALONE.
I NEED YOU, STEVE. PLEASE. I CAN'T DO THIS ALONE.
HEY, KIDDO, WHAT'S WITH THE WATERWORKS?
STEVE?

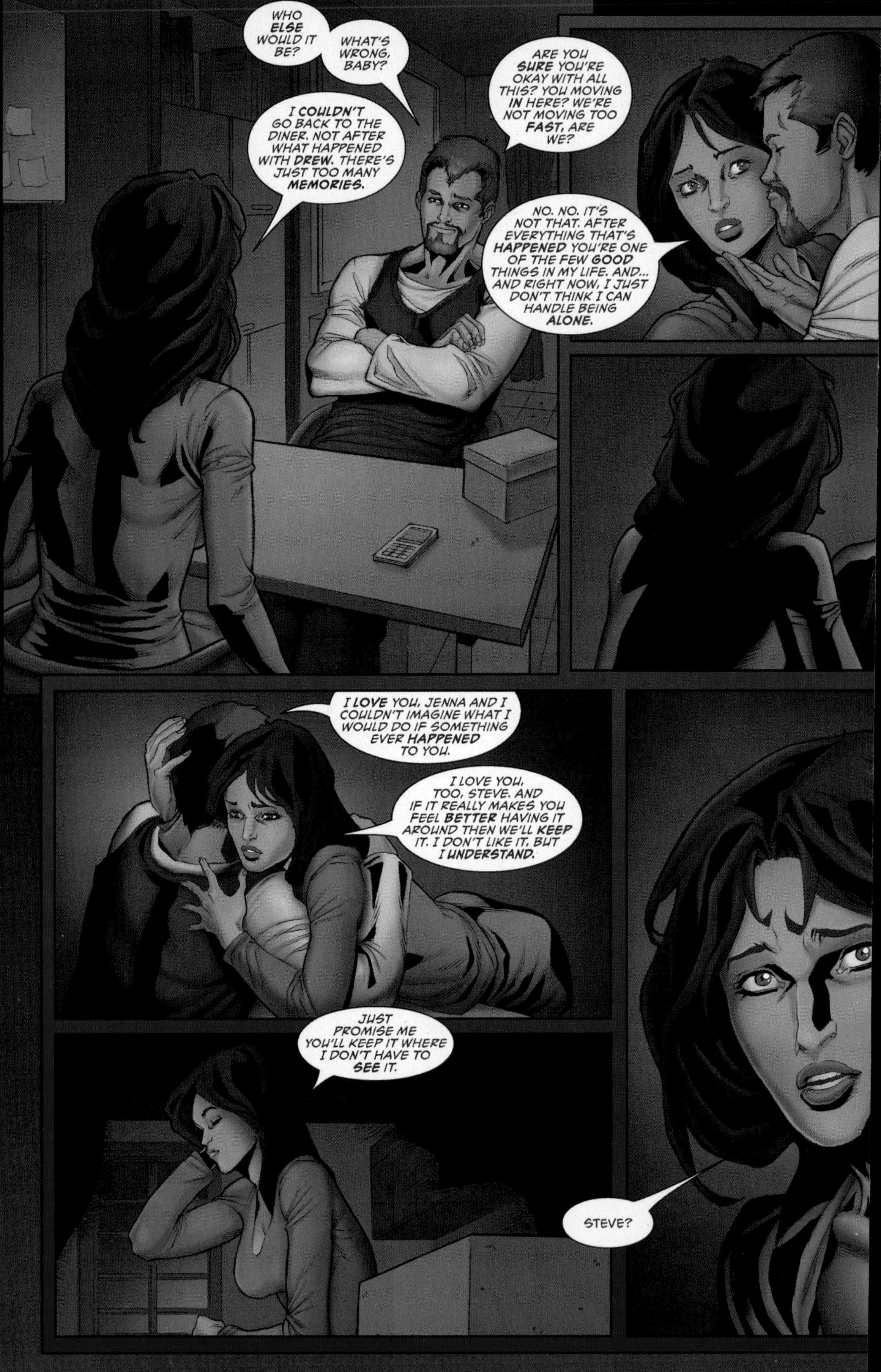
WHO ELSE WOULD IT BE?
WHAT'S WRONG, BABY?
I COULDN'T GO BACK TO THE DINER. NOT AFTER WHAT HAPPENED WITH DREW. THERE'S JUST TOO MANY MEMORIES.
ARE YOU SURE YOU'RE OKAY WITH ALL THIS? YOU MOVING IN HERE? WE'RE NOT MOVING TOO FAST, ARE WE?
NO. NO. IT'S NOT THAT. AFTER EVERYTHING THAT'S HAPPENED YOU'RE ONE OF THE FEW GOOD THINGS IN MY LIFE. AND... AND RIGHT NOW, I JUST DON'T THINK I CAN HANDLE BEING ALONE.
I LOVE YOU, JENNA AND I COULDN'T IMAGINE WHAT I WOULD DO IF SOMETHING EVER HAPPENED TO YOU.
I LOVE YOU, TOO, STEVE. AND IF IT REALLY MAKES YOU FEEL BETTER HAVING IT AROUND THEN WE'LL KEEP IT. I DON'T LIKE IT, BUT I UNDERSTAND.
JUST PROMISE ME YOU'LL KEEP IT WHERE I DON'T HAVE TO SEE IT.
STEVE?

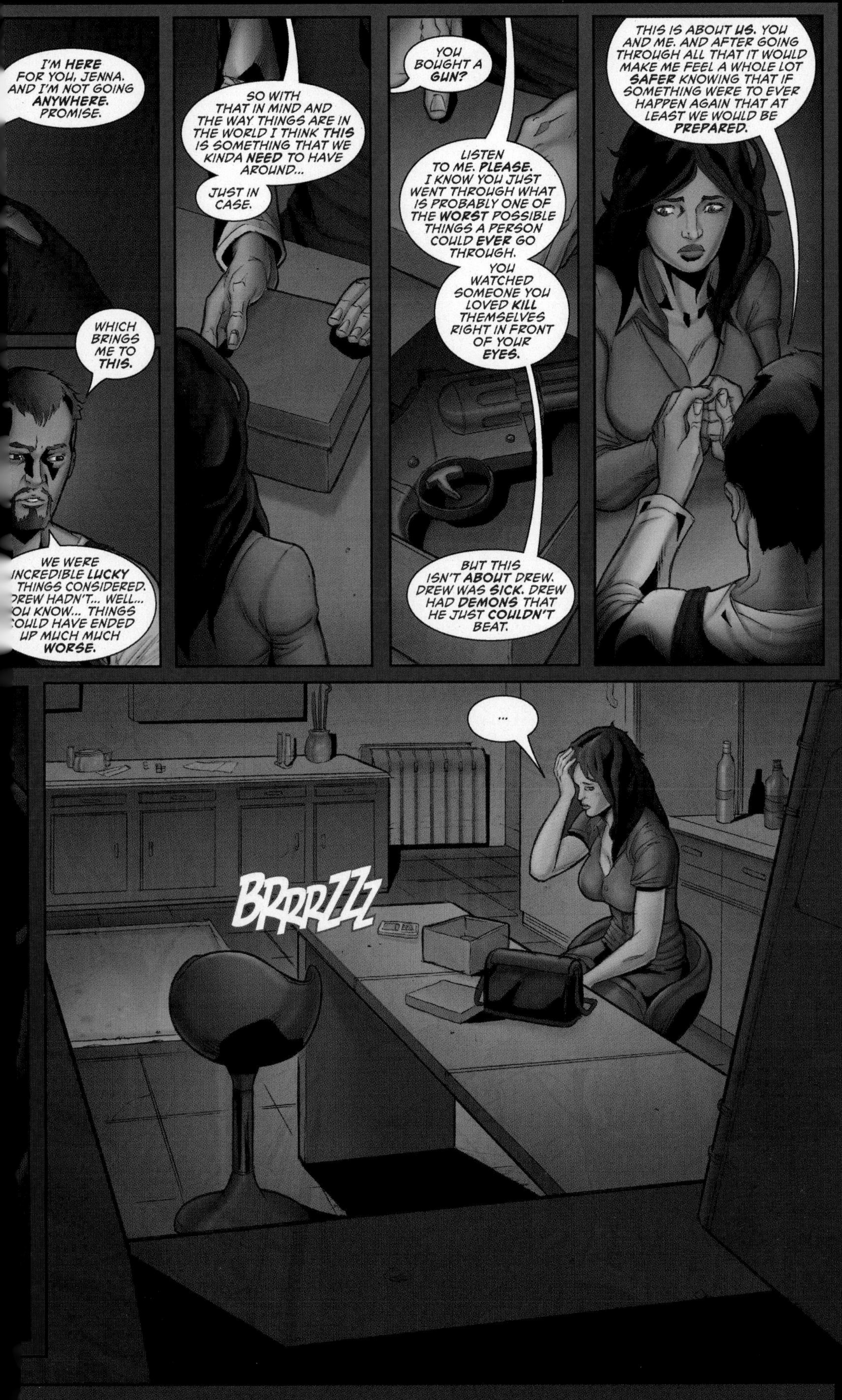

I'M HERE FOR YOU, JENNA. AND I'M NOT GOING ANYWHERE. PROMISE.
WHICH BRINGS ME TO THIS.
WE WERE INCREDIBLE LUCKY THINGS CONSIDERED. DREW HADN'T... WELL... YOU KNOW... THINGS COULD HAVE ENDED UP MUCH MUCH WORSE.
SO WITH THAT IN MIND AND THE WAY THINGS ARE IN THE WORLD I THINK THIS IS SOMETHING THAT WE KINDA NEED TO HAVE AROUND...
JUST IN CASE.
YOU BOUGHT A GUN?
LISTEN TO ME. PLEASE. I KNOW YOU JUST WENT THROUGH WHAT IS PROBABLY ONE OF THE WORST POSSIBLE THINGS A PERSON COULD EVER GO THROUGH.
YOU WATCHED SOMEONE YOU LOVED KILL THEMSELVES RIGHT IN FRONT OF YOUR EYES.
BUT THIS ISN'T ABOUT DREW. DREW WAS SICK. DREW HAD DEMONS THAT HE JUST COULDN'T BEAT.
THIS IS ABOUT US. YOU AND ME. AND AFTER GOING THROUGH ALL THAT IT WOULD MAKE ME FEEL A WHOLE LOT SAFER KNOWING THAT IF SOMETHING WERE TO EVER HAPPEN AGAIN THAT AT LEAST WE WOULD BE PREPARED.
...
BRRRZZZ

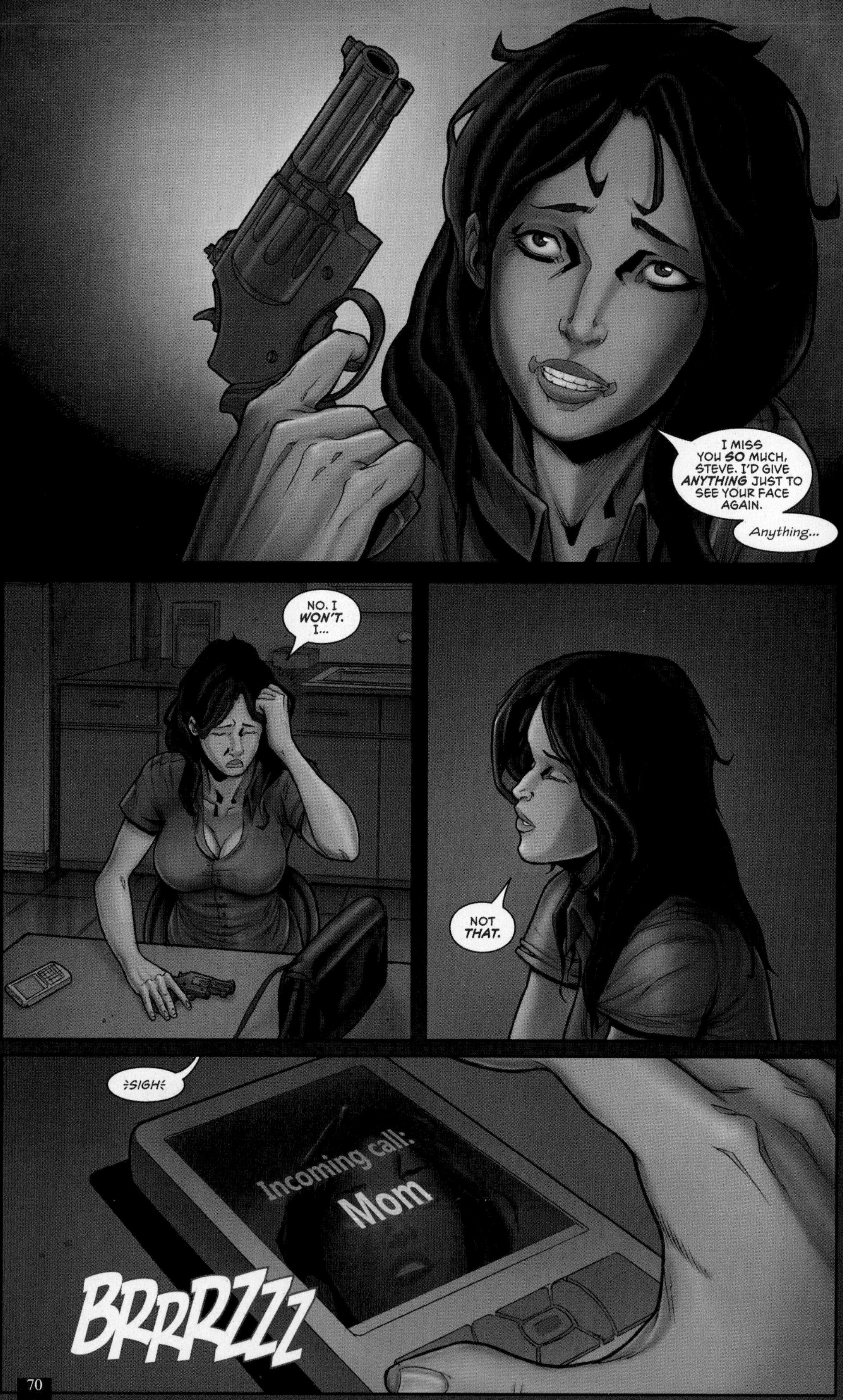
I MISS YOU SO MUCH, STEVE. I'D GIVE ANYTHING JUST TO SEE YOUR FACE AGAIN.
Anything...
NO. I WON'T. I...
NOT THAT.
SIGH
Incoming call: Mom
BRRRZZZZ

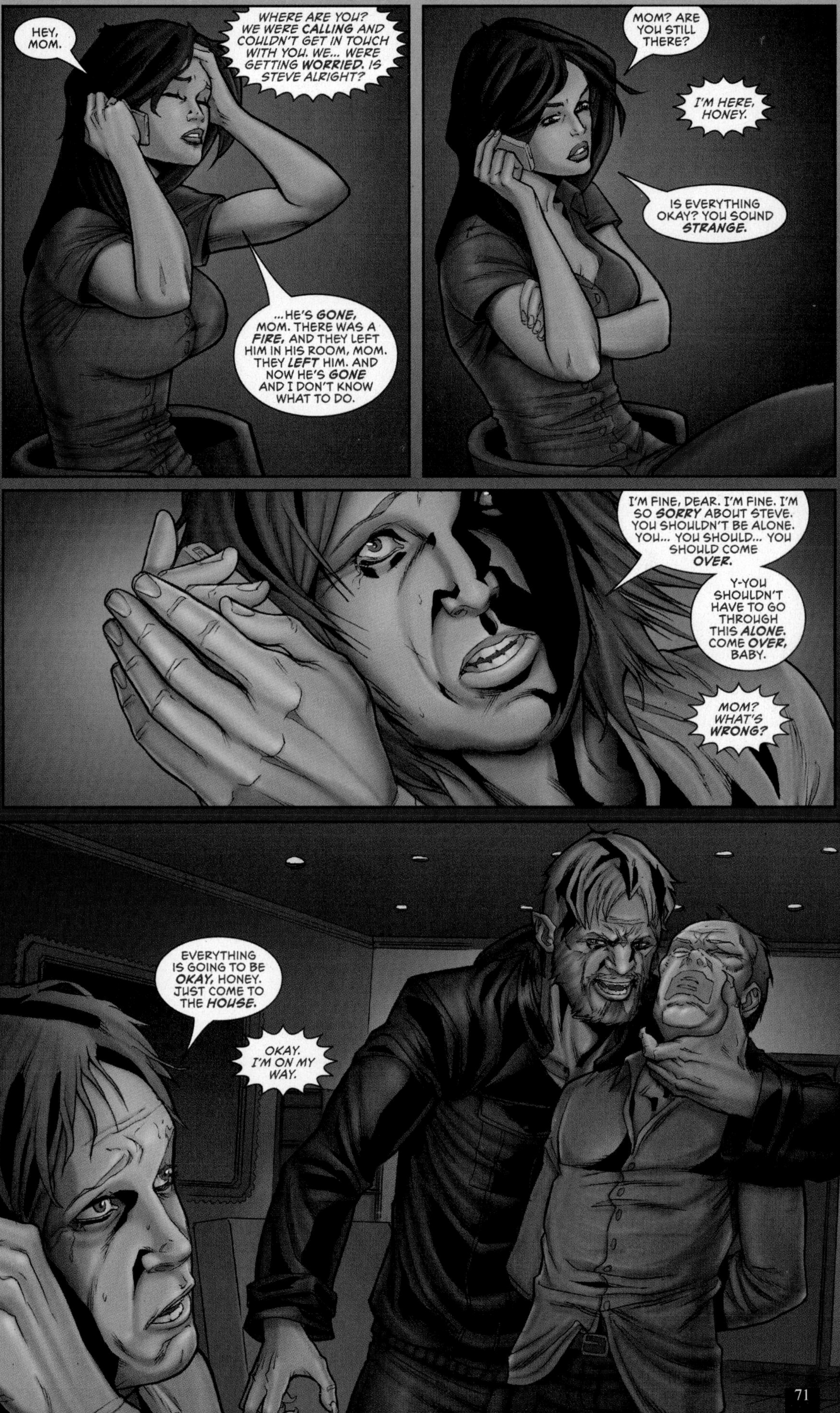
HEY, MOM.
WHERE ARE YOU? WE WERE CALLING AND COULDN'T GET IN TOUCH WITH YOU. WE... WERE GETTING WORRIED. IS STEVE ALRIGHT?
...HE'S GONE, MOM. THERE WAS A FIRE, AND THEY LEFT HIM IN HIS ROOM, MOM. THEY LEFT HIM. AND NOW HE'S GONE AND I DON'T KNOW WHAT TO DO.
MOM? ARE YOU STILL THERE?
I'M HERE, HONEY.
IS EVERYTHING OKAY? YOU SOUND STRANGE.
I'M FINE, DEAR. I'M FINE. I'M SO SORRY ABOUT STEVE. YOU SHOULDN'T BE ALONE. YOU... YOU SHOULD... YOU SHOULD COME OVER.
Y-YOU SHOULDN'T HAVE TO GO THROUGH THIS ALONE. COME OVER, BABY.
MOM? WHAT'S WRONG?
EVERYTHING IS GOING TO BE OKAY, HONEY. JUST COME TO THE HOUSE.
OKAY. I'M ON MY WAY.

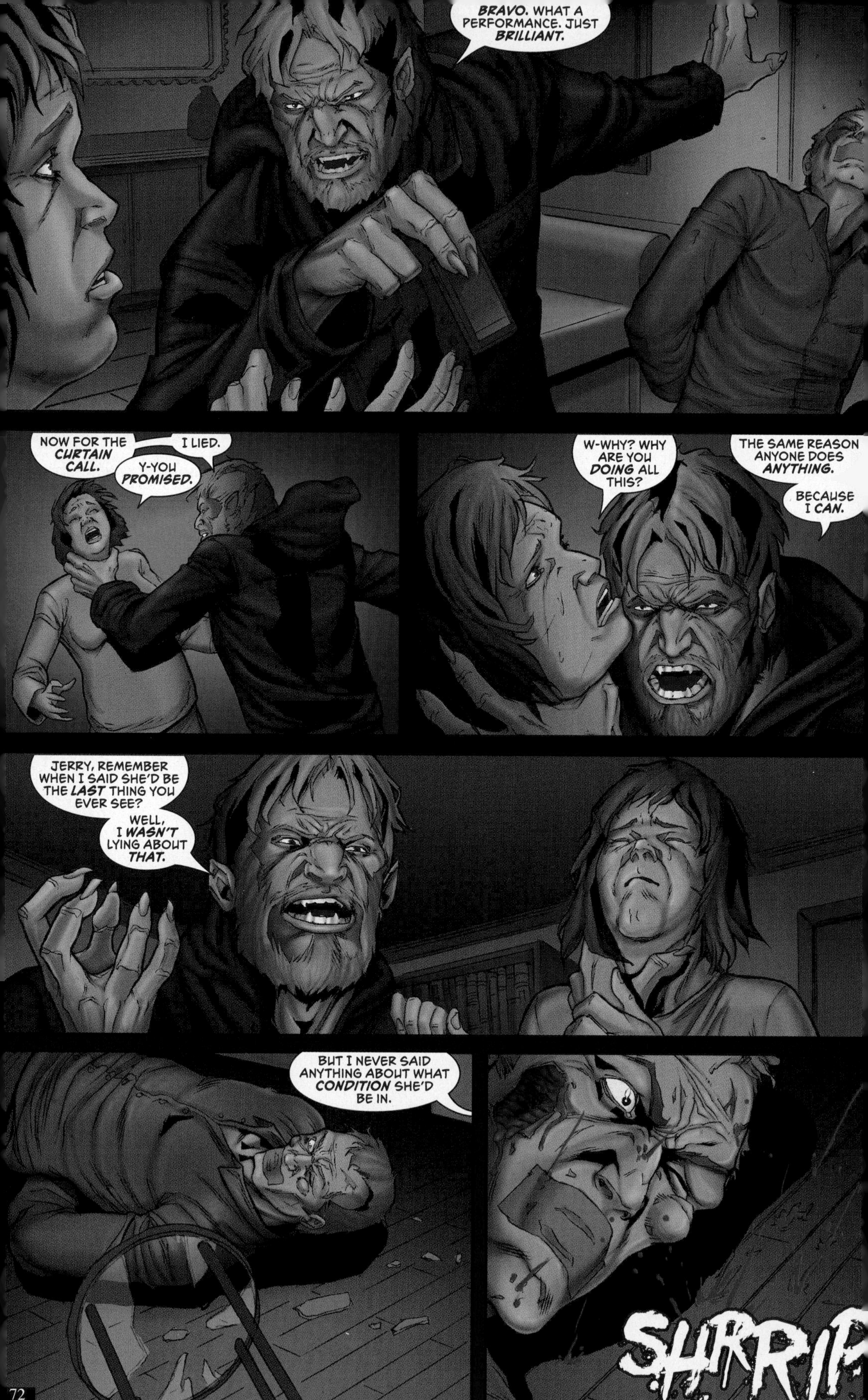
BRAVO. WHAT A PERFORMANCE. JUST BRILLIANT.
NOW FOR THE CURTAIN CALL.
Y-YOU PROMISED.
I LIED.
W-WHY? WHY ARE YOU DOING ALL THIS?
THE SAME REASON ANYONE DOES ANYTHING.
BECAUSE I CAN.
JERRY, REMEMBER WHEN I SAID SHE'D BE THE LAST THING YOU EVER SEE?
WELL, I WASN'T LYING ABOUT THAT.
BUT I NEVER SAID ANYTHING ABOUT WHAT CONDITION SHE'D BE IN.
SHRRIP

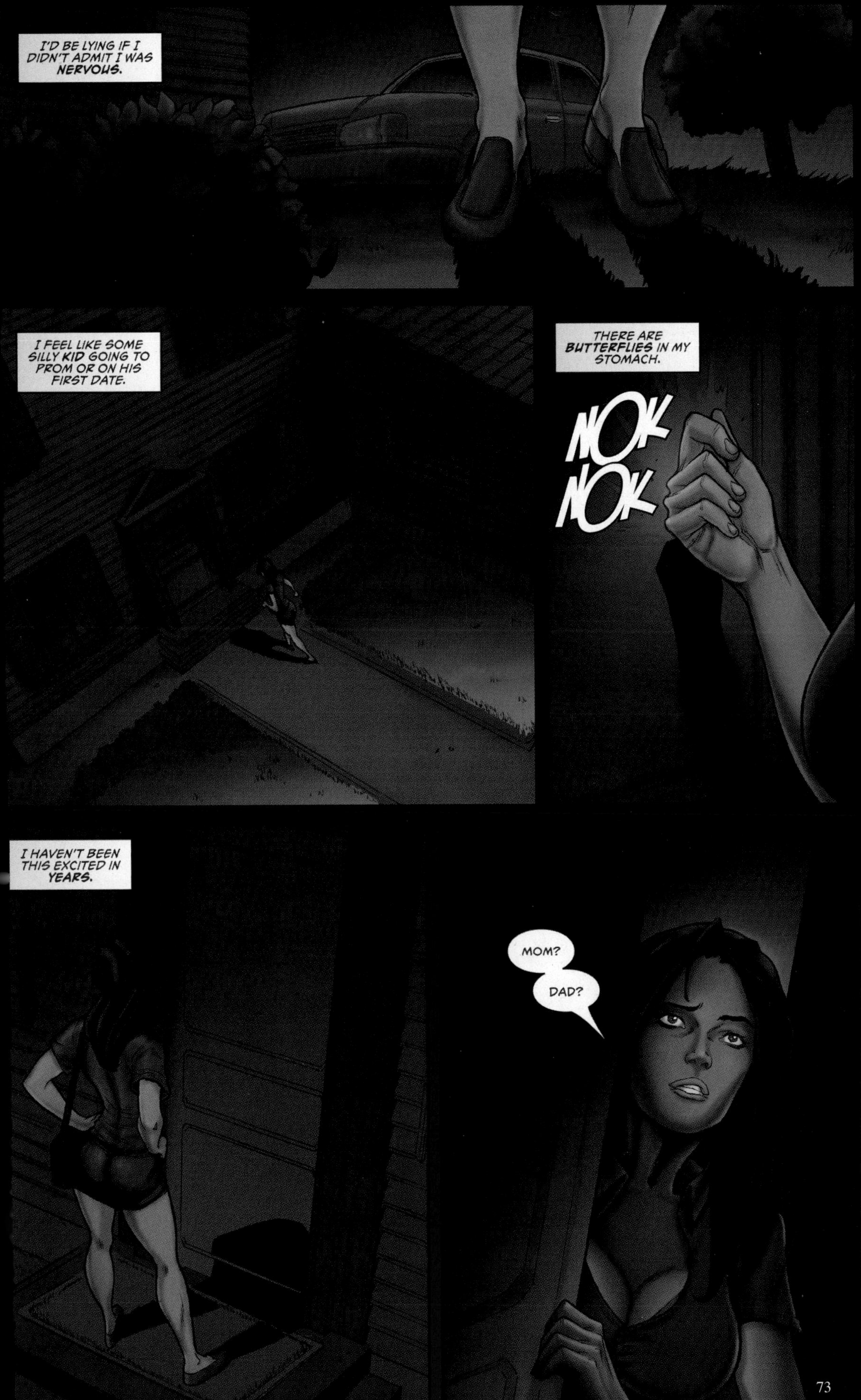

I'D BE LYING IF I DIDN'T ADMIT I WAS NERVOUS.
I FEEL LIKE SOME SILLY KID GOING TO PROM OR ON HIS FIRST DATE.
THERE ARE BUTTERFLIES IN MY STOMACH.
NOK NOK
I HAVEN'T BEEN THIS EXCITED IN YEARS.
MOM?
DAD?

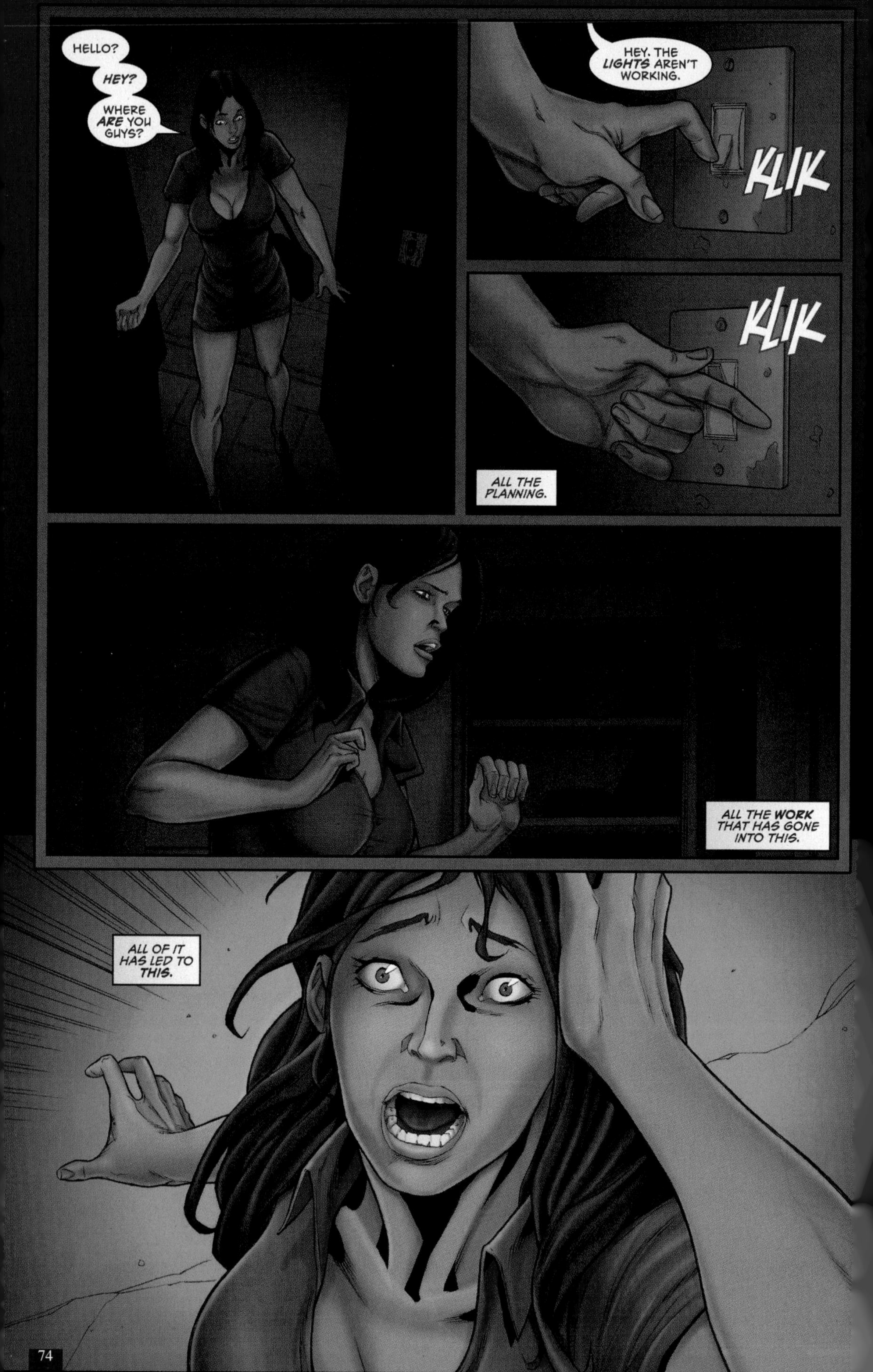
HELLO?
HEY?
WHERE ARE YOU GUYS?
HEY. THE LIGHTS AREN'T WORKING.
KLIK
KLIK
ALL THE PLANNING.
ALL THE WORK THAT HAS GONE INTO THIS.
ALL OF IT HAS LED TO THIS.

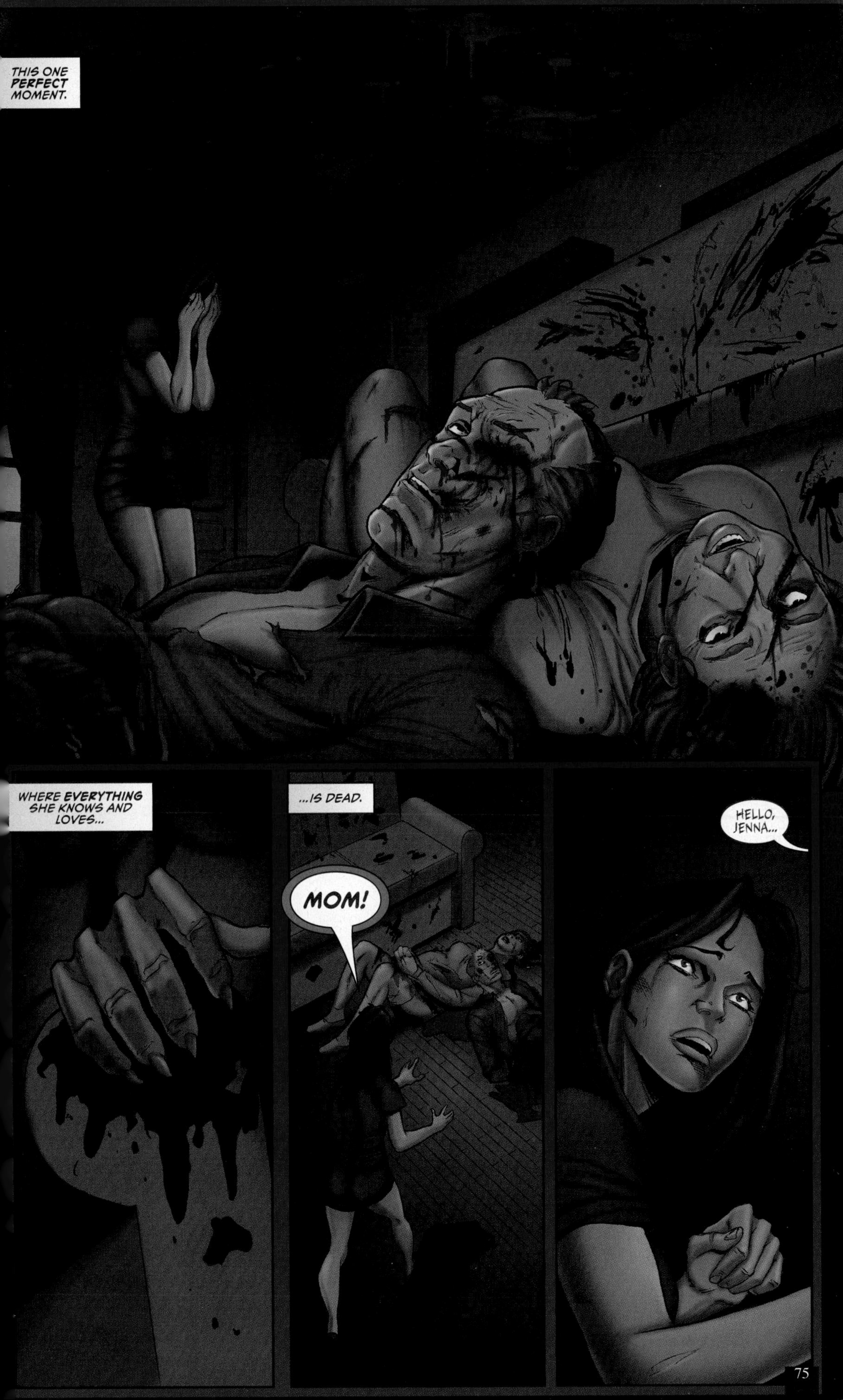
THIS ONE PERFECT MOMENT.
WHERE EVERYTHING SHE KNOWS AND LOVES...
...IS DEAD.
MOM!
HELLO, JENNA...

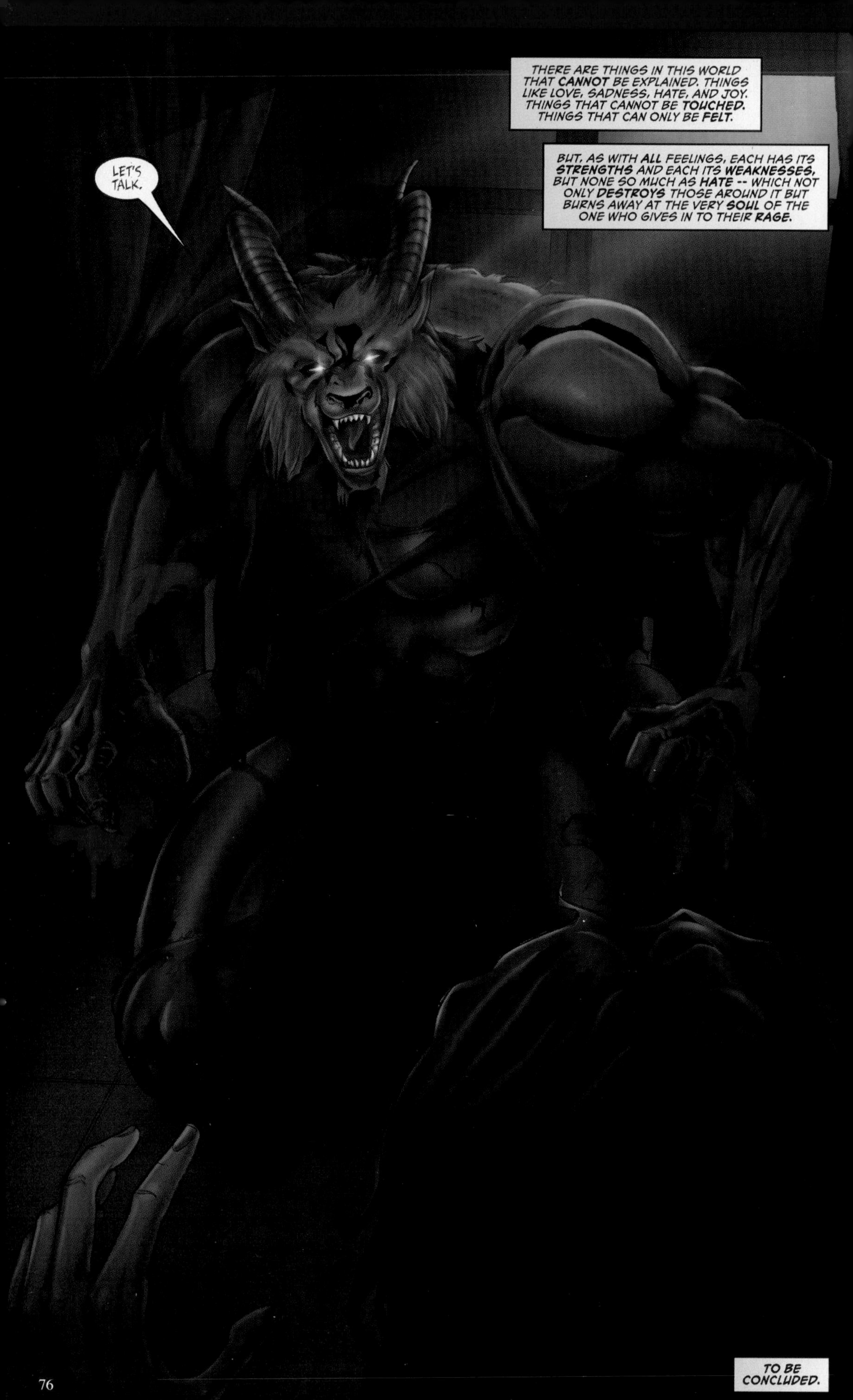
THERE ARE THINGS IN THIS WORLD THAT **CANNOT** BE EXPLAINED. THINGS LIKE LOVE, SADNESS, HATE, AND JOY. THINGS THAT CANNOT BE **TOUCHED**. THINGS THAT CAN ONLY BE **FELT**.
LET'S TALK.
BUT, AS WITH **ALL** FEELINGS, EACH HAS ITS **STRENGTHS** AND EACH ITS **WEAKNESSES**, BUT NONE SO MUCH AS **HATE** -- WHICH NOT ONLY **DESTROYS** THOSE AROUND IT BUT BURNS AWAY AT THE VERY **SOUL** OF THE ONE WHO GIVES IN TO THEIR **RAGE**.
TO BE CONCLUDED.

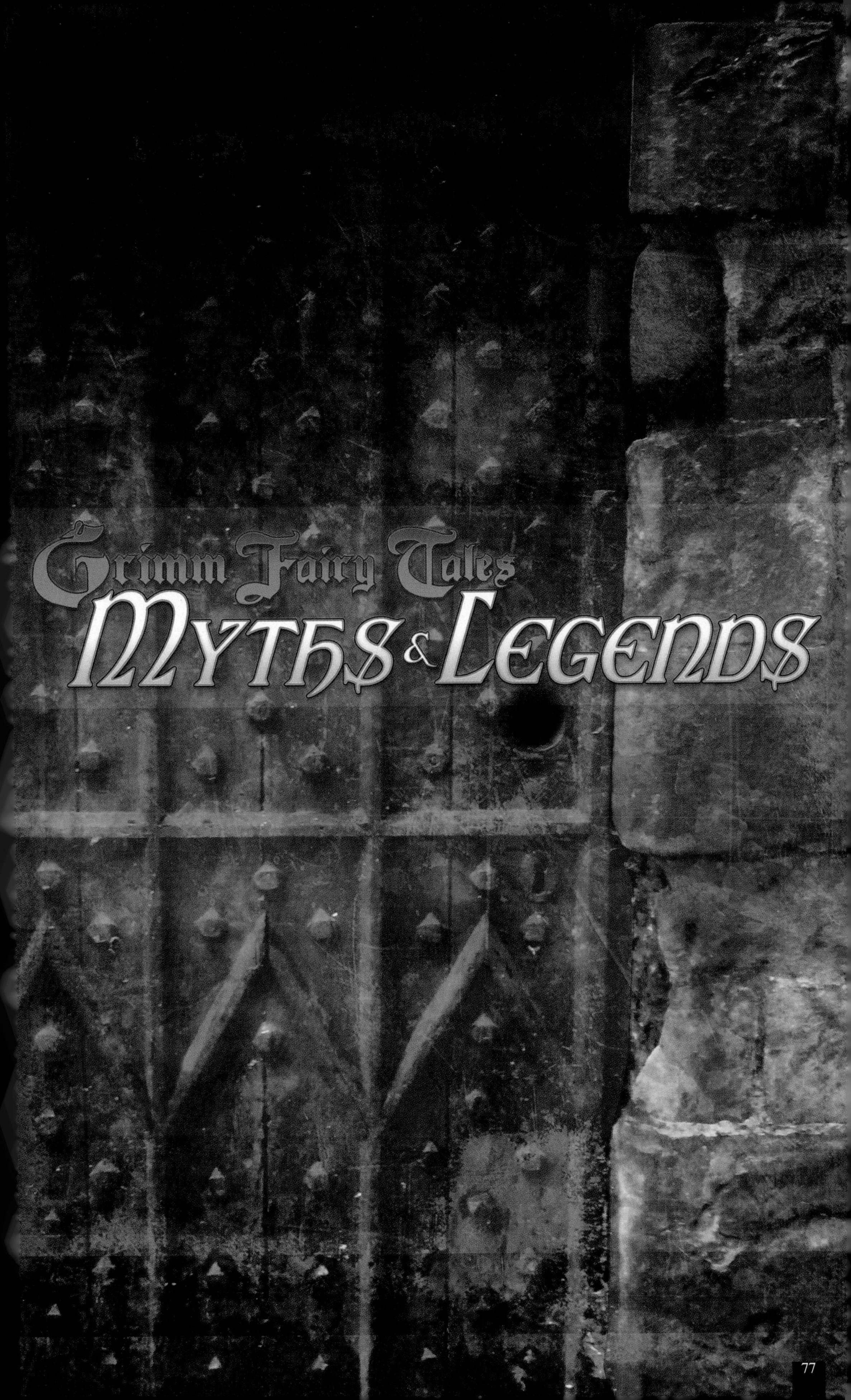

# Grimm Fairy Tales
# Myths & Legends

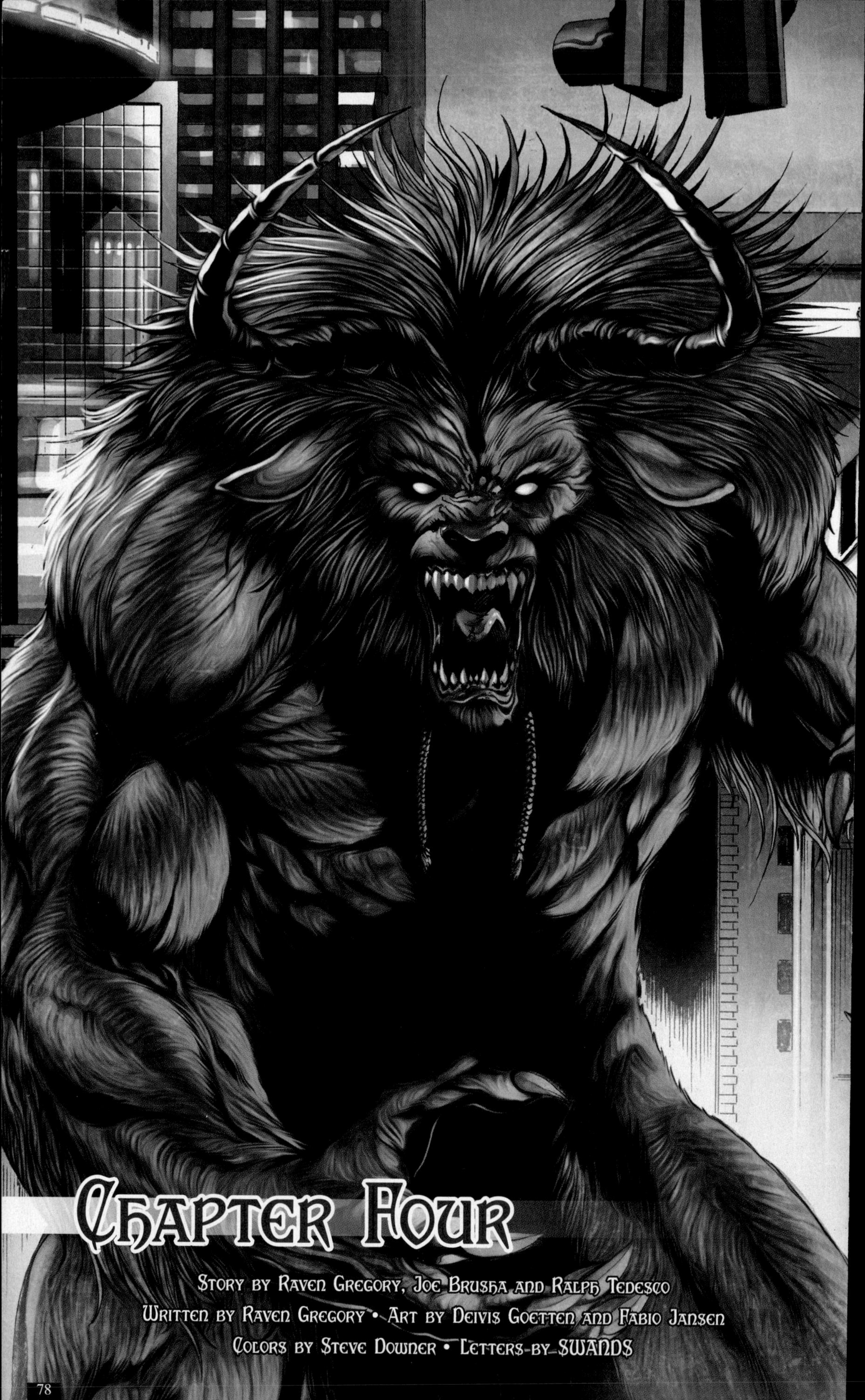
Chapter Four
Story by Raven Gregory, Joe Brusha and Ralph Tedesco
Written by Raven Gregory • Art by Deivis Goetten and Fabio Jansen
Colors by Steve Downer • Letters by SWANDS

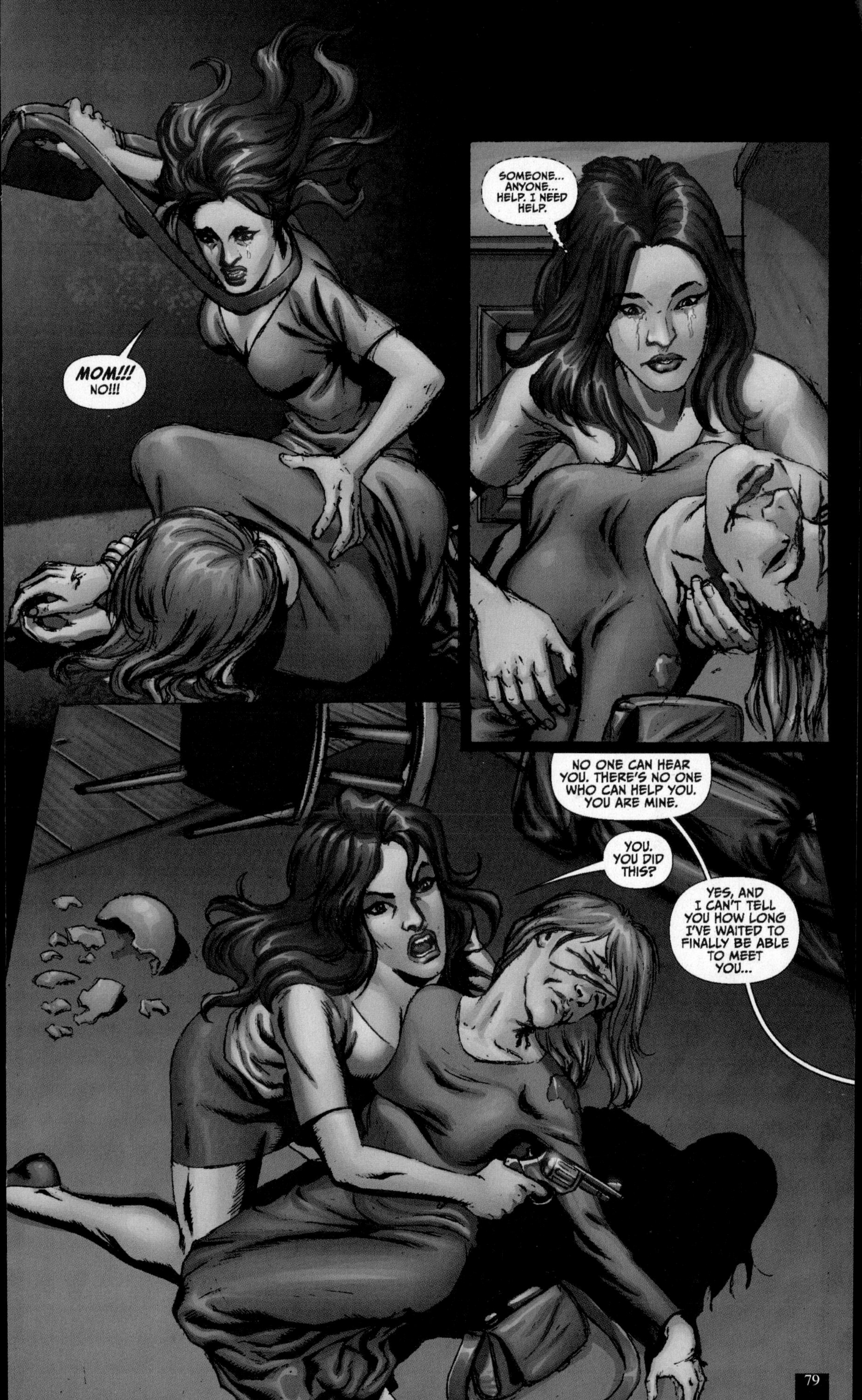
MOM!!! NO!!!
SOMEONE... ANYONE... HELP. I NEED HELP.
NO ONE CAN HEAR YOU. THERE'S NO ONE WHO CAN HELP YOU. YOU ARE MINE.
YOU. YOU DID THIS?
YES, AND I CAN'T TELL YOU HOW LONG I'VE WAITED TO FINALLY BE ABLE TO MEET YOU...

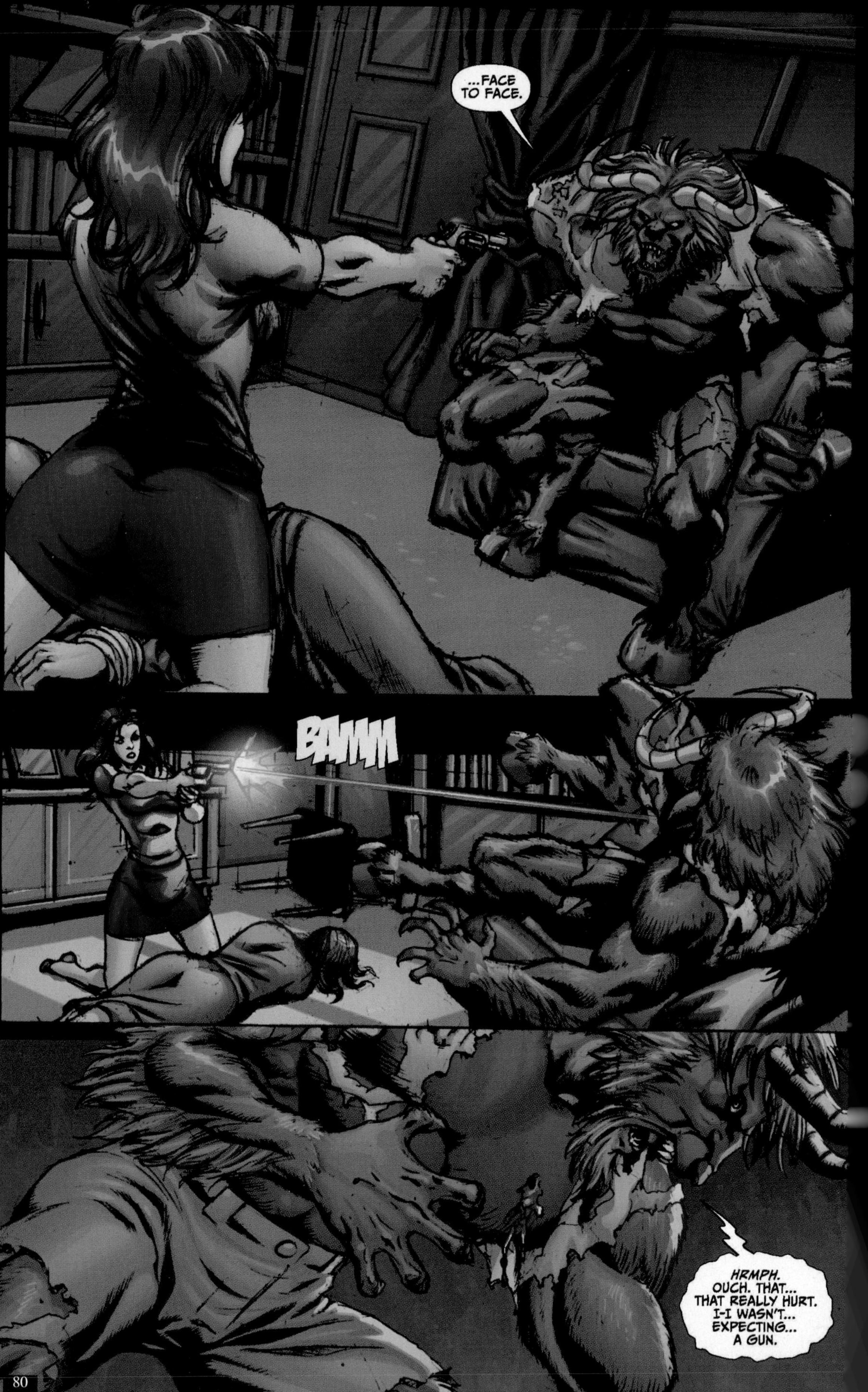
...FACE TO FACE.
BAMM
*HRMPH.* OUCH. THAT... THAT REALLY HURT. I-I WASN'T... EXPECTING... A GUN.

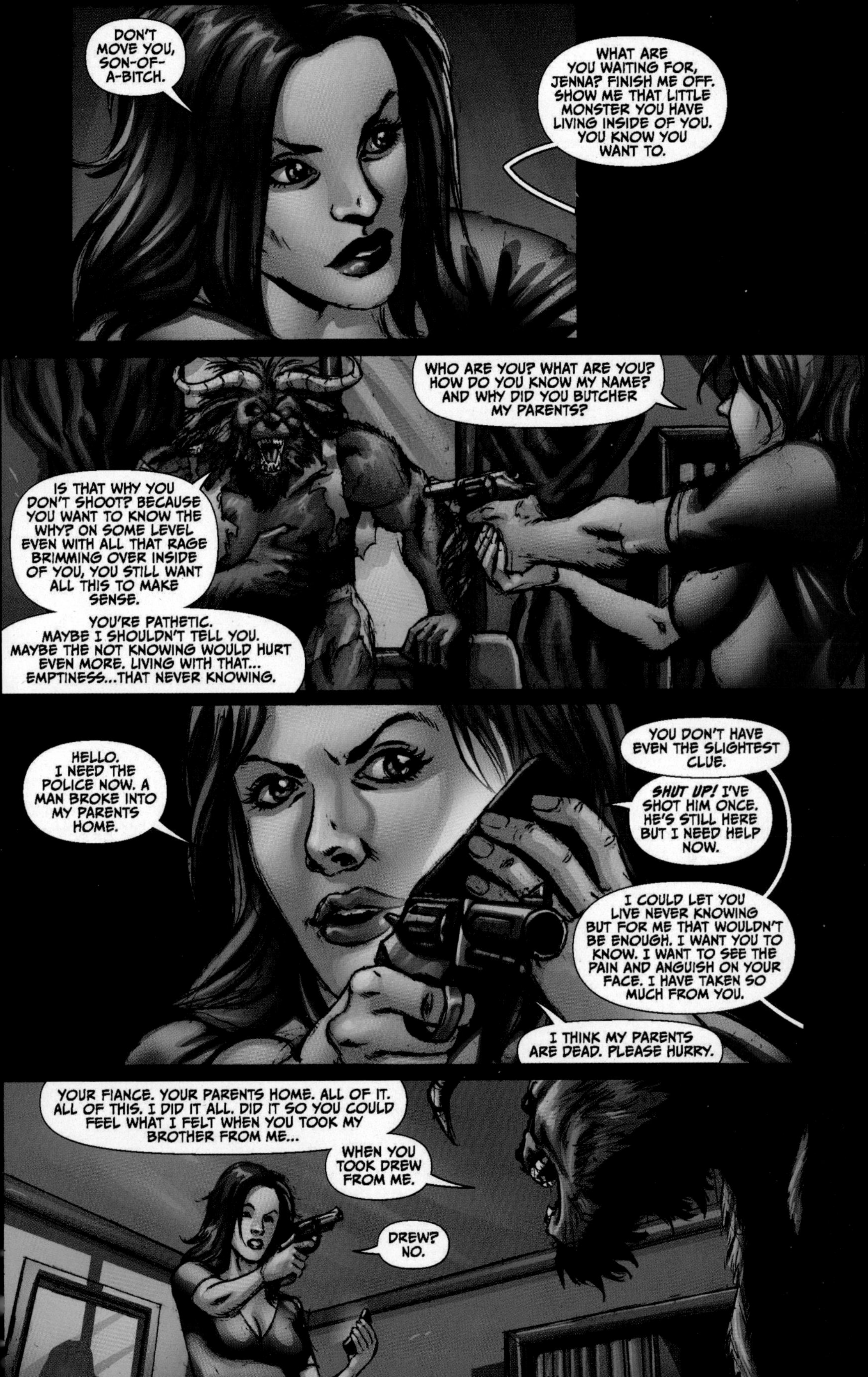
DON'T MOVE YOU, SON-OF-A-BITCH.
WHAT ARE YOU WAITING FOR, JENNA? FINISH ME OFF. SHOW ME THAT LITTLE MONSTER YOU HAVE LIVING INSIDE OF YOU. YOU KNOW YOU WANT TO.
WHO ARE YOU? WHAT ARE YOU? HOW DO YOU KNOW MY NAME? AND WHY DID YOU BUTCHER MY PARENTS?
IS THAT WHY YOU DON'T SHOOT? BECAUSE YOU WANT TO KNOW THE WHY? ON SOME LEVEL EVEN WITH ALL THAT RAGE BRIMMING OVER INSIDE OF YOU, YOU STILL WANT ALL THIS TO MAKE SENSE.
YOU'RE PATHETIC. MAYBE I SHOULDN'T TELL YOU. MAYBE THE NOT KNOWING WOULD HURT EVEN MORE. LIVING WITH THAT... EMPTINESS...THAT NEVER KNOWING.
HELLO. I NEED THE POLICE NOW. A MAN BROKE INTO MY PARENTS HOME.
YOU DON'T HAVE EVEN THE SLIGHTEST CLUE.
SHUT UP! I'VE SHOT HIM ONCE. HE'S STILL HERE BUT I NEED HELP NOW.
I COULD LET YOU LIVE NEVER KNOWING BUT FOR ME THAT WOULDN'T BE ENOUGH. I WANT YOU TO KNOW. I WANT TO SEE THE PAIN AND ANGUISH ON YOUR FACE. I HAVE TAKEN SO MUCH FROM YOU.
I THINK MY PARENTS ARE DEAD. PLEASE HURRY.
YOUR FIANCE. YOUR PARENTS HOME. ALL OF IT. ALL OF THIS. I DID IT ALL. DID IT SO YOU COULD FEEL WHAT I FELT WHEN YOU TOOK MY BROTHER FROM ME...
WHEN YOU TOOK DREW FROM ME.
DREW? NO.

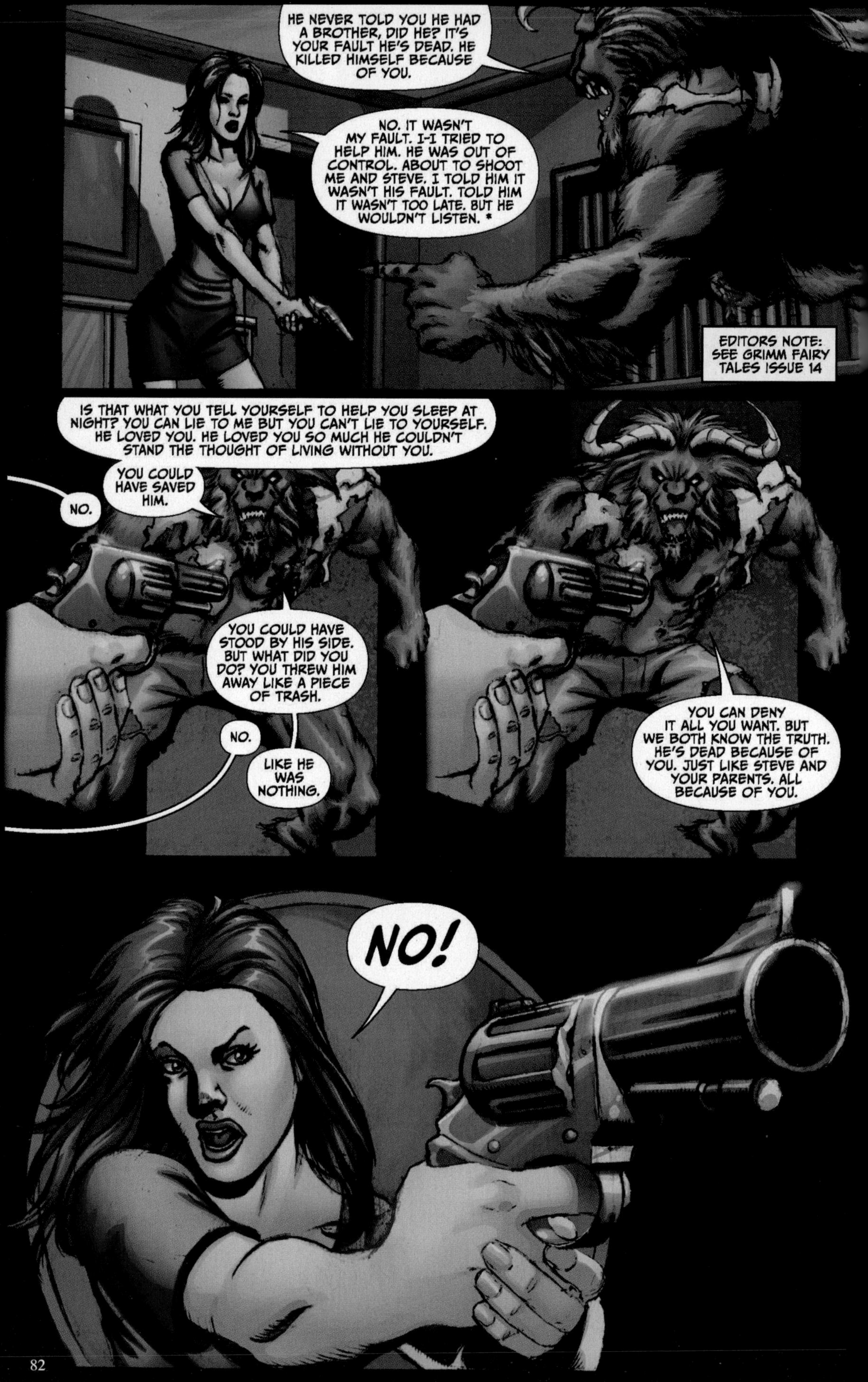
HE NEVER TOLD YOU HE HAD A BROTHER, DID HE? IT'S YOUR FAULT HE'S DEAD. HE KILLED HIMSELF BECAUSE OF YOU.
NO. IT WASN'T MY FAULT. I-I TRIED TO HELP HIM. HE WAS OUT OF CONTROL. ABOUT TO SHOOT ME AND STEVE. I TOLD HIM IT WASN'T HIS FAULT. TOLD HIM IT WASN'T TOO LATE. BUT HE WOULDN'T LISTEN. *
EDITORS NOTE: SEE GRIMM FAIRY TALES ISSUE 14
IS THAT WHAT YOU TELL YOURSELF TO HELP YOU SLEEP AT NIGHT? YOU CAN LIE TO ME BUT YOU CAN'T LIE TO YOURSELF. HE LOVED YOU. HE LOVED YOU SO MUCH HE COULDN'T STAND THE THOUGHT OF LIVING WITHOUT YOU.
YOU COULD HAVE SAVED HIM.
NO.
YOU COULD HAVE STOOD BY HIS SIDE. BUT WHAT DID YOU DO? YOU THREW HIM AWAY LIKE A PIECE OF TRASH.
NO.
LIKE HE WAS NOTHING.
YOU CAN DENY IT ALL YOU WANT. BUT WE BOTH KNOW THE TRUTH. HE'S DEAD BECAUSE OF YOU. JUST LIKE STEVE AND YOUR PARENTS. ALL BECAUSE OF YOU.
NO!

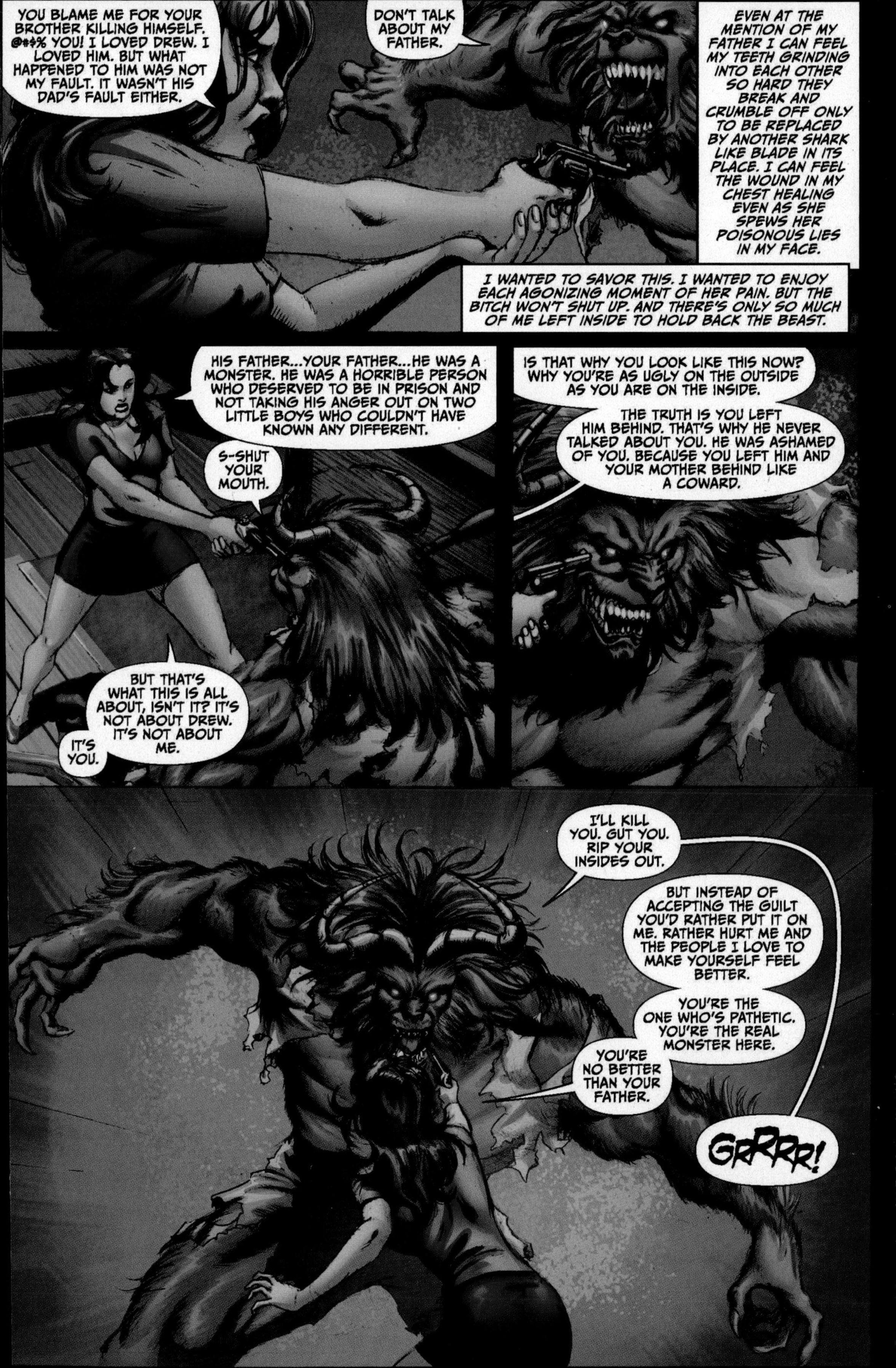
YOU BLAME ME FOR YOUR BROTHER KILLING HIMSELF. @#$% YOU! I LOVED DREW. I LOVED HIM. BUT WHAT HAPPENED TO HIM WAS NOT MY FAULT. IT WASN'T HIS DAD'S FAULT EITHER.
DON'T TALK ABOUT MY FATHER.
EVEN AT THE MENTION OF MY FATHER I CAN FEEL MY TEETH GRINDING INTO EACH OTHER SO HARD THEY BREAK AND CRUMBLE OFF ONLY TO BE REPLACED BY ANOTHER SHARK LIKE BLADE IN ITS PLACE. I CAN FEEL THE WOUND IN MY CHEST HEALING EVEN AS SHE SPEWS HER POISONOUS LIES IN MY FACE.
I WANTED TO SAVOR THIS. I WANTED TO ENJOY EACH AGONIZING MOMENT OF HER PAIN. BUT THE BITCH WON'T SHUT UP. AND THERE'S ONLY SO MUCH OF ME LEFT INSIDE TO HOLD BACK THE BEAST.
HIS FATHER...YOUR FATHER...HE WAS A MONSTER. HE WAS A HORRIBLE PERSON WHO DESERVED TO BE IN PRISON AND NOT TAKING HIS ANGER OUT ON TWO LITTLE BOYS WHO COULDN'T HAVE KNOWN ANY DIFFERENT.
S-SHUT YOUR MOUTH.
BUT THAT'S WHAT THIS IS ALL ABOUT, ISN'T IT? IT'S NOT ABOUT DREW. IT'S NOT ABOUT ME.
IT'S YOU.
IS THAT WHY YOU LOOK LIKE THIS NOW? WHY YOU'RE AS UGLY ON THE OUTSIDE AS YOU ARE ON THE INSIDE.
THE TRUTH IS YOU LEFT HIM BEHIND. THAT'S WHY HE NEVER TALKED ABOUT YOU. HE WAS ASHAMED OF YOU. BECAUSE YOU LEFT HIM AND YOUR MOTHER BEHIND LIKE A COWARD.
I'LL KILL YOU. GUT YOU. RIP YOUR INSIDES OUT.
BUT INSTEAD OF ACCEPTING THE GUILT YOU'D RATHER PUT IT ON ME. RATHER HURT ME AND THE PEOPLE I LOVE TO MAKE YOURSELF FEEL BETTER.
YOU'RE THE ONE WHO'S PATHETIC. YOU'RE THE REAL MONSTER HERE.
YOU'RE NO BETTER THAN YOUR FATHER.
GRRRR!

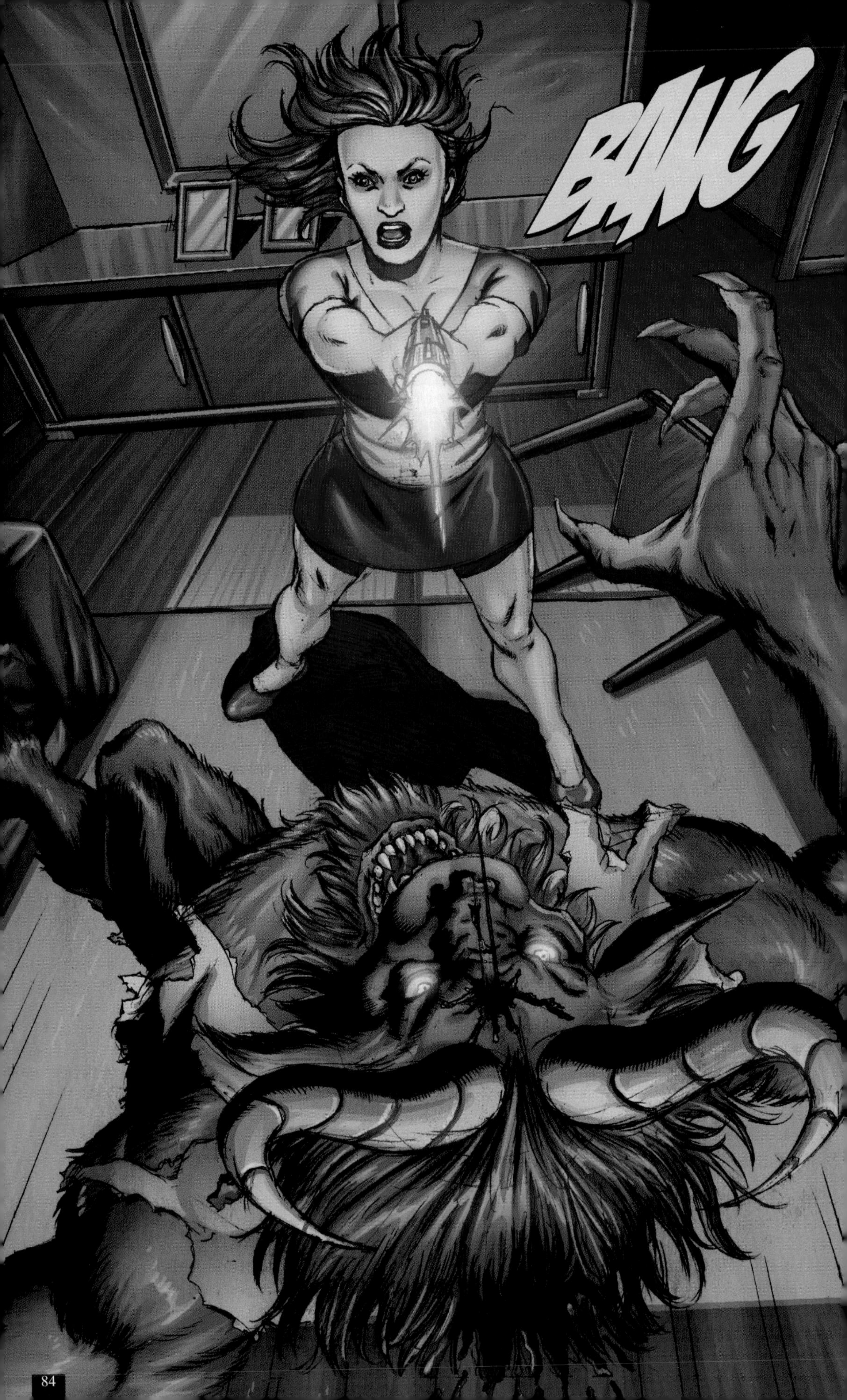
BANG

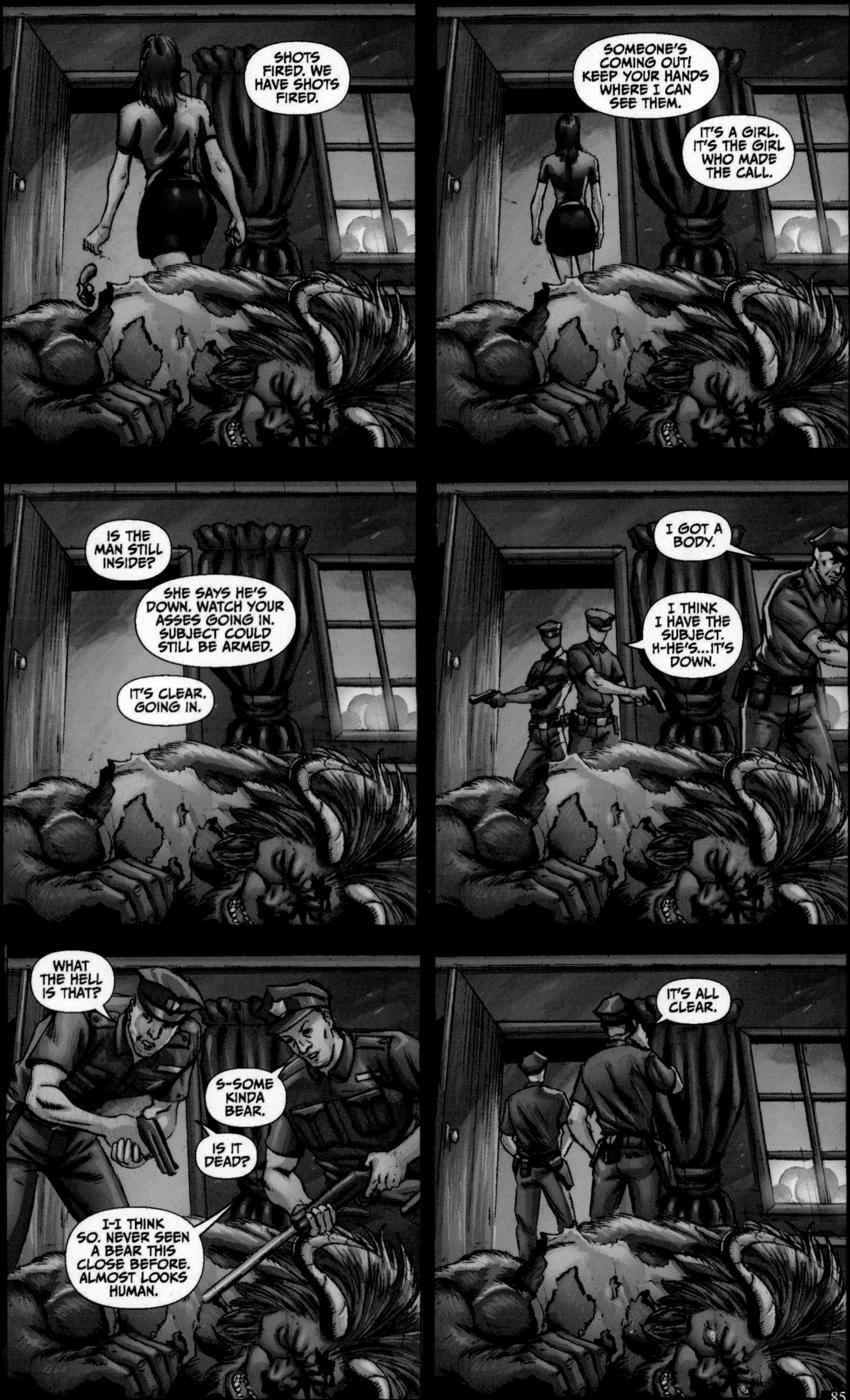
SHOTS FIRED. WE HAVE SHOTS FIRED.
SOMEONE'S COMING OUT! KEEP YOUR HANDS WHERE I CAN SEE THEM.
IT'S A GIRL. IT'S THE GIRL WHO MADE THE CALL.
IS THE MAN STILL INSIDE?
SHE SAYS HE'S DOWN. WATCH YOUR ASSES GOING IN. SUBJECT COULD STILL BE ARMED.
IT'S CLEAR. GOING IN.
I GOT A BODY.
I THINK I HAVE THE SUBJECT. H-HE'S...IT'S DOWN.
WHAT THE HELL IS THAT?
S-SOME KINDA BEAR.
IS IT DEAD?
I-I THINK SO. NEVER SEEN A BEAR THIS CLOSE BEFORE. ALMOST LOOKS HUMAN.
IT'S ALL CLEAR.

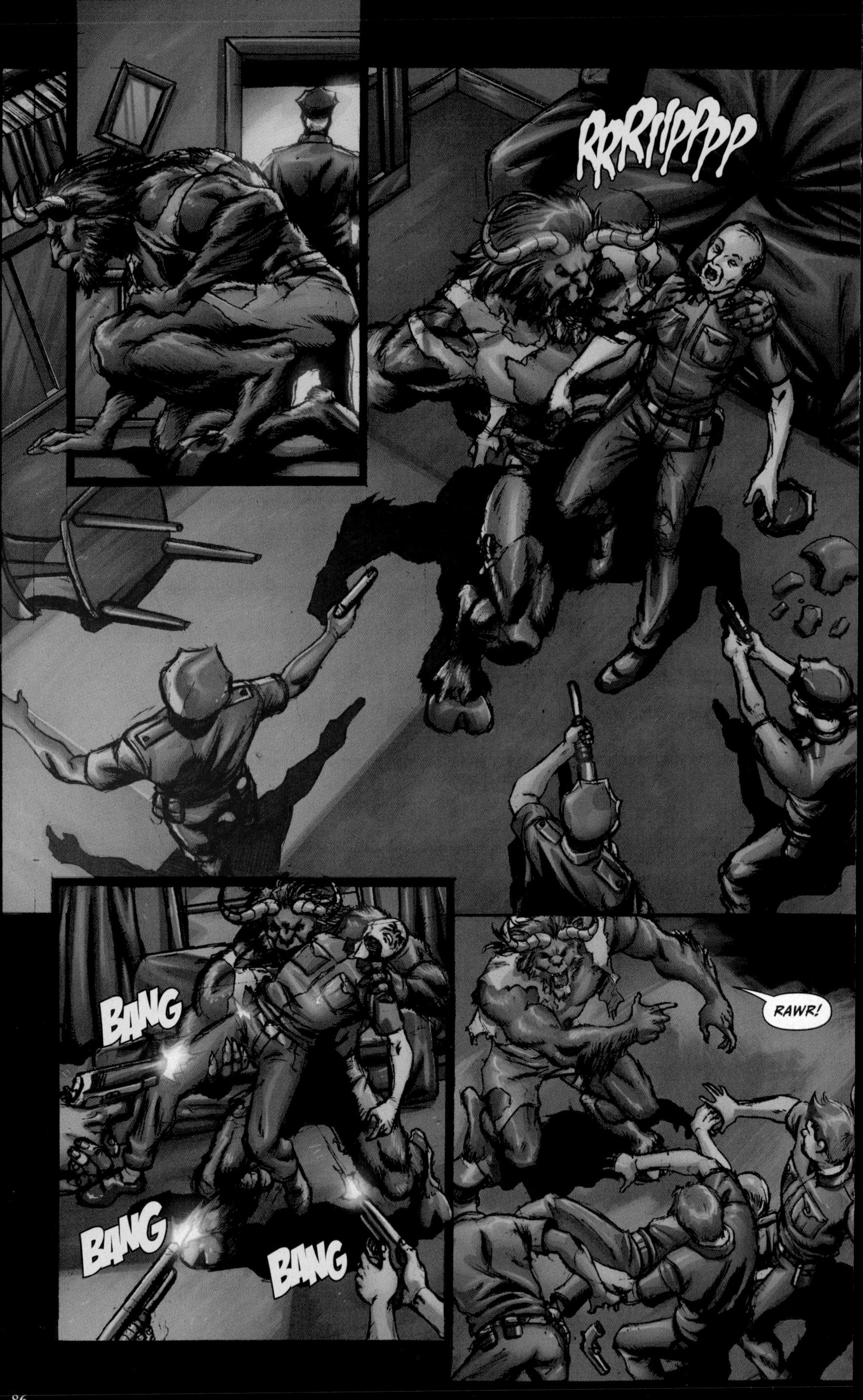
RRRIIIPPPP
BANG
BANG
BANG
RAWR!

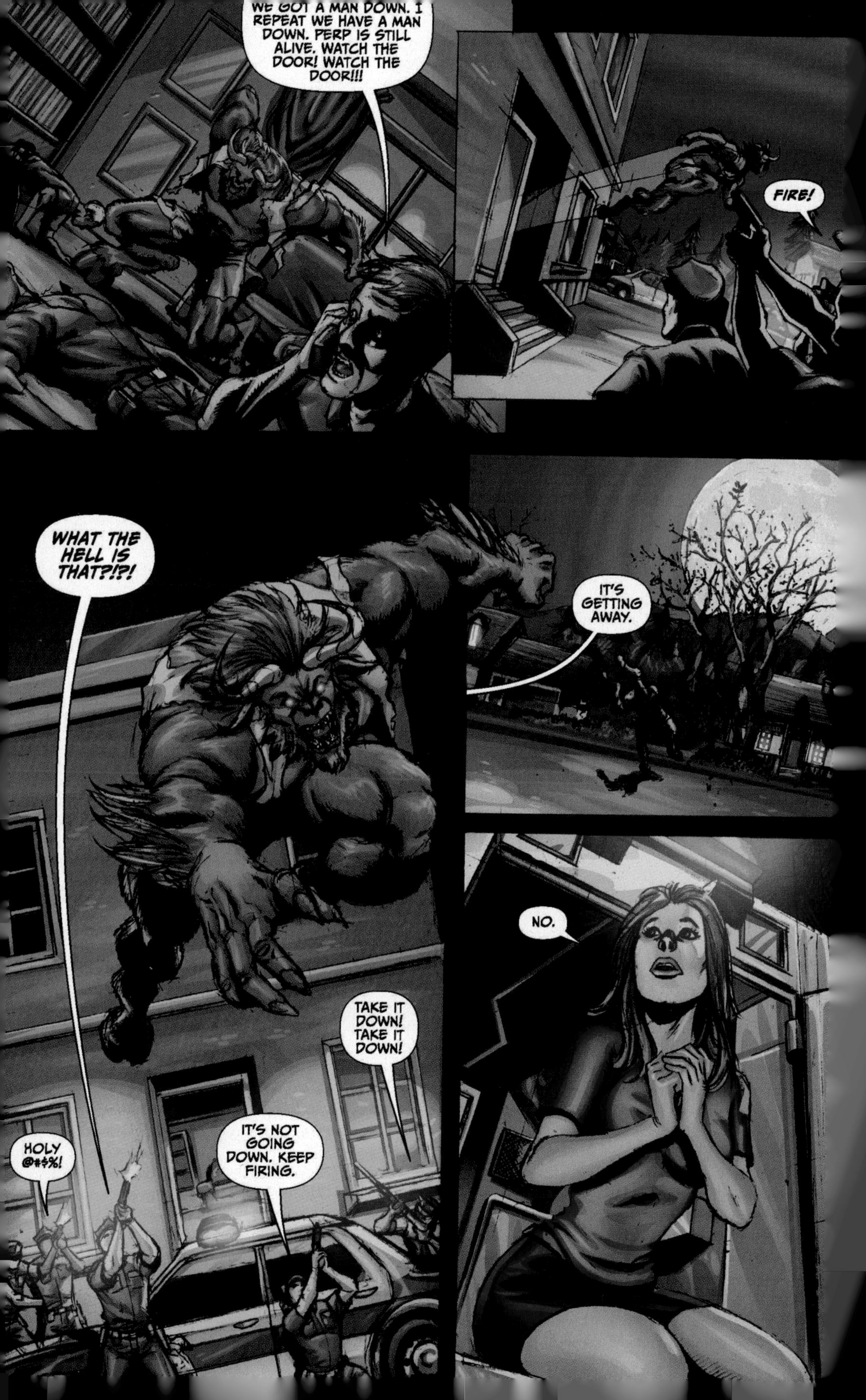
WE GOT A MAN DOWN. I REPEAT WE HAVE A MAN DOWN. PERP IS STILL ALIVE. WATCH THE DOOR! WATCH THE DOOR!!!
FIRE!
WHAT THE HELL IS THAT?!?!
TAKE IT DOWN! TAKE IT DOWN!
IT'S NOT GOING DOWN. KEEP FIRING.
HOLY @#$%!
IT'S GETTING AWAY.
NO.

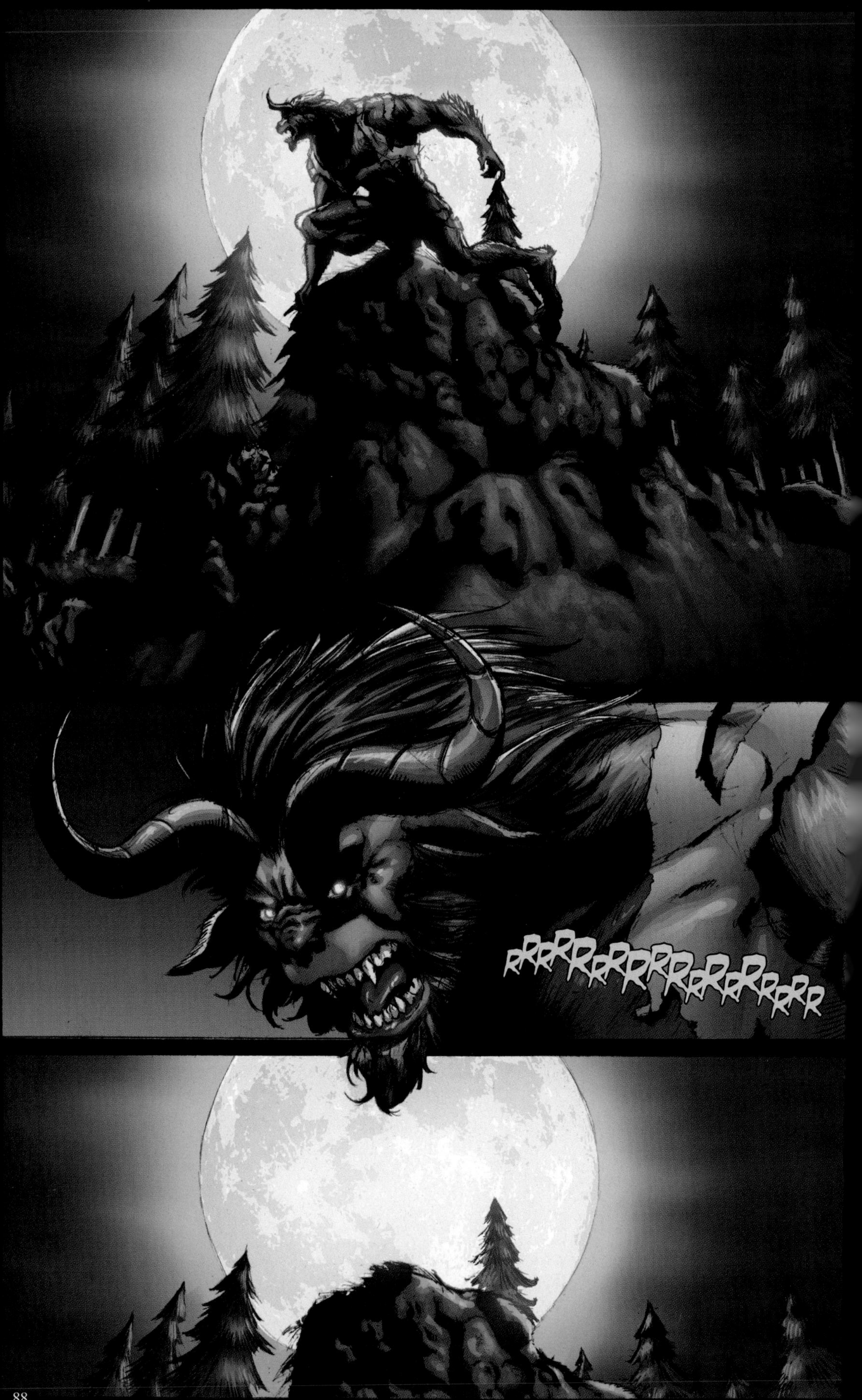
RRRRRRRRRRRRRRRRRRRRR

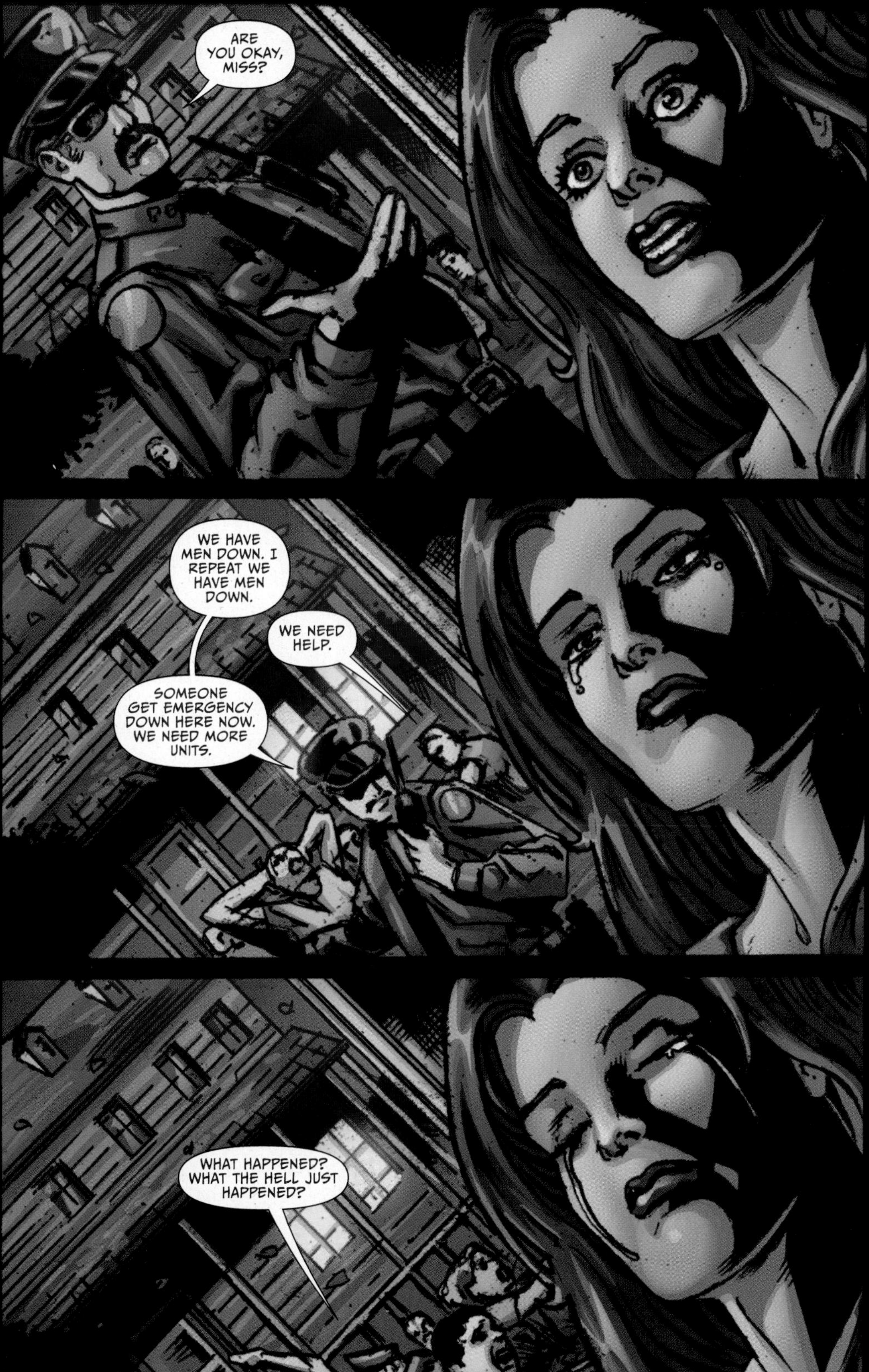
ARE YOU OKAY, MISS?
WE HAVE MEN DOWN. I REPEAT WE HAVE MEN DOWN.
WE NEED HELP.
SOMEONE GET EMERGENCY DOWN HERE NOW. WE NEED MORE UNITS.
WHAT HAPPENED? WHAT THE HELL JUST HAPPENED?

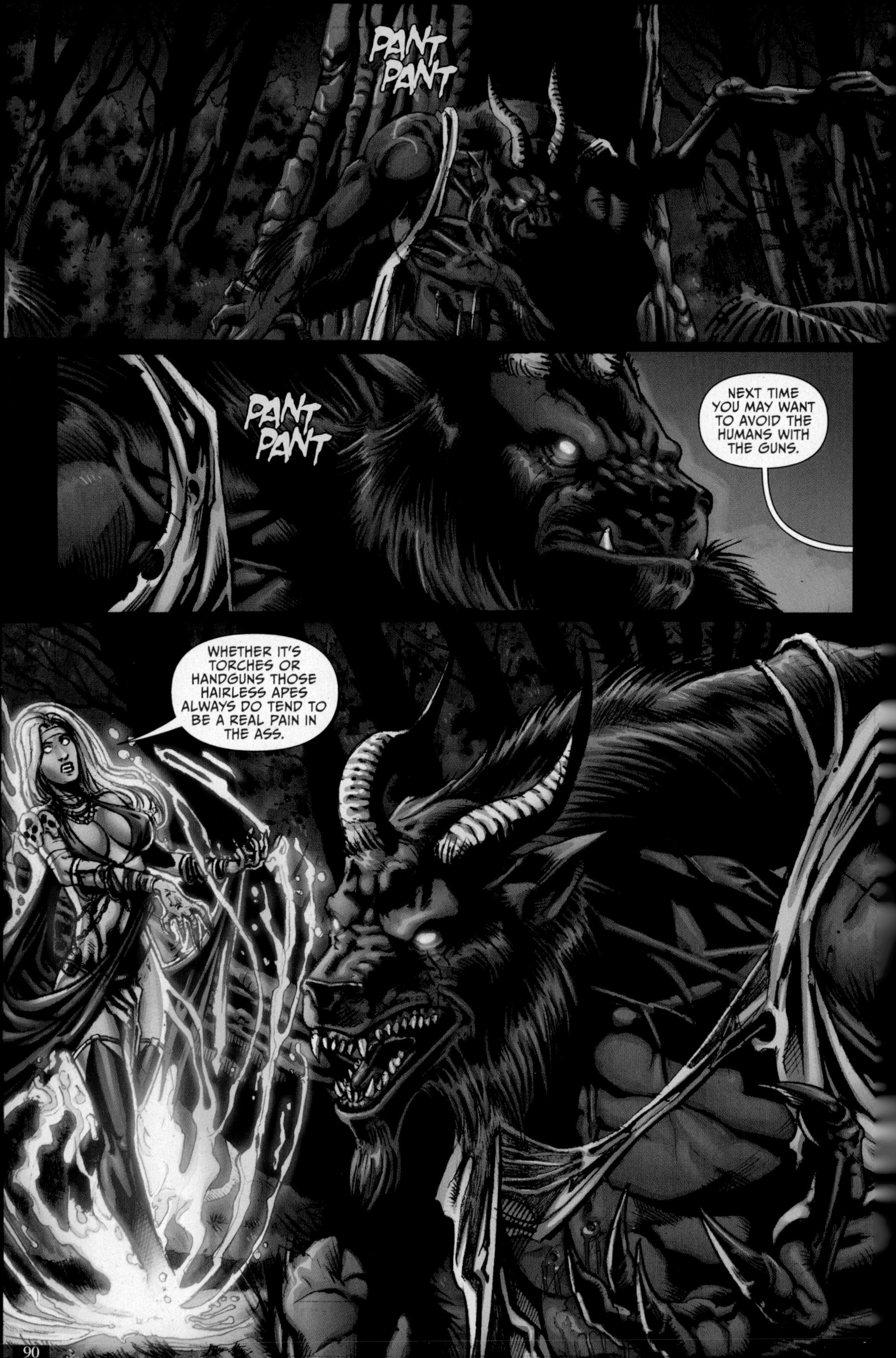
PANT PANT
PANT PANT
NEXT TIME YOU MAY WANT TO AVOID THE HUMANS WITH THE GUNS.
WHETHER IT'S TORCHES OR HANDGUNS THOSE HAIRLESS APES ALWAYS DO TEND TO BE A REAL PAIN IN THE ASS.

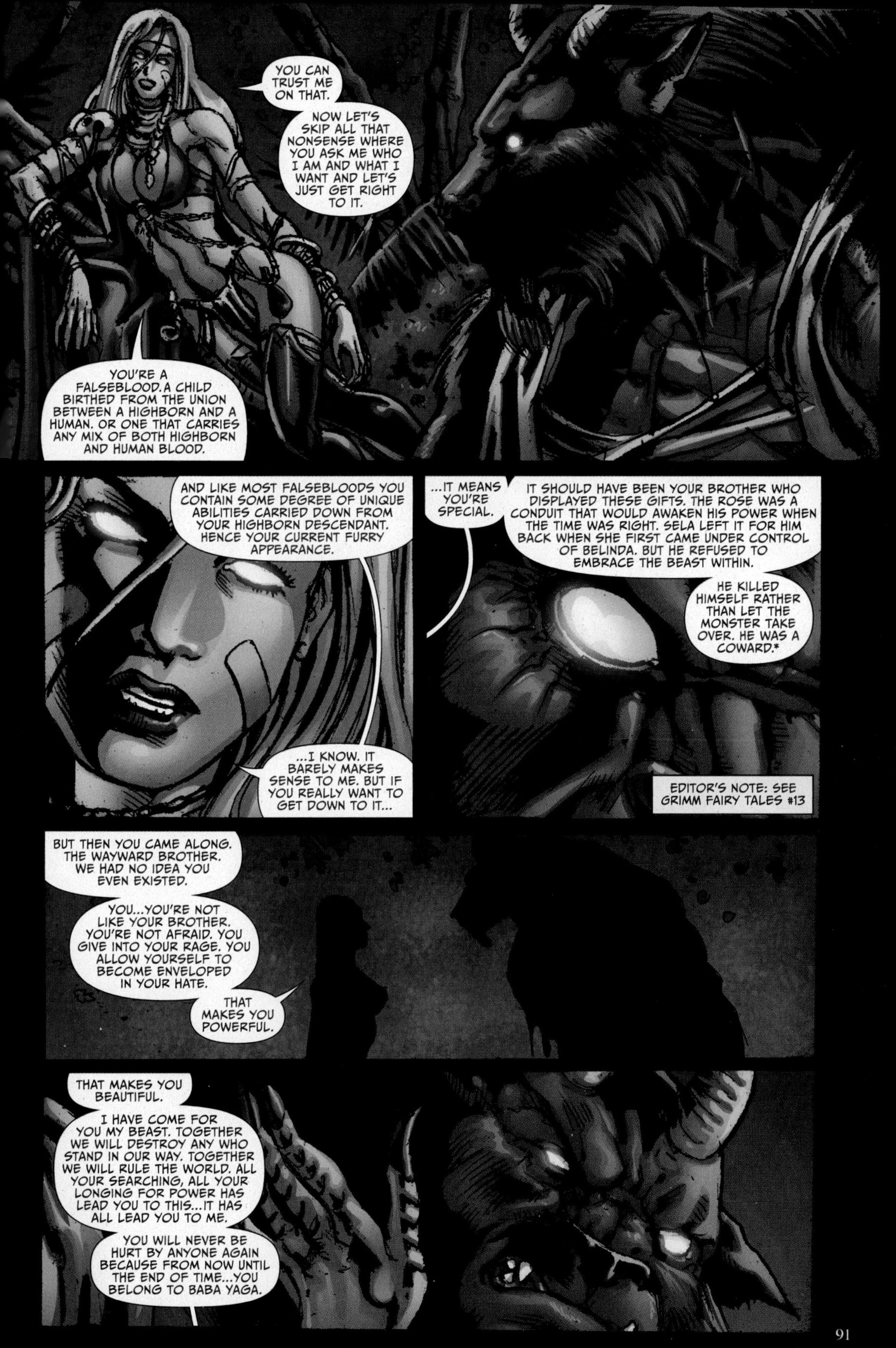
YOU CAN TRUST ME ON THAT.
NOW LET'S SKIP ALL THAT NONSENSE WHERE YOU ASK ME WHO I AM AND WHAT I WANT AND LET'S JUST GET RIGHT TO IT.
YOU'RE A FALSEBLOOD. A CHILD BIRTHED FROM THE UNION BETWEEN A HIGHBORN AND A HUMAN. OR ONE THAT CARRIES ANY MIX OF BOTH HIGHBORN AND HUMAN BLOOD.
AND LIKE MOST FALSEBLOODS YOU CONTAIN SOME DEGREE OF UNIQUE ABILITIES CARRIED DOWN FROM YOUR HIGHBORN DESCENDANT. HENCE YOUR CURRENT FURRY APPEARANCE.
...I KNOW. IT BARELY MAKES SENSE TO ME. BUT IF YOU REALLY WANT TO GET DOWN TO IT...
...IT MEANS YOU'RE SPECIAL.
IT SHOULD HAVE BEEN YOUR BROTHER WHO DISPLAYED THESE GIFTS. THE ROSE WAS A CONDUIT THAT WOULD AWAKEN HIS POWER WHEN THE TIME WAS RIGHT. SELA LEFT IT FOR HIM BACK WHEN SHE FIRST CAME UNDER CONTROL OF BELINDA. BUT HE REFUSED TO EMBRACE THE BEAST WITHIN.
HE KILLED HIMSELF RATHER THAN LET THE MONSTER TAKE OVER. HE WAS A COWARD.*
EDITOR'S NOTE: SEE GRIMM FAIRY TALES #13
BUT THEN YOU CAME ALONG. THE WAYWARD BROTHER. WE HAD NO IDEA YOU EVEN EXISTED.
YOU...YOU'RE NOT LIKE YOUR BROTHER. YOU'RE NOT AFRAID. YOU GIVE INTO YOUR RAGE. YOU ALLOW YOURSELF TO BECOME ENVELOPED IN YOUR HATE.
THAT MAKES YOU POWERFUL.
THAT MAKES YOU BEAUTIFUL.
I HAVE COME FOR YOU MY BEAST. TOGETHER WE WILL DESTROY ANY WHO STAND IN OUR WAY. TOGETHER WE WILL RULE THE WORLD. ALL YOUR SEARCHING, ALL YOUR LONGING FOR POWER HAS LEAD YOU TO THIS...IT HAS ALL LEAD YOU TO ME.
YOU WILL NEVER BE HURT BY ANYONE AGAIN BECAUSE FROM NOW UNTIL THE END OF TIME...YOU BELONG TO BABA YAGA.

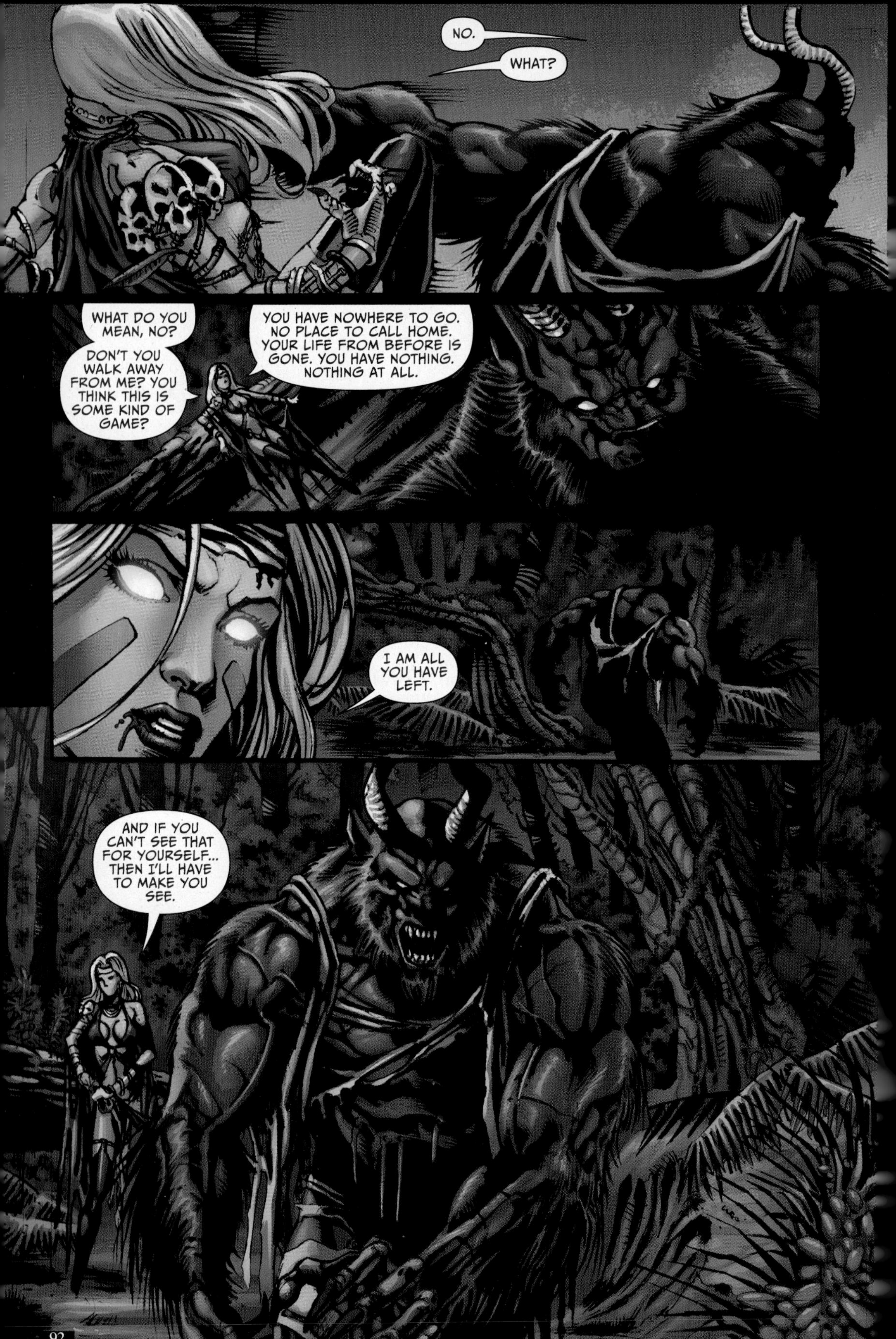
NO.
WHAT?
WHAT DO YOU MEAN, NO?
DON'T YOU WALK AWAY FROM ME? YOU THINK THIS IS SOME KIND OF GAME?
YOU HAVE NOWHERE TO GO. NO PLACE TO CALL HOME. YOUR LIFE FROM BEFORE IS GONE. YOU HAVE NOTHING. NOTHING AT ALL.
I AM ALL YOU HAVE LEFT.
AND IF YOU CAN'T SEE THAT FOR YOURSELF... THEN I'LL HAVE TO MAKE YOU SEE.

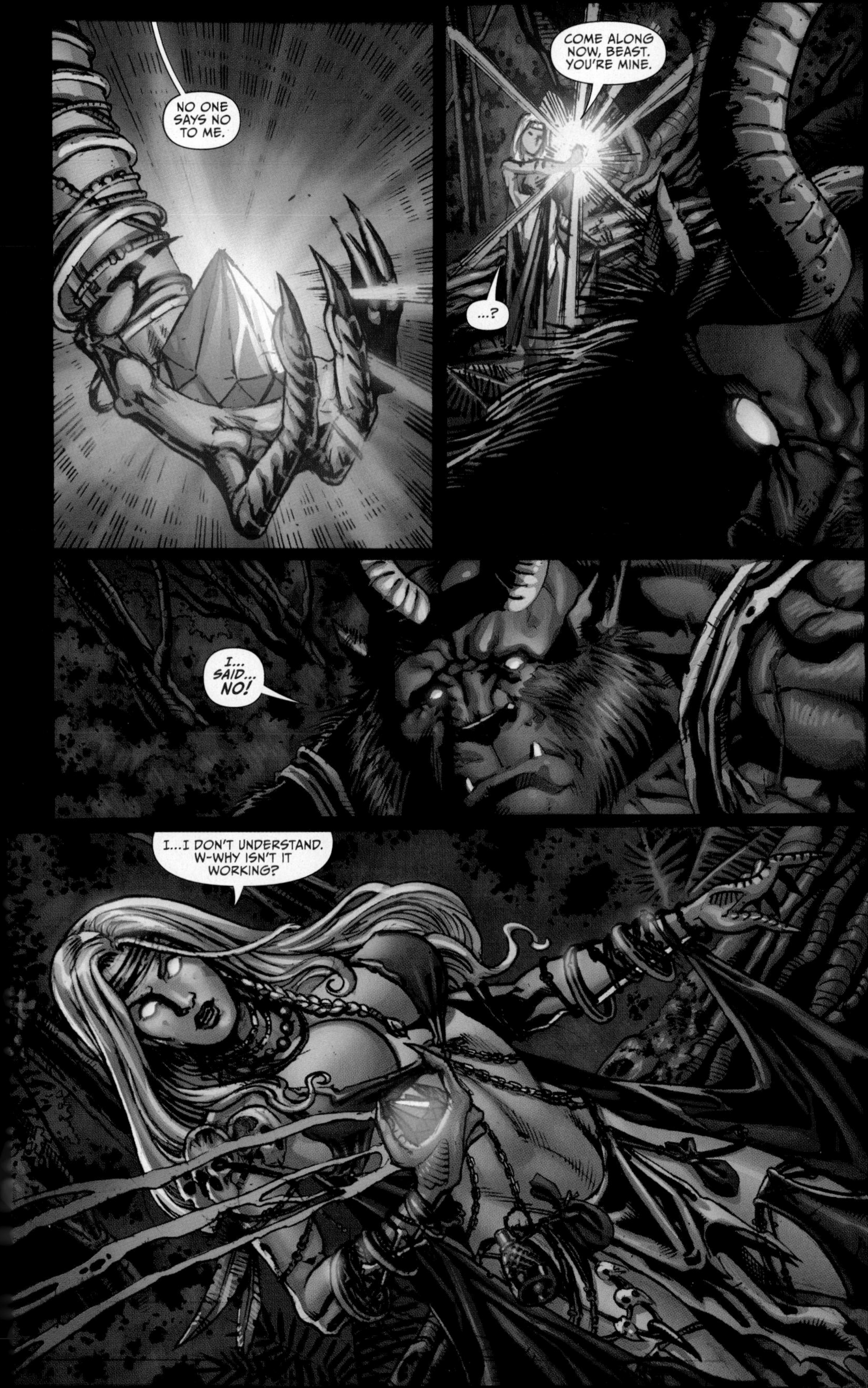
NO ONE SAYS NO TO ME.
COME ALONG NOW, BEAST. YOU'RE MINE.
...?
I... SAID... NO!
I...I DON'T UNDERSTAND. W-WHY ISN'T IT WORKING?

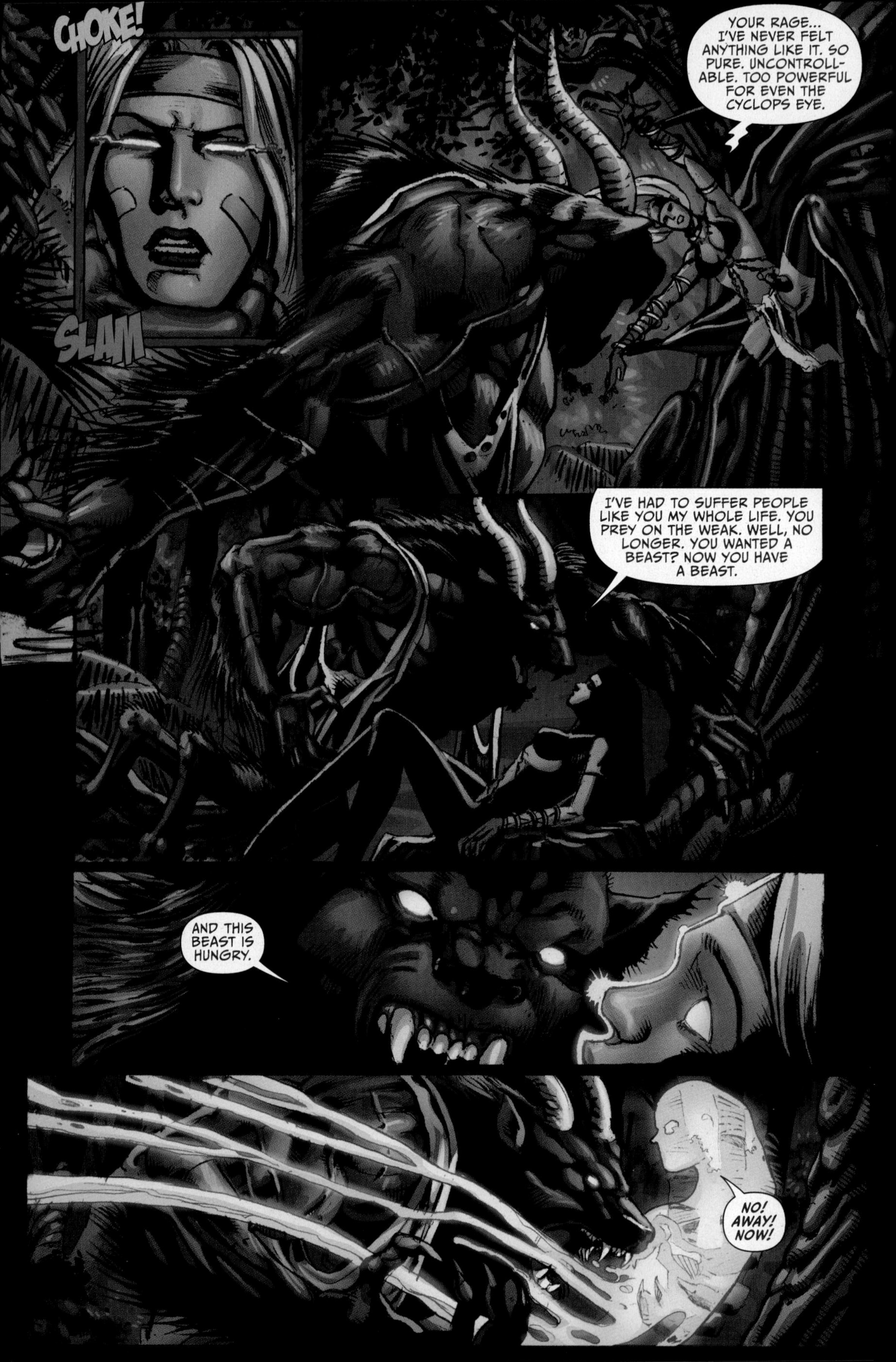
CHOKE!
SLAM
YOUR RAGE... I'VE NEVER FELT ANYTHING LIKE IT. SO PURE. UNCONTROLL-ABLE. TOO POWERFUL FOR EVEN THE CYCLOPS EYE.
I'VE HAD TO SUFFER PEOPLE LIKE YOU MY WHOLE LIFE. YOU PREY ON THE WEAK. WELL, NO LONGER. YOU WANTED A BEAST? NOW YOU HAVE A BEAST.
AND THIS BEAST IS HUNGRY.
NO! AWAY! NOW!

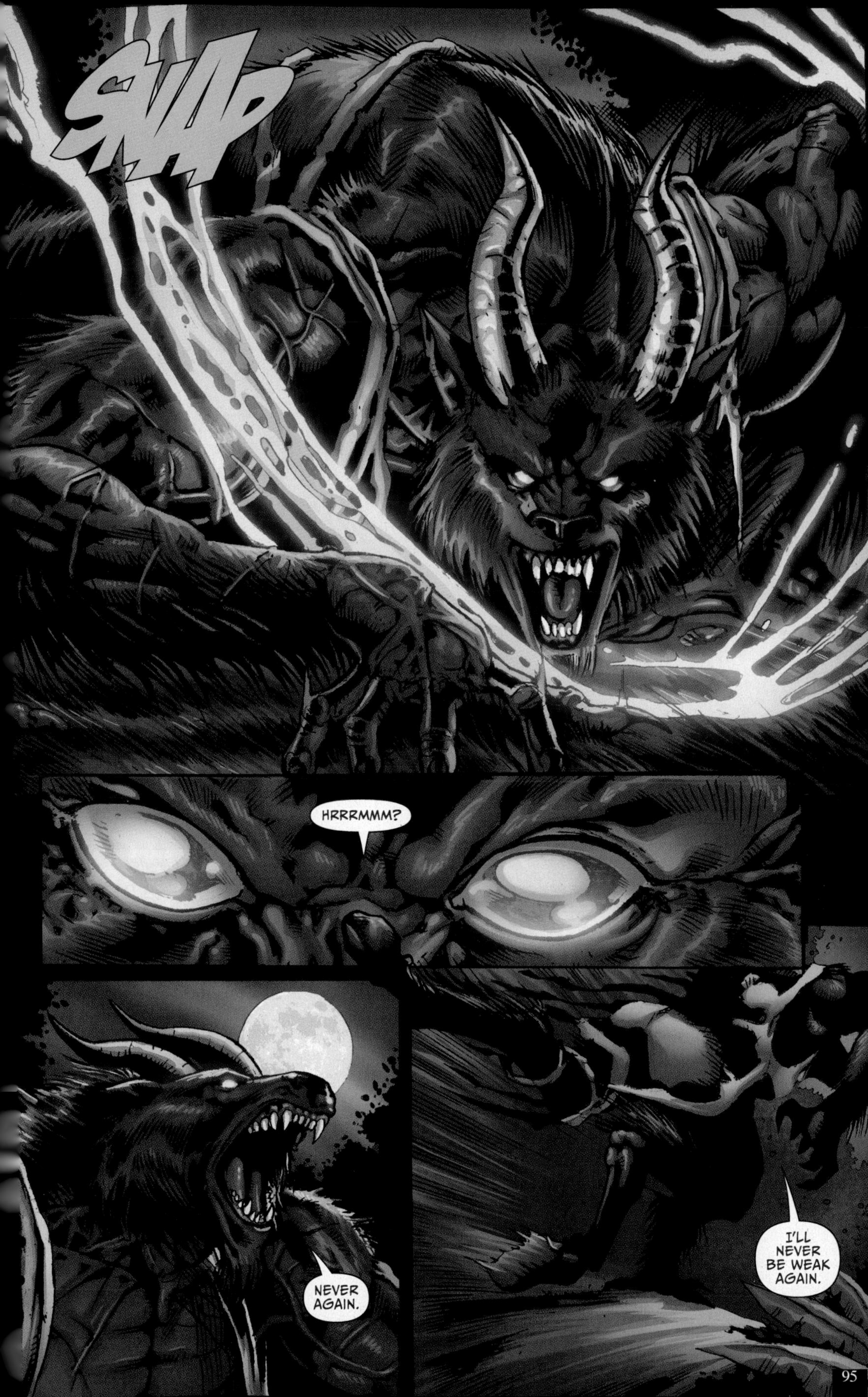
SNAP
HRRRMMM?
NEVER AGAIN.
I'LL NEVER BE WEAK AGAIN.

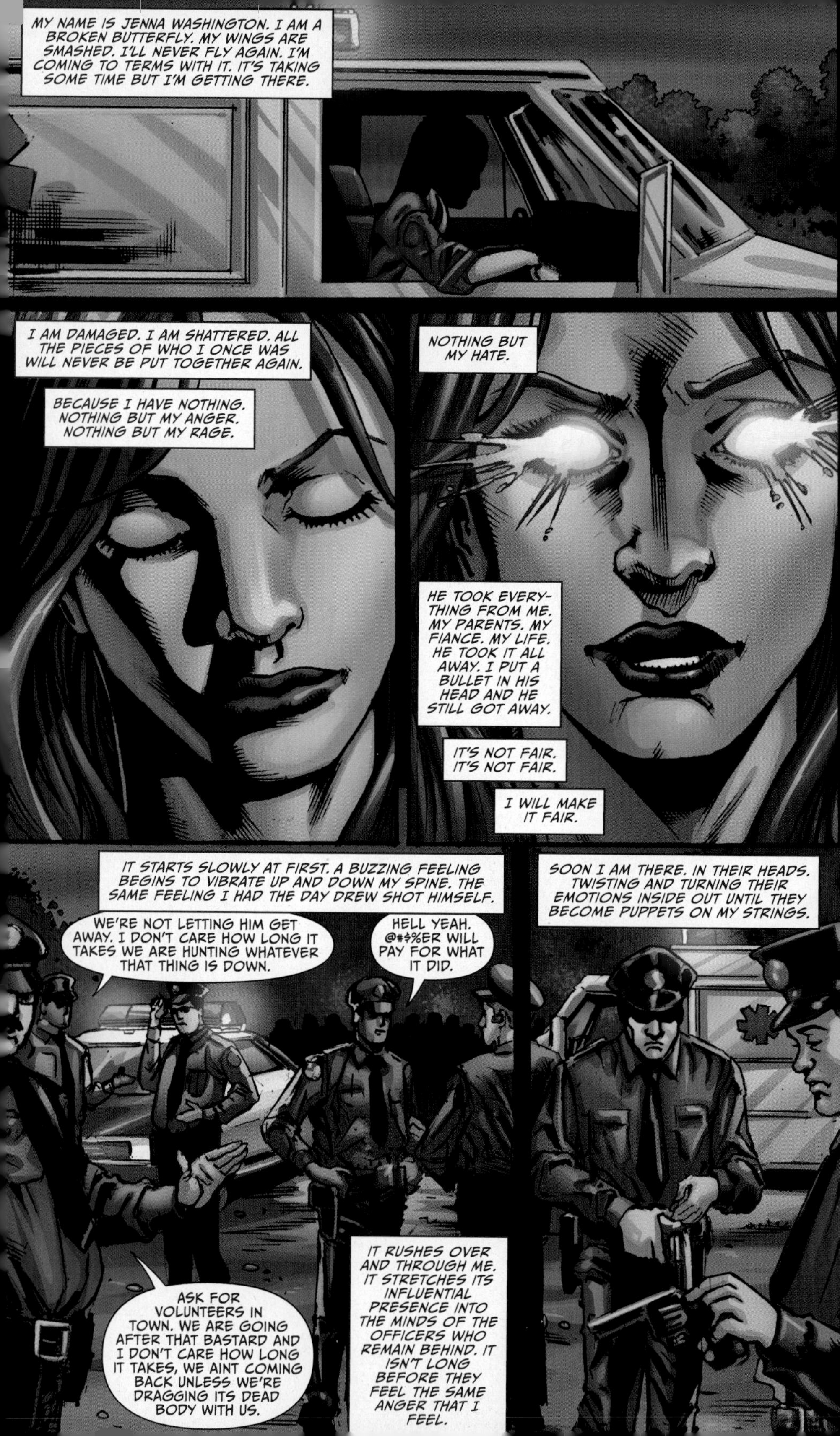
MY NAME IS JENNA WASHINGTON. I AM A BROKEN BUTTERFLY. MY WINGS ARE SMASHED. I'LL NEVER FLY AGAIN. I'M COMING TO TERMS WITH IT. IT'S TAKING SOME TIME BUT I'M GETTING THERE.
I AM DAMAGED. I AM SHATTERED. ALL THE PIECES OF WHO I ONCE WAS WILL NEVER BE PUT TOGETHER AGAIN.
BECAUSE I HAVE NOTHING. NOTHING BUT MY ANGER. NOTHING BUT MY RAGE.
NOTHING BUT MY HATE.
HE TOOK EVERYTHING FROM ME. MY PARENTS. MY FIANCE. MY LIFE. HE TOOK IT ALL AWAY. I PUT A BULLET IN HIS HEAD AND HE STILL GOT AWAY.
IT'S NOT FAIR. IT'S NOT FAIR.
I WILL MAKE IT FAIR.
IT STARTS SLOWLY AT FIRST. A BUZZING FEELING BEGINS TO VIBRATE UP AND DOWN MY SPINE. THE SAME FEELING I HAD THE DAY DREW SHOT HIMSELF.
WE'RE NOT LETTING HIM GET AWAY. I DON'T CARE HOW LONG IT TAKES WE ARE HUNTING WHATEVER THAT THING IS DOWN.
HELL YEAH. @#$%ER WILL PAY FOR WHAT IT DID.
ASK FOR VOLUNTEERS IN TOWN. WE ARE GOING AFTER THAT BASTARD AND I DON'T CARE HOW LONG IT TAKES, WE AINT COMING BACK UNLESS WE'RE DRAGGING ITS DEAD BODY WITH US.
IT RUSHES OVER AND THROUGH ME. IT STRETCHES ITS INFLUENTIAL PRESENCE INTO THE MINDS OF THE OFFICERS WHO REMAIN BEHIND. IT ISN'T LONG BEFORE THEY FEEL THE SAME ANGER THAT I FEEL.
SOON I AM THERE. IN THEIR HEADS. TWISTING AND TURNING THEIR EMOTIONS INSIDE OUT UNTIL THEY BECOME PUPPETS ON MY STRINGS.

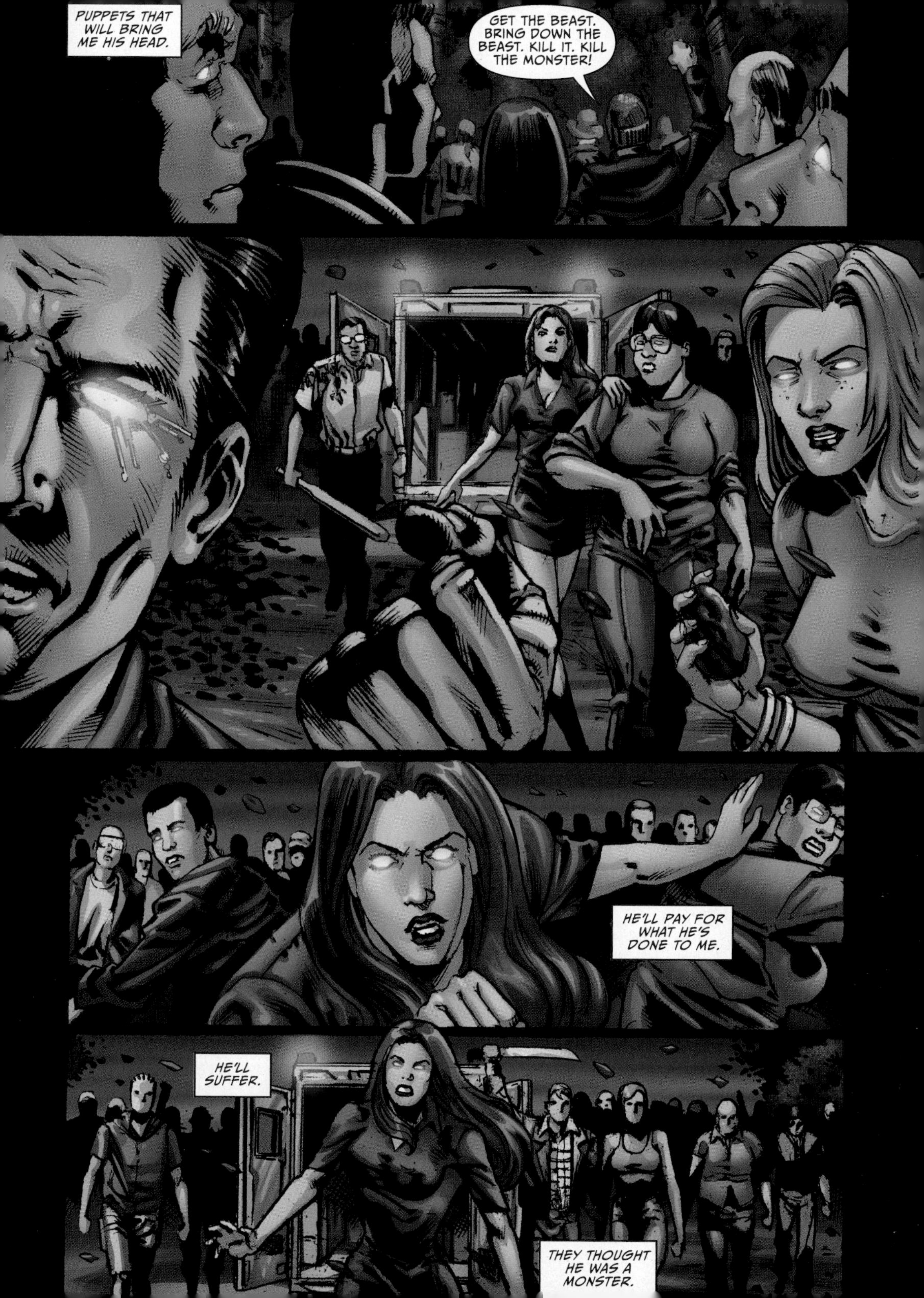
PUPPETS THAT WILL BRING ME HIS HEAD.
GET THE BEAST. BRING DOWN THE BEAST. KILL IT. KILL THE MONSTER!
HE'LL PAY FOR WHAT HE'S DONE TO ME.
HE'LL SUFFER.
THEY THOUGHT HE WAS A MONSTER.

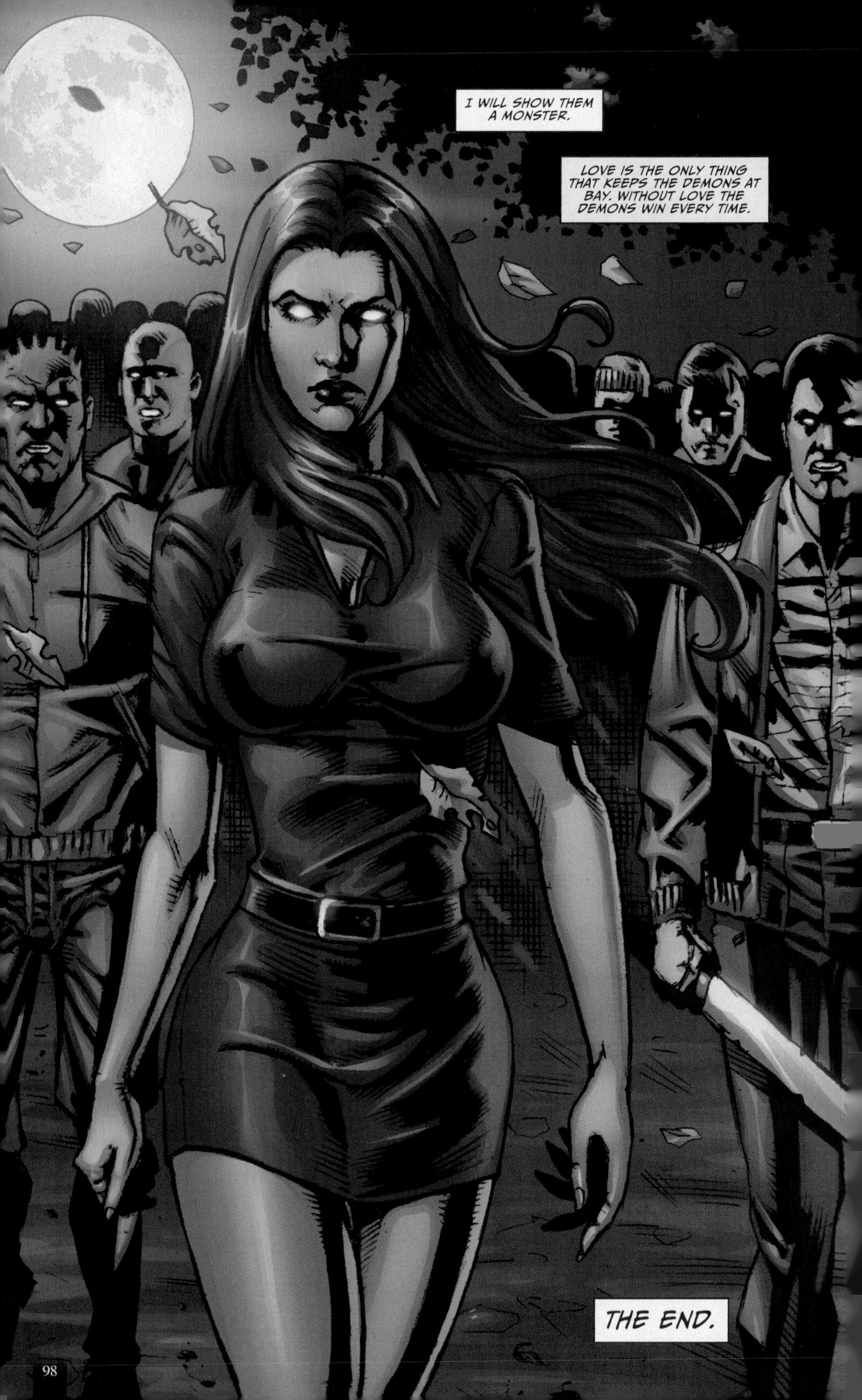
I WILL SHOW THEM A MONSTER.
LOVE IS THE ONLY THING THAT KEEPS THE DEMONS AT BAY. WITHOUT LOVE THE DEMONS WIN EVERY TIME.
THE END.

# Grimm Fairy Tales
# Myths & Legends

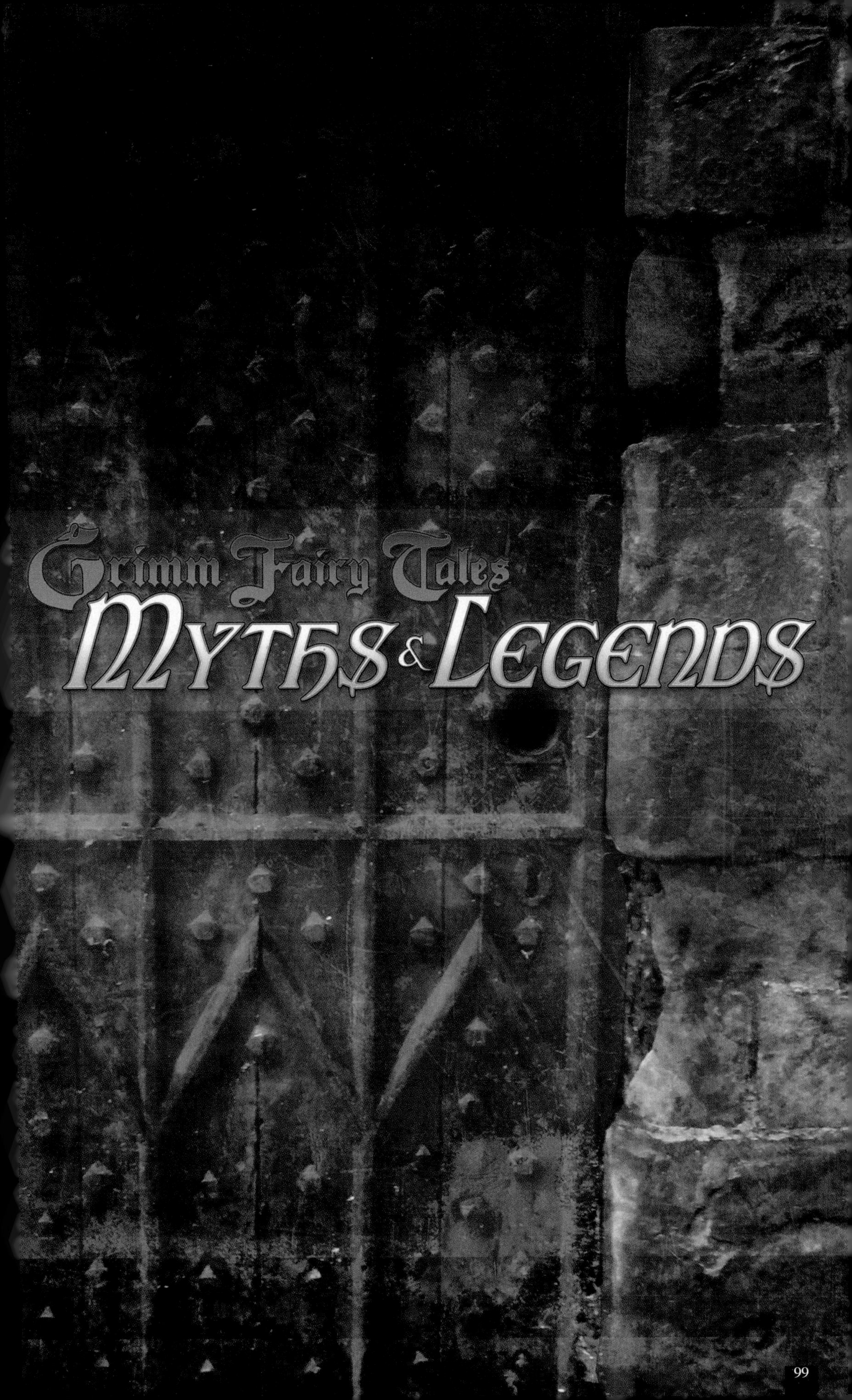

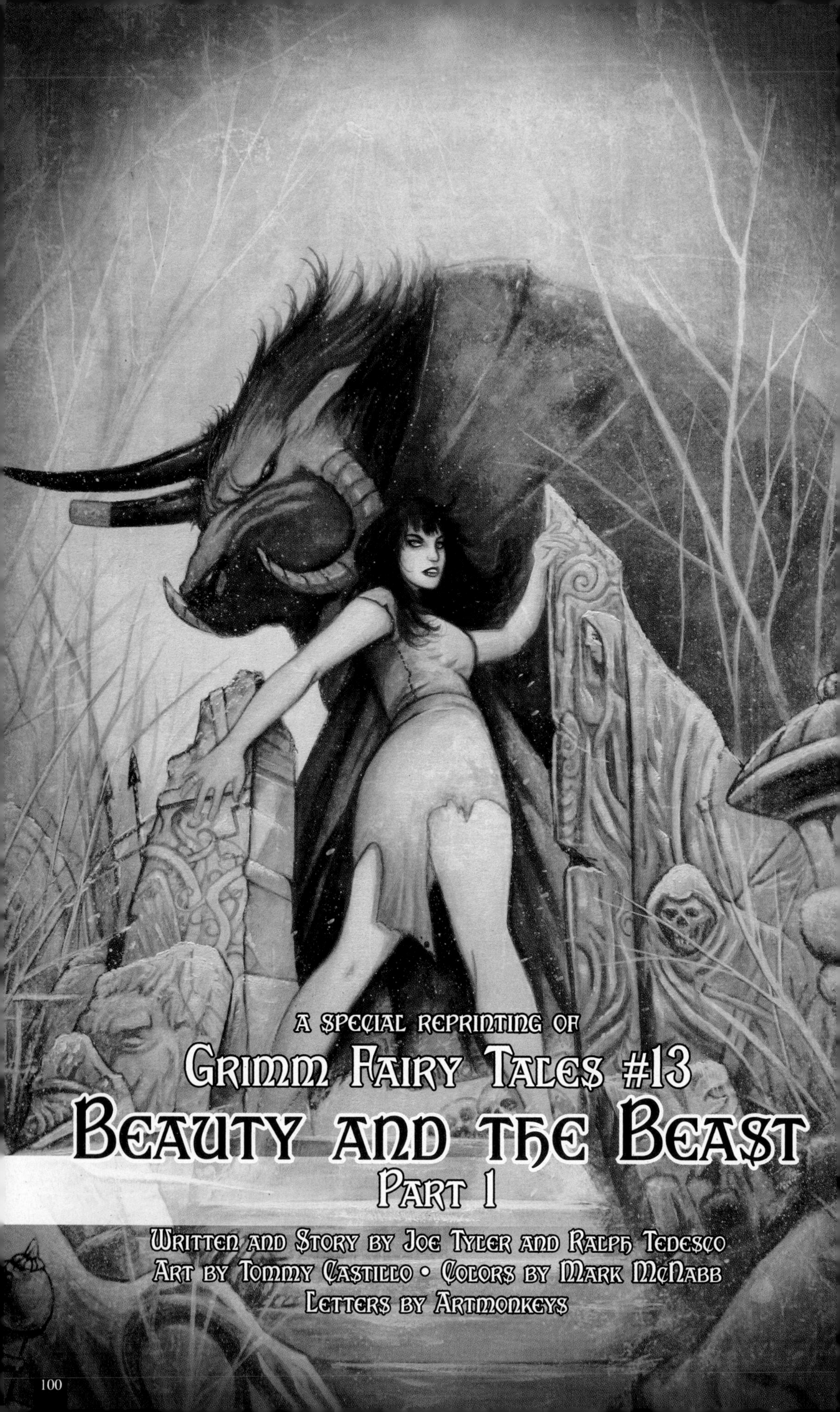

A Special Reprinting of

# Grimm Fairy Tales #13

# Beauty and the Beast

## Part 1

Written and Story by Joe Tyler and Ralph Tedesco
Art by Tommy Castillo • Colors by Mark McNabb
Letters by Artmonkeys

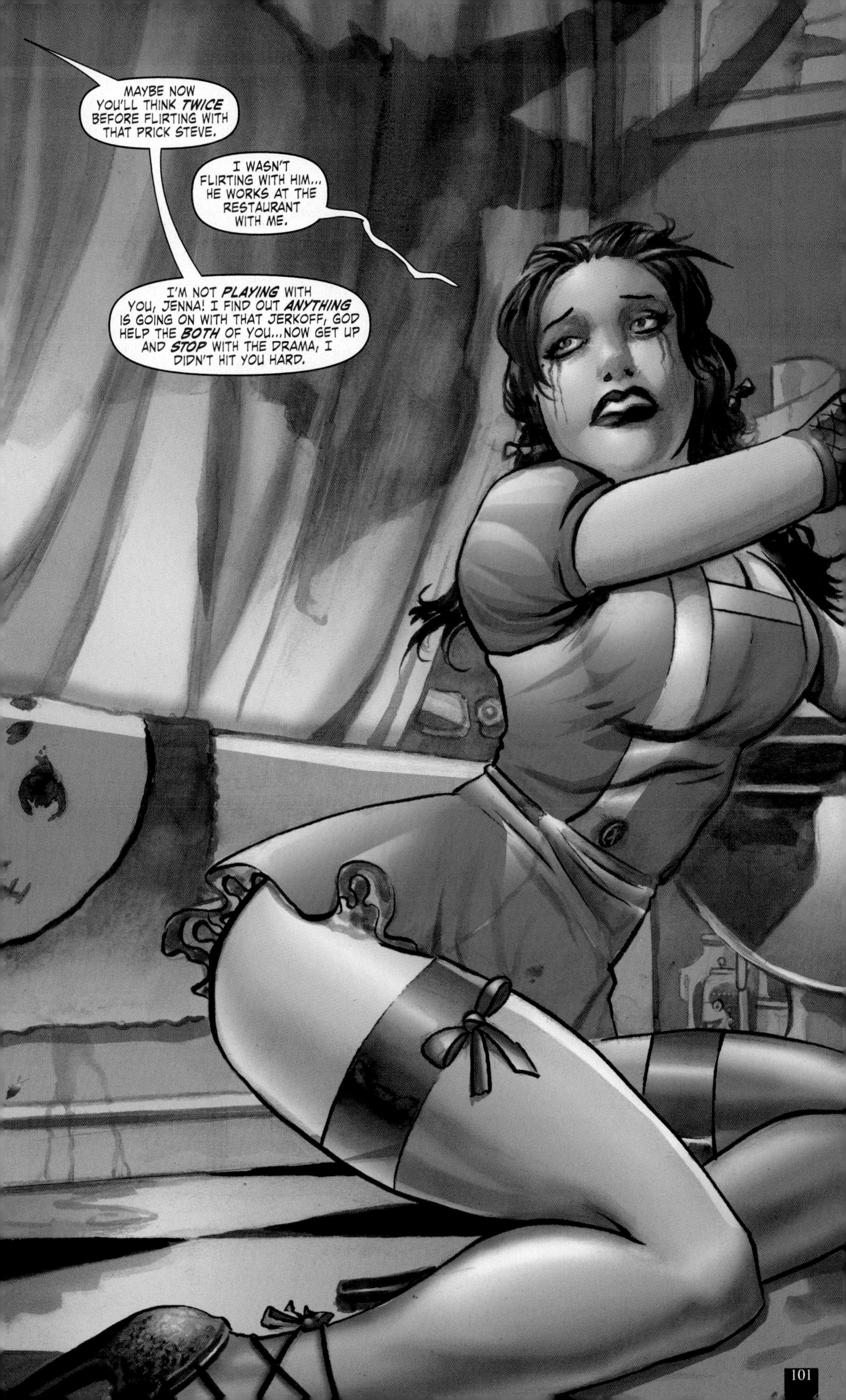
MAYBE NOW YOU'LL THINK TWICE BEFORE FLIRTING WITH THAT PRICK STEVE.
I WASN'T FLIRTING WITH HIM... HE WORKS AT THE RESTAURANT WITH ME.
I'M NOT PLAYING WITH YOU, JENNA! I FIND OUT ANYTHING IS GOING ON WITH THAT JERKOFF, GOD HELP THE BOTH OF YOU...NOW GET UP AND STOP WITH THE DRAMA, I DIDN'T HIT YOU HARD.

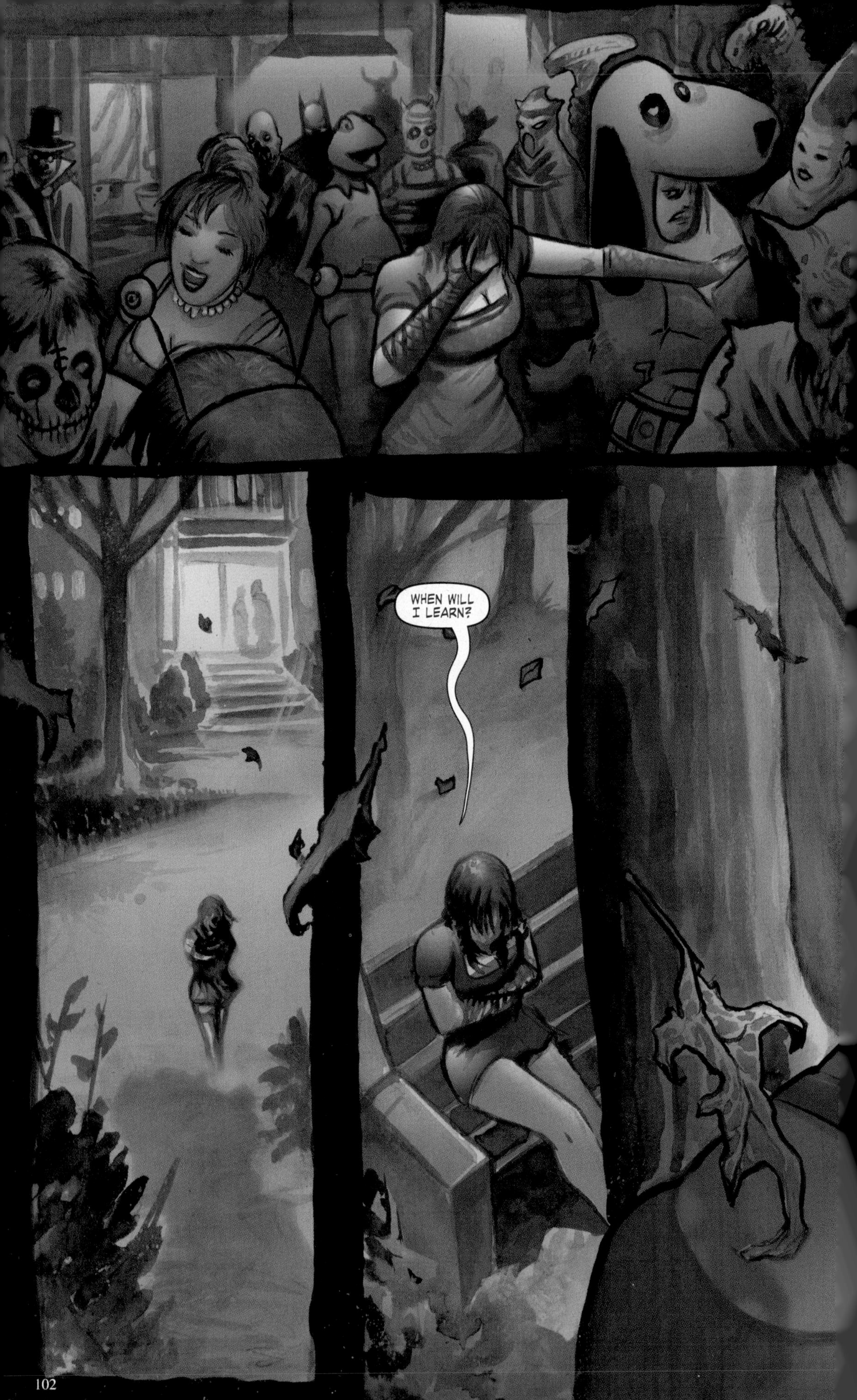
WHEN WILL I LEARN?

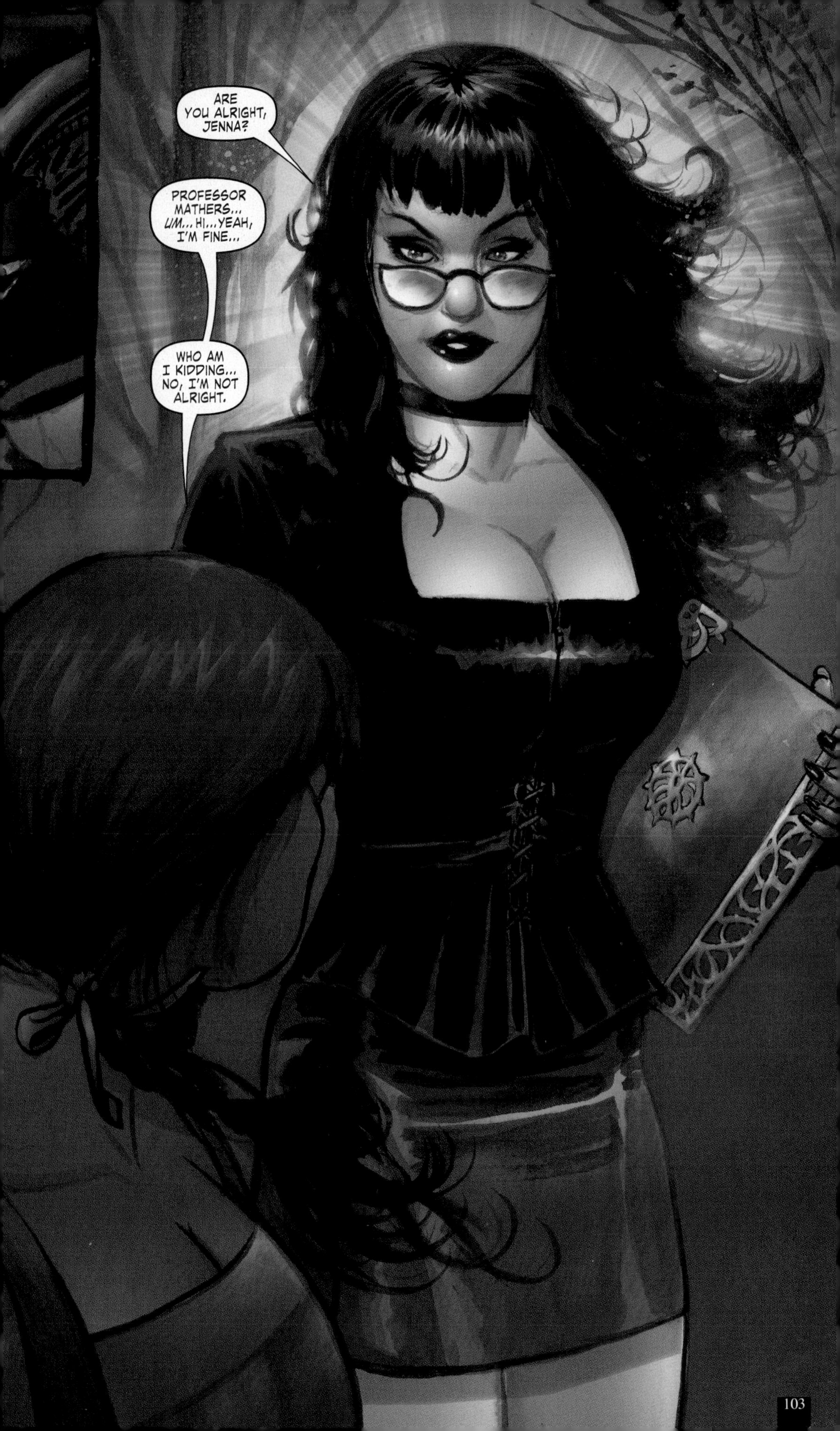
ARE YOU ALRIGHT, JENNA?
PROFESSOR MATHERS... UM... HI...YEAH, I'M FINE...
WHO AM I KIDDING... NO, I'M NOT ALRIGHT.

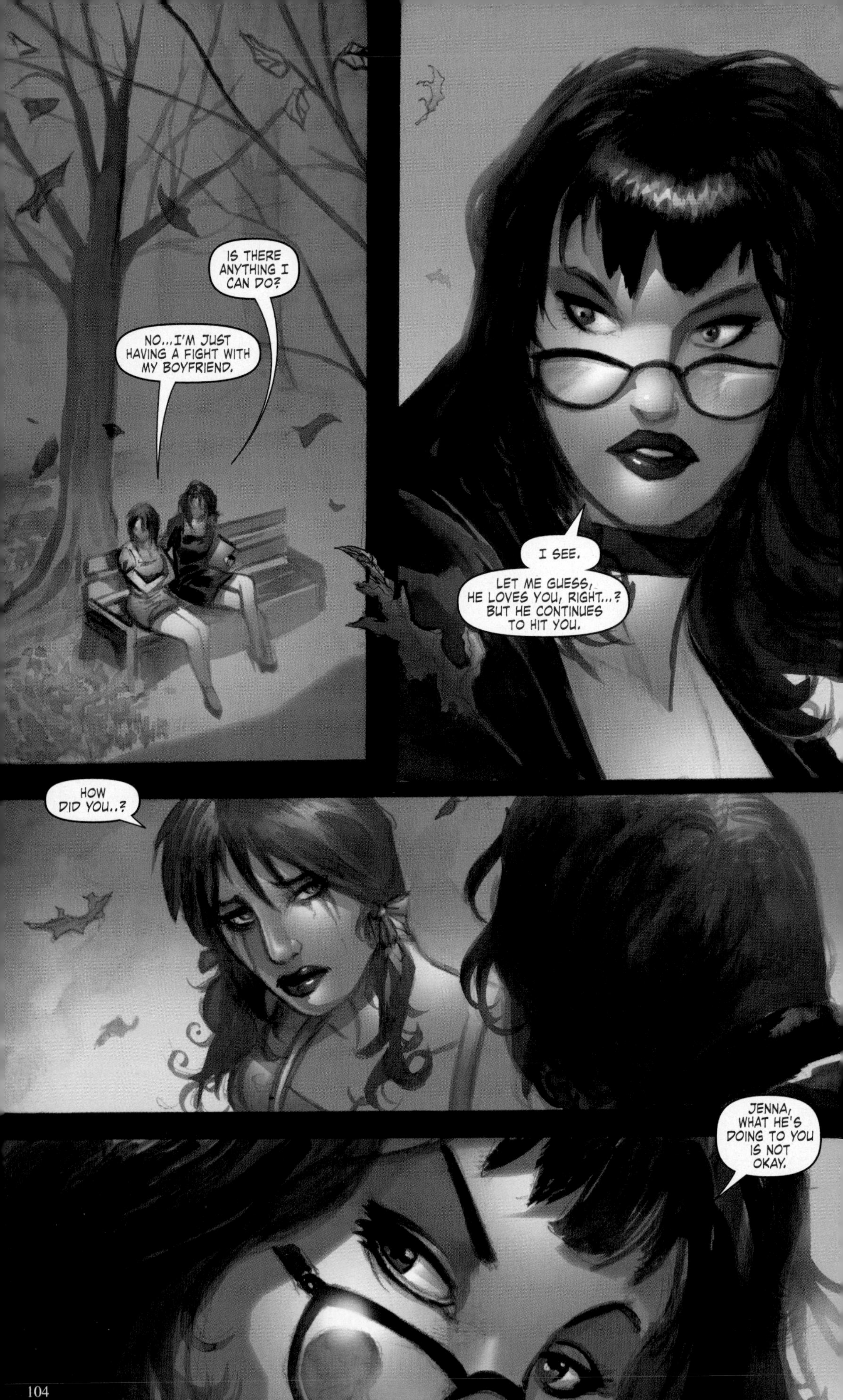
IS THERE ANYTHING I CAN DO?
NO...I'M JUST HAVING A FIGHT WITH MY BOYFRIEND.
I SEE.
LET ME GUESS, HE LOVES YOU, RIGHT...? BUT HE CONTINUES TO HIT YOU.
HOW DID YOU..?
JENNA, WHAT HE'S DOING TO YOU IS NOT OKAY.

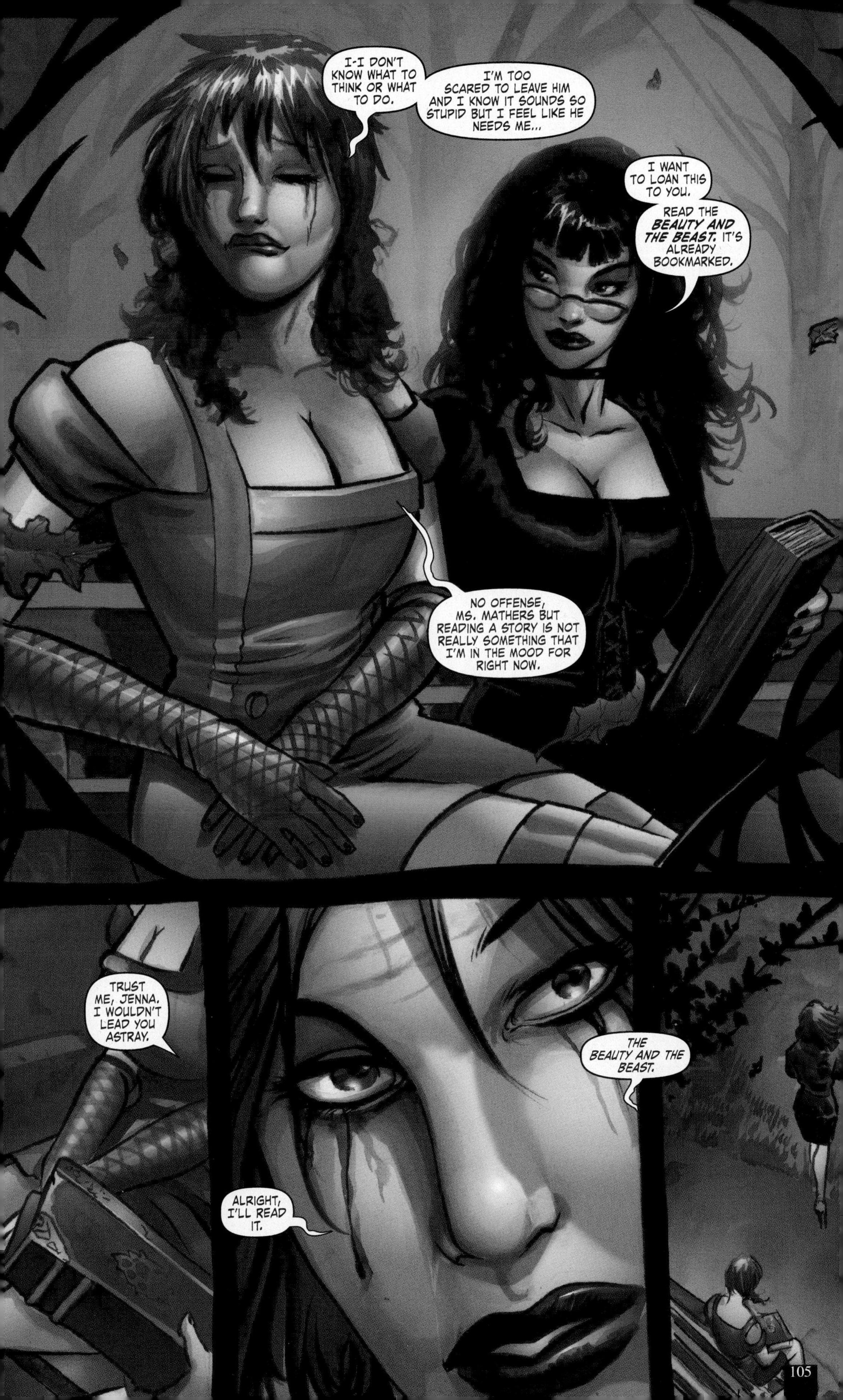
I-I DON'T KNOW WHAT TO THINK OR WHAT TO DO.
I'M TOO SCARED TO LEAVE HIM AND I KNOW IT SOUNDS SO STUPID BUT I FEEL LIKE HE NEEDS ME...
I WANT TO LOAN THIS TO YOU.
READ THE ***BEAUTY AND THE BEAST.*** IT'S ALREADY BOOKMARKED.
NO OFFENSE, MS. MATHERS BUT READING A STORY IS NOT REALLY SOMETHING THAT I'M IN THE MOOD FOR RIGHT NOW.
TRUST ME, JENNA. I WOULDN'T LEAD YOU ASTRAY.
ALRIGHT, I'LL READ IT.
*THE BEAUTY AND THE BEAST.*

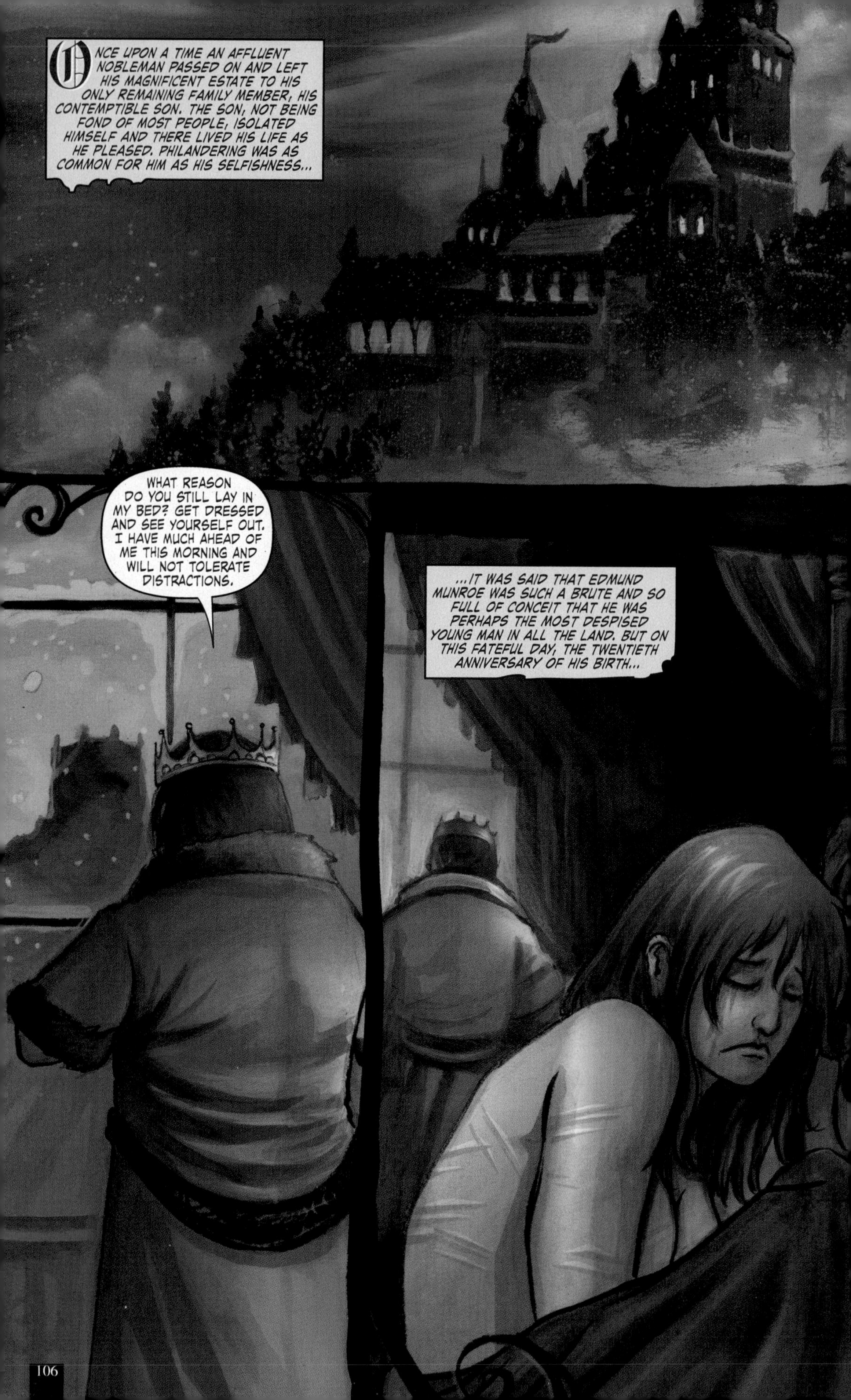
ONCE UPON A TIME AN AFFLUENT NOBLEMAN PASSED ON AND LEFT HIS MAGNIFICENT ESTATE TO HIS ONLY REMAINING FAMILY MEMBER, HIS CONTEMPTIBLE SON. THE SON, NOT BEING FOND OF MOST PEOPLE, ISOLATED HIMSELF AND THERE LIVED HIS LIFE AS HE PLEASED. PHILANDERING WAS AS COMMON FOR HIM AS HIS SELFISHNESS...
WHAT REASON DO YOU STILL LAY IN MY BED? GET DRESSED AND SEE YOURSELF OUT. I HAVE MUCH AHEAD OF ME THIS MORNING AND WILL NOT TOLERATE DISTRACTIONS.
...IT WAS SAID THAT EDMUND MUNROE WAS SUCH A BRUTE AND SO FULL OF CONCEIT THAT HE WAS PERHAPS THE MOST DESPISED YOUNG MAN IN ALL THE LAND. BUT ON THIS FATEFUL DAY, THE TWENTIETH ANNIVERSARY OF HIS BIRTH...

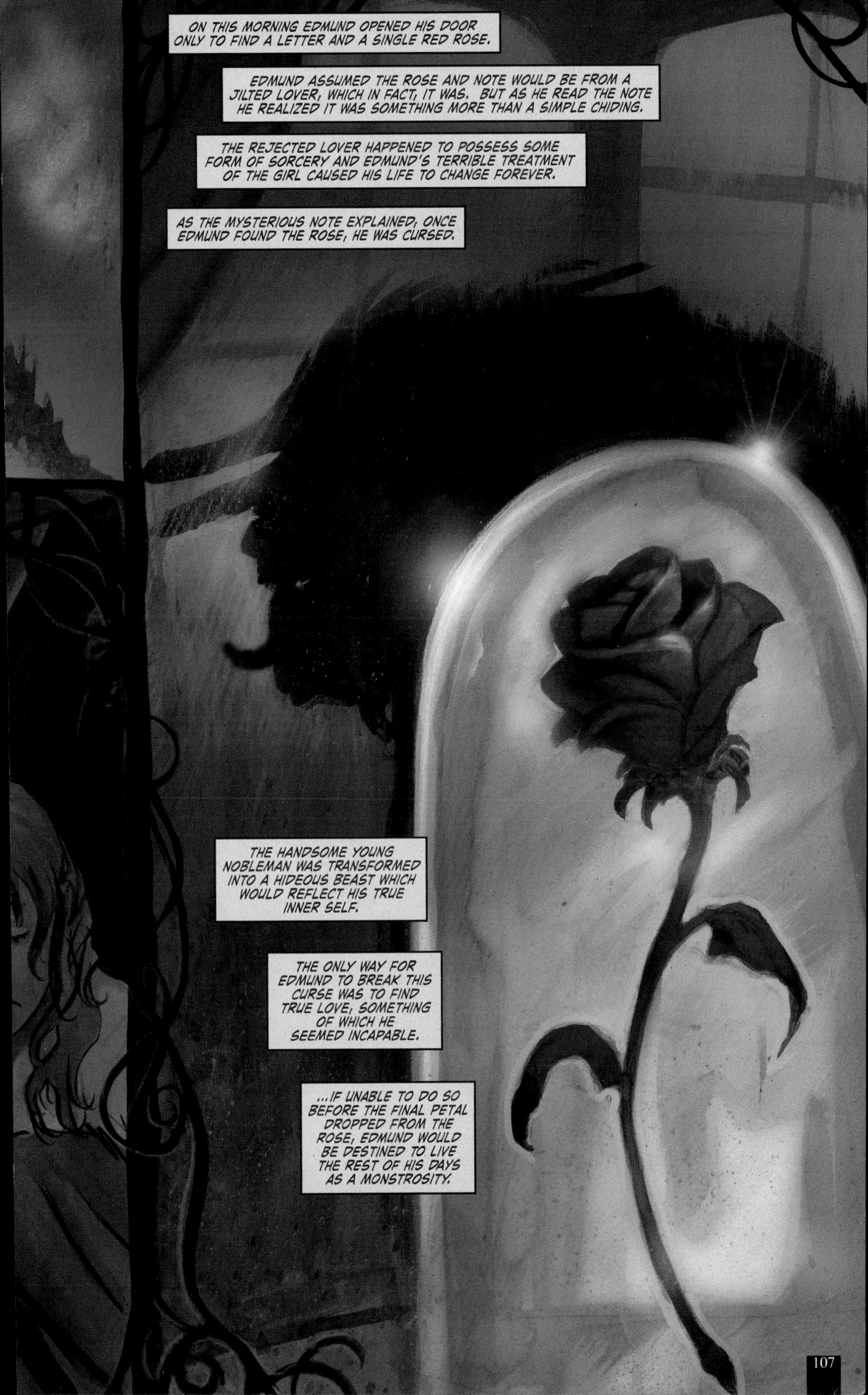
ON THIS MORNING EDMUND OPENED HIS DOOR ONLY TO FIND A LETTER AND A SINGLE RED ROSE.
EDMUND ASSUMED THE ROSE AND NOTE WOULD BE FROM A JILTED LOVER, WHICH IN FACT, IT WAS. BUT AS HE READ THE NOTE HE REALIZED IT WAS SOMETHING MORE THAN A SIMPLE CHIDING.
THE REJECTED LOVER HAPPENED TO POSSESS SOME FORM OF SORCERY AND EDMUND'S TERRIBLE TREATMENT OF THE GIRL CAUSED HIS LIFE TO CHANGE FOREVER.
AS THE MYSTERIOUS NOTE EXPLAINED, ONCE EDMUND FOUND THE ROSE, HE WAS CURSED.
THE HANDSOME YOUNG NOBLEMAN WAS TRANSFORMED INTO A HIDEOUS BEAST WHICH WOULD REFLECT HIS TRUE INNER SELF.
THE ONLY WAY FOR EDMUND TO BREAK THIS CURSE WAS TO FIND TRUE LOVE, SOMETHING OF WHICH HE SEEMED INCAPABLE.
...IF UNABLE TO DO SO BEFORE THE FINAL PETAL DROPPED FROM THE ROSE, EDMUND WOULD BE DESTINED TO LIVE THE REST OF HIS DAYS AS A MONSTROSITY.

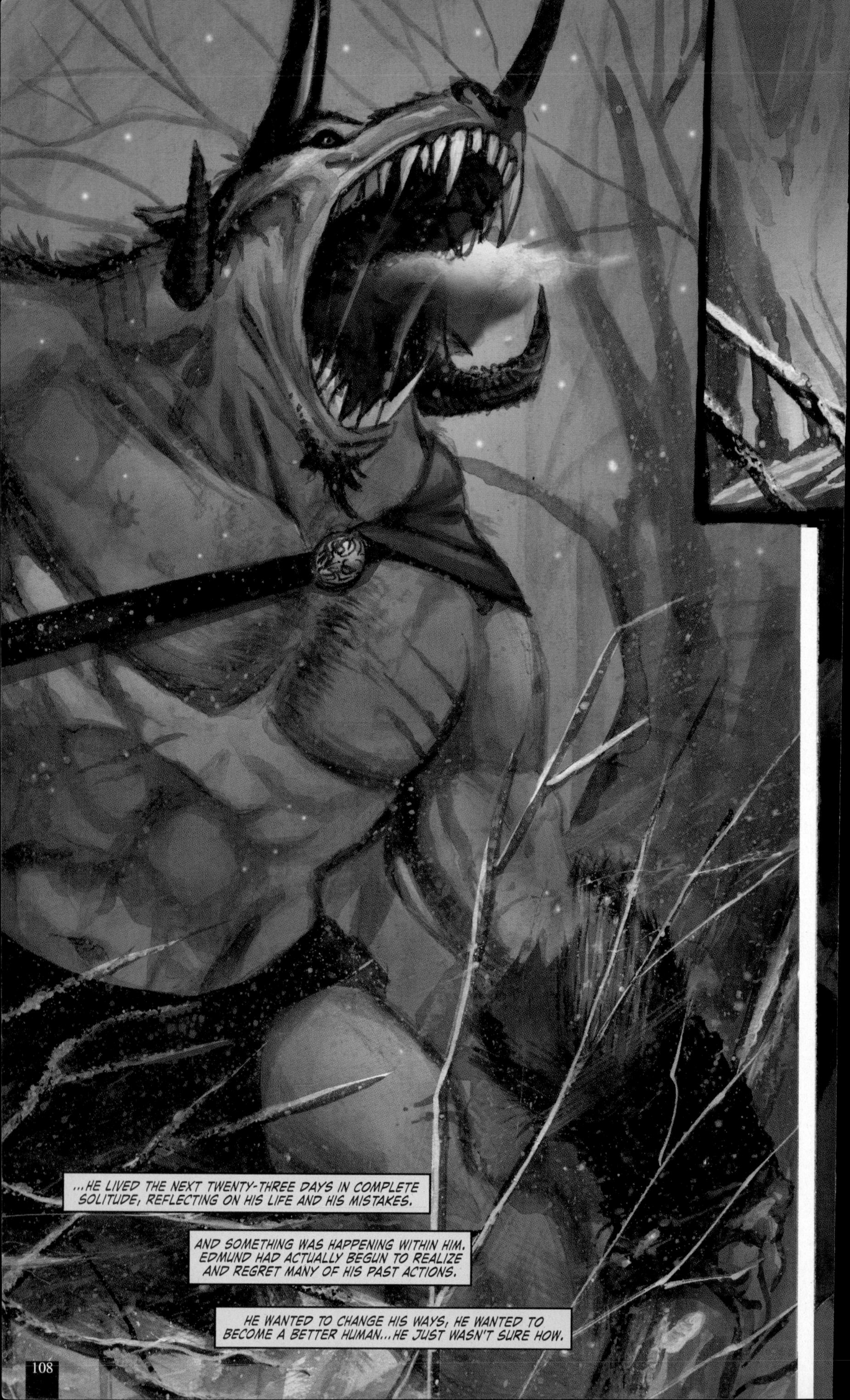
...HE LIVED THE NEXT TWENTY-THREE DAYS IN COMPLETE SOLITUDE, REFLECTING ON HIS LIFE AND HIS MISTAKES.
AND SOMETHING WAS HAPPENING WITHIN HIM. EDMUND HAD ACTUALLY BEGUN TO REALIZE AND REGRET MANY OF HIS PAST ACTIONS.
HE WANTED TO CHANGE HIS WAYS, HE WANTED TO BECOME A BETTER HUMAN...HE JUST WASN'T SURE HOW.

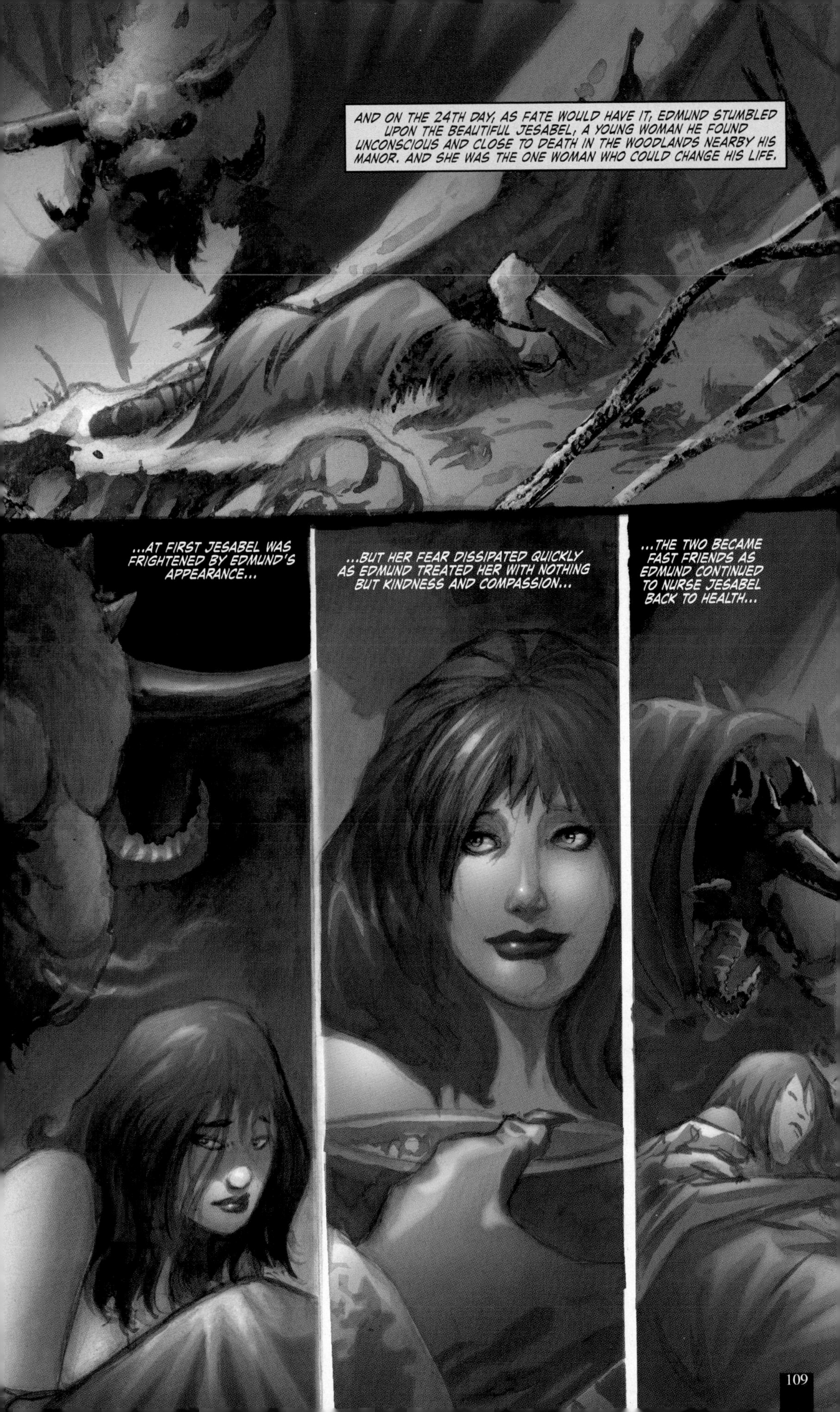
AND ON THE 24TH DAY, AS FATE WOULD HAVE IT, EDMUND STUMBLED UPON THE BEAUTIFUL JESABEL, A YOUNG WOMAN HE FOUND UNCONSCIOUS AND CLOSE TO DEATH IN THE WOODLANDS NEARBY HIS MANOR. AND SHE WAS THE ONE WOMAN WHO COULD CHANGE HIS LIFE.
...AT FIRST JESABEL WAS FRIGHTENED BY EDMUND'S APPEARANCE...
...BUT HER FEAR DISSIPATED QUICKLY AS EDMUND TREATED HER WITH NOTHING BUT KINDNESS AND COMPASSION...
...THE TWO BECAME FAST FRIENDS AS EDMUND CONTINUED TO NURSE JESABEL BACK TO HEALTH...

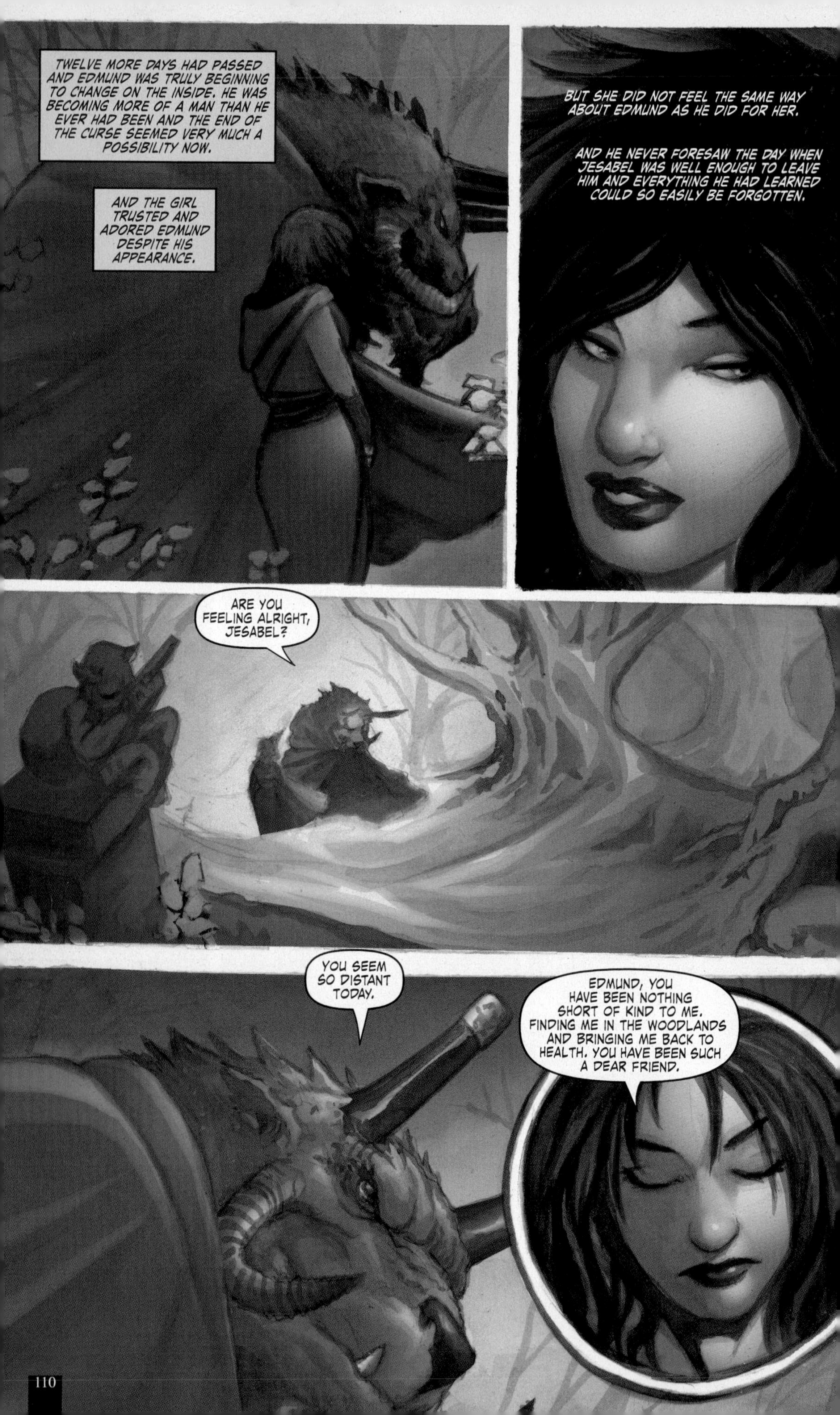
TWELVE MORE DAYS HAD PASSED AND EDMUND WAS TRULY BEGINNING TO CHANGE ON THE INSIDE. HE WAS BECOMING MORE OF A MAN THAN HE EVER HAD BEEN AND THE END OF THE CURSE SEEMED VERY MUCH A POSSIBILITY NOW.
AND THE GIRL TRUSTED AND ADORED EDMUND DESPITE HIS APPEARANCE.
BUT SHE DID NOT FEEL THE SAME WAY ABOUT EDMUND AS HE DID FOR HER.
AND HE NEVER FORESAW THE DAY WHEN JESABEL WAS WELL ENOUGH TO LEAVE HIM AND EVERYTHING HE HAD LEARNED COULD SO EASILY BE FORGOTTEN.
ARE YOU FEELING ALRIGHT, JESABEL?
YOU SEEM SO DISTANT TODAY.
EDMUND, YOU HAVE BEEN NOTHING SHORT OF KIND TO ME. FINDING ME IN THE WOODLANDS AND BRINGING ME BACK TO HEALTH. YOU HAVE BEEN SUCH A DEAR FRIEND.

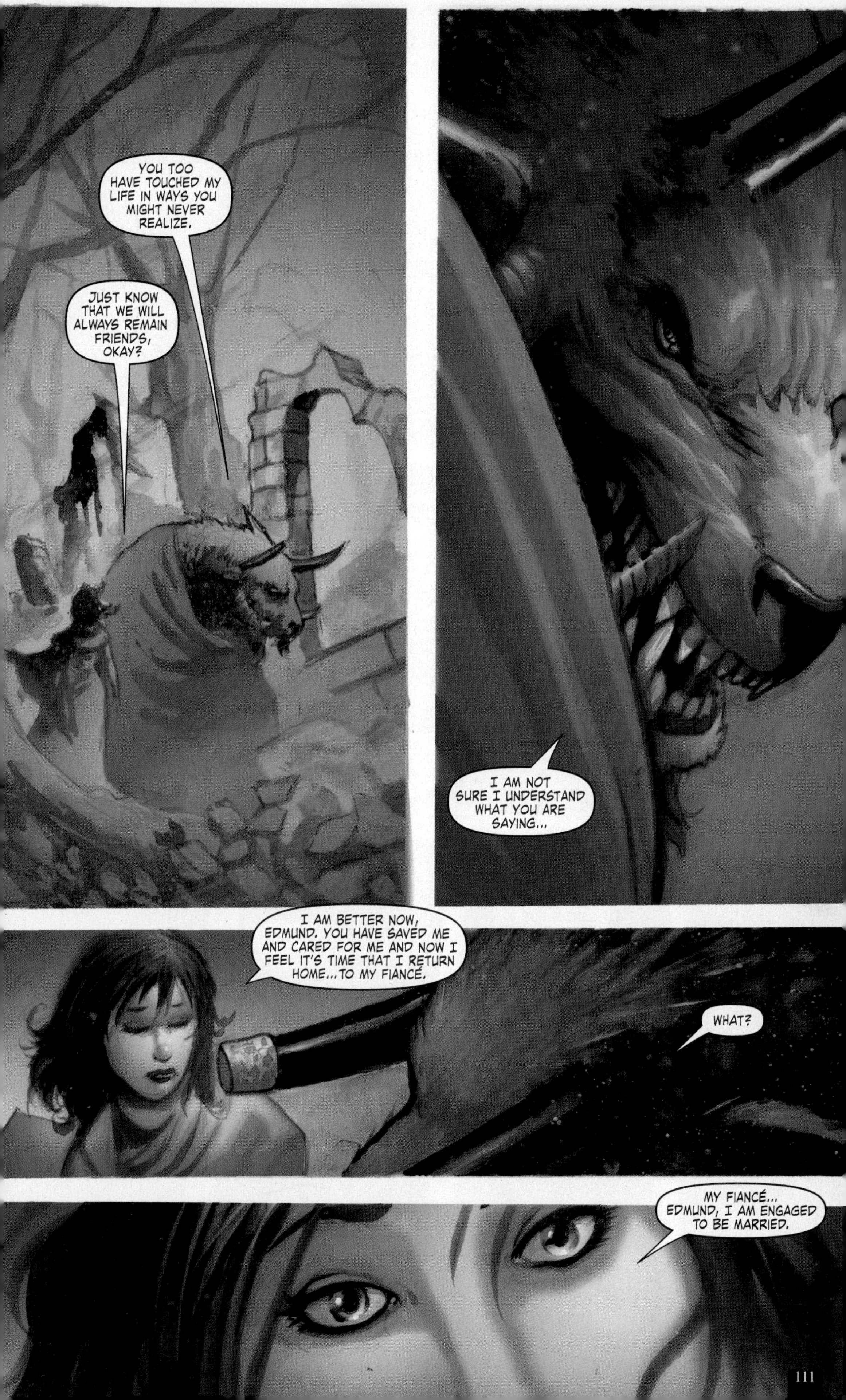
YOU TOO HAVE TOUCHED MY LIFE IN WAYS YOU MIGHT NEVER REALIZE.
JUST KNOW THAT WE WILL ALWAYS REMAIN FRIENDS, OKAY?
I AM NOT SURE I UNDERSTAND WHAT YOU ARE SAYING...
I AM BETTER NOW, EDMUND. YOU HAVE SAVED ME AND CARED FOR ME AND NOW I FEEL IT'S TIME THAT I RETURN HOME...TO MY FIANCÉ.
WHAT?
MY FIANCÉ... EDMUND, I AM ENGAGED TO BE MARRIED.

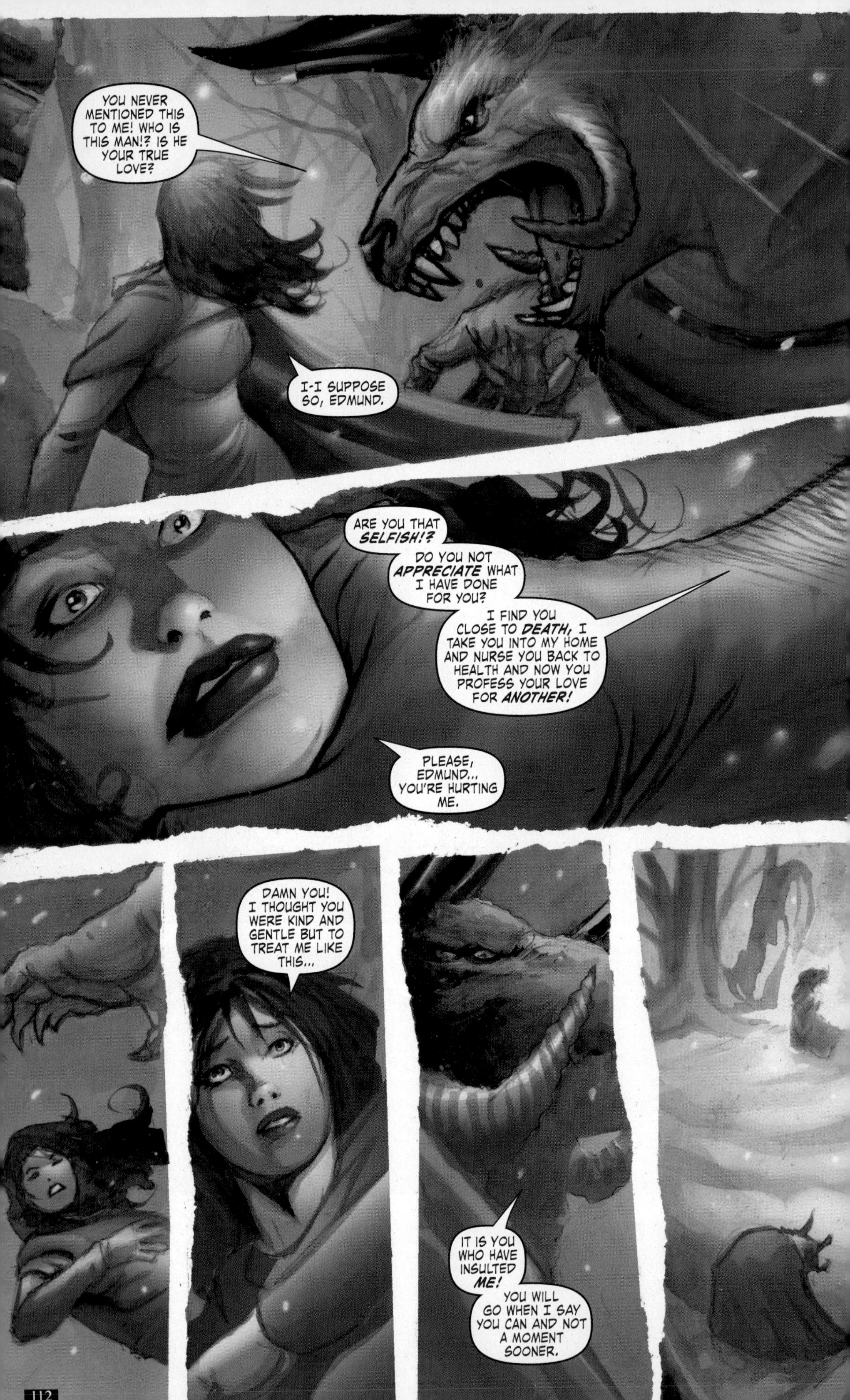

YOU NEVER MENTIONED THIS TO ME! WHO IS THIS MAN!? IS HE YOUR TRUE LOVE?
I-I SUPPOSE SO, EDMUND.
ARE YOU THAT SELFISH!?
DO YOU NOT APPRECIATE WHAT I HAVE DONE FOR YOU?
I FIND YOU CLOSE TO DEATH, I TAKE YOU INTO MY HOME AND NURSE YOU BACK TO HEALTH AND NOW YOU PROFESS YOUR LOVE FOR ANOTHER!
PLEASE, EDMUND... YOU'RE HURTING ME.
DAMN YOU! I THOUGHT YOU WERE KIND AND GENTLE BUT TO TREAT ME LIKE THIS...
IT IS YOU WHO HAVE INSULTED ME!
YOU WILL GO WHEN I SAY YOU CAN AND NOT A MOMENT SOONER.

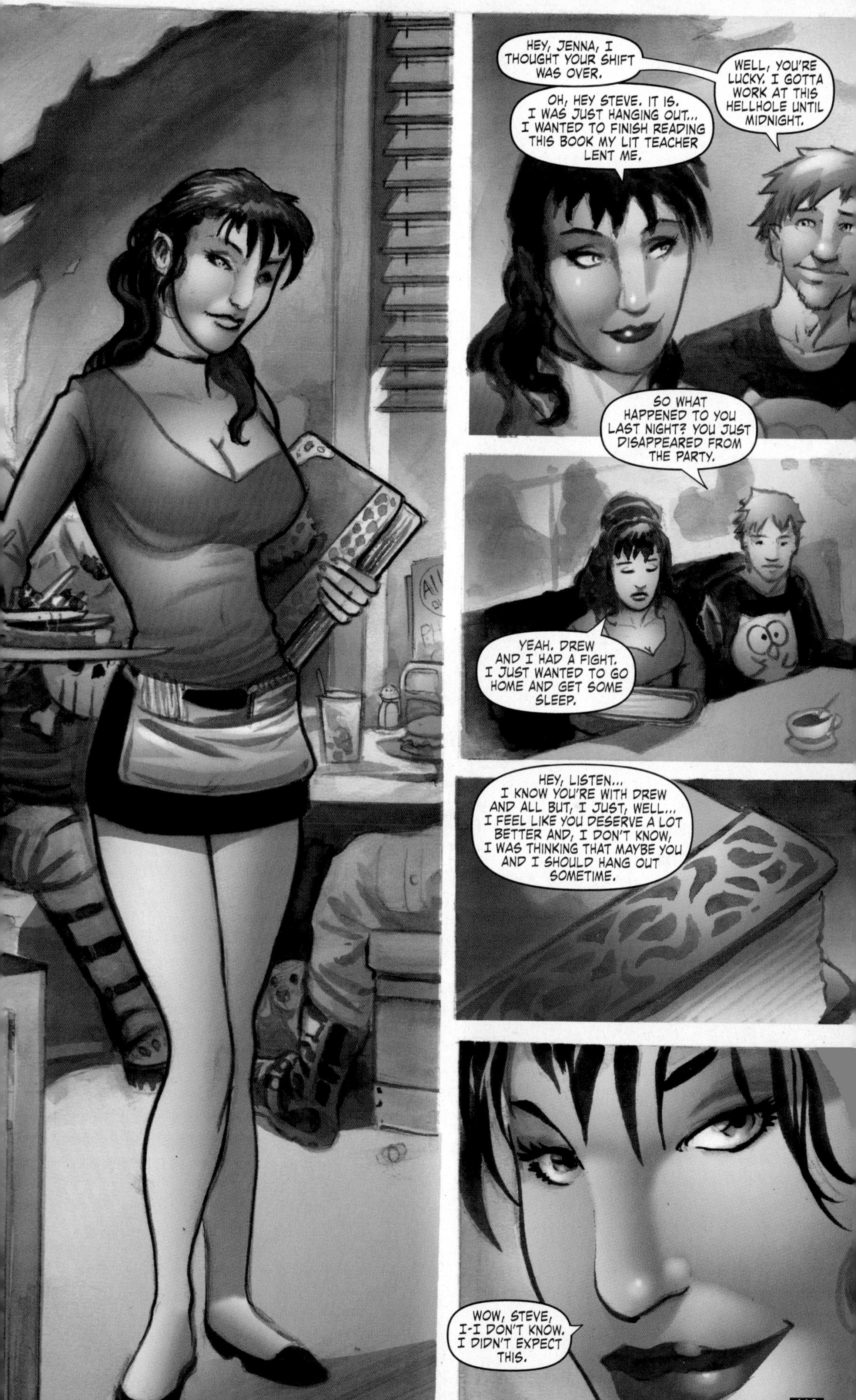

HEY, JENNA, I THOUGHT YOUR SHIFT WAS OVER.
OH, HEY STEVE. IT IS. I WAS JUST HANGING OUT... I WANTED TO FINISH READING THIS BOOK MY LIT TEACHER LENT ME.
WELL, YOU'RE LUCKY. I GOTTA WORK AT THIS HELLHOLE UNTIL MIDNIGHT.
SO WHAT HAPPENED TO YOU LAST NIGHT? YOU JUST DISAPPEARED FROM THE PARTY.
YEAH. DREW AND I HAD A FIGHT. I JUST WANTED TO GO HOME AND GET SOME SLEEP.
HEY, LISTEN... I KNOW YOU'RE WITH DREW AND ALL BUT, I JUST, WELL... I FEEL LIKE YOU DESERVE A LOT BETTER AND, I DON'T KNOW, I WAS THINKING THAT MAYBE YOU AND I SHOULD HANG OUT SOMETIME.
WOW, STEVE, I-I DON'T KNOW. I DIDN'T EXPECT THIS.

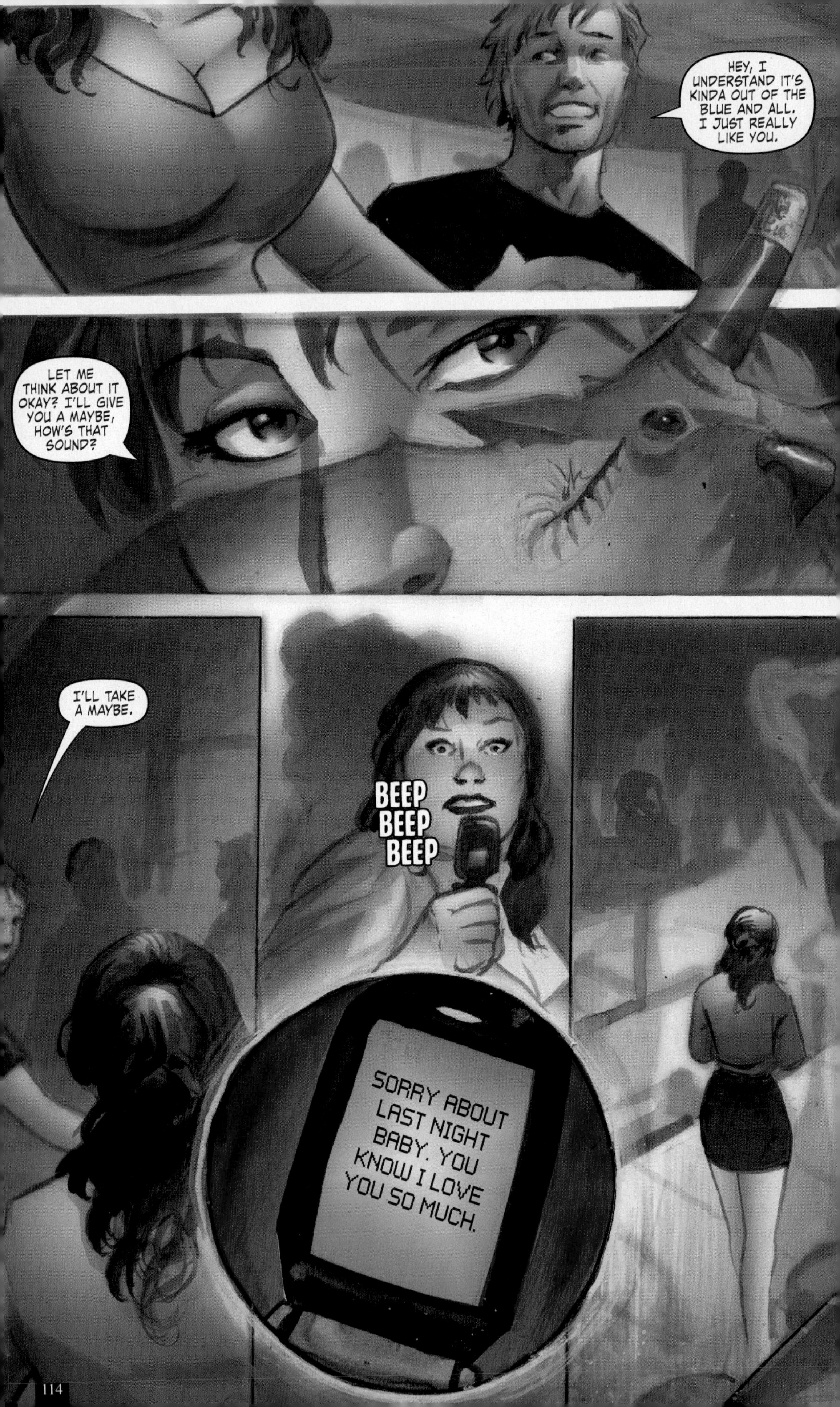
HEY, I UNDERSTAND IT'S KINDA OUT OF THE BLUE AND ALL. I JUST REALLY LIKE YOU.
LET ME THINK ABOUT IT OKAY? I'LL GIVE YOU A MAYBE, HOW'S THAT SOUND?
I'LL TAKE A MAYBE.
BEEP BEEP BEEP
SORRY ABOUT LAST NIGHT BABY. YOU KNOW I LOVE YOU SO MUCH.

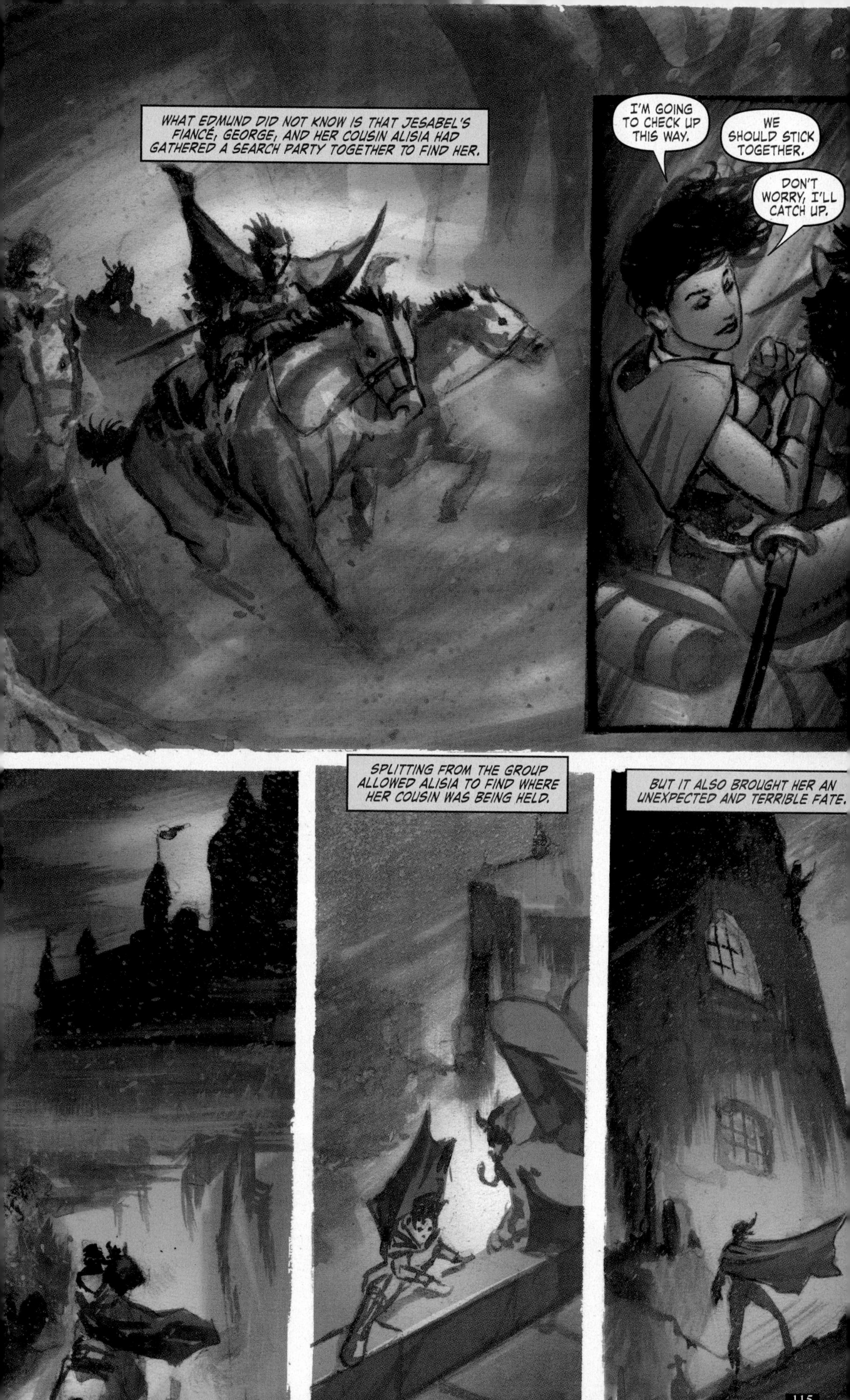

WHAT EDMUND DID NOT KNOW IS THAT JESABEL'S FIANCÉ, GEORGE, AND HER COUSIN ALISIA HAD GATHERED A SEARCH PARTY TOGETHER TO FIND HER.
I'M GOING TO CHECK UP THIS WAY.
WE SHOULD STICK TOGETHER.
DON'T WORRY, I'LL CATCH UP.
SPLITTING FROM THE GROUP ALLOWED ALISIA TO FIND WHERE HER COUSIN WAS BEING HELD.
BUT IT ALSO BROUGHT HER AN UNEXPECTED AND TERRIBLE FATE.

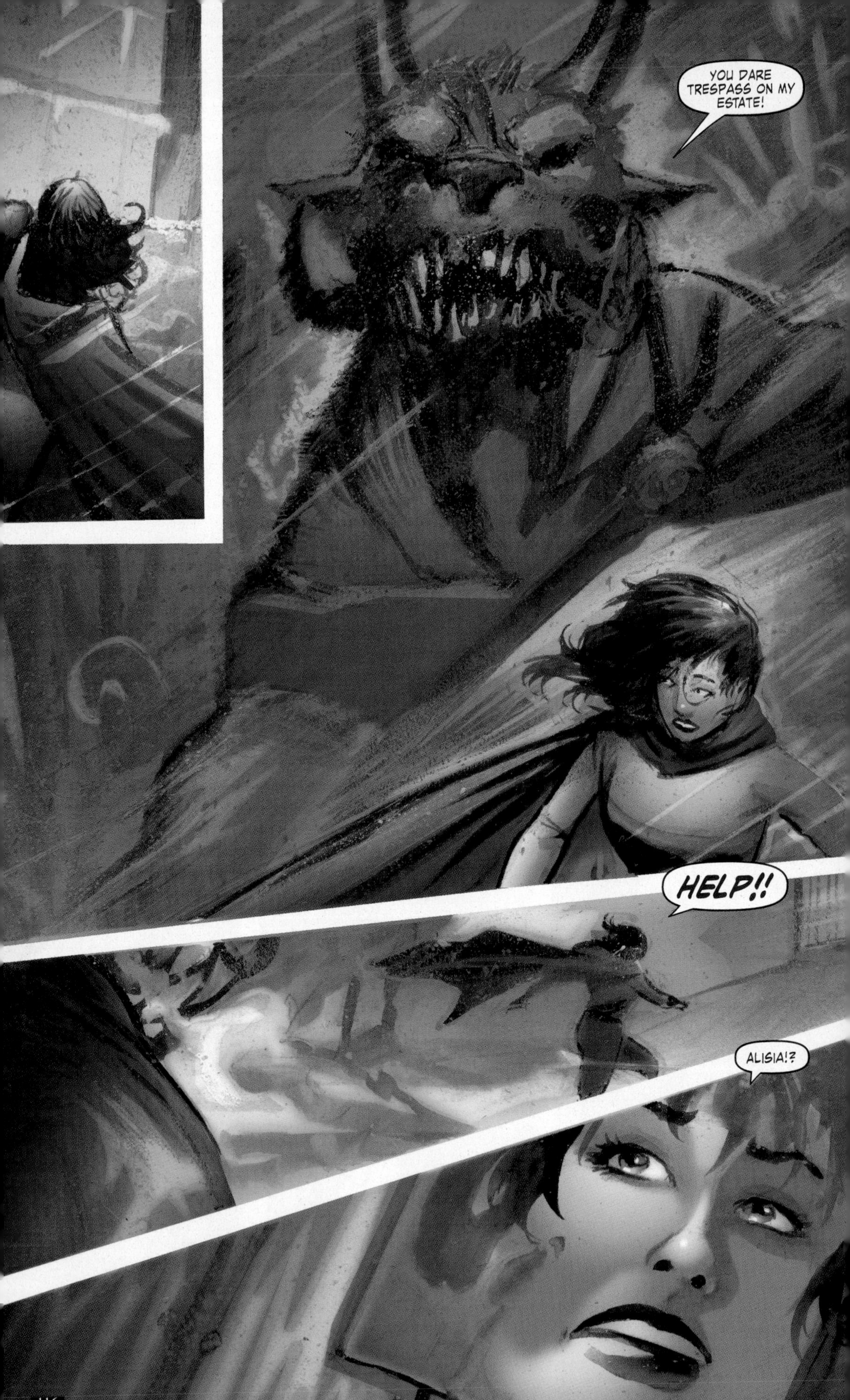
YOU DARE TRESPASS ON MY ESTATE!
HELP!!
ALISIA!?

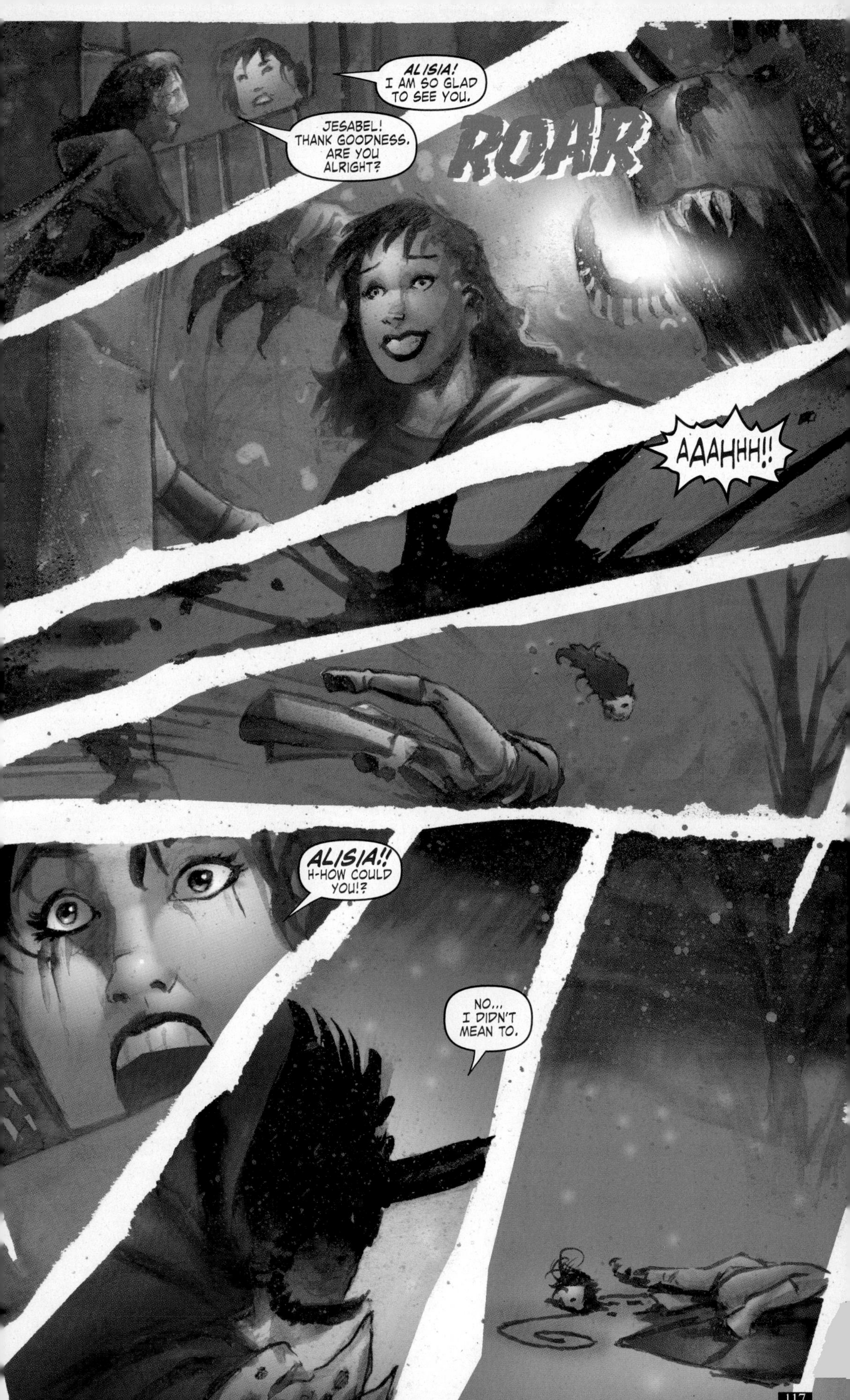
ALISIA! I AM SO GLAD TO SEE YOU.
JESABEL! THANK GOODNESS. ARE YOU ALRIGHT?
ROAR
AAAHHH!!
ALISIA!! H-HOW COULD YOU!?
NO... I DIDN'T MEAN TO.

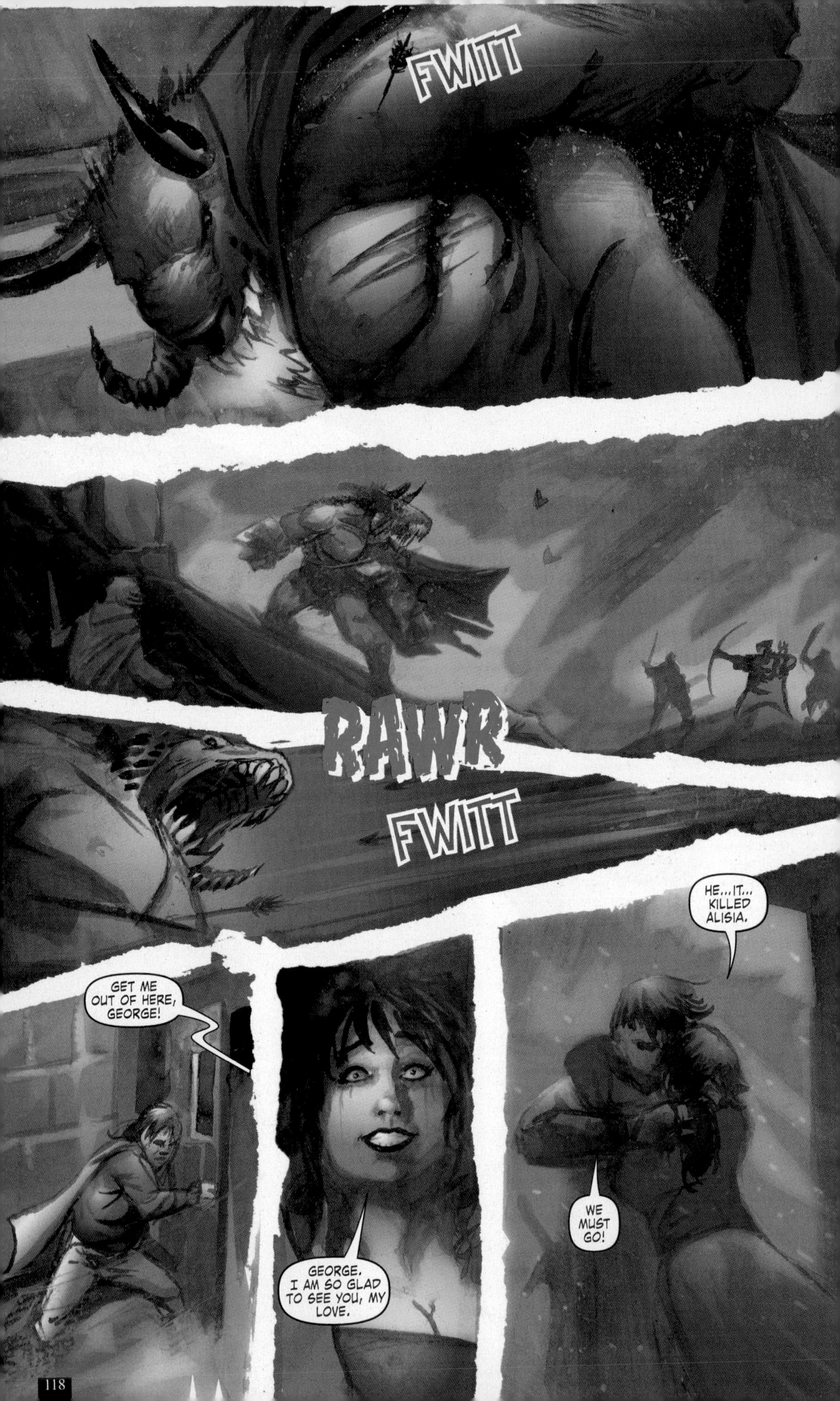
FWITT
RAWR
FWITT
GET ME OUT OF HERE, GEORGE!
GEORGE. I AM SO GLAD TO SEE YOU, MY LOVE.
HE... IT... KILLED ALISIA.
WE MUST GO!

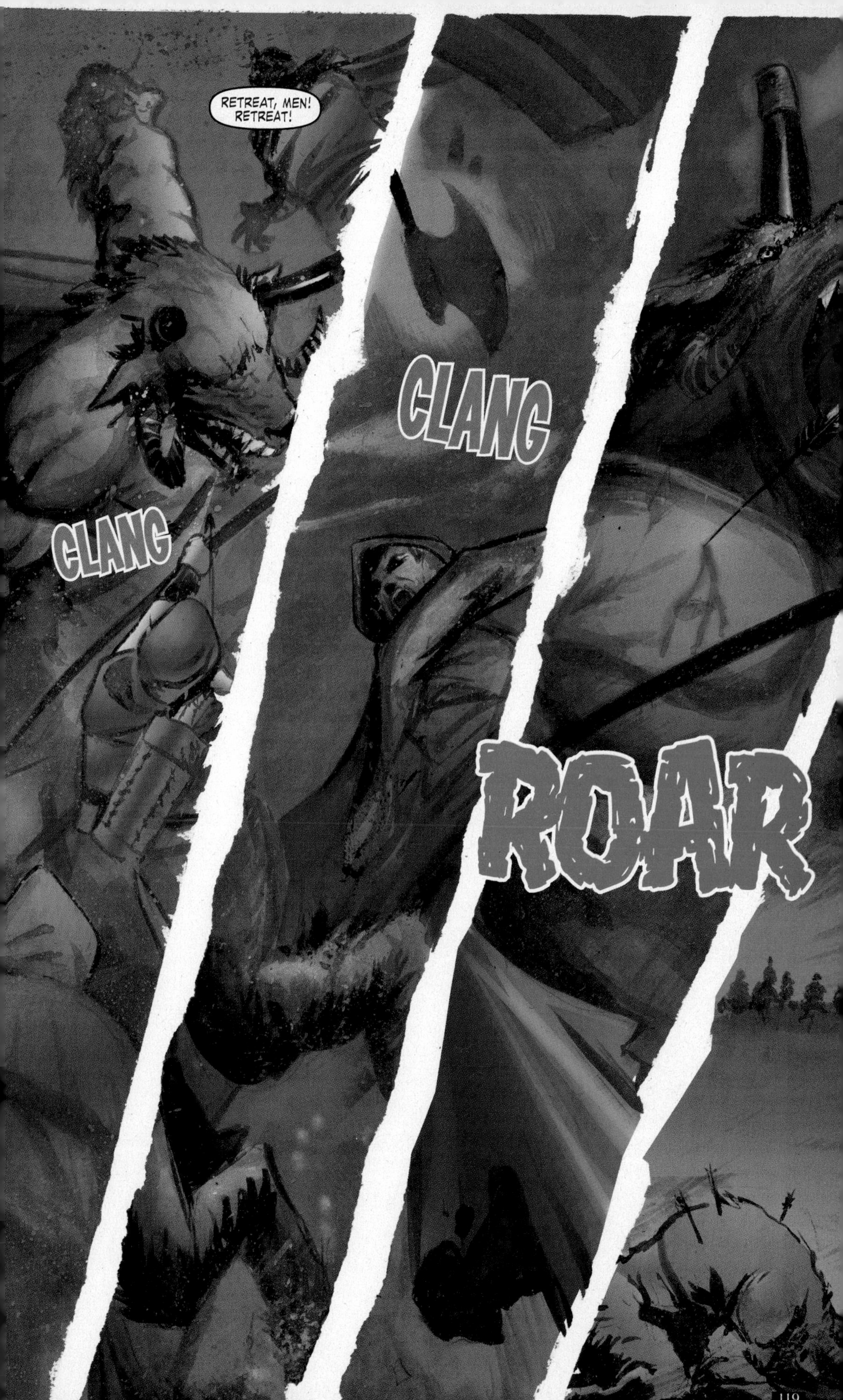
RETREAT, MEN! RETREAT!
CLANG
CLANG
ROAR

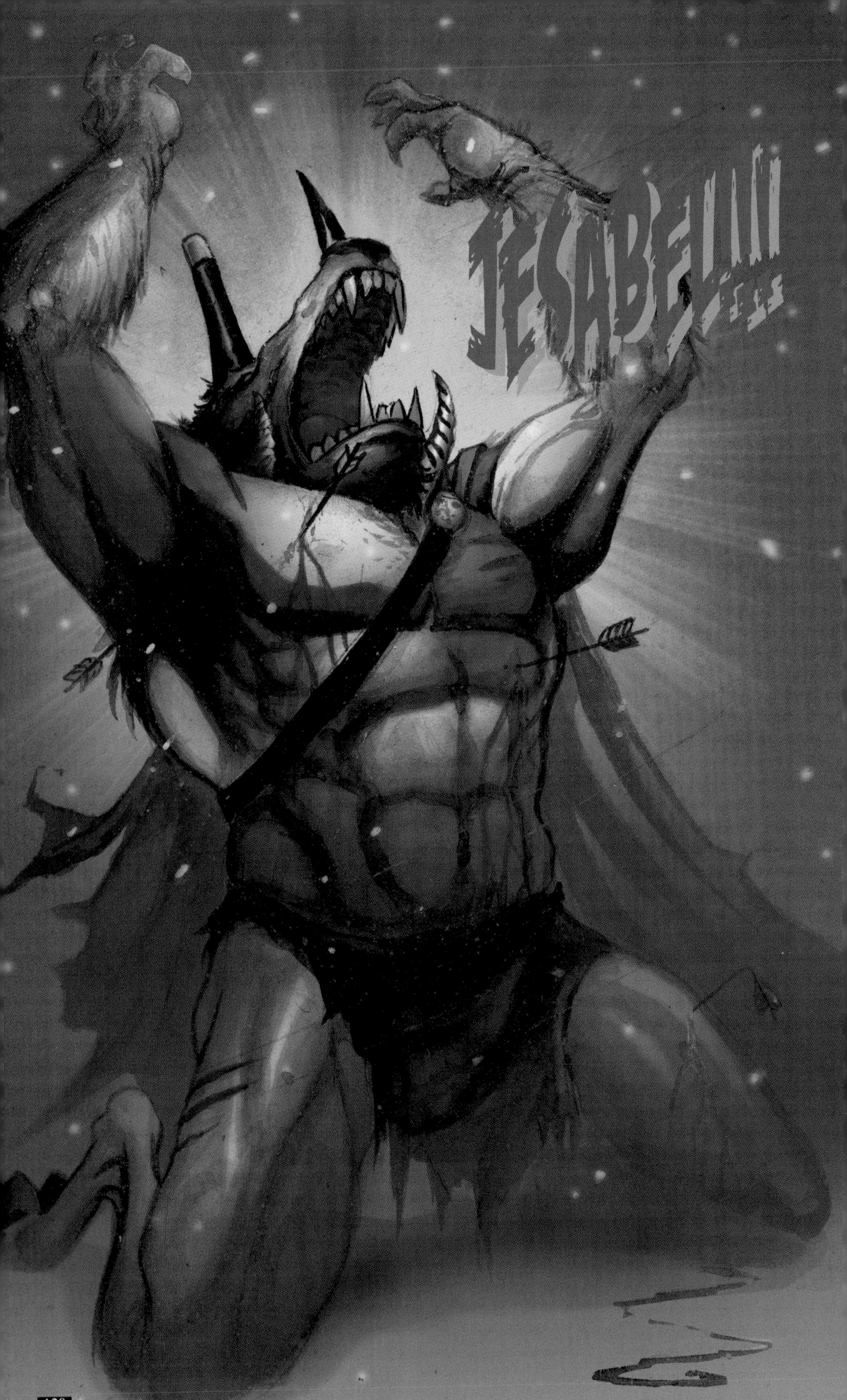
JESABEL!!!

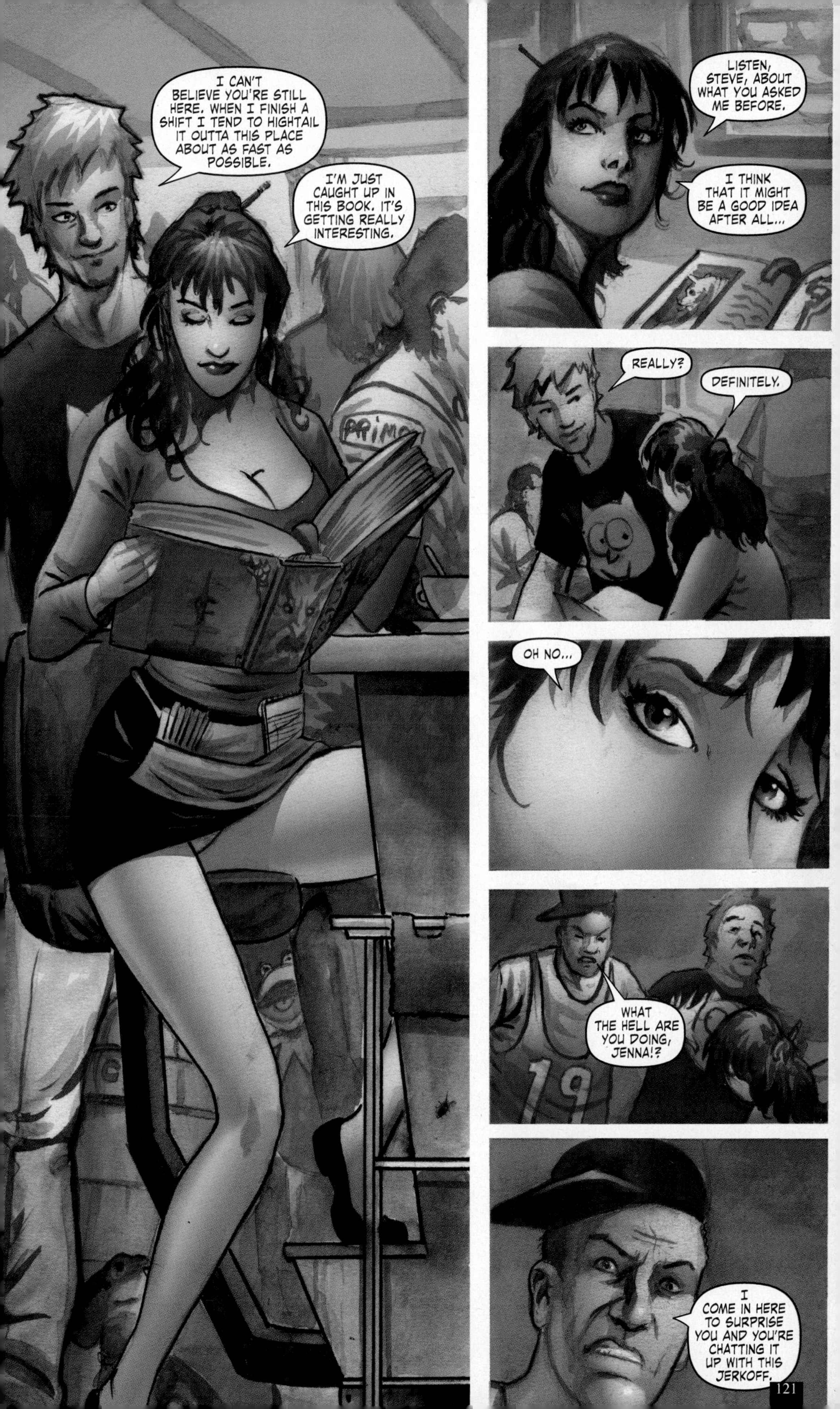
I CAN'T BELIEVE YOU'RE STILL HERE. WHEN I FINISH A SHIFT I TEND TO HIGHTAIL IT OUTTA THIS PLACE ABOUT AS FAST AS POSSIBLE.
I'M JUST CAUGHT UP IN THIS BOOK. IT'S GETTING REALLY INTERESTING.
LISTEN, STEVE, ABOUT WHAT YOU ASKED ME BEFORE.
I THINK THAT IT MIGHT BE A GOOD IDEA AFTER ALL...
REALLY?
DEFINITELY.
OH NO...
WHAT THE HELL ARE YOU DOING, JENNA!?
I COME IN HERE TO SURPRISE YOU AND YOU'RE CHATTING IT UP WITH THIS JERKOFF.

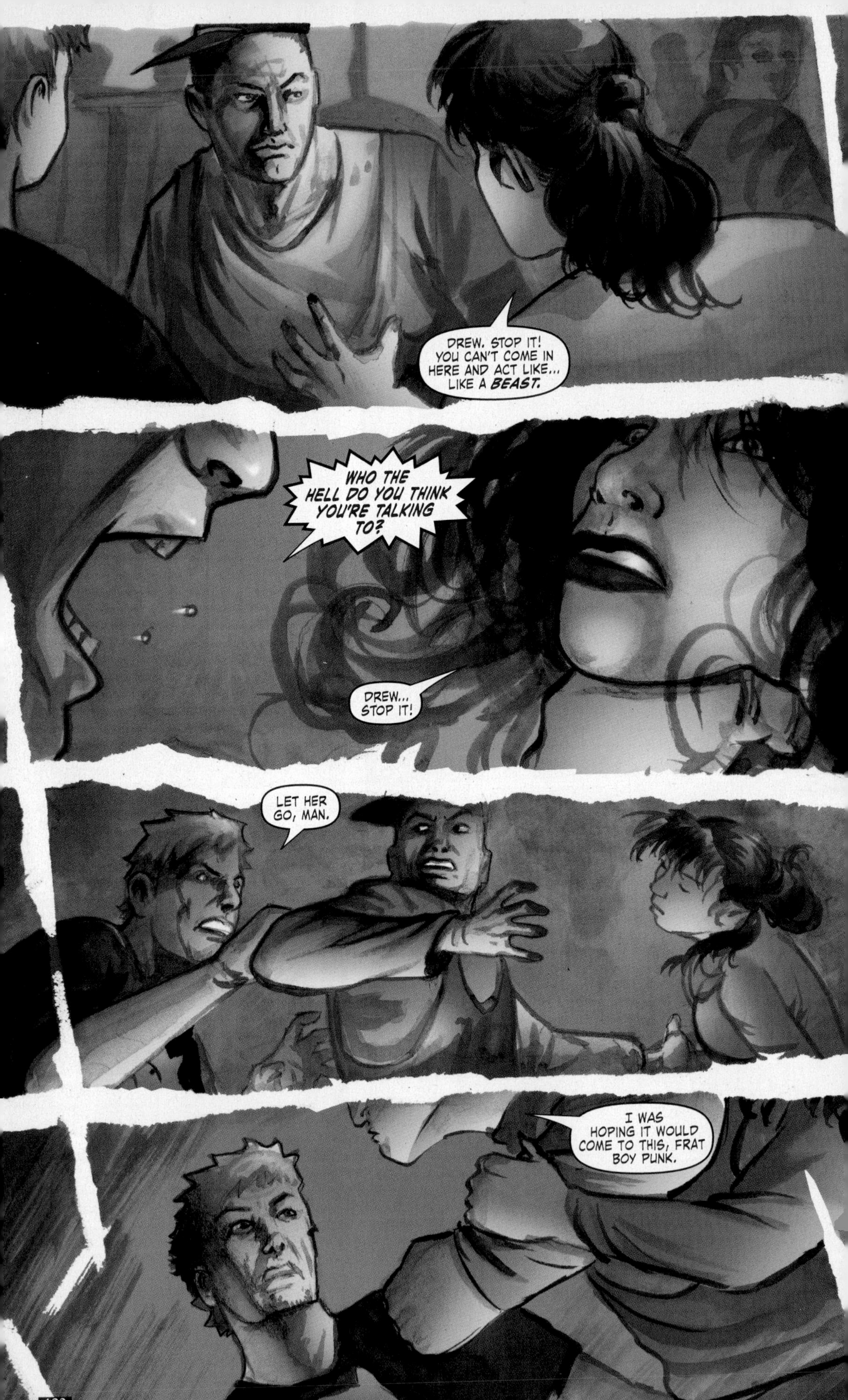
DREW. STOP IT! YOU CAN'T COME IN HERE AND ACT LIKE... LIKE A BEAST.
WHO THE HELL DO YOU THINK YOU'RE TALKING TO?
DREW... STOP IT!
LET HER GO, MAN.
I WAS HOPING IT WOULD COME TO THIS, FRAT BOY PUNK.

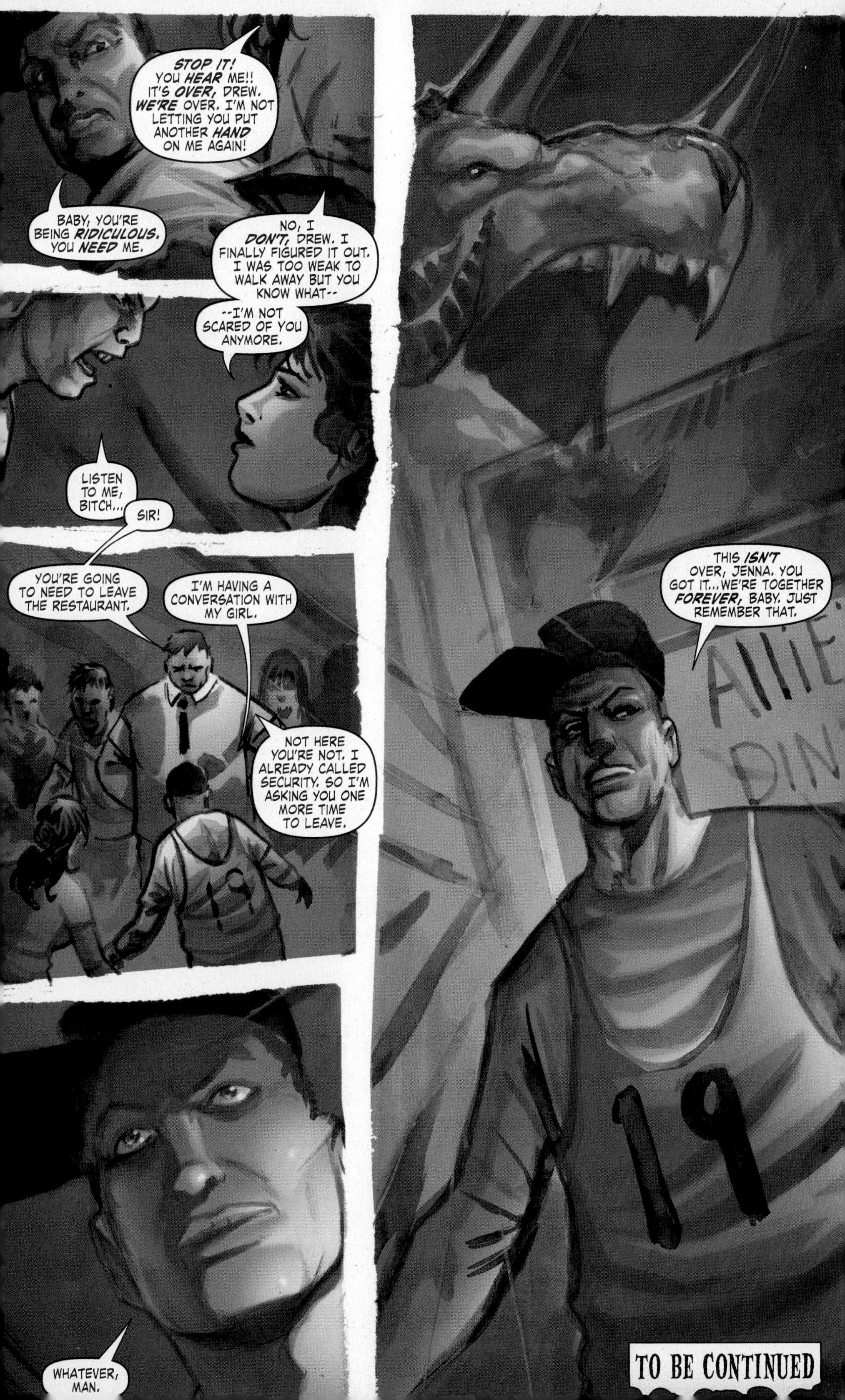
STOP IT! YOU HEAR ME!! IT'S OVER, DREW. WE'RE OVER. I'M NOT LETTING YOU PUT ANOTHER HAND ON ME AGAIN!
BABY, YOU'RE BEING RIDICULOUS. YOU NEED ME.
NO, I DON'T, DREW. I FINALLY FIGURED IT OUT. I WAS TOO WEAK TO WALK AWAY BUT YOU KNOW WHAT--
--I'M NOT SCARED OF YOU ANYMORE.
LISTEN TO ME, BITCH...
SIR!
YOU'RE GOING TO NEED TO LEAVE THE RESTAURANT.
I'M HAVING A CONVERSATION WITH MY GIRL.
NOT HERE YOU'RE NOT. I ALREADY CALLED SECURITY. SO I'M ASKING YOU ONE MORE TIME TO LEAVE.
WHATEVER, MAN.
THIS ISN'T OVER, JENNA. YOU GOT IT...WE'RE TOGETHER FOREVER, BABY. JUST REMEMBER THAT.
TO BE CONTINUED

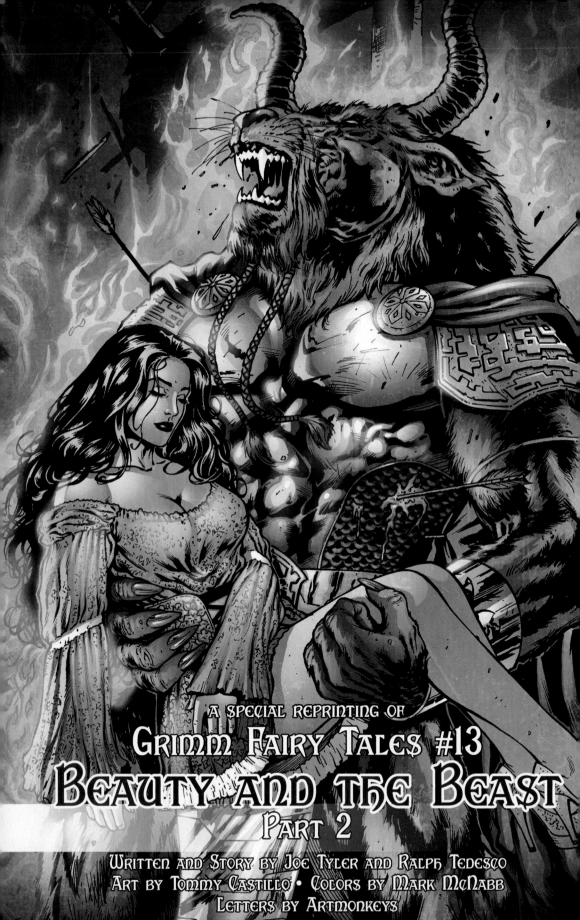

A SPECIAL REPRINTING OF
# Grimm Fairy Tales #13
# Beauty and the Beast
## Part 2

Written and Story by Joe Tyler and Ralph Tedesco
Art by Tommy Castillo • Colors by Mark McNabb
Letters by Artmonkeys

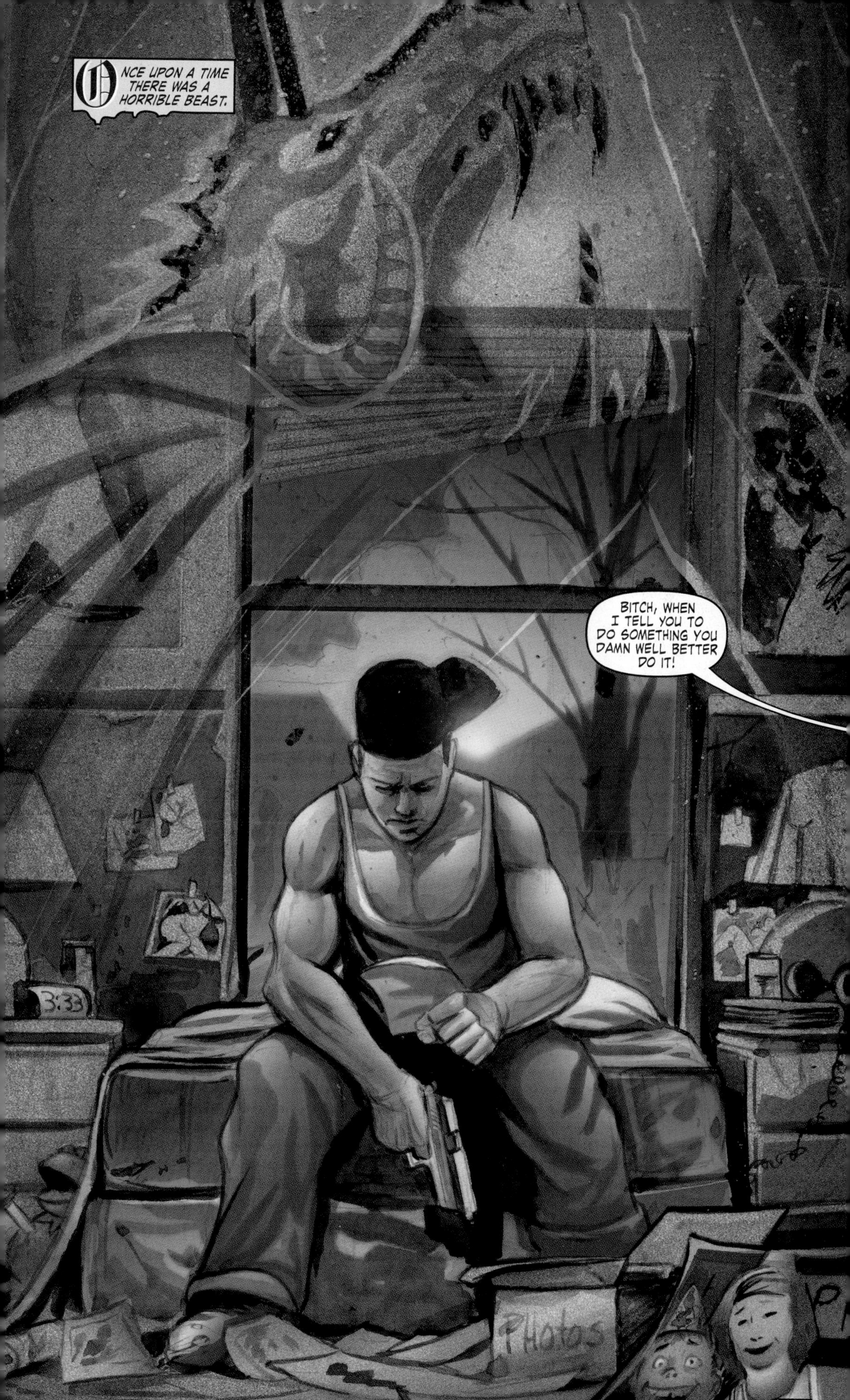
ONCE UPON A TIME THERE WAS A HORRIBLE BEAST.
BITCH, WHEN I TELL YOU TO DO SOMETHING YOU DAMN WELL BETTER DO IT!
3:33
Photos

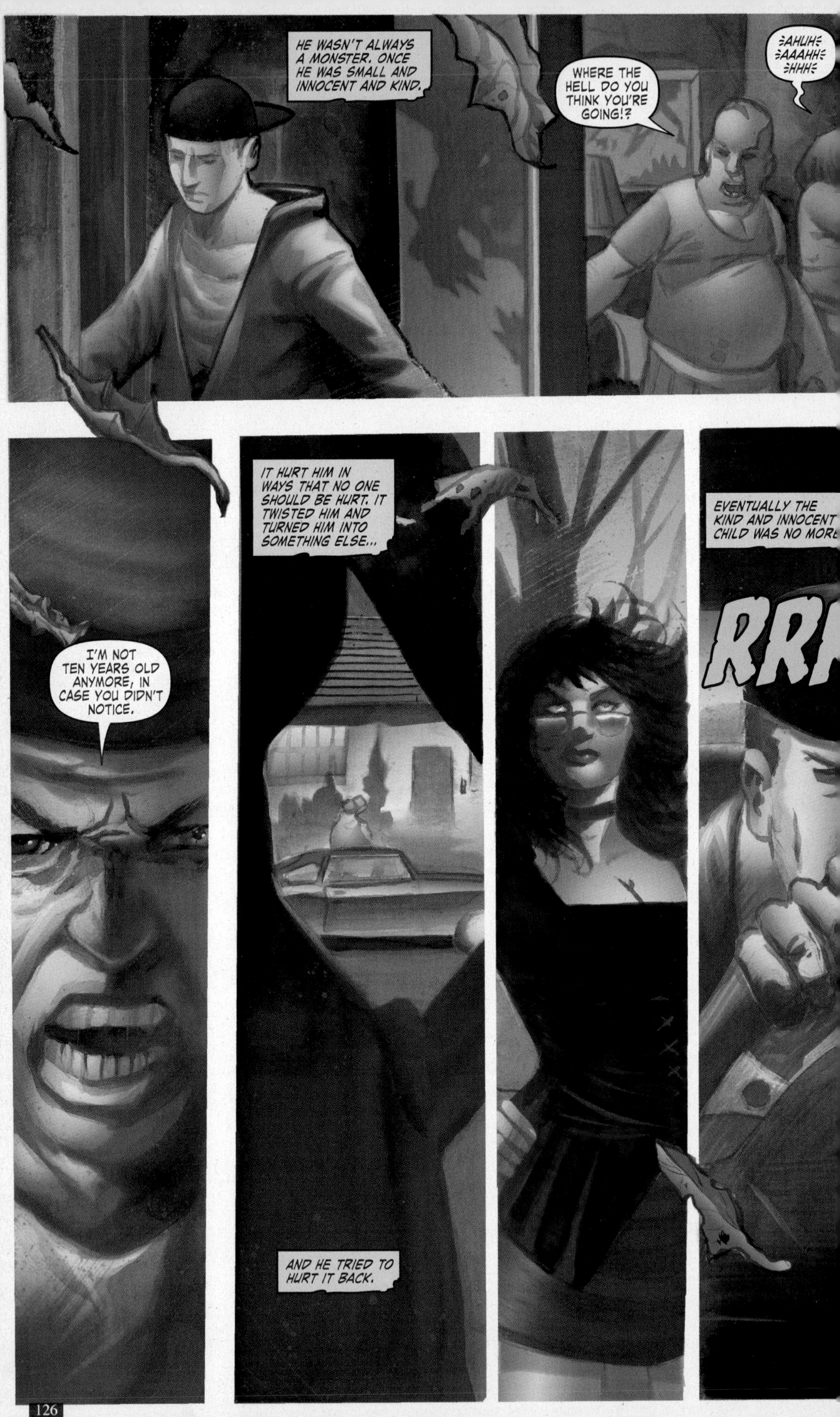
HE WASN'T ALWAYS A MONSTER. ONCE HE WAS SMALL AND INNOCENT AND KIND.
WHERE THE HELL DO YOU THINK YOU'RE GOING!?
AHUH AAAAHH HHH
I'M NOT TEN YEARS OLD ANYMORE, IN CASE YOU DIDN'T NOTICE.
IT HURT HIM IN WAYS THAT NO ONE SHOULD BE HURT. IT TWISTED HIM AND TURNED HIM INTO SOMETHING ELSE...
AND HE TRIED TO HURT IT BACK.
EVENTUALLY THE KIND AND INNOCENT CHILD WAS NO MORE

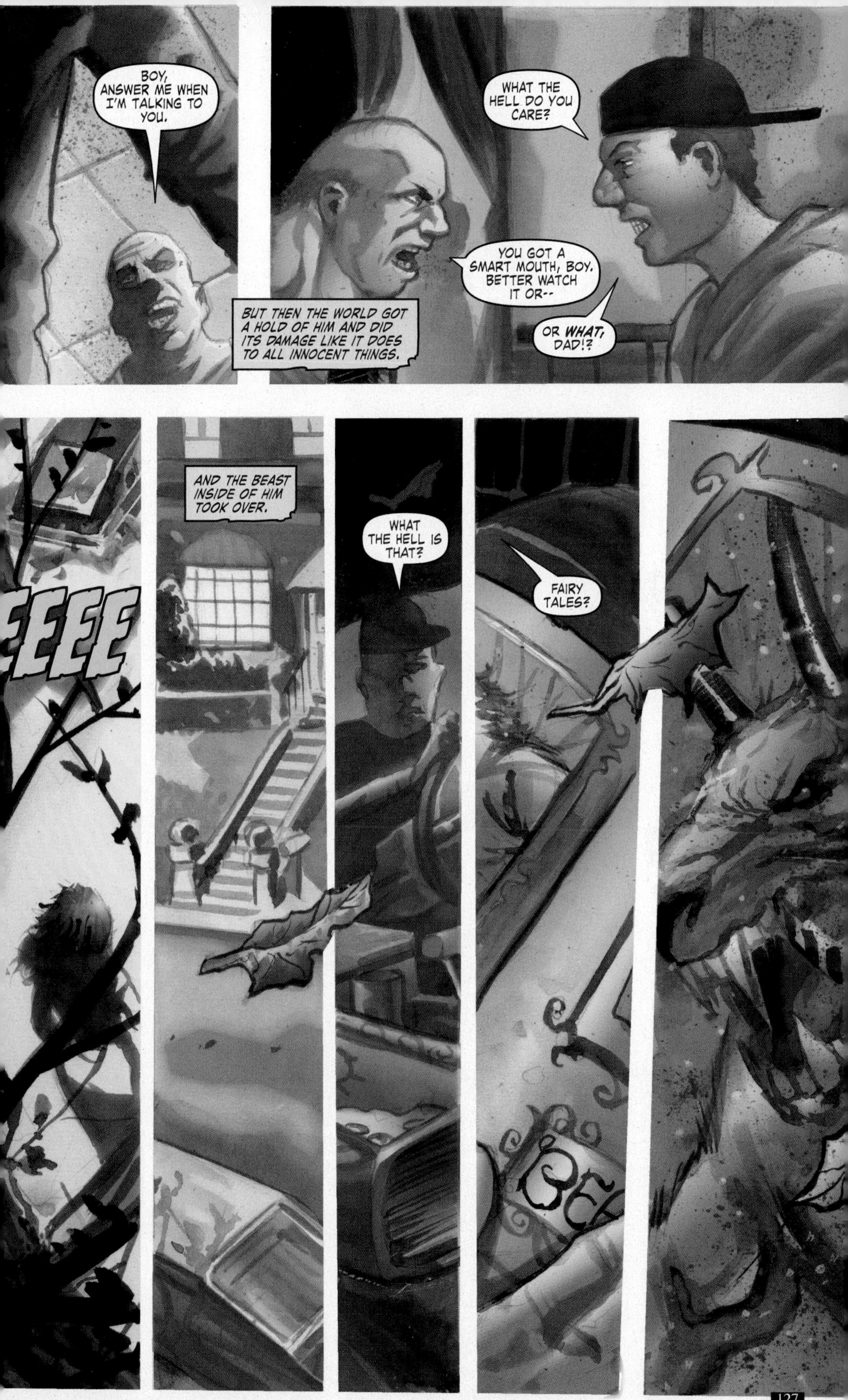

BOY, ANSWER ME WHEN I'M TALKING TO YOU.
WHAT THE HELL DO YOU CARE?
YOU GOT A SMART MOUTH, BOY. BETTER WATCH IT OR--
BUT THEN THE WORLD GOT A HOLD OF HIM AND DID ITS DAMAGE LIKE IT DOES TO ALL INNOCENT THINGS.
OR WHAT, DAD!?
EEEE
AND THE BEAST INSIDE OF HIM TOOK OVER.
WHAT THE HELL IS THAT?
FAIRY TALES?

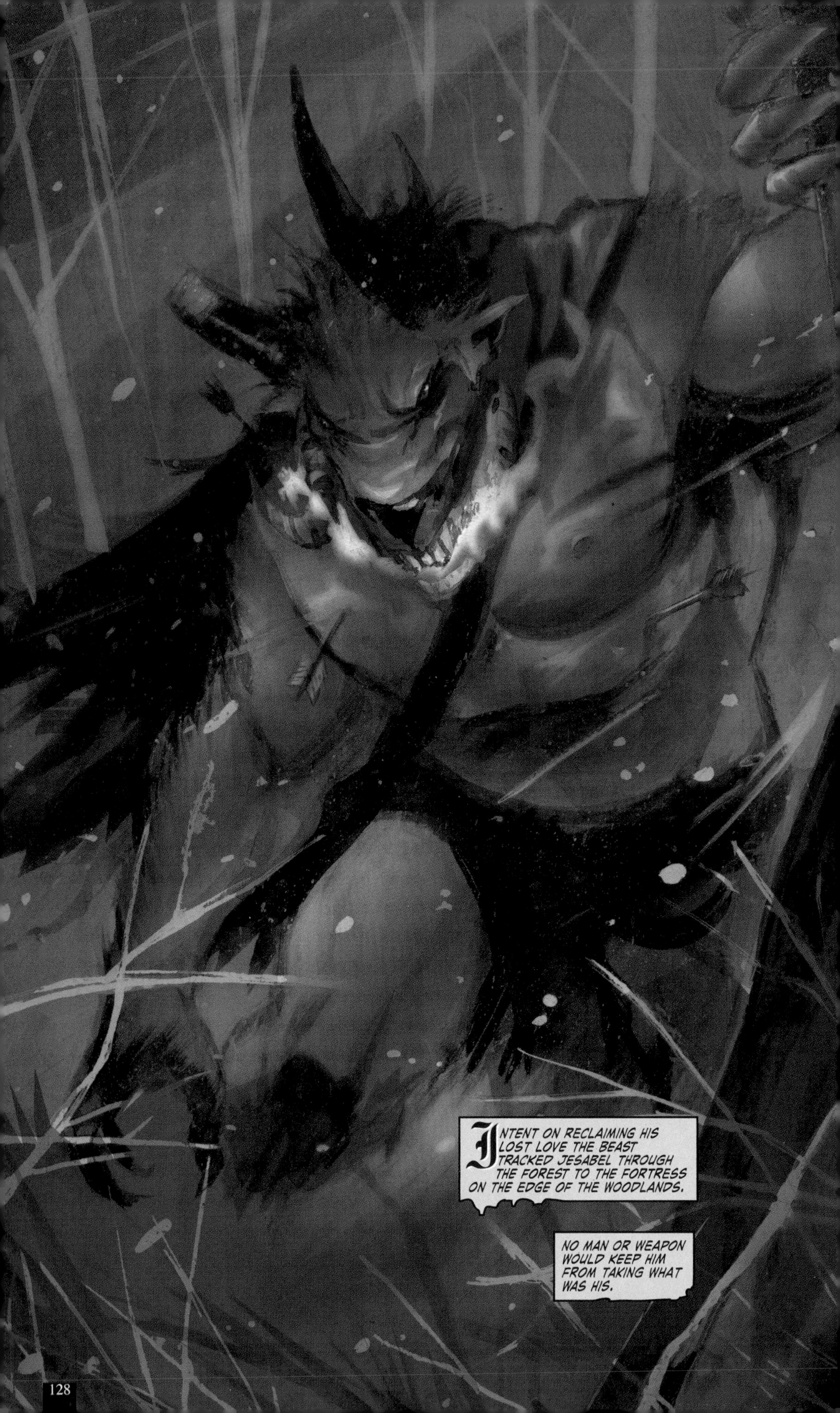
INTENT ON RECLAIMING HIS LOST LOVE THE BEAST TRACKED JESABEL THROUGH THE FOREST TO THE FORTRESS ON THE EDGE OF THE WOODLANDS.
NO MAN OR WEAPON WOULD KEEP HIM FROM TAKING WHAT WAS HIS.

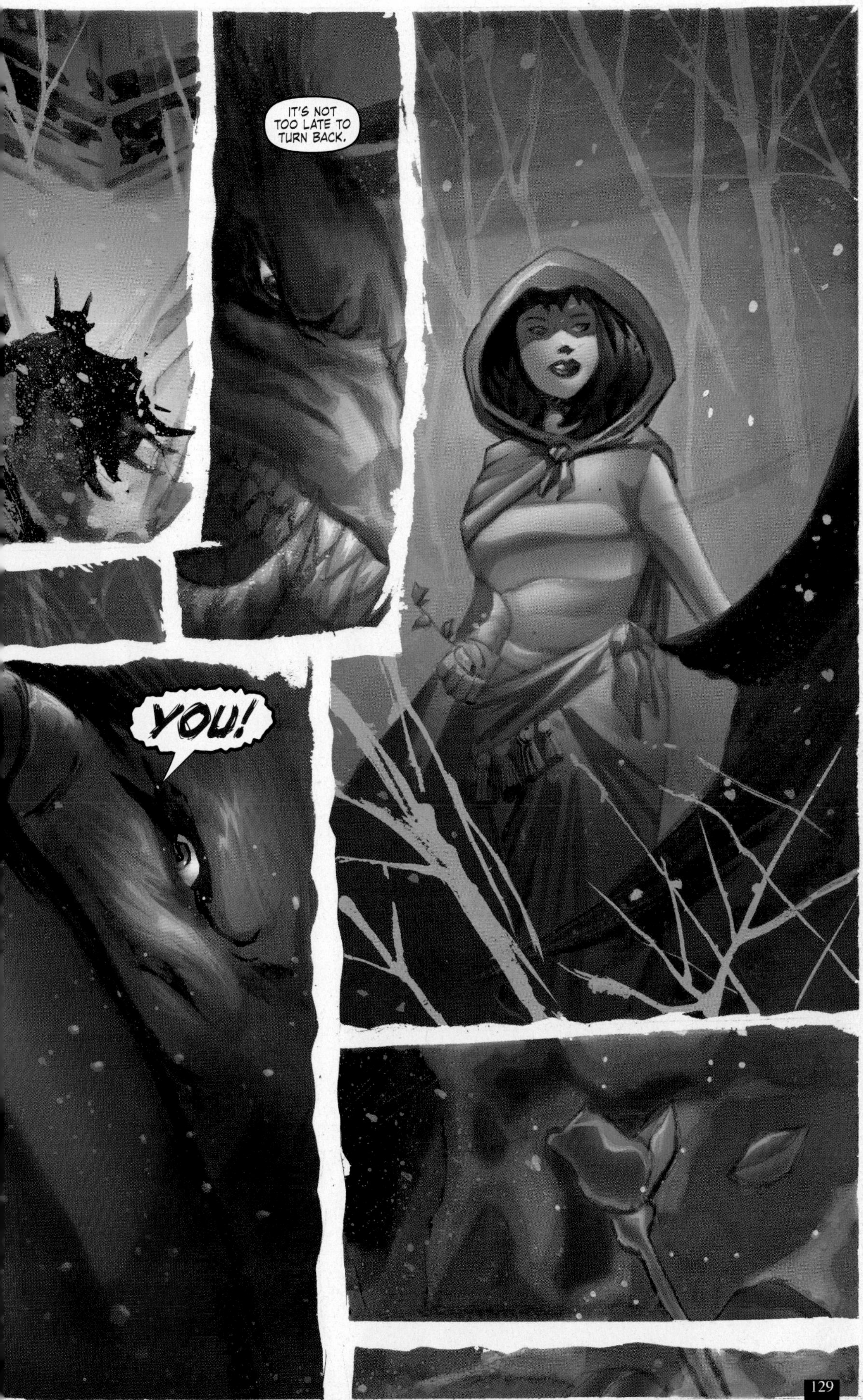
IT'S NOT TOO LATE TO TURN BACK.
YOU!

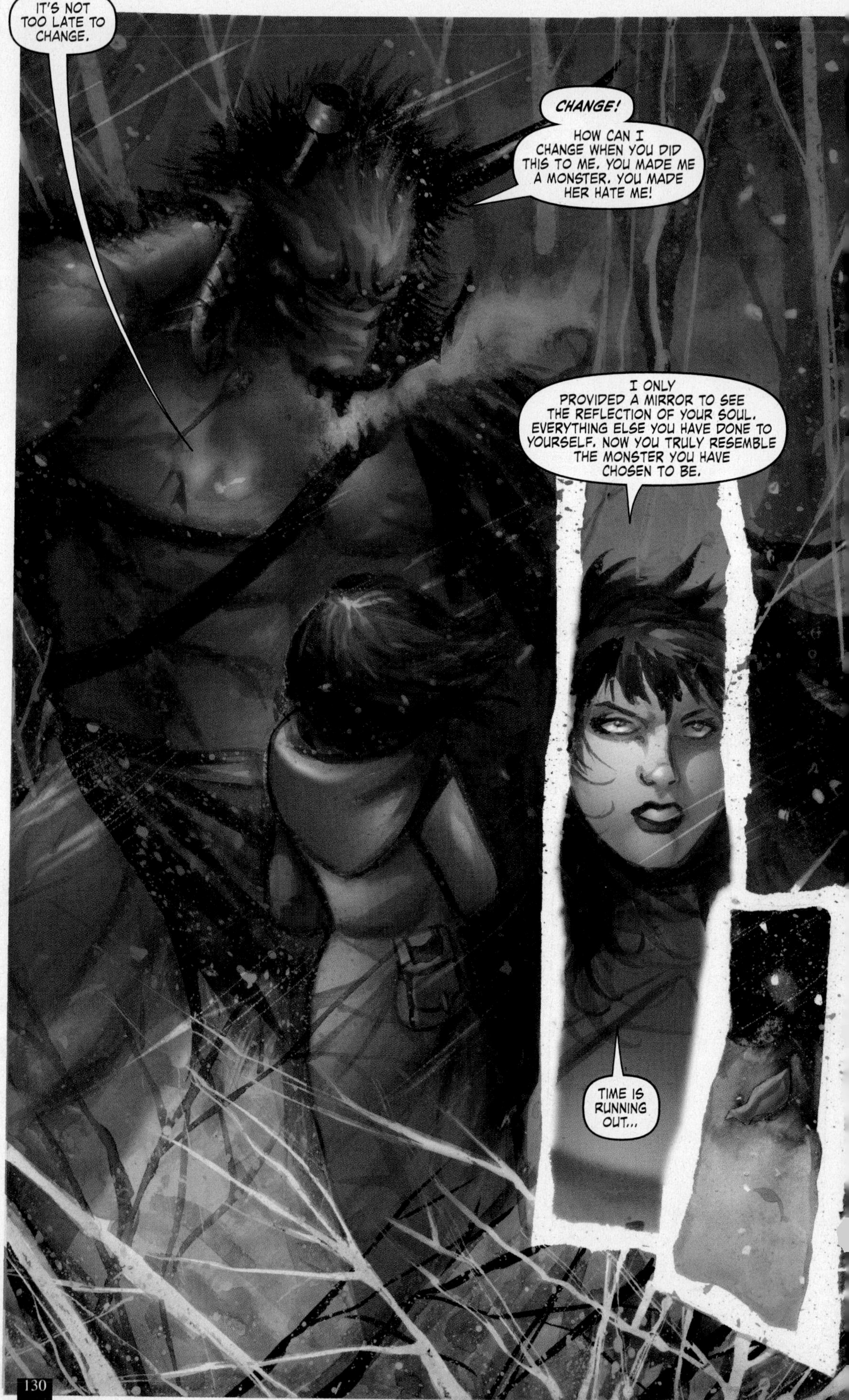
IT'S NOT TOO LATE TO CHANGE.
CHANGE!
HOW CAN I CHANGE WHEN YOU DID THIS TO ME. YOU MADE ME A MONSTER. YOU MADE HER HATE ME!
I ONLY PROVIDED A MIRROR TO SEE THE REFLECTION OF YOUR SOUL. EVERYTHING ELSE YOU HAVE DONE TO YOURSELF. NOW YOU TRULY RESEMBLE THE MONSTER YOU HAVE CHOSEN TO BE.
TIME IS RUNNING OUT...

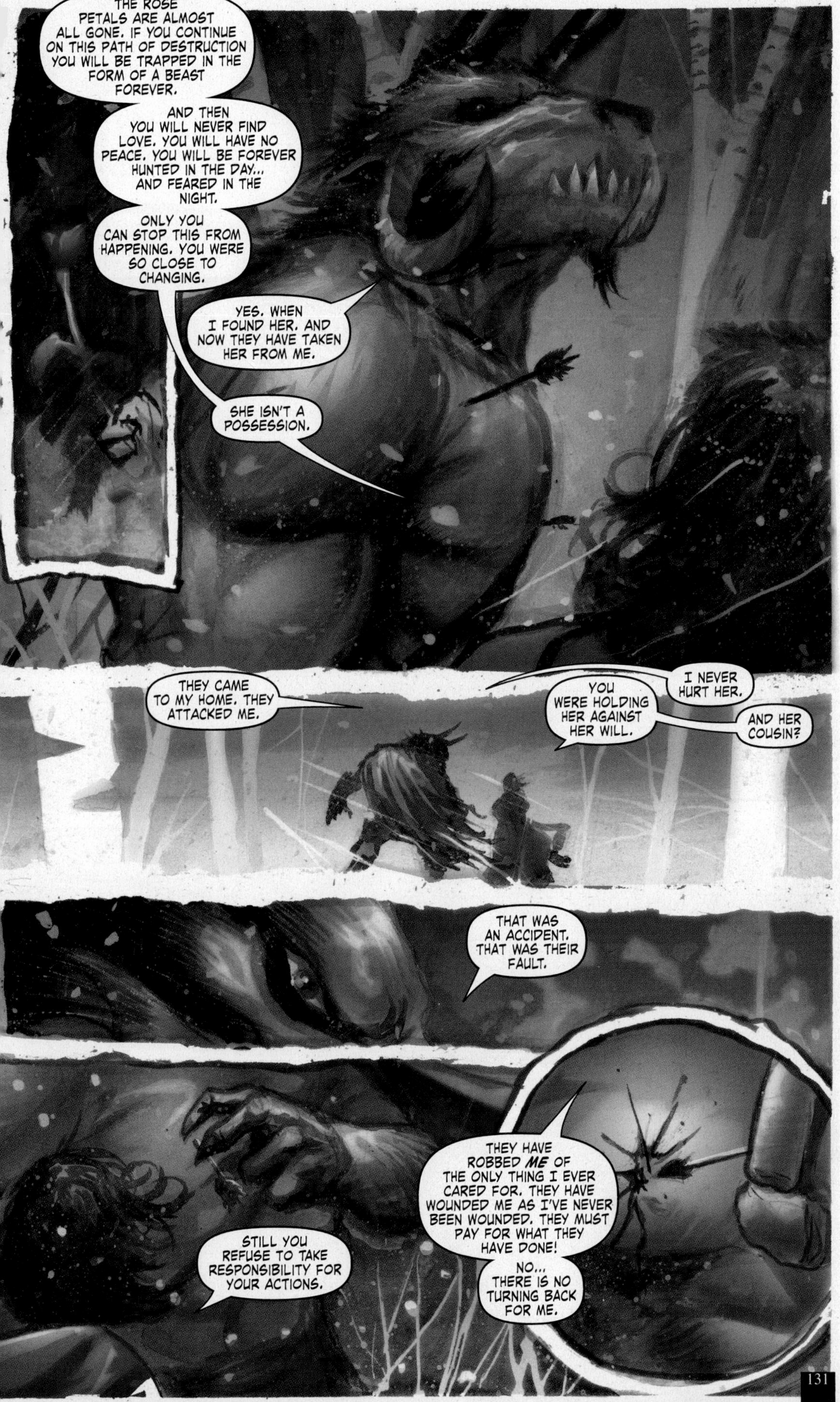
THE ROSE PETALS ARE ALMOST ALL GONE. IF YOU CONTINUE ON THIS PATH OF DESTRUCTION YOU WILL BE TRAPPED IN THE FORM OF A BEAST FOREVER.
AND THEN YOU WILL NEVER FIND LOVE. YOU WILL HAVE NO PEACE. YOU WILL BE FOREVER HUNTED IN THE DAY... AND FEARED IN THE NIGHT.
ONLY YOU CAN STOP THIS FROM HAPPENING. YOU WERE SO CLOSE TO CHANGING.
YES. WHEN I FOUND HER. AND NOW THEY HAVE TAKEN HER FROM ME.
SHE ISN'T A POSSESSION.
THEY CAME TO MY HOME. THEY ATTACKED ME.
YOU WERE HOLDING HER AGAINST HER WILL.
I NEVER HURT HER.
AND HER COUSIN?
THAT WAS AN ACCIDENT. THAT WAS THEIR FAULT.
STILL YOU REFUSE TO TAKE RESPONSIBILITY FOR YOUR ACTIONS.
THEY HAVE ROBBED *ME* OF THE ONLY THING I EVER CARED FOR. THEY HAVE WOUNDED ME AS I'VE NEVER BEEN WOUNDED. THEY MUST PAY FOR WHAT THEY HAVE DONE!
NO... THERE IS NO TURNING BACK FOR ME.

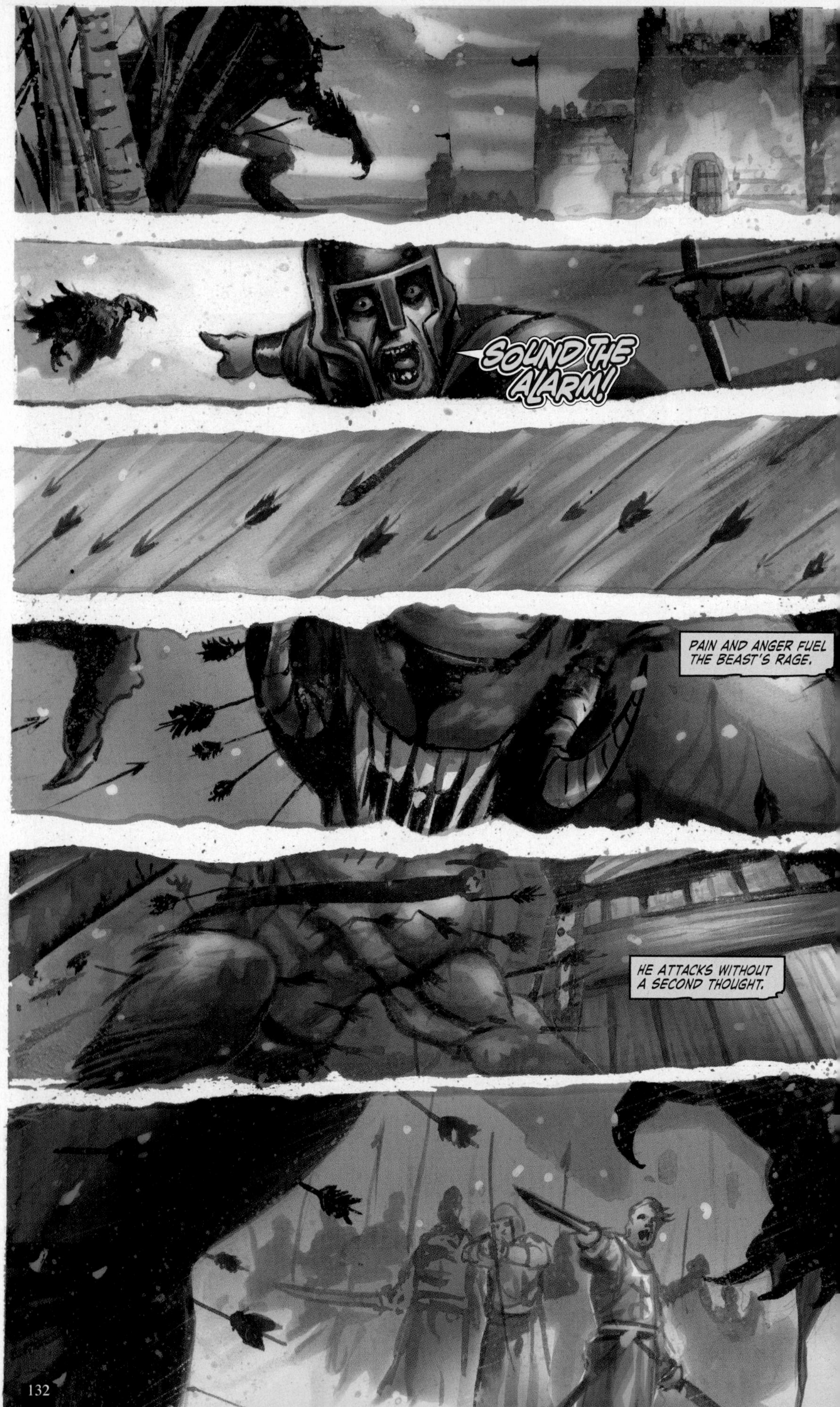
SOUND THE ALARM!
PAIN AND ANGER FUEL THE BEAST'S RAGE.
HE ATTACKS WITHOUT A SECOND THOUGHT.

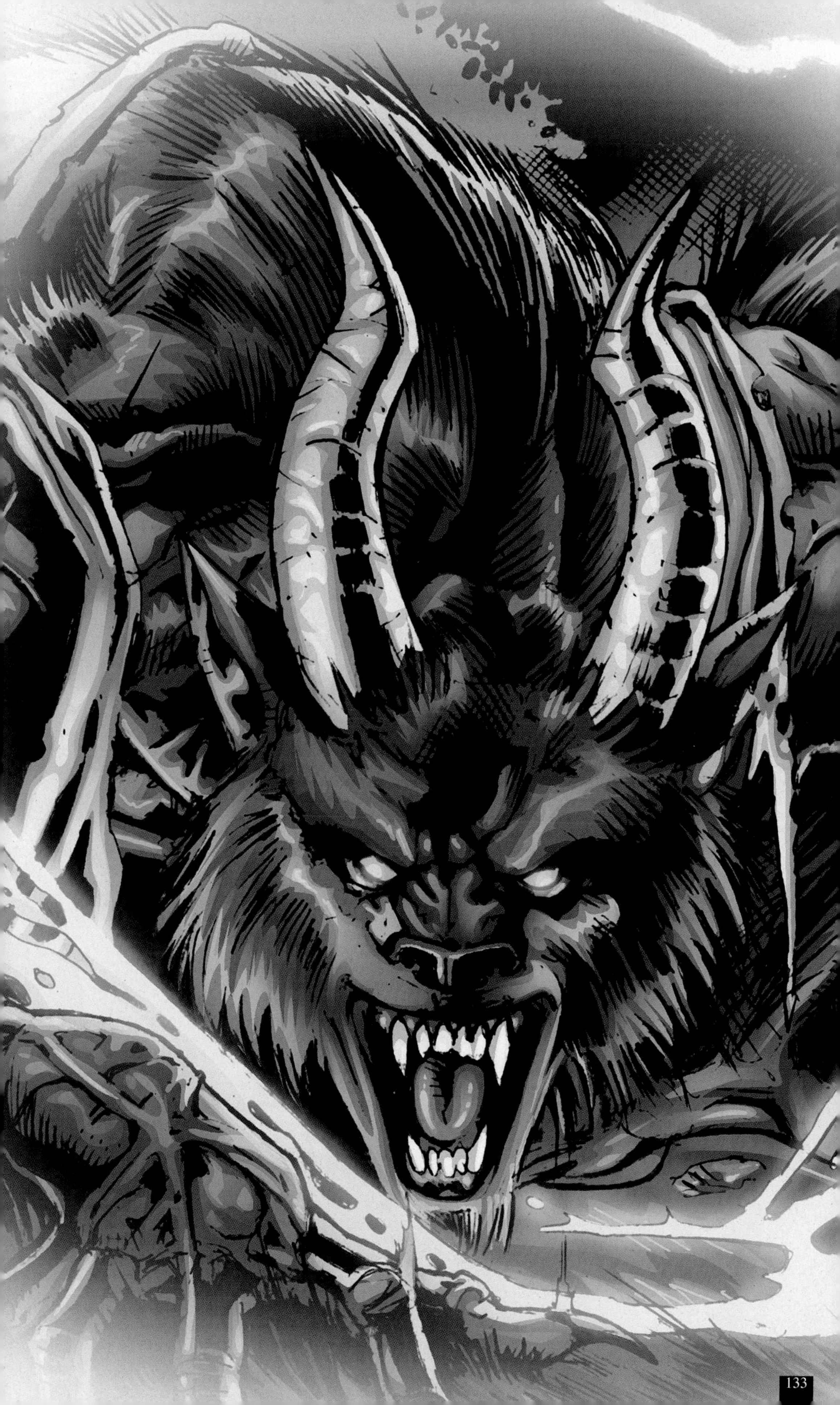

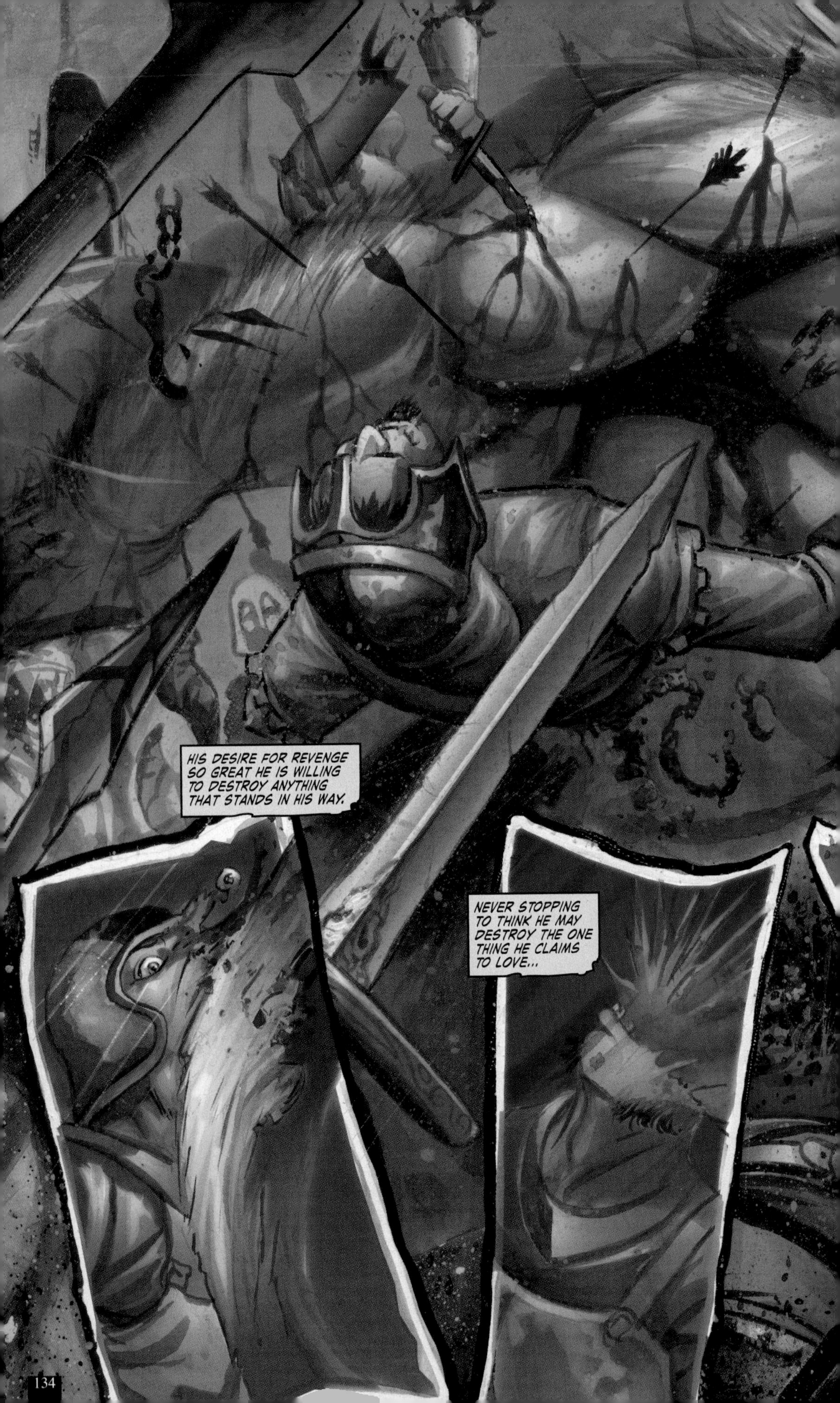
HIS DESIRE FOR REVENGE SO GREAT HE IS WILLING TO DESTROY ANYTHING THAT STANDS IN HIS WAY.
NEVER STOPPING TO THINK HE MAY DESTROY THE ONE THING HE CLAIMS TO LOVE...

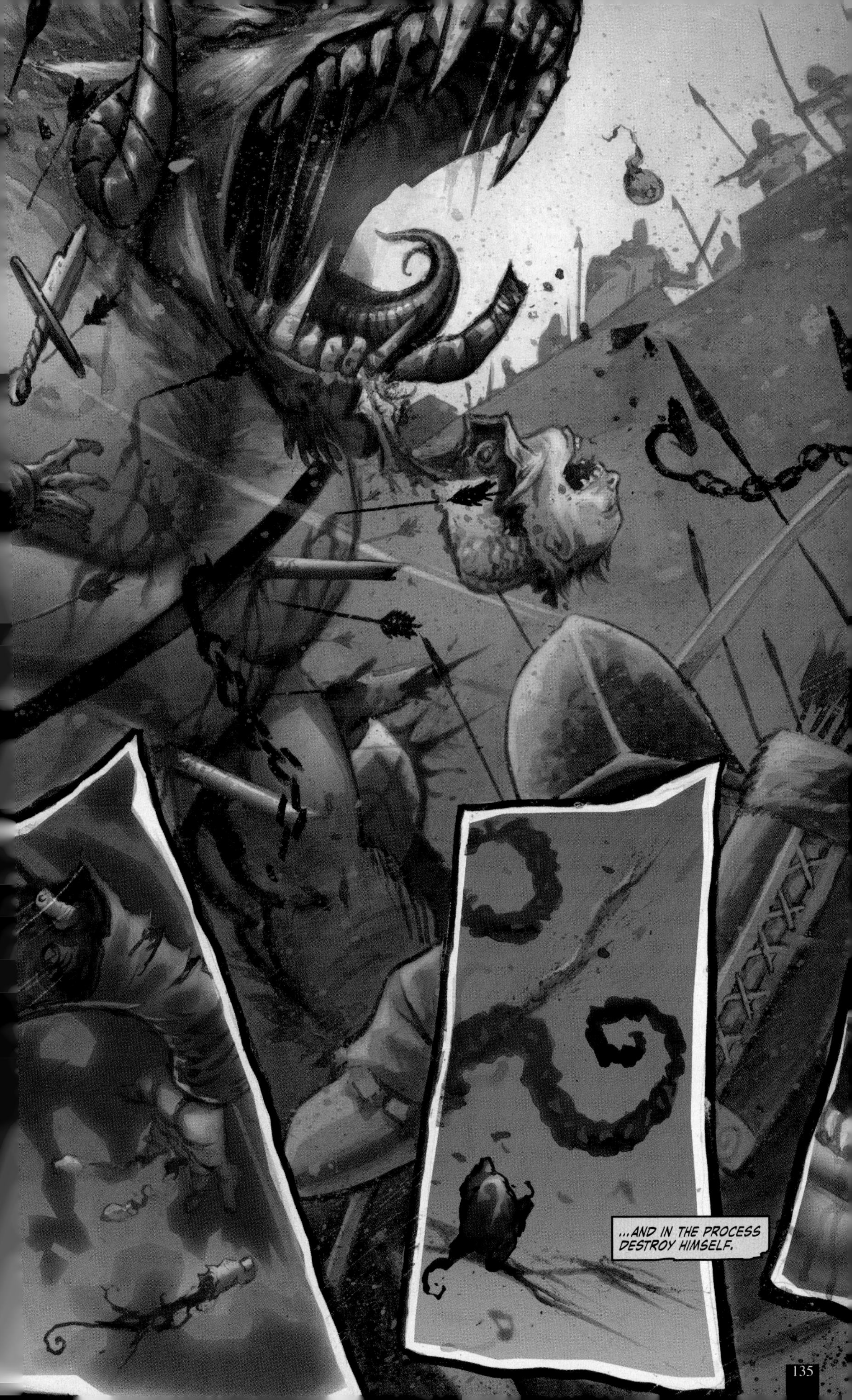
...AND IN THE PROCESS DESTROY HIMSELF.

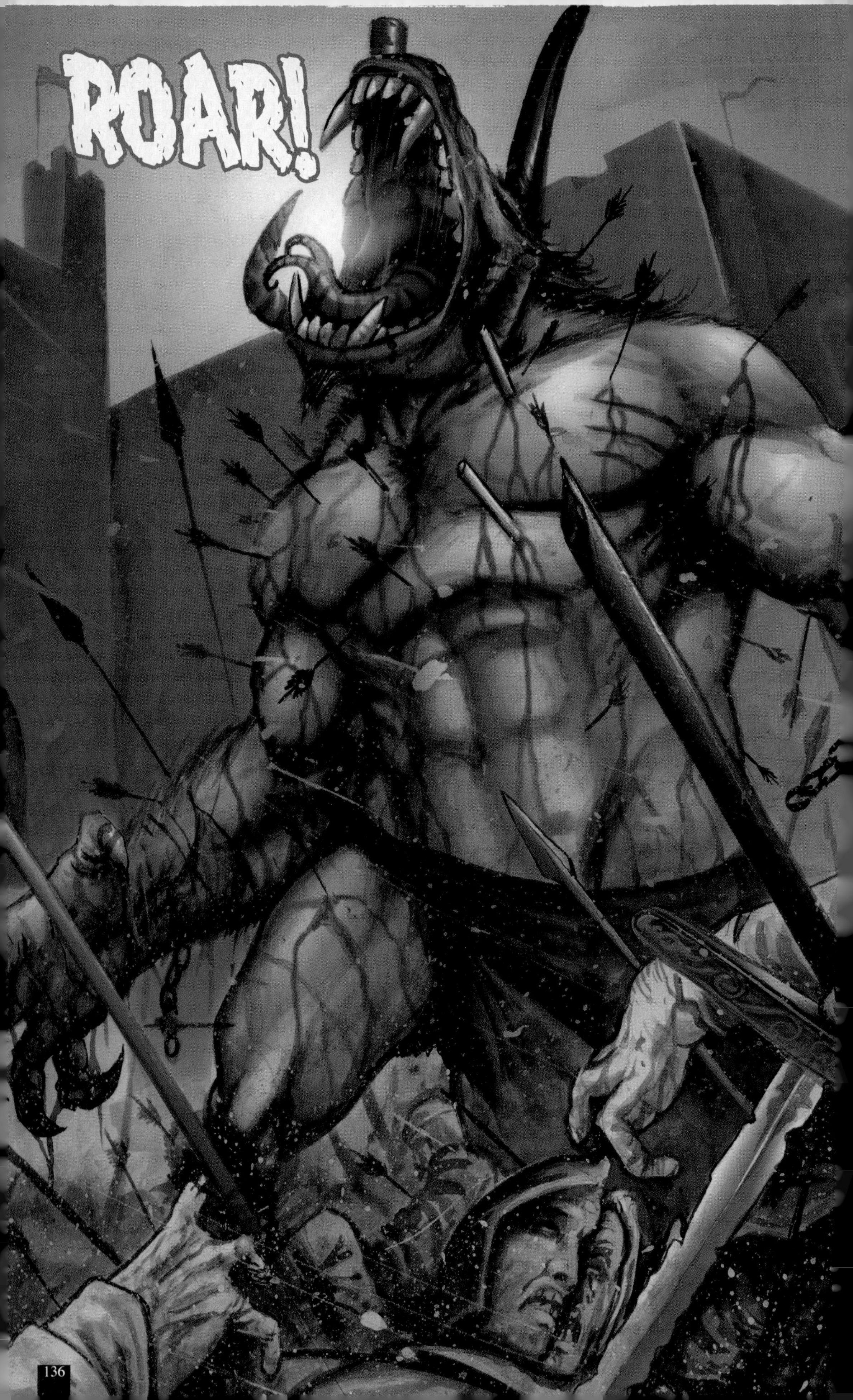
ROAR!

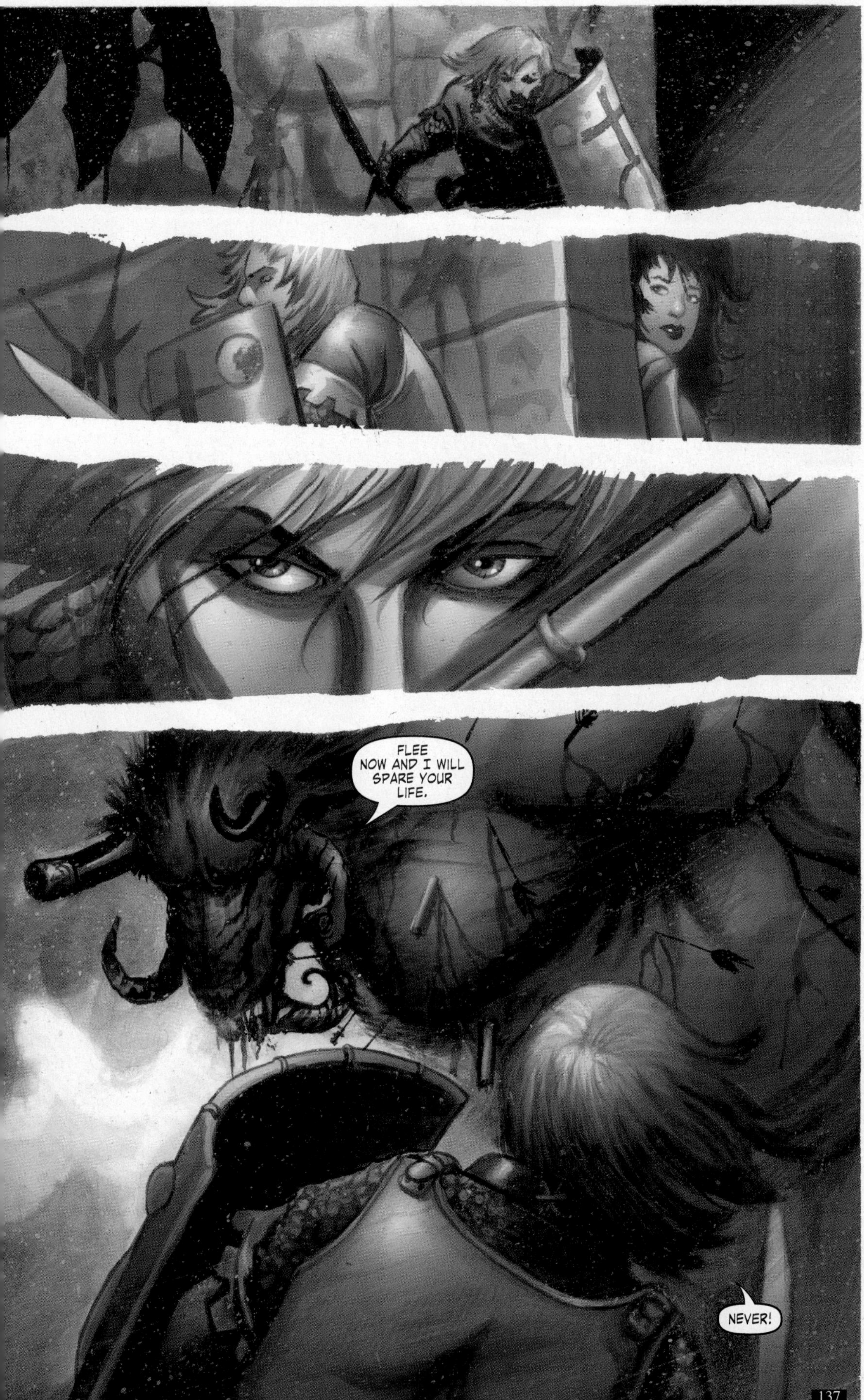
FLEE NOW AND I WILL SPARE YOUR LIFE.
NEVER!

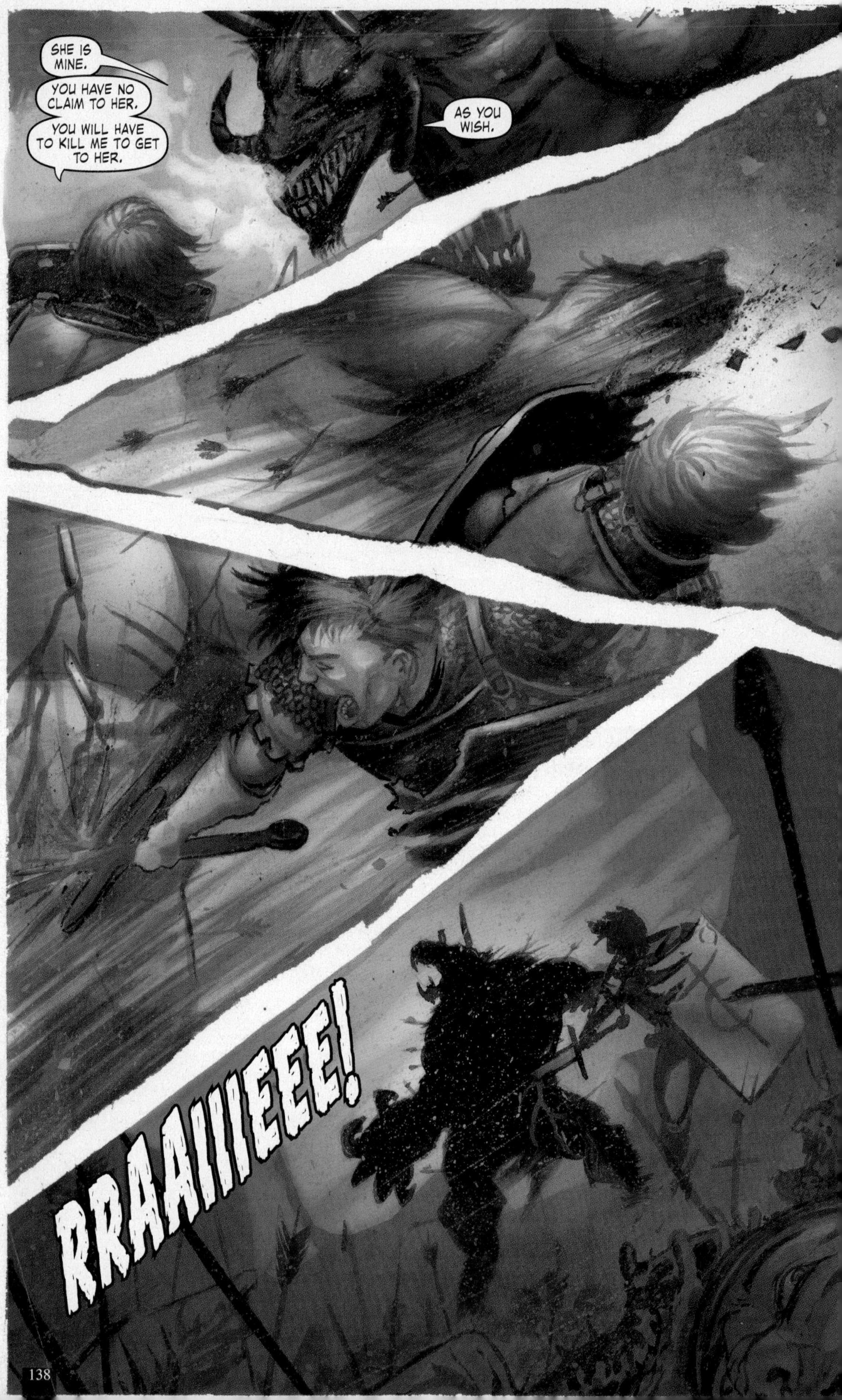
SHE IS MINE.
YOU HAVE NO CLAIM TO HER.
YOU WILL HAVE TO KILL ME TO GET TO HER.
AS YOU WISH.
RRAAIIIEEE!

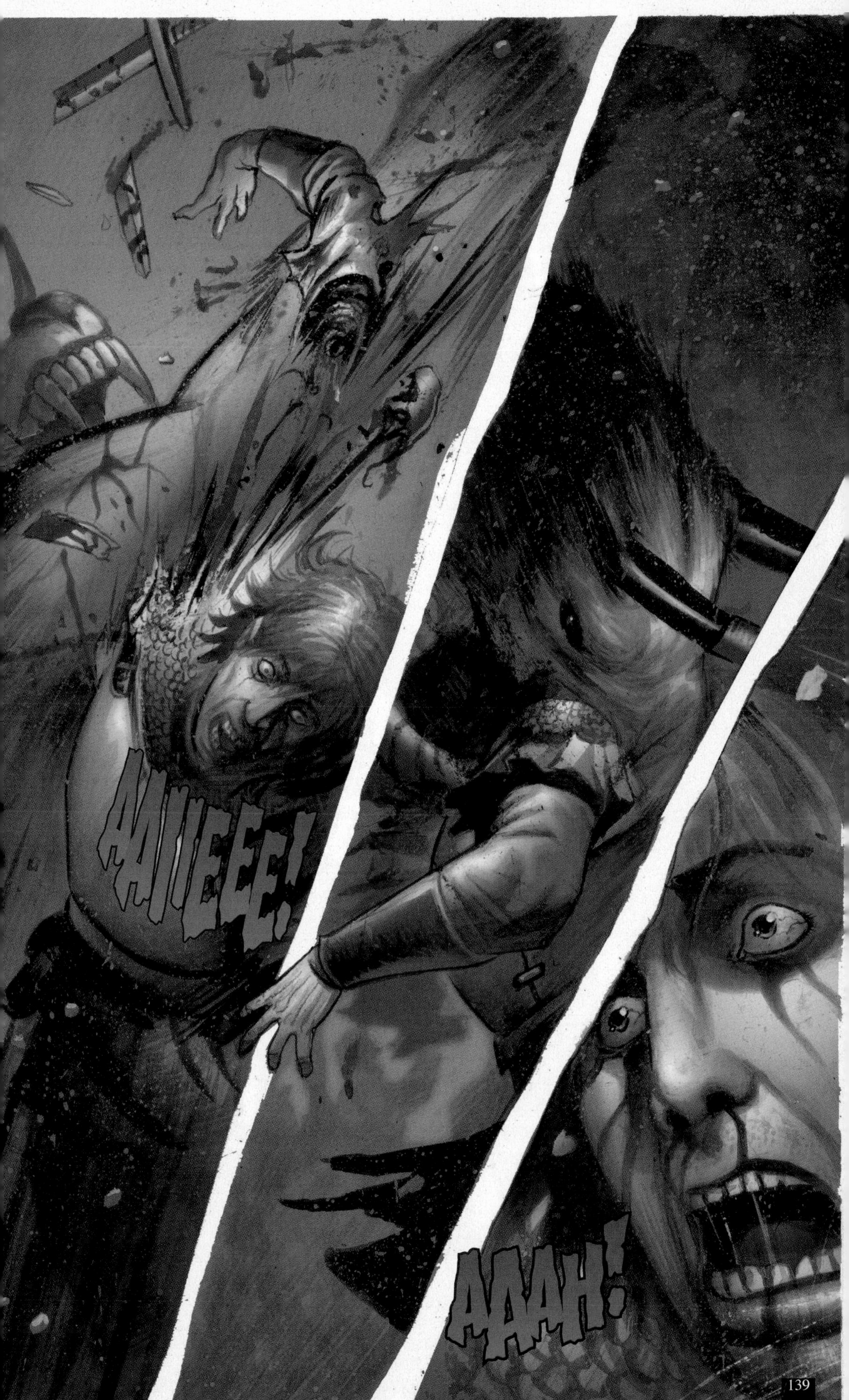
AAIIEEE!
AAAH!

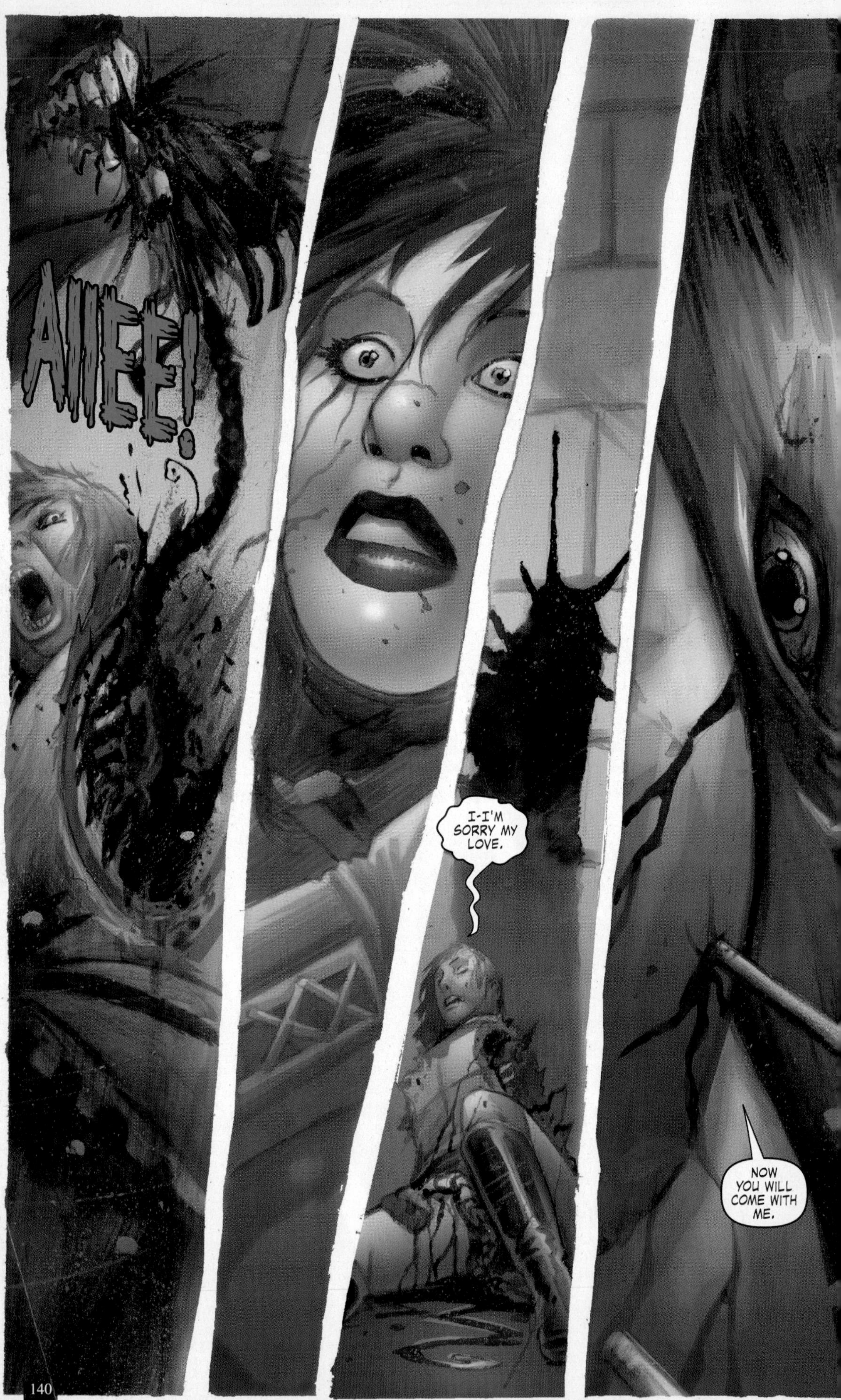
AIIEE!
I-I'M SORRY MY LOVE.
NOW YOU WILL COME WITH ME.

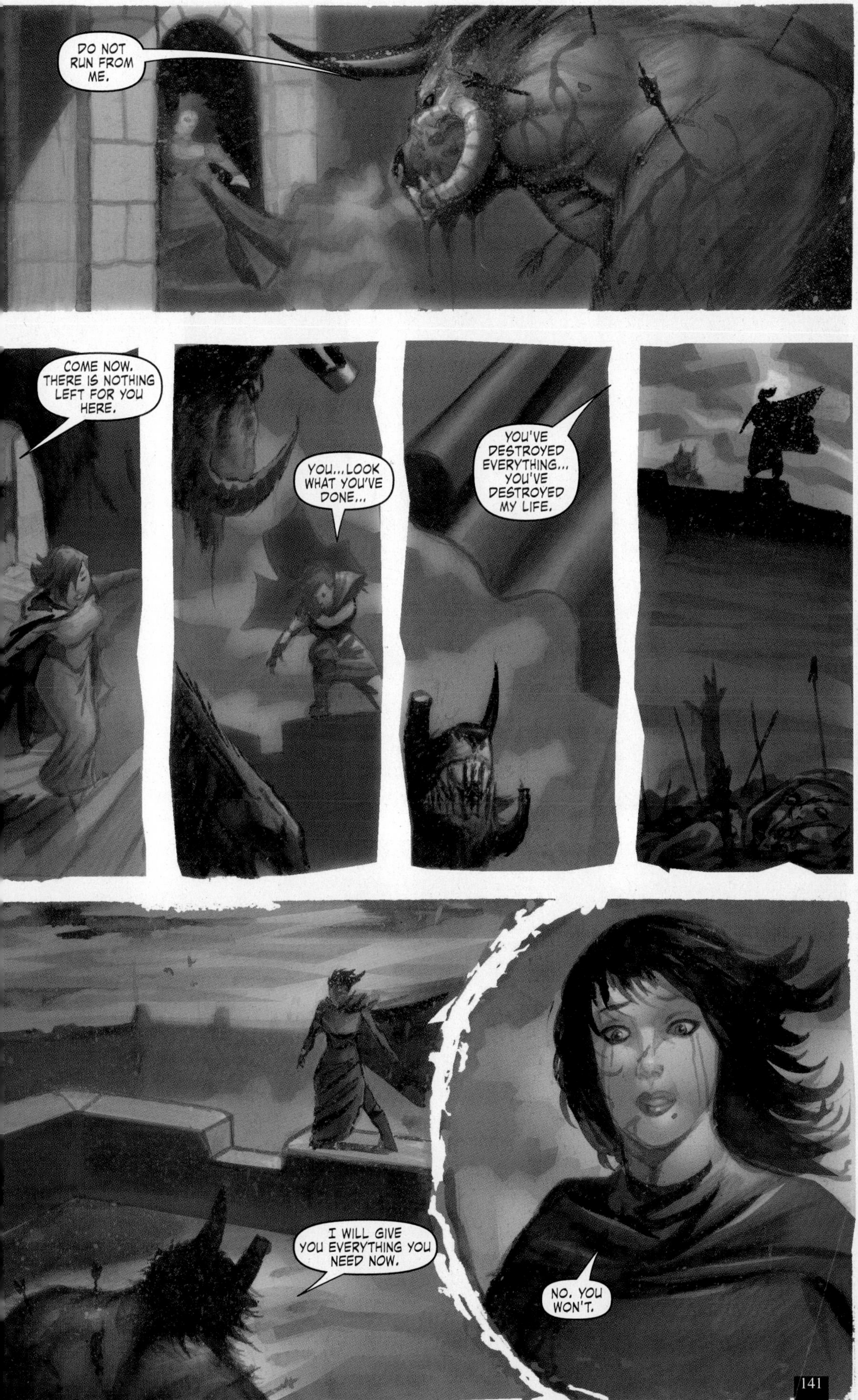
DO NOT RUN FROM ME.
COME NOW. THERE IS NOTHING LEFT FOR YOU HERE.
YOU...LOOK WHAT YOU'VE DONE...
YOU'VE DESTROYED EVERYTHING... YOU'VE DESTROYED MY LIFE.
I WILL GIVE YOU EVERYTHING YOU NEED NOW.
NO. YOU WON'T.

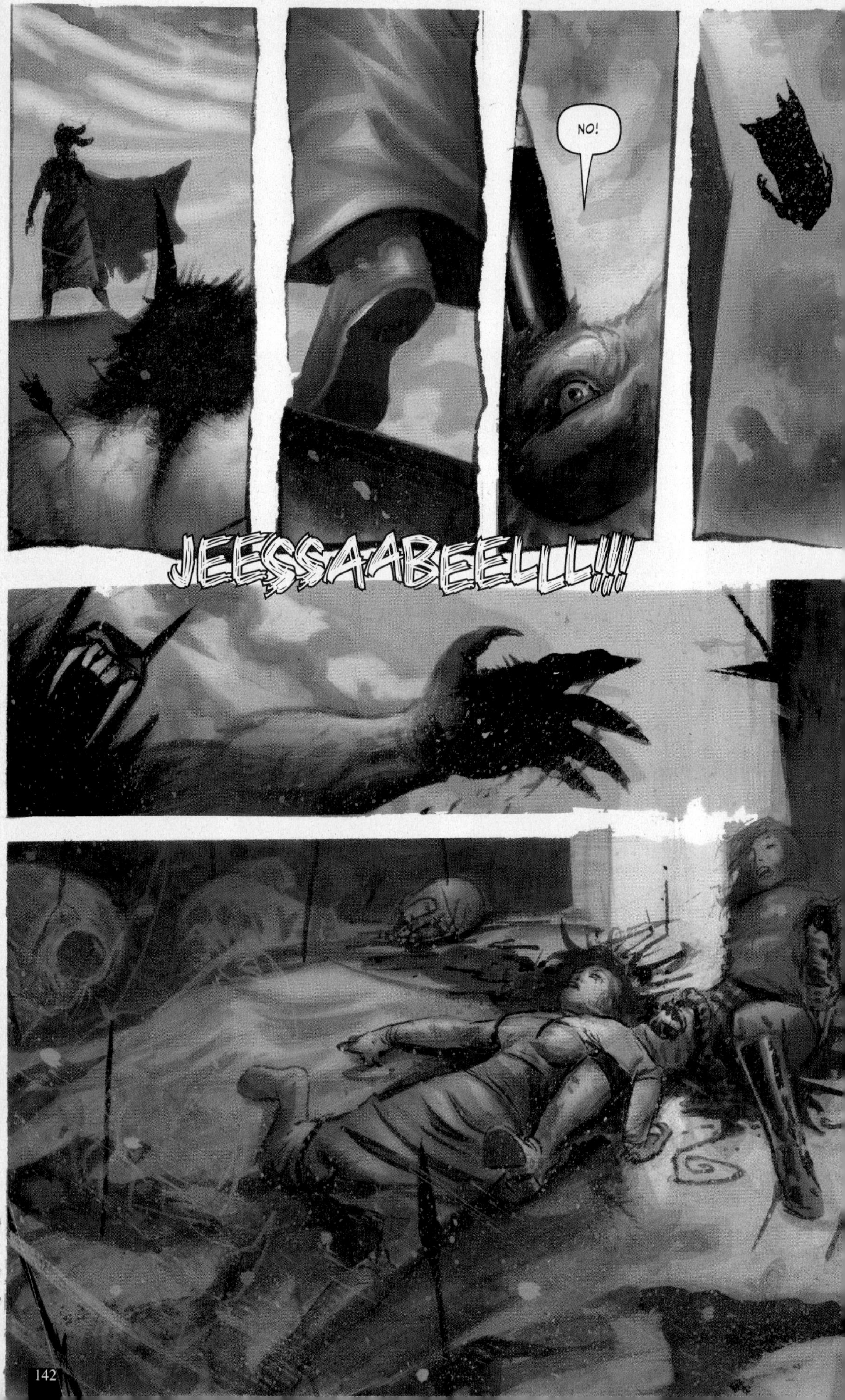
NO!
JEESSAABEELLLL!!!

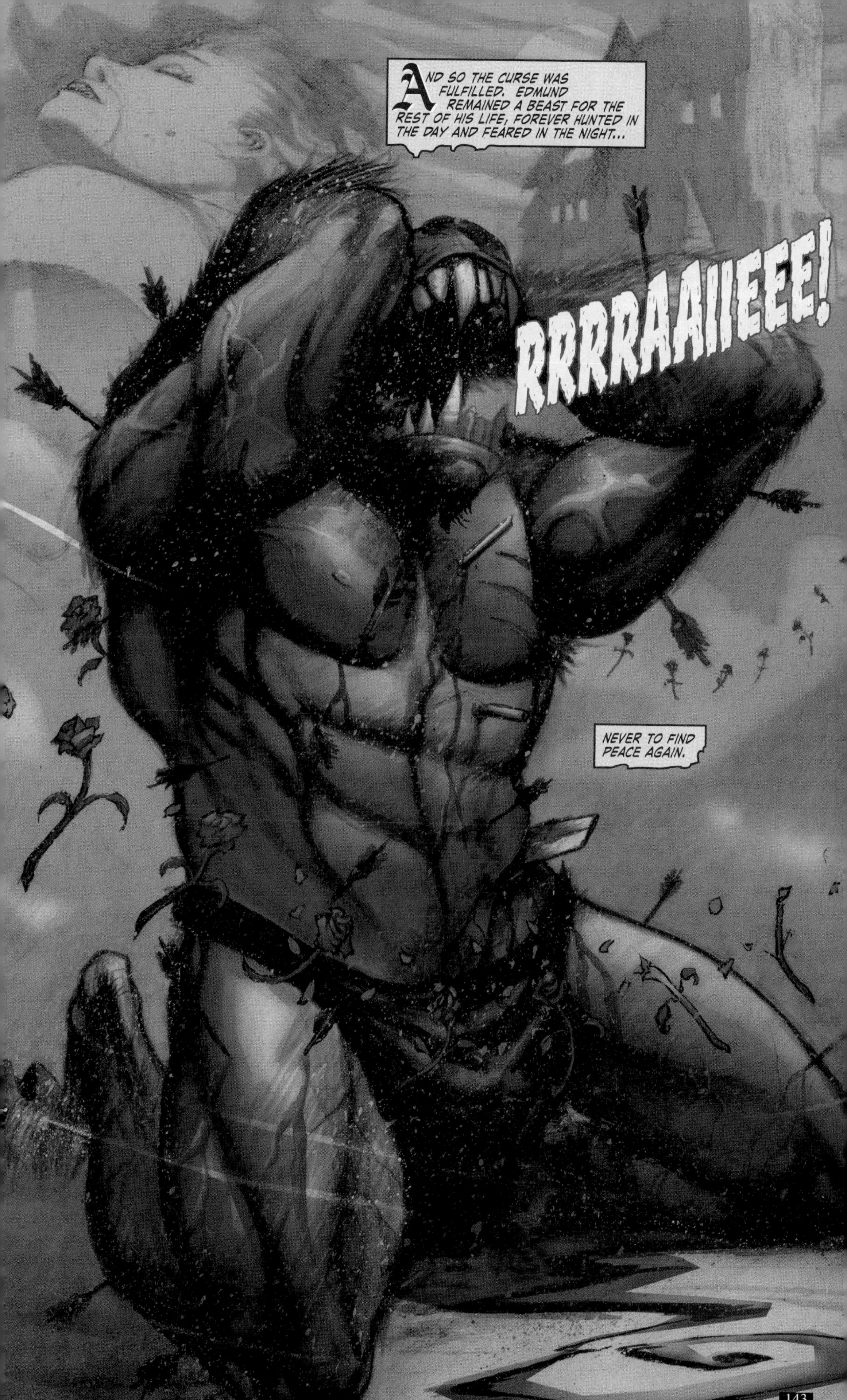
AND SO THE CURSE WAS FULFILLED. EDMUND REMAINED A BEAST FOR THE REST OF HIS LIFE, FOREVER HUNTED IN THE DAY AND FEARED IN THE NIGHT...
RRRRAAIIEEE!
NEVER TO FIND PEACE AGAIN.

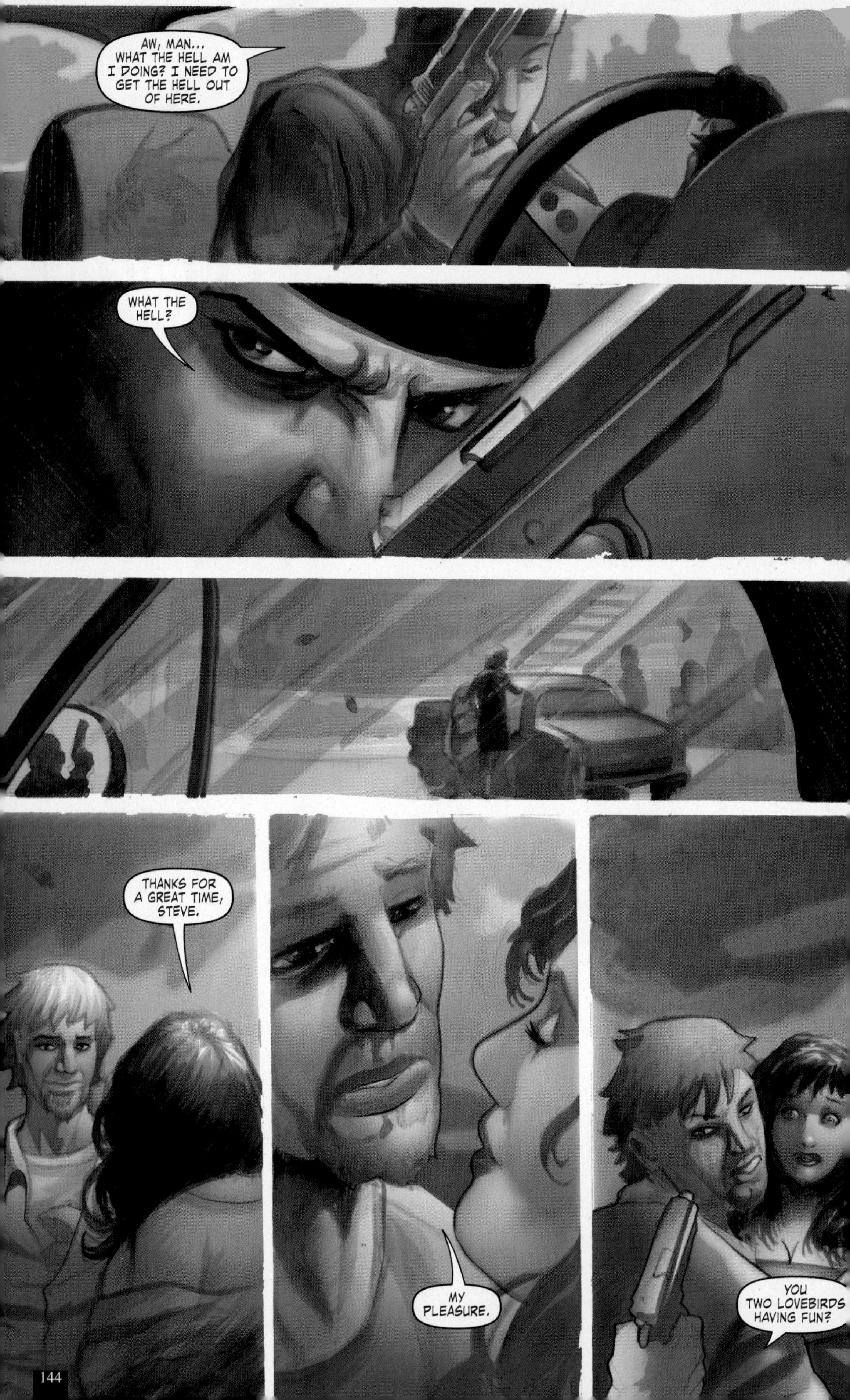
AW, MAN... WHAT THE HELL AM I DOING? I NEED TO GET THE HELL OUT OF HERE.
WHAT THE HELL?
THANKS FOR A GREAT TIME, STEVE.
MY PLEASURE.
YOU TWO LOVEBIRDS HAVING FUN?

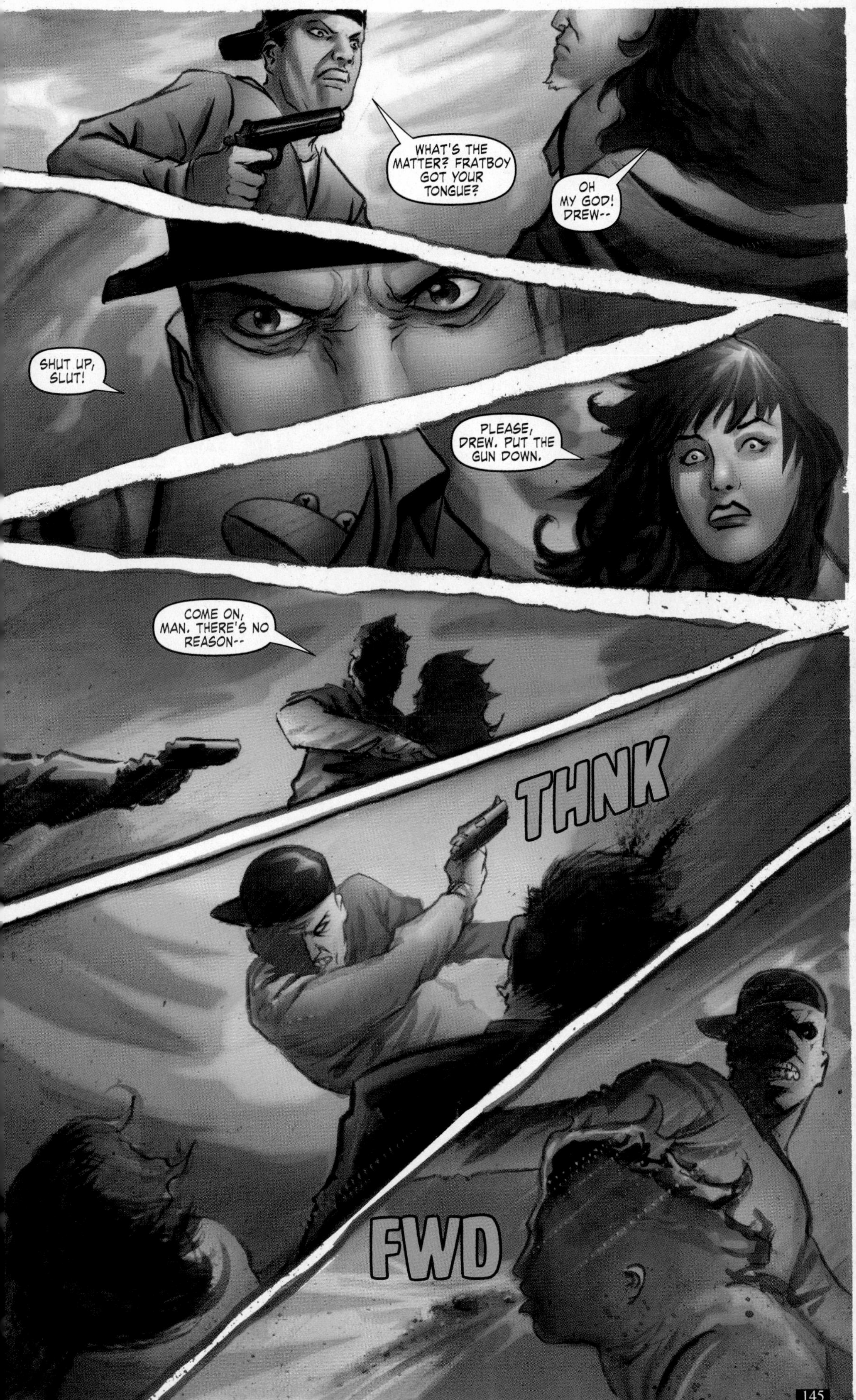
WHAT'S THE MATTER? FRATBOY GOT YOUR TONGUE?
OH MY GOD! DREW--
SHUT UP, SLUT!
PLEASE, DREW. PUT THE GUN DOWN.
COME ON, MAN. THERE'S NO REASON--
THNK
FWD

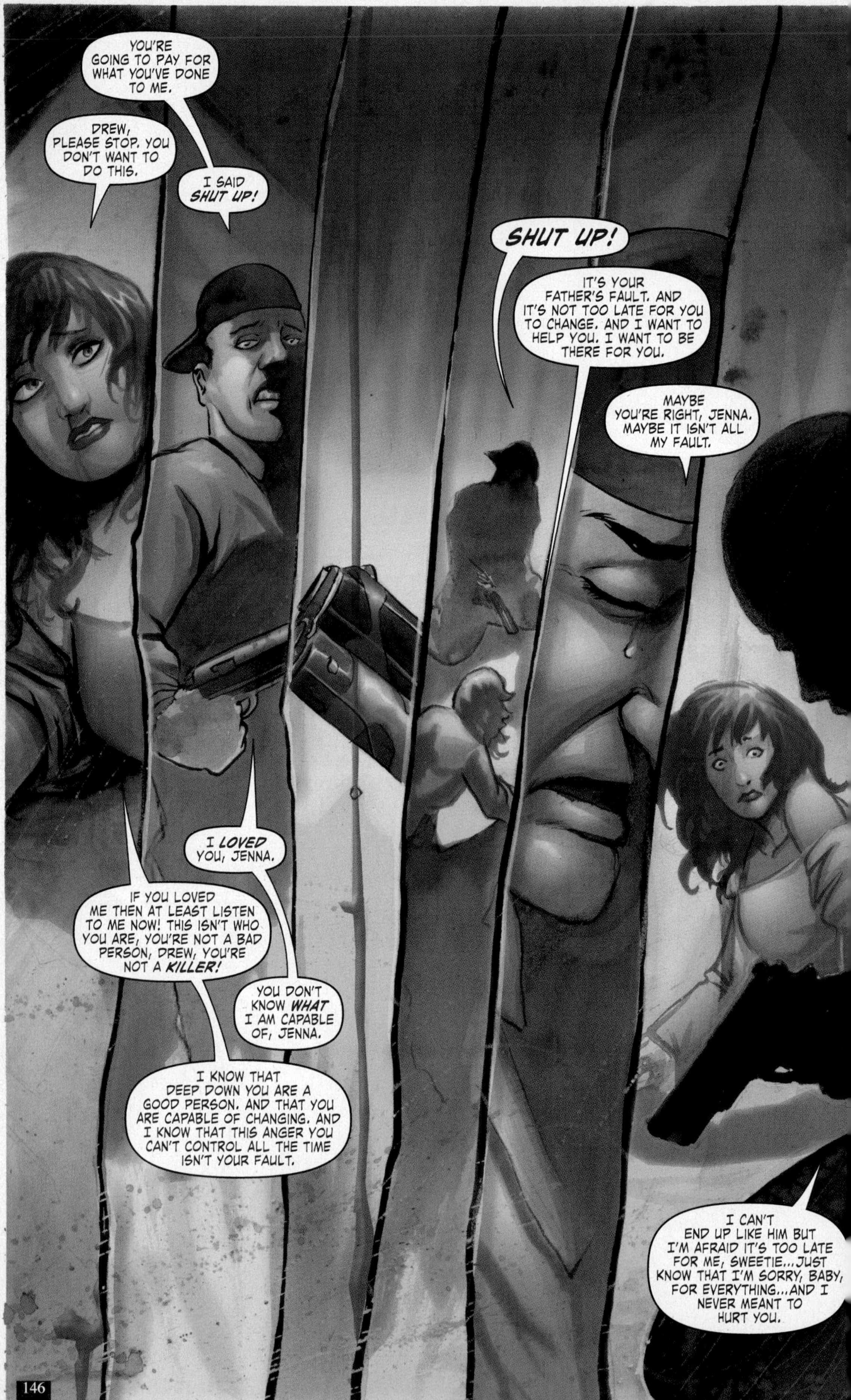
YOU'RE GOING TO PAY FOR WHAT YOU'VE DONE TO ME.
DREW, PLEASE STOP. YOU DON'T WANT TO DO THIS.
I SAID *SHUT UP!*
*SHUT UP!*
IT'S YOUR FATHER'S FAULT. AND IT'S NOT TOO LATE FOR YOU TO CHANGE. AND I WANT TO HELP YOU. I WANT TO BE THERE FOR YOU.
MAYBE YOU'RE RIGHT, JENNA. MAYBE IT ISN'T ALL MY FAULT.
I *LOVED* YOU, JENNA.
IF YOU LOVED ME THEN AT LEAST LISTEN TO ME NOW! THIS ISN'T WHO YOU ARE, YOU'RE NOT A BAD PERSON, DREW, YOU'RE NOT A *KILLER!*
YOU DON'T KNOW *WHAT* I AM CAPABLE OF, JENNA.
I KNOW THAT DEEP DOWN YOU ARE A GOOD PERSON. AND THAT YOU ARE CAPABLE OF CHANGING. AND I KNOW THAT THIS ANGER YOU CAN'T CONTROL ALL THE TIME ISN'T YOUR FAULT.
I CAN'T END UP LIKE HIM BUT I'M AFRAID IT'S TOO LATE FOR ME, SWEETIE...JUST KNOW THAT I'M SORRY, BABY, FOR EVERYTHING...AND I NEVER MEANT TO HURT YOU.

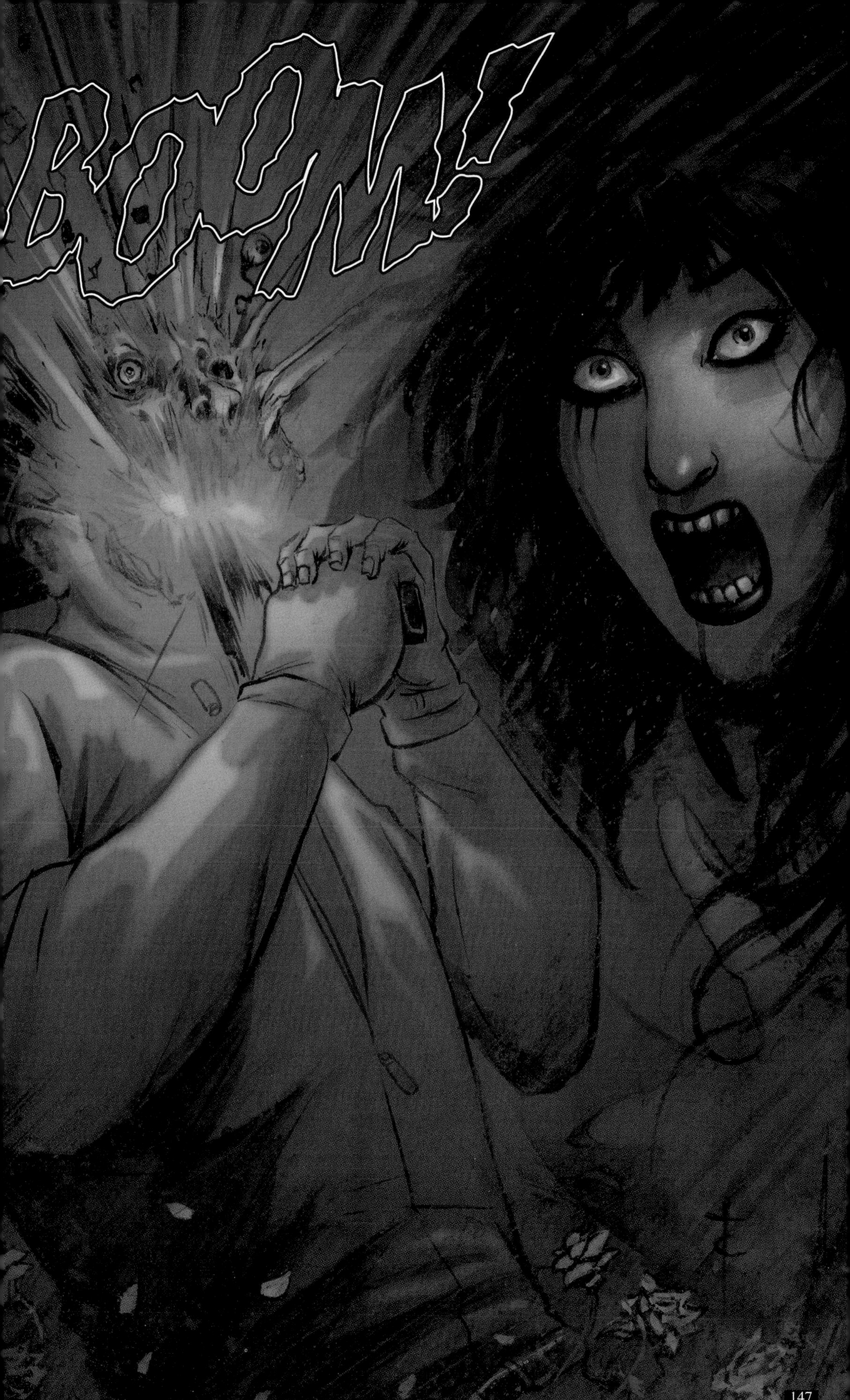
BOOM!

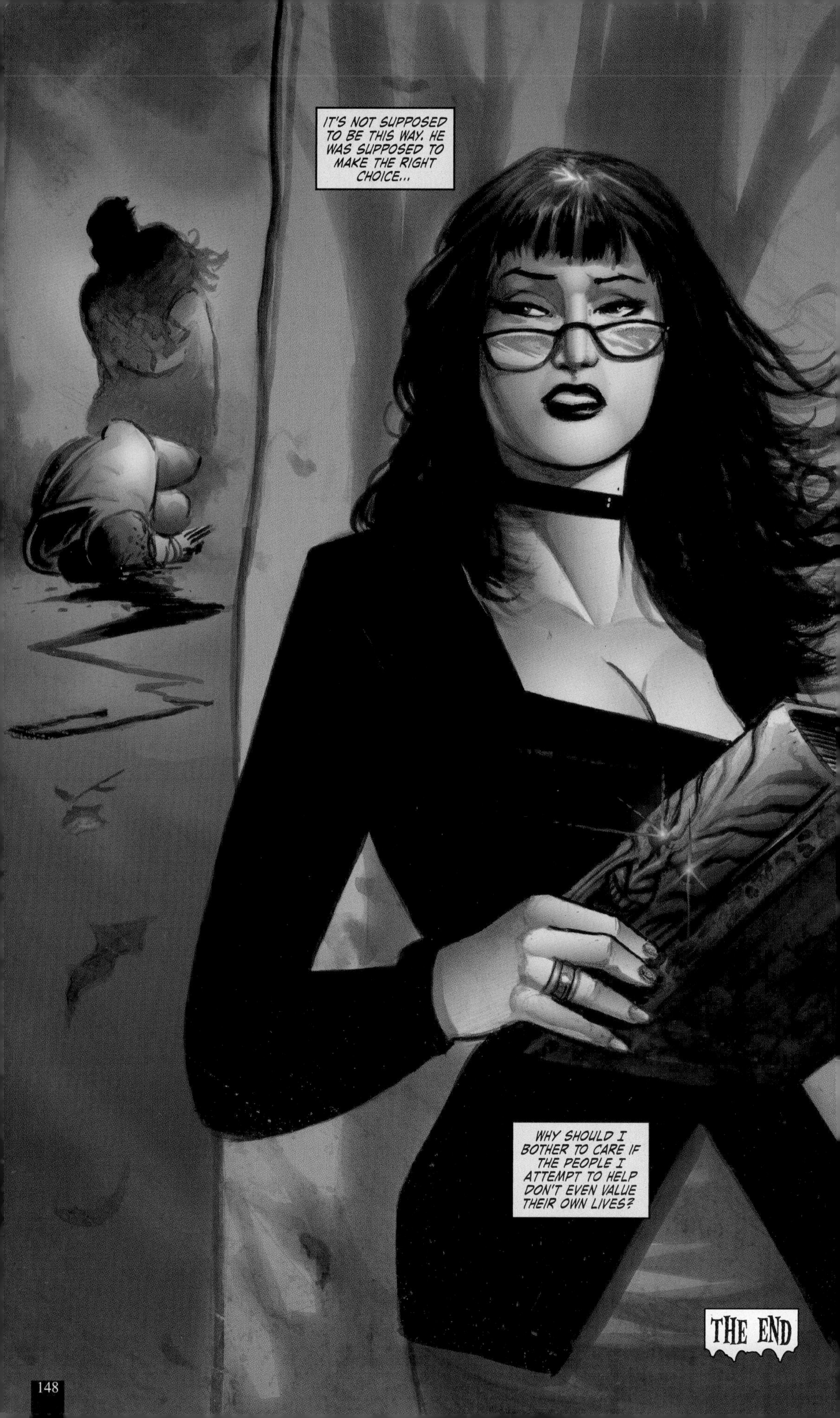
IT'S NOT SUPPOSED TO BE THIS WAY. HE WAS SUPPOSED TO MAKE THE RIGHT CHOICE...
WHY SHOULD I BOTHER TO CARE IF THE PEOPLE I ATTEMPT TO HELP DON'T EVEN VALUE THEIR OWN LIVES?
THE END

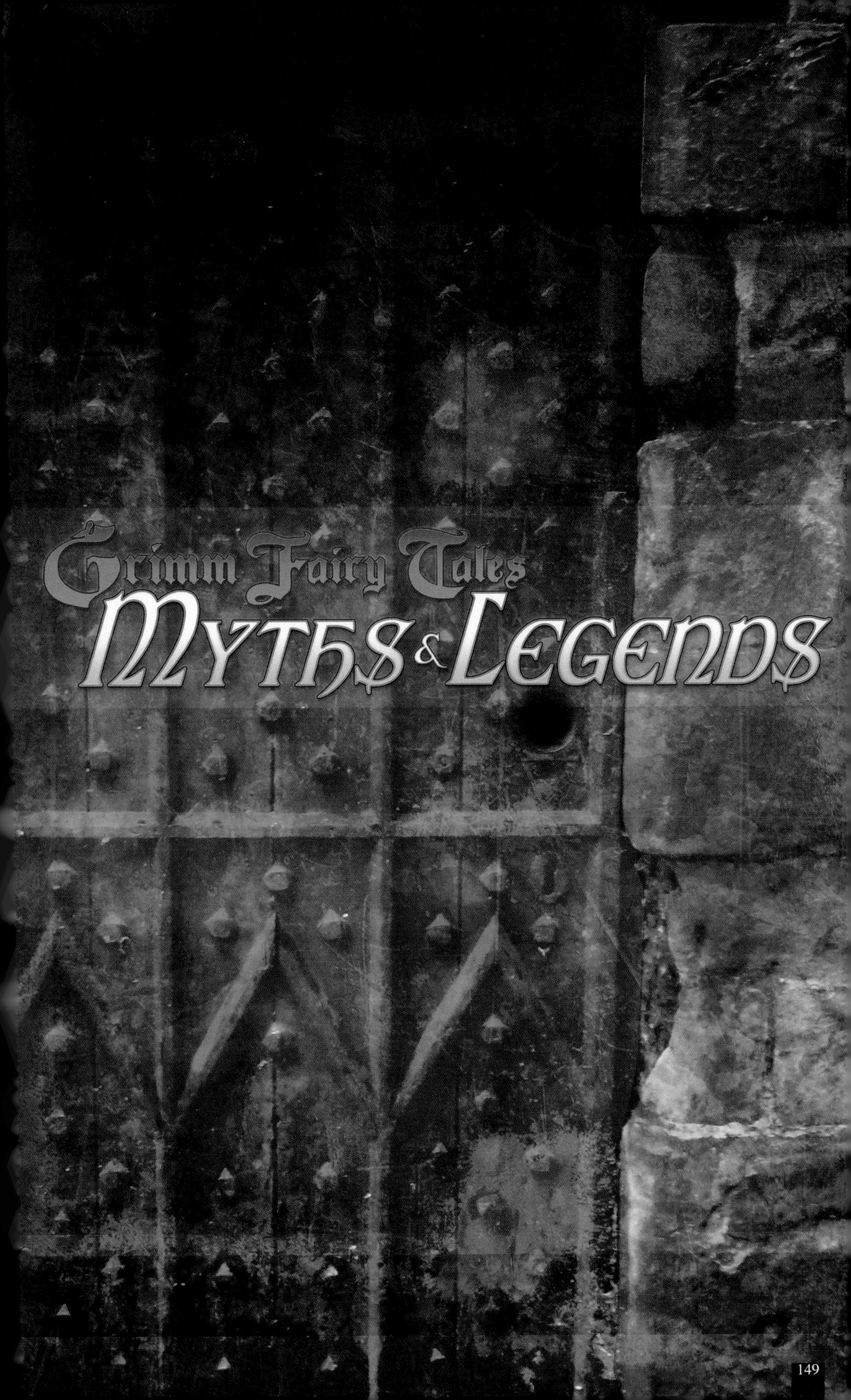

# Grimm Fairy Tales
# Myths & Legends

# Cover Gallery

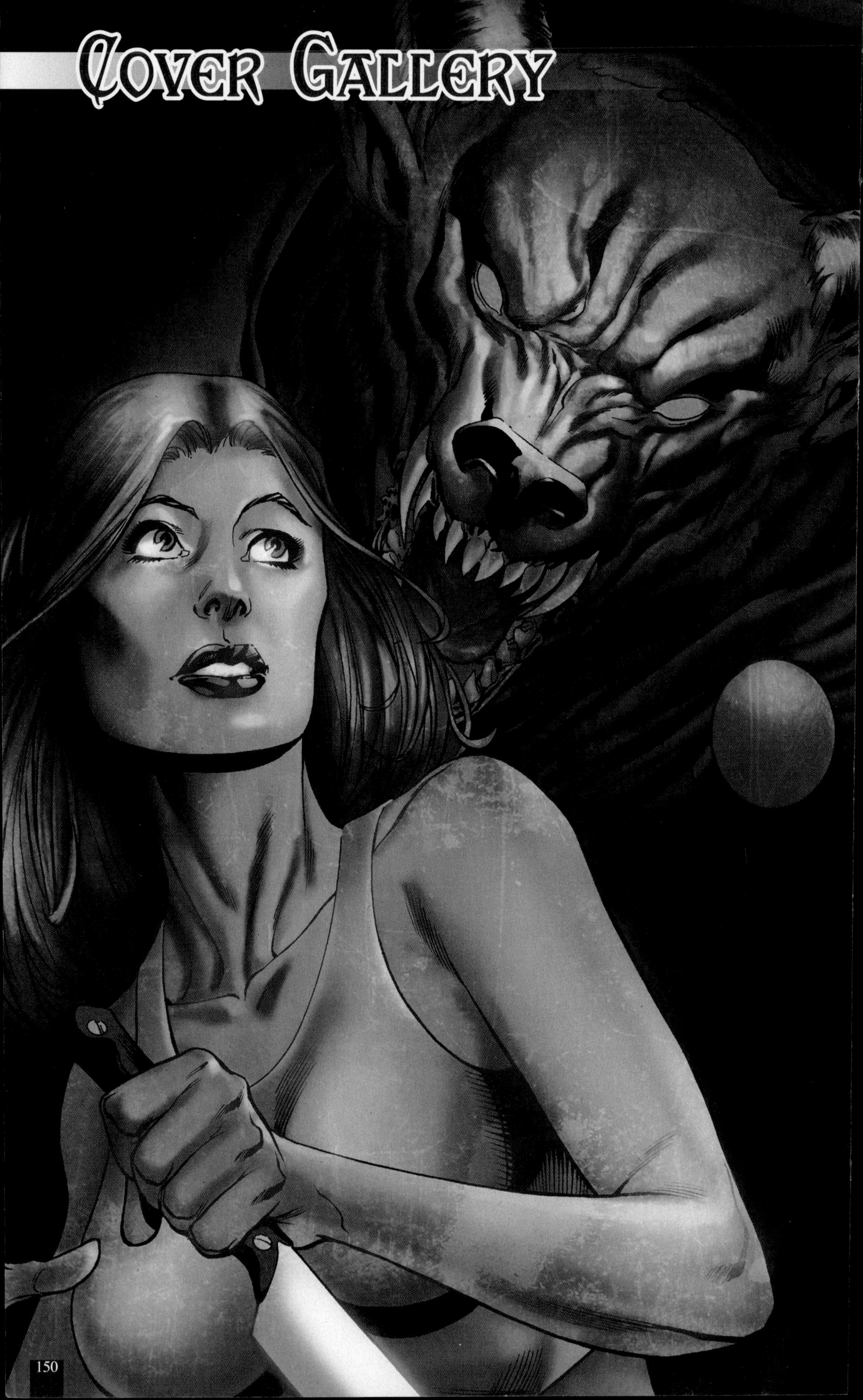

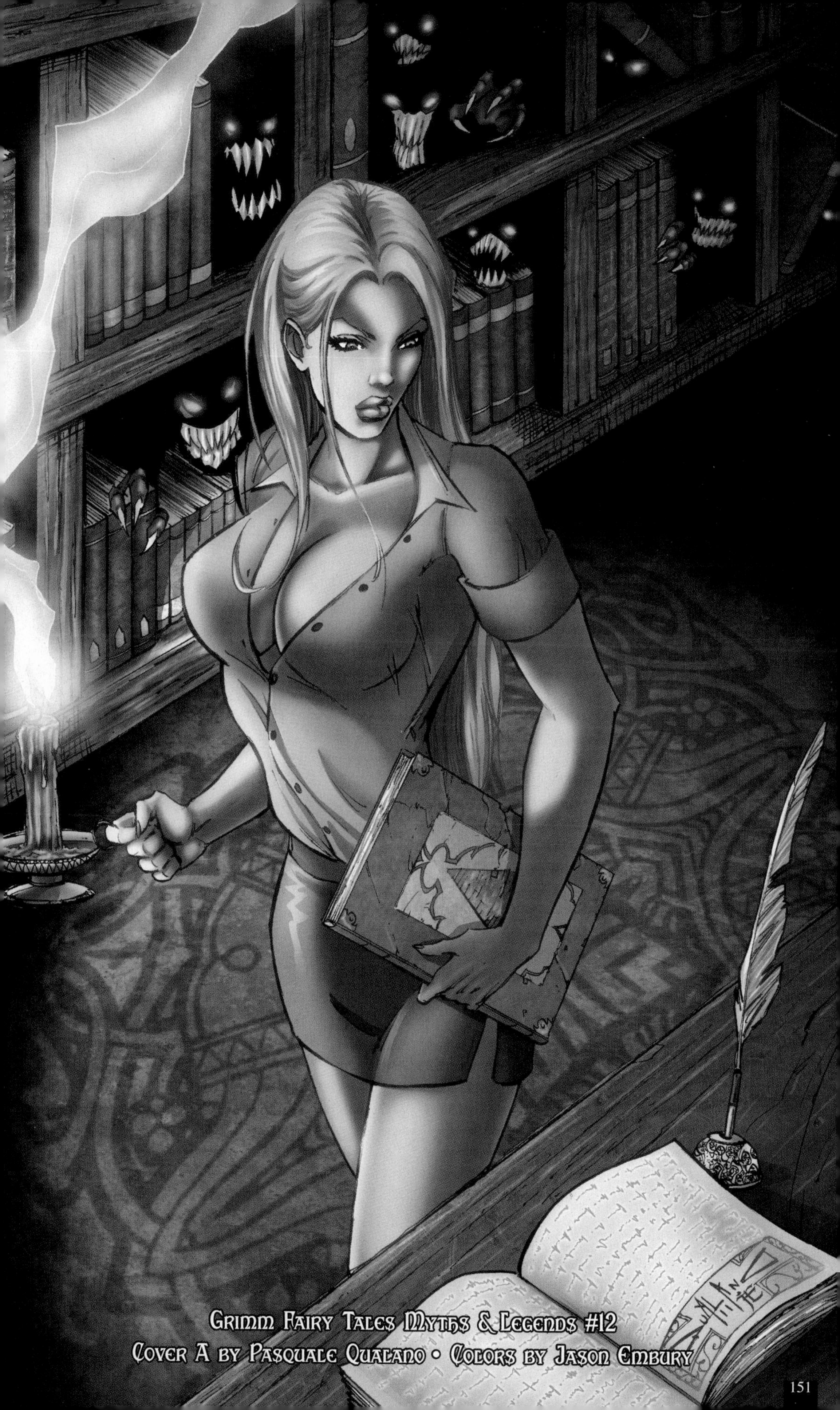

Grimm Fairy Tales Myths & Legends #12
Cover A by Pasquale Qualano • Colors by Jason Embury

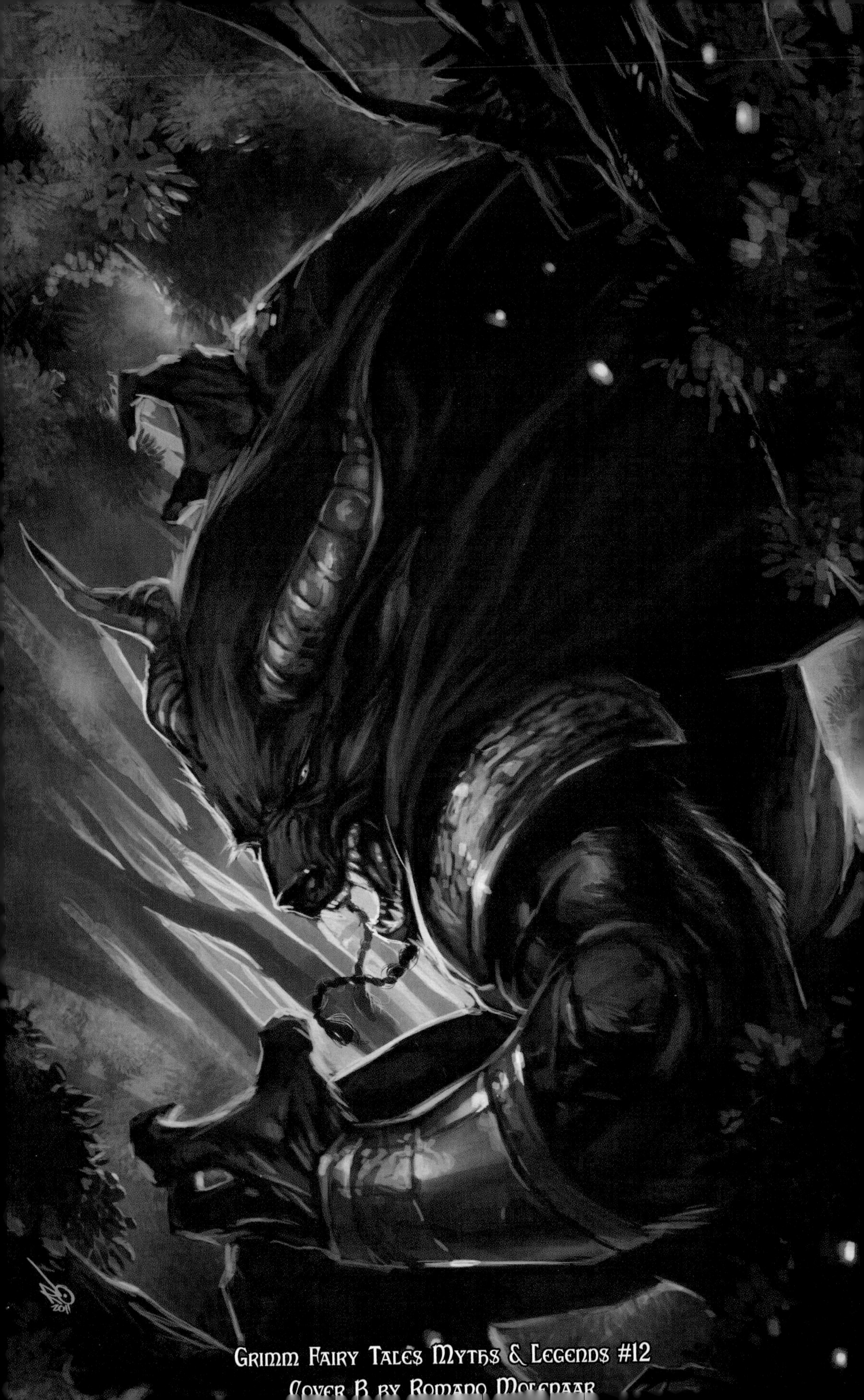

Grimm Fairy Tales Myths & Legends #12
Cover B by Romano Molenaar

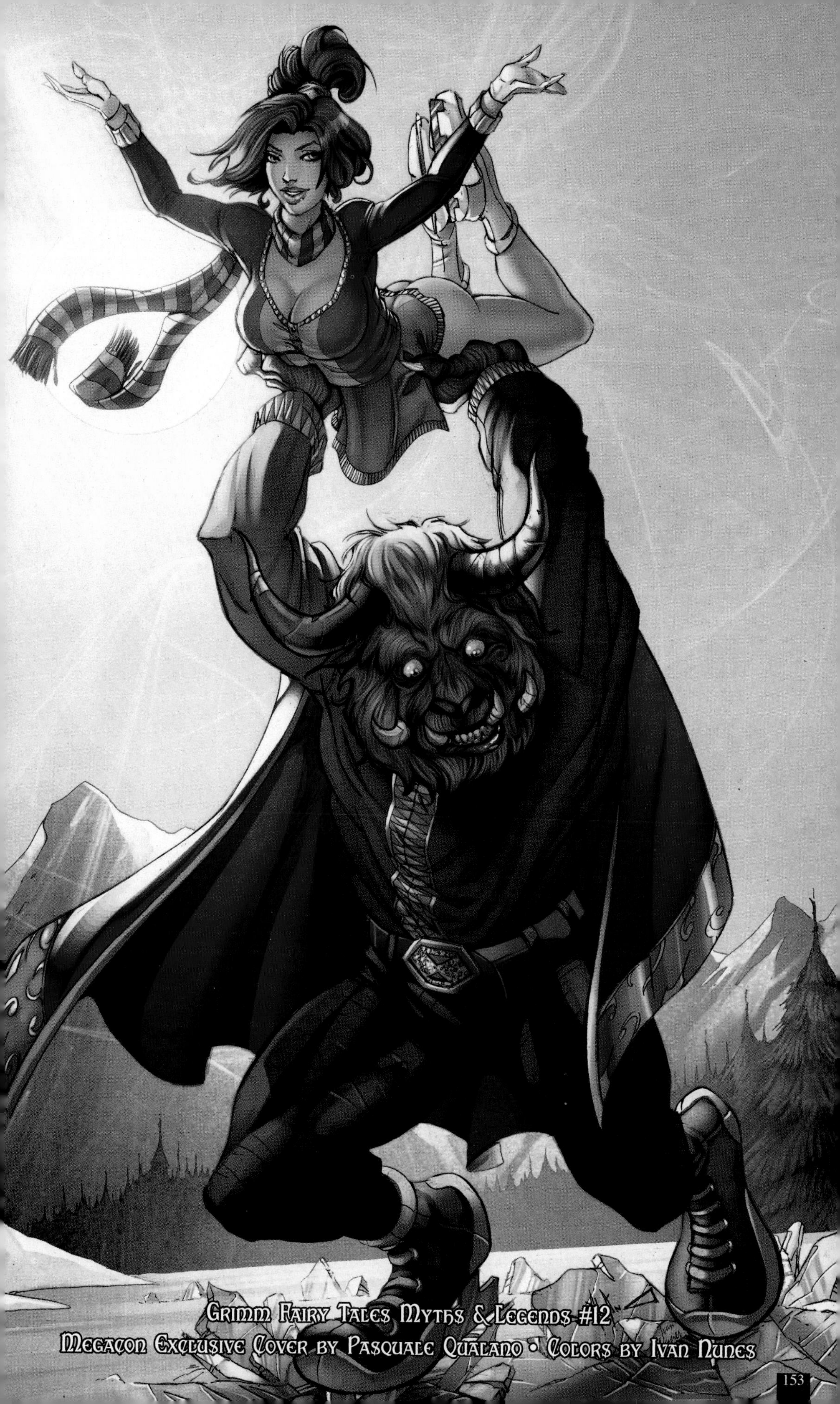

Grimm Fairy Tales Myths & Legends #12
Megacon Exclusive Cover by Pasquale Qualano • Colors by Ivan Nunes

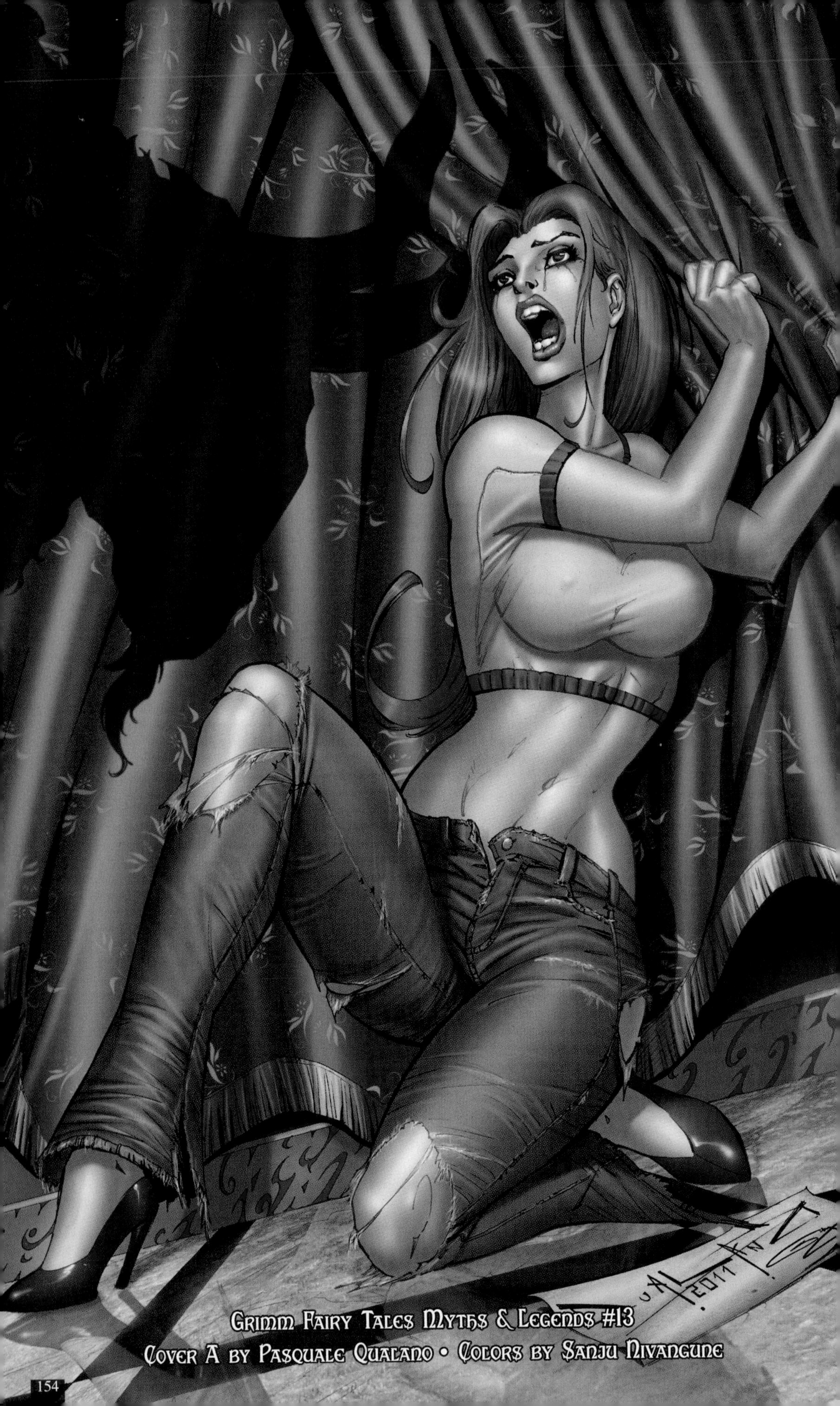

Grimm Fairy Tales Myths & Legends #13
Cover A by Pasquale Qualano • Colors by Sanju Nivangune

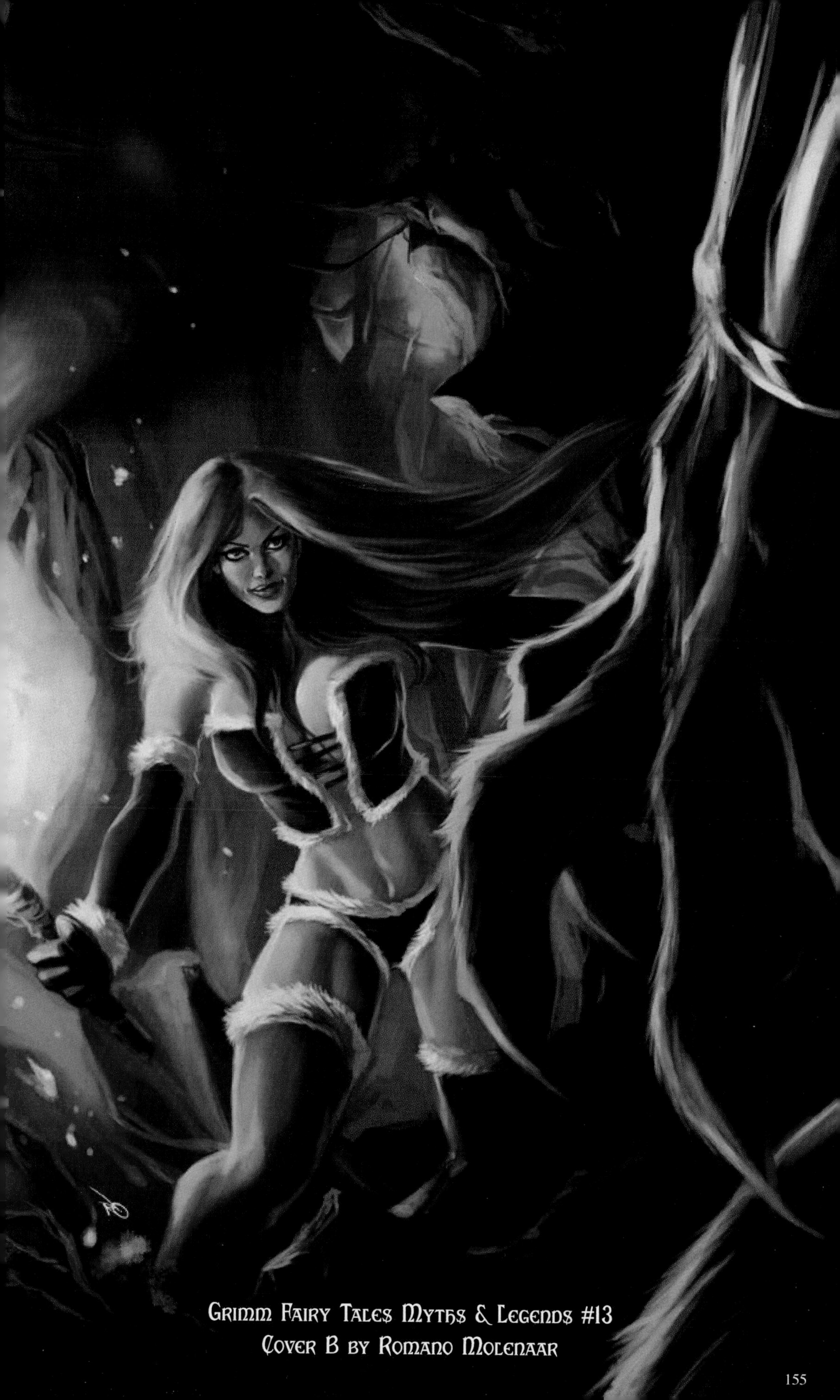

Grimm Fairy Tales Myths & Legends #13
Cover B by Romano Molenaar

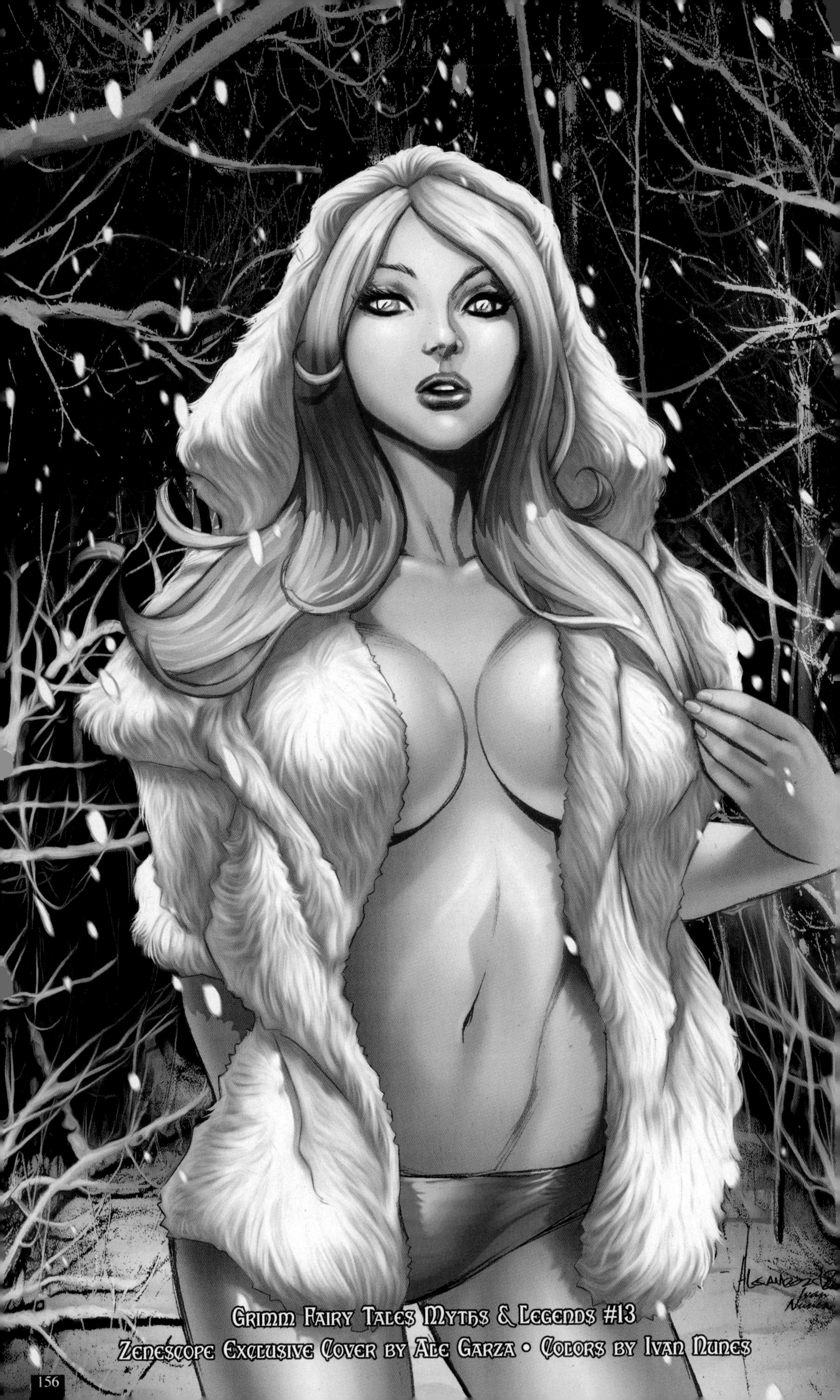

Grimm Fairy Tales Myths & Legends #13
Zenescope Exclusive Cover by Ale Garza • Colors by Ivan Nunes

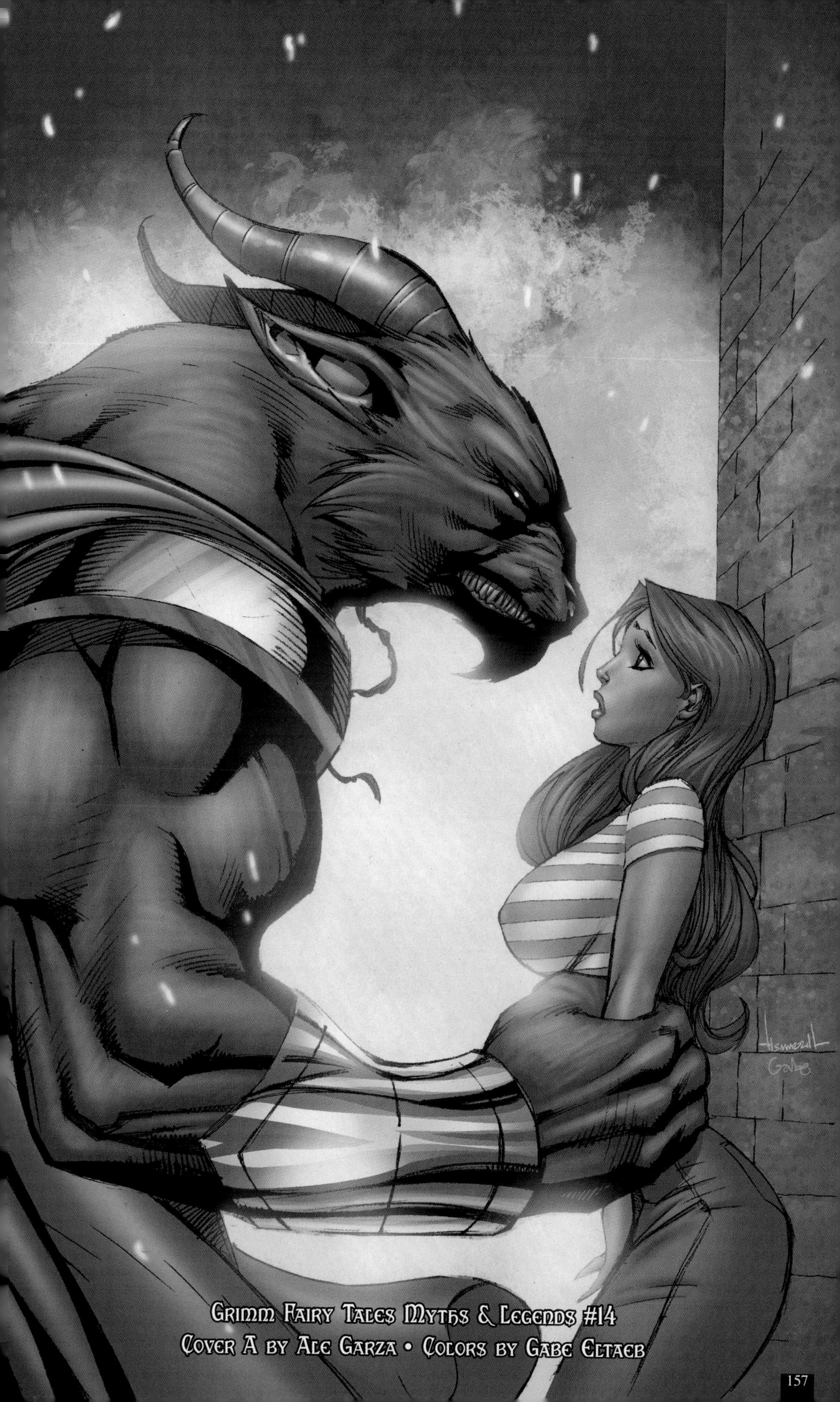

Hammer
Gabe


Grimm Fairy Tales Myths & Legends #14
Cover A by Ale Garza • Colors by Gabe Eltaeb

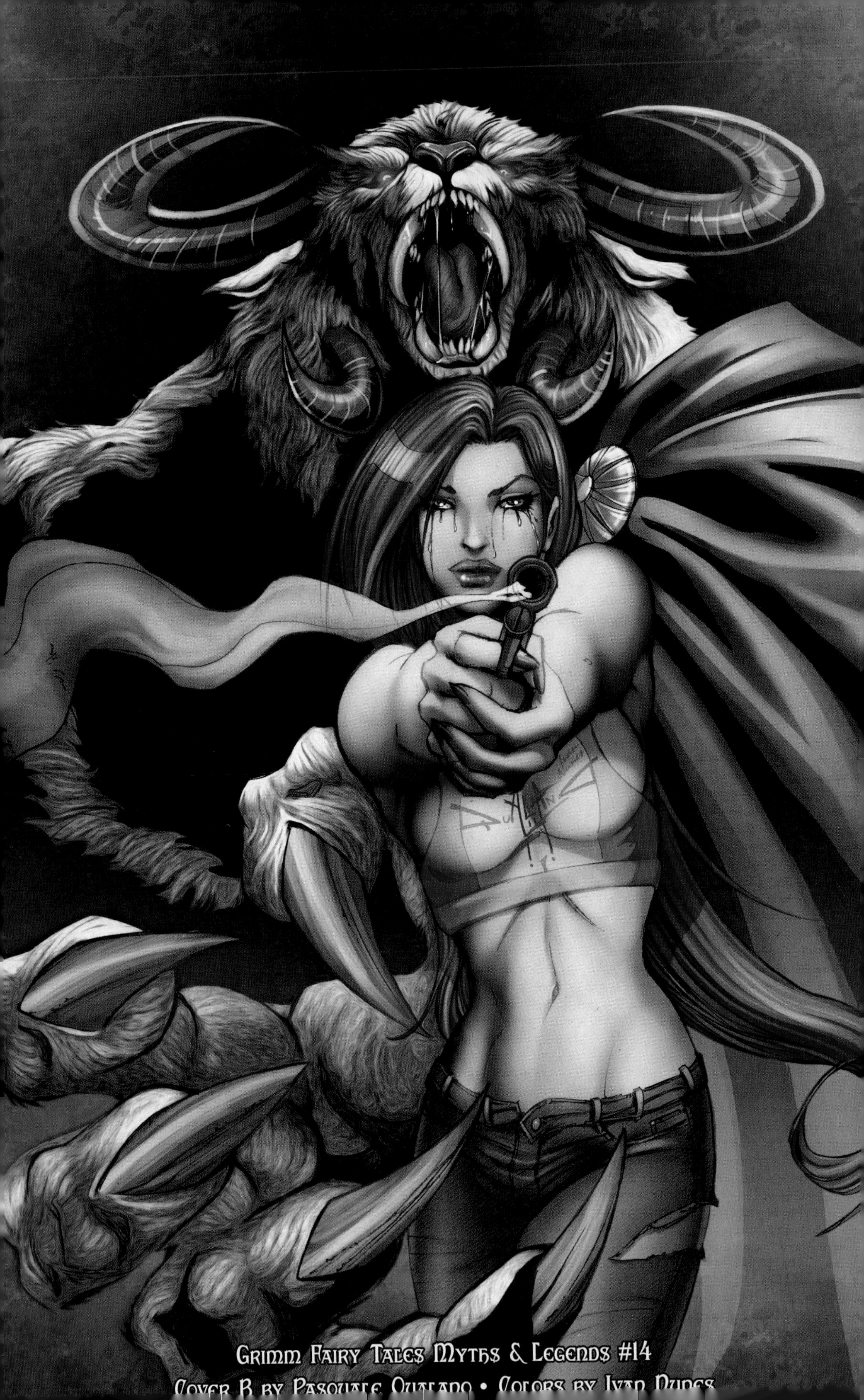

Grimm Fairy Tales Myths & Legends #14
Cover B by Pasquale Qualano • Colors by Ivan Nunes

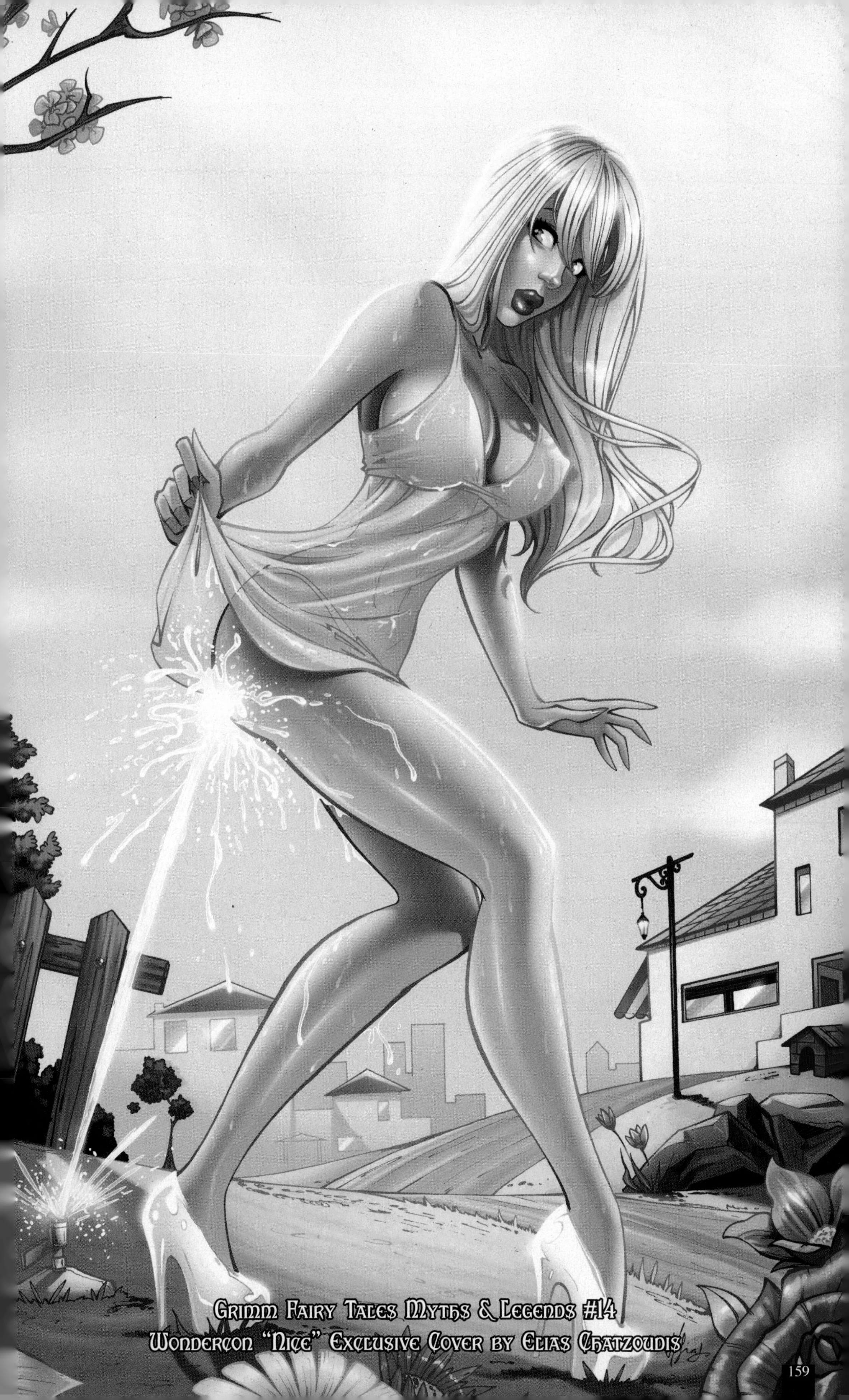

Grimm Fairy Tales Myths & Legends #14
Wondercon "Nice" Exclusive Cover by Elias Chatzoudis

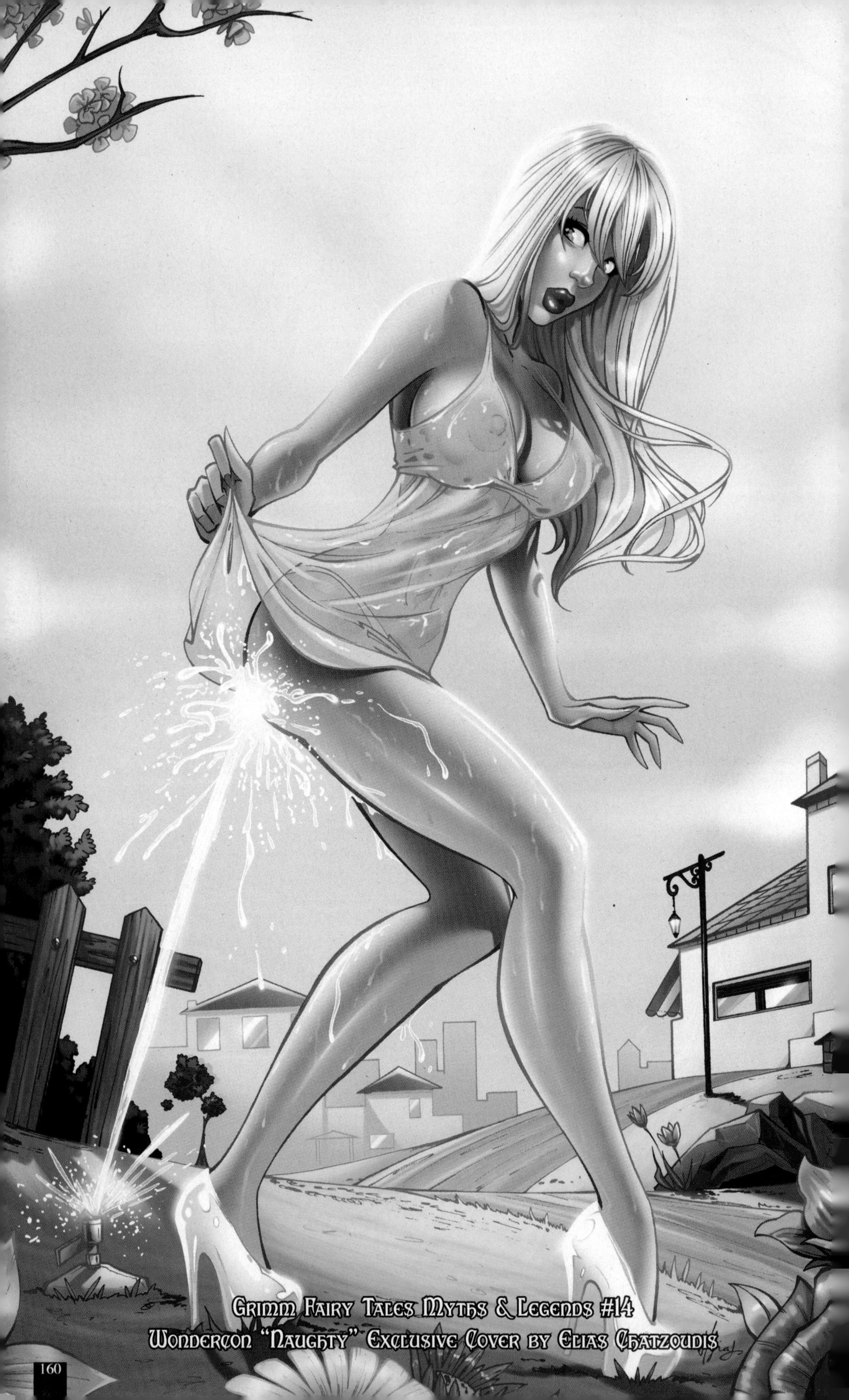

Grimm Fairy Tales Myths & Legends #14
WonderCon "Naughty" Exclusive Cover by Elias Chatzoudis

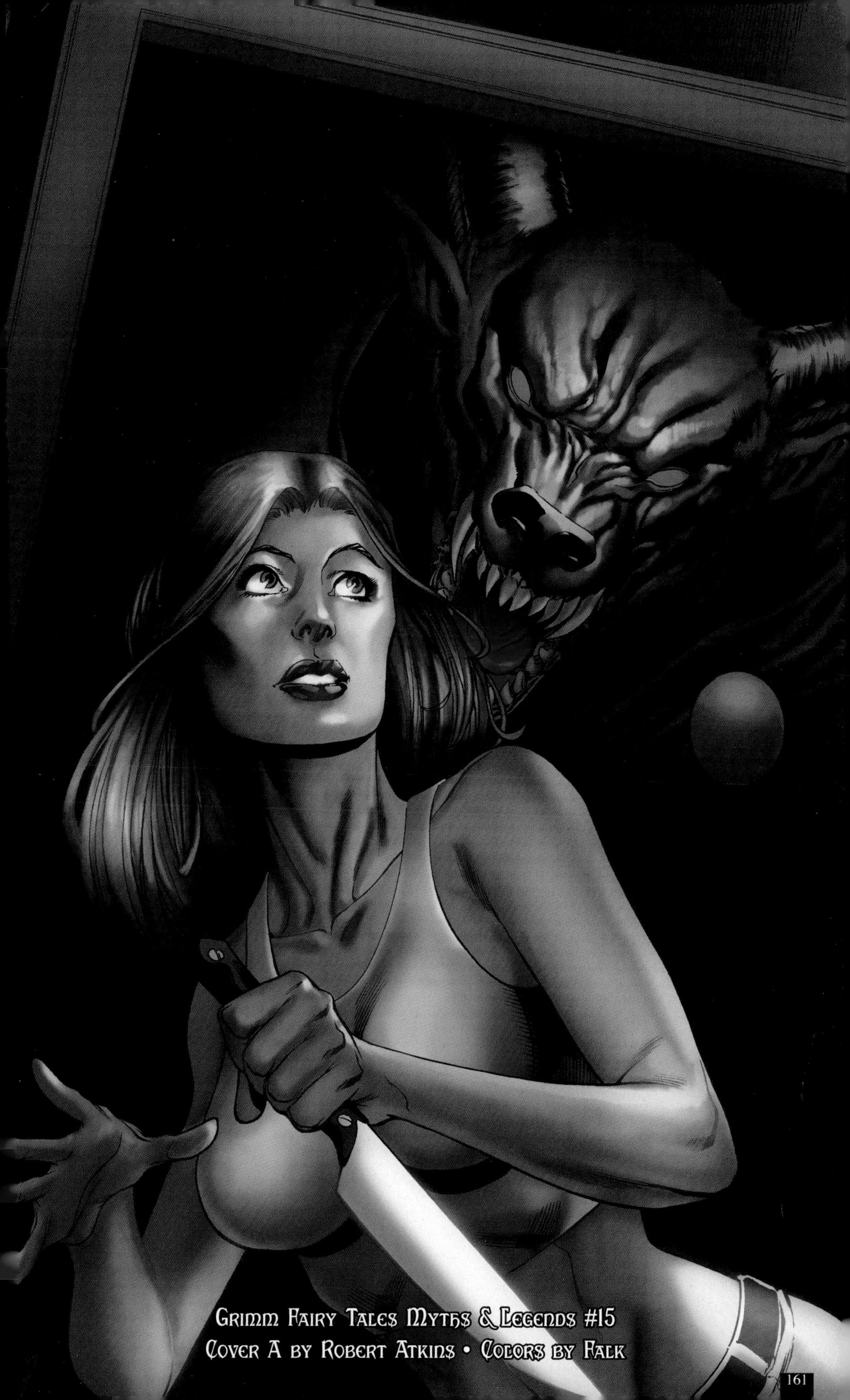

Grimm Fairy Tales Myths & Legends #15
Cover A by Robert Atkins • Colors by Falk

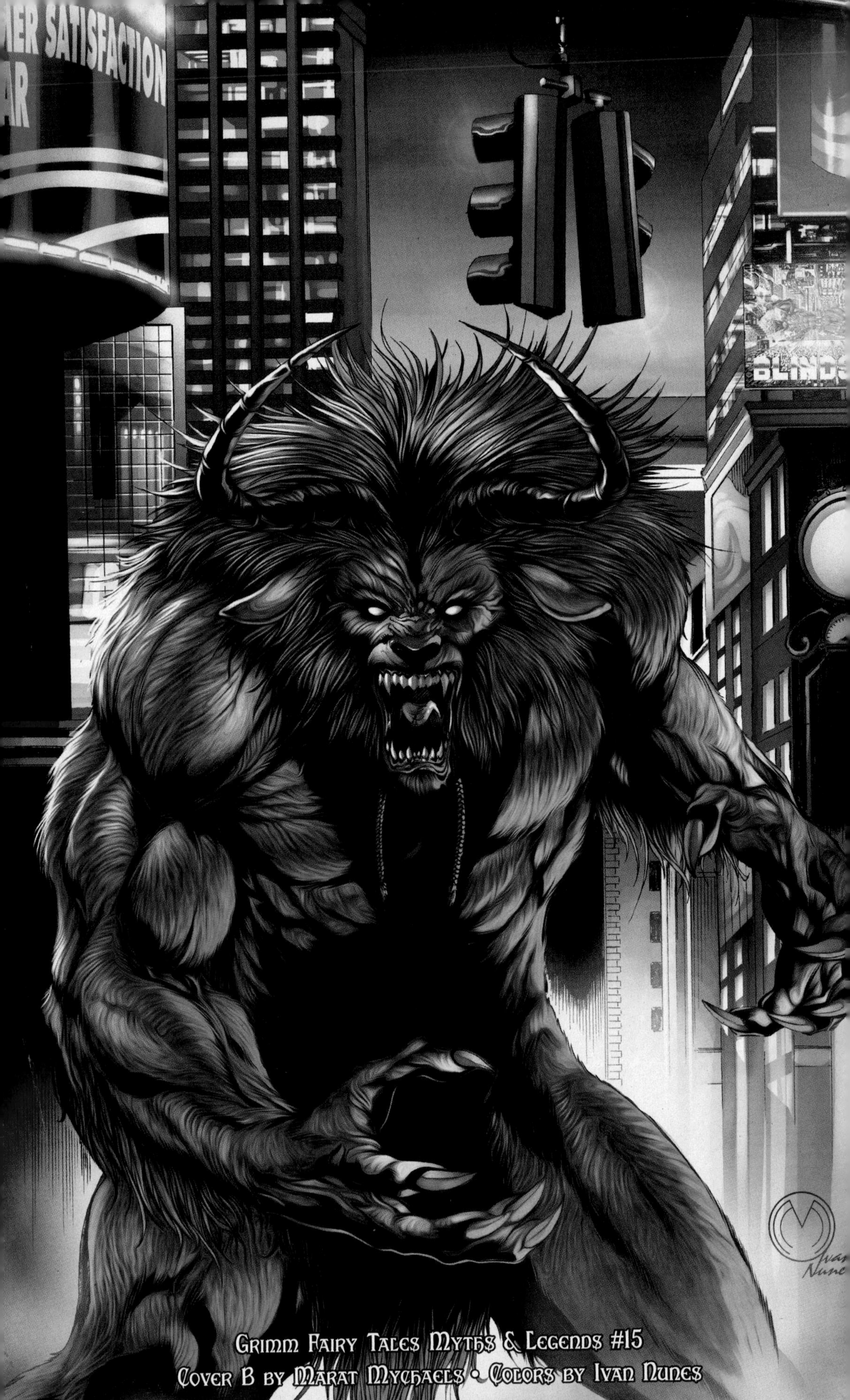
SATISFACTION

Grimm Fairy Tales Myths & Legends #15
Cover B by Marat Mychaels • Colors by Ivan Nunes

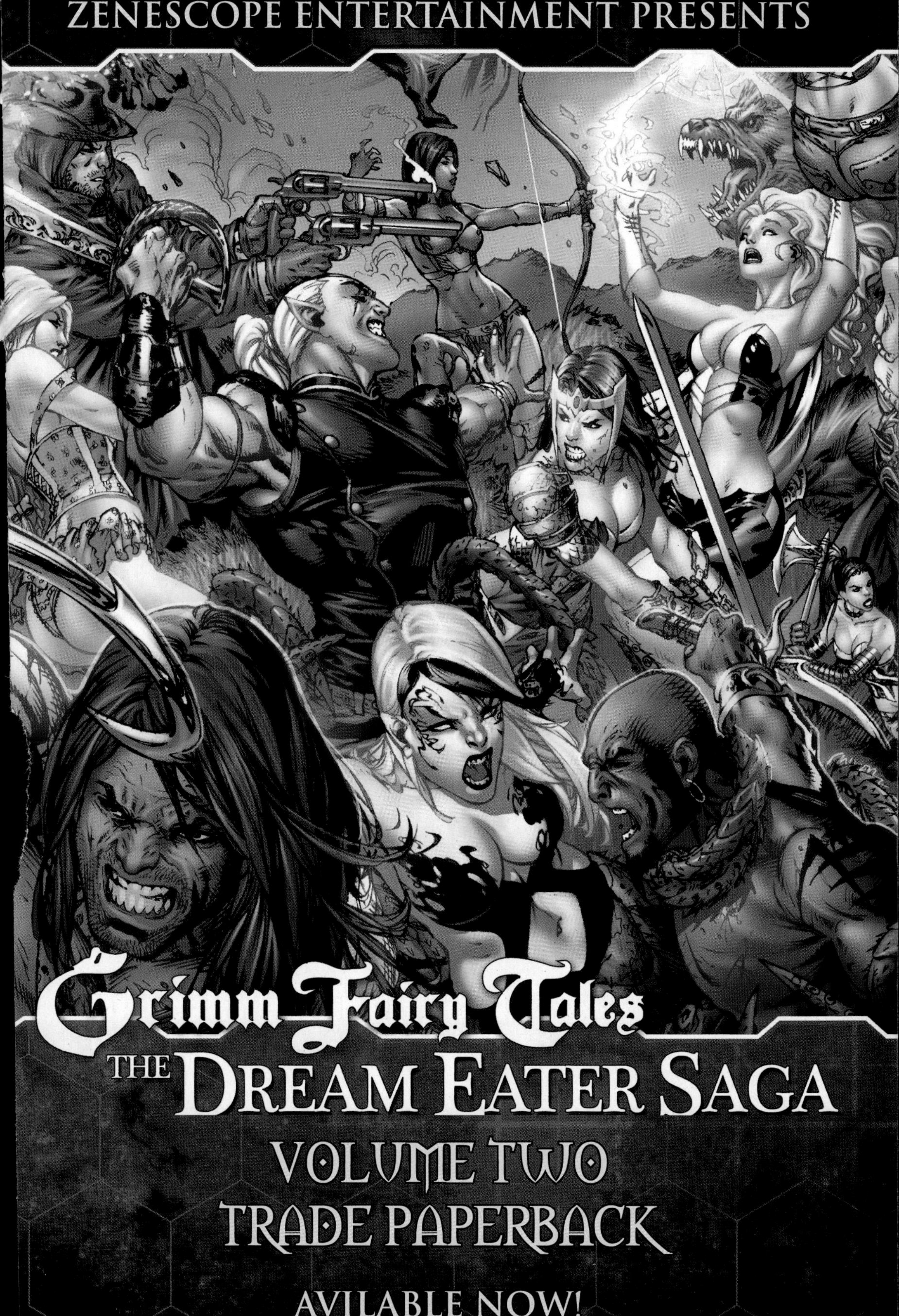
ZENESCOPE ENTERTAINMENT PRESENTS
Grimm Fairy Tales
THE DREAM EATER SAGA
VOLUME TWO
TRADE PAPERBACK
AVILABLE NOW!

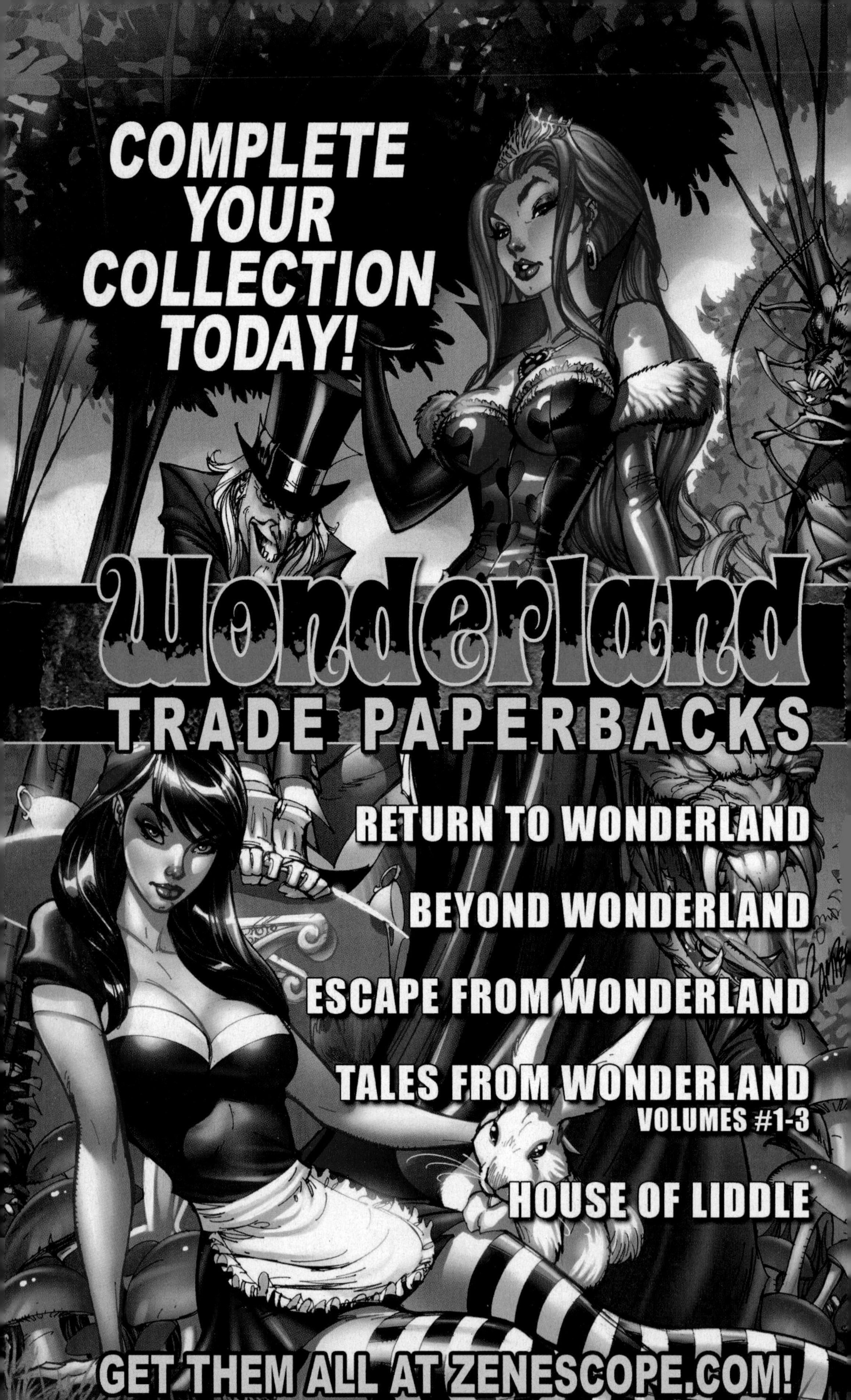
COMPLETE YOUR COLLECTION TODAY!
Wonderland
TRADE PAPERBACKS
RETURN TO WONDERLAND
BEYOND WONDERLAND
ESCAPE FROM WONDERLAND
TALES FROM WONDERLAND
VOLUMES #1-3
HOUSE OF LIDDLE
GET THEM ALL AT ZENESCOPE.COM!

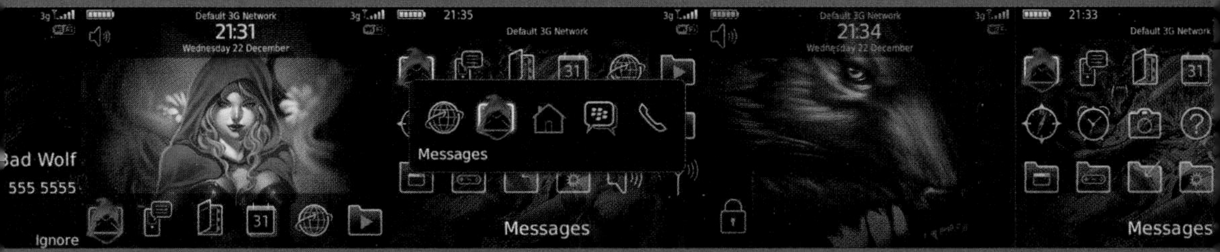
Bad Wolf
555 5555
Ignore
Messages
Messages
Messages



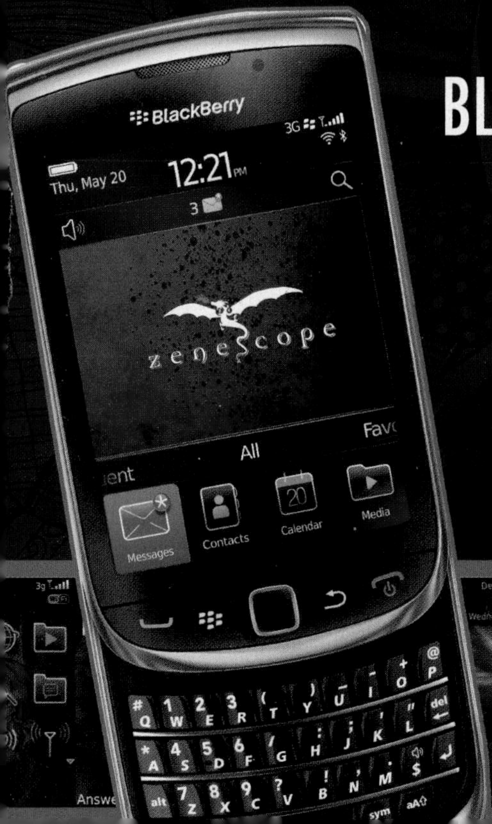
BlackBerry
12:21
Thu, May 20
zenescope
All
Messages
Contacts
Calendar
Media

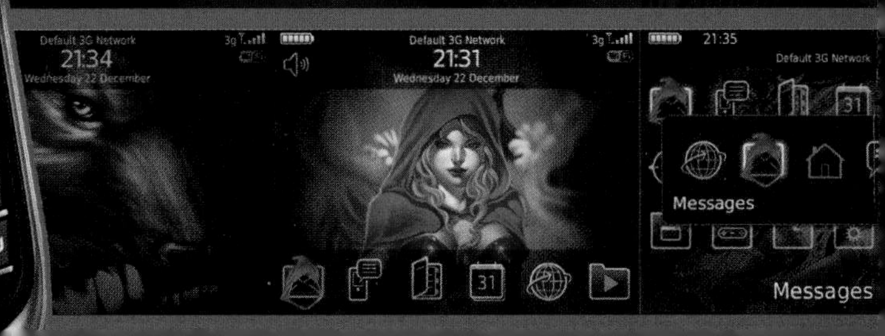
Messages
Messages

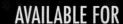

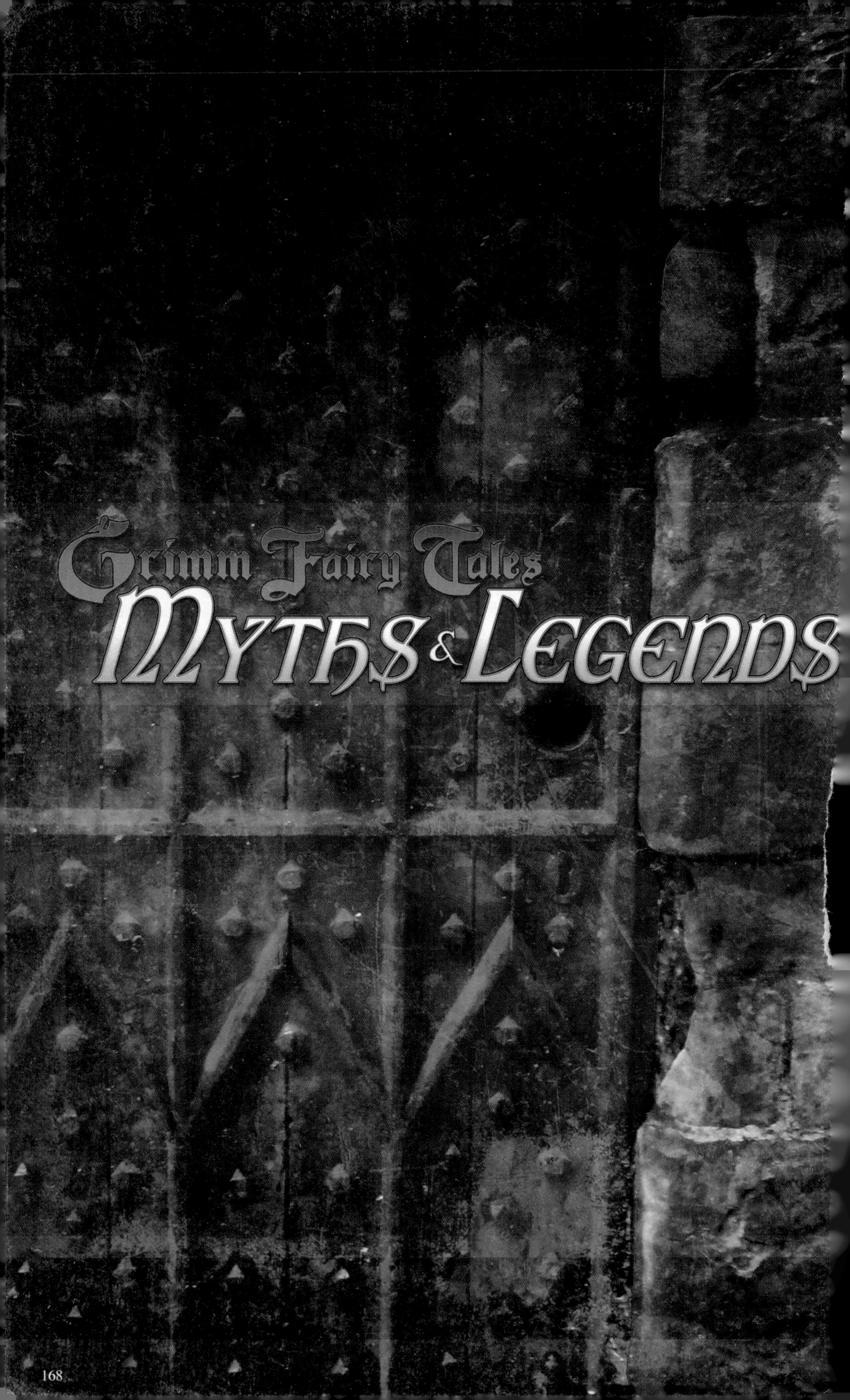
Grimm Fairy Tales
Myths & Legends